Guidebook: A Manual For Students

The American Pageant

FOURTEENTH EDITION

David M. Kennedy
Stanford University

Lizabeth Cohen
Harvard University

Thomas A. Bailey

Prepared by

Mel Piehl
Valparaiso University

WADSWORTH
CENGAGE Learning

Australia • Brazil • Japan • Korea • Mexico • Singapore • Spain • United Kingdom • United States

ISBN-13: 978-0-547-16696-4
ISBN-10: 0-547-16696-6

Wadsworth
25 Thomson Place
Boston, MA 02210
USA

Cengage Learning is a leading provider of customized learning solutions with office locations around the globe, including Singapore, the United Kingdom, Australia, Mexico, Brazil, and Japan. Locate your local office at: **international.cengage.com/region**

Cengage Learning products are represented in Canada by Nelson Education, Ltd.

For your course and learning solutions, visit **academic.cengage.com**

Purchase any of our products at your local college store or at our preferred online store **www.ichapters.com**

Printed in the United States of America
3 4 5 6 13 12 11 10

Contents

CHAPTER 1

New World Beginnings, 33,000 B.C.–A.D. 1769

PART I: REVIEWING THE CHAPTER

A. Checklist of Learning Objectives

After mastering this chapter, you should be able to:

1. Describe the geological and geographical conditions that set the stage for North American history.

2. Describe the origin and development of the major Indian cultures of the Americas.

3. Explain the developments in Europe and Africa that led to Columbus's voyage to America.

4. Explain the changes and conflicts that occurred when the diverse worlds and peoples of Europe, Africa, and the Americas collided after 1492.

5. Describe the Spanish conquest of Mexico and South America, and of the later Spanish colonial expansion into North America.

6. Describe the major features of Spain's New World Empire, including relations with the native Indian populations.

B. Glossary

To build your social science vocabulary, familiarize yourself with the following terms.

1. **nation-state** The form of political society that combines centralized government with a high degree of ethnic and cultural unity. ". . . the complex, large-scale, centralized Aztec and Incan nation-states that eventually emerged."

2. **matrilinear** The form of society in which family line, power, and wealth are passed primarily through the female side. ". . . many North American native peoples, including the Iroquois, developed matrilinear cultures. . . ."

3. **confederacy** An alliance or league of nations or peoples looser than a federation. "The Iroquois Confederacy developed the political and organizational skills. . . ."

4. **primeval** Concerning the earliest origin of things. ". . . the whispering, primeval forests. . . ."

5. **saga** A lengthy story or poem recounting the great deeds and adventures of a people and their heroes. ". . . their discovery was forgotten, except in Scandinavian saga and song."

6. **middlemen** In trading systems, those dealers who operate between the original buyers and the retail merchants who sell to consumers. "Muslim middlemen exacted a heavy toll en route."

7. **caravel** A small vessel with a high deck and three triangular sails. ". . . they developed the caravel, a ship that could sail more closely into the wind. . . ."

8. **plantation** A large-scale agricultural enterprise growing commercial crops and usually employing coerced or slave labor. "They built up their own systematic traffic in slaves to work the sugar plantations. . . ."

9. **ecosystem** A naturally evolved network of relations among organisms in a stable environment. "Two ecosystems . . . commingled and clashed when Columbus waded ashore."

10. **demographic** Concerning the general characteristics of a given population, including such factors as numbers, age, gender, birth and death rates, and so on. ". . . a demographic catastrophe without parallel in human history."

11. **conquistador(es)** A Spanish conqueror or adventurer in the Americas. "Spanish *conquistadores* (conquerors) fanned out across . . . American continents."

12. **capitalism** An economic system characterized by private property, free trade, and open and accessible markets. ". . . the fuel that fed the growth of the economic system known as capitalism."

13. **encomienda** The Spanish labor system in which persons were held to unpaid service under the permanent control of their masters, though not legally owned by them. ". . . the institution known as *encomienda*."

14. **mestizo** A person of mixed Native American and European ancestry. " . . . the new race of *mestizos* formed a cultural and biological bridge. . . ."

15. **province** A medium-sized subunit of territory and governmental administration within a larger nation or empire. "They proclaimed the area to be the province of New Mexico. . . ."

PART II: CHECKING YOUR PROGRESS

A. True-False

Where the statement is true, circle **T**; where it is false, circle **F**.

1. T F The geography of the North American continent was fundamentally shaped by the advance and retreat of glaciers during the Great Ice Age.

2. T F Native peoples of northeast Asia continued to migrate across the land bridge from Siberia to Alaska until the time of Columbus.

3. T F The early Indian civilizations of Mexico and Peru were built on the economic foundations of cattle herding and wheat growing.

4. T F Most American Indians north of Mexico lived in small, seminomadic agricultural and hunting communities.

5. T F Many Indian cultures like the Iroquois traced descent and passed possessions through the female line.

6. T F No Europeans had ever set foot on the American continents prior to Columbus's arrival in 1492.

7. T F A primary motive for the European voyages of discovery was the desire to find a less expensive route to Asian luxury goods and markets.

8. T F African slavery first developed in the aftermath of the Spanish conquest of the Americas.

9. T F Columbus immediately recognized in 1492 that he had come across vast new continents previously unknown to Europeans.

10. T F The greatest effect of the European intrusion into the Americas was to increase the Indian and *mestizo* population through intermarriage with the whites.

11.   T   F   The primary cause of the massive population decline among native Americans after the European arrival was not warfare but disease.

12.   T   F   The Spanish *conquistadores* had little to do with the native peoples of Mexico and refused to intermarry with them.

13.   T   F   The Spanish were able to defeat the Aztecs because the Aztecs had no experience with a sophisticated, urban civilization.

14.   T   F   Spain expanded its empire north into Florida and Texas partly to block French ambitions and protect their Caribbean Sea lanes.

15.   T   F   The Spanish Empire in the New World was larger, richer, and longer-lasting than that later established by the English.

B. Multiple Choice

Select the best answer and write the proper letter in the space provided.

1.   The geologically oldest mountains in North America are the
     a.   Appalachians.
     b.   Rockies.
     c.   Cascades.
     d.   Sierra Nevada.
     e.   Ozarks.

2.   The Indian peoples of the Americas
     a.   developed no advanced forms of civilization.
     b.   migrated by boat from the South Pacific region about 10,000 B.C.
     c.   were under the control of the two large empires of the Incas and the Aztecs.
     d.   relied primarily on nomadic hunting for their sustenance.
     e.   were divided into many diverse cultures speaking more than two thousand different languages.

3.   Which of the following was *not* among the ancient Indian cultures established in North America prior to 1300 A.D.?
     a.   The Incas
     b.   The Pueblos
     c.   The Anasazis
     d.   The Mississippian culture (Cahokia)
     e.   The Mound Builders

4.   One of the important factors that first stimulated European interest in trade and discovery was
     a.   the Christian crusaders who brought back a taste for the silks and spices of Asia.
     b.   the Arab slave traders on the east coast of Africa.
     c.   the Scandinavian sailors who had kept up continuous trade contacts with North America.
     d.   the division of Spain into small kingdoms competing for wealth and power.
     e.   Copernicus's discovery that the earth revolved around the sun.

5.   Among the most important American Indian products or discoveries to spread to the Old World were
     a.   animals such as buffalo and horses.
     b.   technologies such as the compass and the wheel.
     c.   clothing such as buckskin and beaver fur hats.
     d.   foodstuffs such as corn, beans, and tomatoes.
     e.   methods of calculating time such as the lunar calendar and the sundial.

6. The primary staples of Indian agriculture before the European arrival were

    a.   potatoes, beets, and sugar cane.
    b.   rice, sweet potatoes, and peanuts.
    c.   fruit, nuts, and honey.
    d.   wheat, oats, and barley.
    e.   corn, beans, and squash.

7. The number of Indians in North America at the time Columbus arrived was approximately

    a.   one million.
    b.   four million.
    c.   twenty million.
    d.   one hundred and fifty million.
    e.   three hundred million.

8. Before Columbus arrived, the only Europeans known to have visited North America, temporarily, were the

    a.   Greeks.
    b.   Irish.
    c.   Norse.
    d.   Italians.
    e.   Portuguese.

9. Even before the discovery of the Americas, Portugal became the first nation to enter the slave trade and establish large-scale plantations using slave labor in

    a.   West Africa.
    b.   the Mediterranean islands of Sardinia and Sicily.
    c.   the West Indies.
    d.   Brazil.
    e.   the sugar islands off the coast of Africa.

10. Much of the impetus for Spanish exploration and pursuit of glory in the early 1500s came from Spain's recent

    a.   successful wars with England.
    b.   national unification and expulsion of the Muslim Moors.
    c.   voyages of discovery along the coast of Africa.
    d.   conversion to Roman Catholicism.
    e.   founding of the Jesuit order by the Spanish soldier Ignatius Loyola.

11. A crucial political development that paved the way for the European colonization of America was the

    a.   rise of Italian city-states like Venice and Genoa.
    b.   feudal nobles' political domination of the merchant class.
    c.   rise of the centralized national monarchies such as those of Spain, Portugal, and France.
    d.   political alliance between the Christian papacy and Muslim Arab traders.
    e.   decline of religious conflict between Roman Catholics and Protestants.

12. The primary reason for the drastic decline in the Indian population after the encounter with the Europeans was the

    a.   rise of intertribal warfare.
    b.   destruction of major Indian cities and their dispersal into small, nomadic groups.
    c.   sharp decline in the Indian birthrate due to the killing of Indian males by the Europeans.
    d.   sudden introduction of the deadly disease syphilis to the New World.
    e.   Indians' lack of resistance to European diseases such as smallpox and malaria.

13. Cortés and his men were able to conquer the Aztec capital Tenochtitlán partly because
    a. they had larger forces than the Aztecs.
    b. the Aztec ruler Montezuma believed that Cortés was a god whose return had been predicted.
    c. the Aztecs were a peaceful people with no experience of war or conquest.
    d. the city of Tenochtitlán already had been devastated by a disease epidemic.
    e. Cortes was able to bribe many Aztec warriors to betray their people.

14. The flood of gold and silver from Spain's New World Empire into Europe after 1500 played a large role in the
    a. rise of capitalism and modern merchant banking.
    b. Protestant Reformation.
    c. development of an industrial working class.
    d. expansion of the jewelry industry.
    e. development of a modern system of precious metal currency.

15. The belief that the Spanish only killed, tortured, and stole in the Americas, while contributing nothing good, is called the
    a. *encomienda*.
    b. Inquisition.
    c. Evil Empire.
    d. *conquistadore* thesis.
    e. Black Legend.

C. Identification

Supply the correct identification for each numbered description.

1. _____   Extended period when glaciers covered most of the North American continent

2. _____   Staple crop that formed the economic foundation of Indian civilizations

3. _____   Important ancient Anasazi Indian center in New Mexico that included a pueblo of six hundred interconnected rooms

4. _____   First European nation to send explorers around the west coast of Africa

5. _____   Flourishing West African kingdom that had a major Islamic university in the city of Timbuktu

6. _____   The two smaller kingdoms that were united by King Ferdinand and Queen Isabella to create the powerful nation of Spain

7. _____   Animal introduced to North America by Europeans that transformed the Indian way of life on the Great Plains

8. _____   Name *one* of the major European diseases that devastated Native American populations after 1492

9. _____   Sexually transmitted disease originating in the Americas that was transmitted and spread among Europeans after 1492

10. _____   Treaty of 1492 that aimed to divide all of the Americas between Spain and Portugal

11. _____   Wealthy and populous capital of the Aztec empire

12. _____   Term for a person of mixed European and Indian ancestry

13. _____   A major Pueblo uprising of 1680 caused by Spanish efforts to suppress the Indians' religious practices

14. _____   Spanish term for the night of June 30, 1520, when war began between Aztecs and Spanish, leading to Spanish conquest of Mexico

15. _____   Roman Catholic religious order of friars that organized a chain of missions in California

D. Matching People, Places, and Events

Match the person, place, or event in the left column with the proper description in the right column by inserting the correct letter on the blank line.

1. ___   Ferdinand and Isabella

2. ___   Hernan Cortés and Francisco Pizarro

3. ___   Lake Bonneville

4. ___   Días and da Gama

5. ___   Christopher Columbus

6. ___   Malinche

7. ___   Moctezuma

8. ___   Hiawatha

9. ___   Tenochtitlán

10. ___   St. Augustine

11. ___   Giovanni Caboto (John Cabot)

12. ___   Junipero Serra

13. ___   Bartolome de Las Casas

a.   Female Indian slave who served as interpreter for Cortés

b.   Legendary founder of the powerful Iroquois Confederacy

c.   Wealthy capital of the Aztec empire

d.   Financiers and beneficiaries of Columbus's voyages to the New World

e.   Portuguese navigators who sailed around the African coast

f.   Dominican friar who sympathized with Indians and protested cruel Spanish policies in the New World

g.   Founded in 1565, the oldest continually inhabited European settlement in United States territory

h.   Italian-born navigator sent by English to explore North American coast in 1498

i.   Italian-born explorer who thought that he had arrived off the coast of Asia rather than on unknown continents

j.   Powerful Aztec monarch who fell to Spanish conquerors

k.   Spanish conquerors of great Indian civilizations

l.   Franciscan missionary who settled California

m.   Inland sea left by melting glaciers whose remnant is the Great Salt Lake

E. Putting Things in Order

Put the following events in correct order by numbering them from 1 to 5.

1. _____   The wealthy Aztec civilization falls to Cortés.

2. _____   Portuguese navigators sail down the west coast of Africa.

3. _____   The first human inhabitants cross into North America from Siberia across a temporary land bridge.

4. _____   Coronado explores present-day American Southwest.

5. _____   Spanish conquerors move into the Rio Grande valley of New Mexico.

F. Matching Cause and Effect

Match the historical cause in the left column with the proper effect in the right column by writing the correct letter on the blank line.

Cause

1. ___   The Great Ice Age

2. ___   Cultivation of corn (maize)

3. ___   New sailing technology and desire for spices

4. ___   Portugal's creation of sugar plantations on Atlantic coastal islands

5. ___   Columbus's first encounter with the New World

6. ___   Native Americans' lack of immunity to smallpox, malaria, and yellow fever

7. ___   The Spanish conquest of large quantities of New World gold and silver

8. ___   Aztec legends of a returning god, Quetzalcoatl

9. ___   The Spanish need to protect Mexico against French and English encroachment

10. ___   Franciscan friars' desire to convert Pacific coast Indians to Catholicism

Effect

a.   Rapid expansion of global economic commerce and manufacturing

b.   European voyages around Africa and across the Atlantic attempting to reach Asia

c.   Establishment of Spanish settlements in Florida and New Mexico

d.   Exposure of a land bridge between Asia and North America

e.   Formation of a chain of mission settlements in California

f.   A global exchange of animals, plants, and diseases

g.   The formation of large, sophisticated civilizations in Mexico and South America

h.   Cortés's relatively easy conquest of Tenochtitlán

i.   A decline of 90 percent in the New World Indian population

j.   The rapid expansion of the African slave trade

G. Developing Historical Skills

Connecting History with Geology and Geography

Because human history takes place across the surface of the earth, both the physical science of geology and the social science of geography are important to historians. Answer the following questions about the geological and geographical setting of North American history.

1.   What are the two major mountain chains that border the great mid-continental basin drained by the Mississippi River system?

2.   What great geological event explains the formation of the Great Lakes, the St. Lawrence River system, the Columbia-Snake River system, and Great Salt Lake?

3.   How did this same geological event isolate the human population of the Americas from that of Asia?

4.   Given the original geographical origins of the Indian populations, in which direction did their earliest migrations across North America occur: from southeast to north and west, from southwest to north and east, or from northwest to south and east?

H. Map Mastery

Map Discrimination

Using the maps and charts in Chapter 1, answer the following questions.

1.   *Chronological Chart*: The American Declaration of Independence occurred exactly 169 years between what other two major events in American history?

2.   *The First Discoverers of America*: When the first migrants crossed the Bering Land Bridge from Siberia to North America, approximately how many miles did they have to walk before they were south of the large ice caps to either side of the only open route?

     a.   200 miles

     b.   500 miles

     c.   2000 miles

     d.   3000 miles

3.   North American Indian Peoples at the Time of First Contact with Europeans: List five Indian tribes that lived in each of the following regions of North America:

     a.   Southwest

     b.   Great Plains

     c.   Northeast

     d.   Southeast

4. *Trade Routes with the East*: In the early European trading routes with Asia and the East Indies, what one common destination could be reached by the Middle Route, the Southern route, and da Gama's ocean route?

    a. Constantinople

    b. Persia

    c. China

    d. India

5. *Principal Early Spanish Explorations and Conquests*: Of the principal Spanish explorers—Columbus, Balboa, de León, Cortés, Pizarro, de Soto, and Coronado—which four *never* visited the territory or territorial waters of the land that eventually became part of the United States?

6. *Spain's North American Frontier, 1542–1823*:

    a. What were the two easternmost Spanish settlements on the northern frontier of Spanish Mexico?

    b. About how many years was Mission San Antonio founded before the first Spanish settlements in California?

        (1)   10

        (2)   25

        (3)   50

        (4)   100

7. *Principal Voyages of Discovery:*

    a. Who was the first explorer of the Pacific Ocean?

    b. According to the 1494 Treaty of Tordesillas, about how much of North America was allotted to the Portuguese?

        (1)   one-half

        (2)   one-third

        (3)   one-tenth

        (4)   none

Map Challenge

Using the text and the map on p. 9 of *North American Indian Peoples at the Time of First Contact with Europeans*, write a brief essay describing the geographical distributions of the more dense North American Indian populations at the time of European arrival. Include some discussion of why certain regions were densely populated and others less so.

PART III: APPLYING WHAT YOU HAVE LEARNED[*]

1. How did the geographic setting of North America—including its relation to Asia, Europe, and Africa—affect its subsequent history?

2. What were the common characteristics of all Indian cultures in the New World, and what were the important differences among them?

3. What fundamental factors drew the Europeans to the exploration, conquest, and settlement of the New World?

4. What was the impact on the Indians, Europeans, and Africans when each of their previously separate worlds collided with one another?

5. What were the greatest achievements of Spain's New World Empire, and what were its greatest evils and disasters?

6. Should the European encounter with the Indian peoples of the Americas be understood primarily as a story of conquest and exploitation, or as one of mutual cultural encounter that brought beneficial as well as tragic results for both?

---

[*]   Space is provided at the end of each chapter for answering the essay questions. Students needing more room should answer on separate sheets of paper.

CHAPTER 2

The Planting of English America, 1500–1733

PART I: REVIEWING THE CHAPTER

A. Checklist of Learning Objectives

After mastering this chapter, you should be able to:

1. Explain why England was slow to enter the colonization race and what factors finally led it to launch colonies in the early seventeenth century.

2. Describe the development of the Jamestown colony from its disastrous beginnings to its later prosperity.

3. Describe the cultural and social interaction and exchange between English settlers and Indians in Virginia and the effects of the Virginians' policy of warfare and forced removal on Indians and whites.

4. Compare the tobacco-based economic development of Virginia and Maryland with South Carolina's reliance on large-plantation rice-growing and African slavery based on West Indian models.

5. Identify the major similarities and differences among the southern colonies of Virginia, Maryland, North Carolina, South Carolina, and Georgia.

B. Glossary

To build your social science vocabulary, familiarize yourself with the following terms.

1. **nationalism** Fervent belief and loyalty given to the political unit of the nation-state. "Indeed England now had . . . a vibrant sense of nationalism and national destiny."

2. **primogeniture** The legal principle that the oldest son inherits all family property or land. ". . . laws of primogeniture decreed that only eldest sons were eligible to inherit landed estates."

3. **joint-stock companies** An economic arrangement by which a number of investors pool their capital for investment. "Joint-stock companies provided the financial means."

4. **charter** A legal document granted by a government to some group or agency to implement a stated purpose, and spelling out the attending rights and obligations. ". . . the Virginia Company of London received a charter from King James I of England. . . ."

5. **census** An official count of population, often also including other information about the population. "By 1669 an official census revealed that only about two thousand Indians remained in Virginia. . . ."

6. **feudal** Concerning the hierarchical, decentralized medieval social system of personal obligations between rulers and ruled. "Absentee proprietor Lord Baltimore hoped that . . . Maryland . . . would be the vanguard of a vast new feudal domain."

7. **indentured servant** A poor person obligated to a fixed term of unpaid labor, often in exchange for a benefit such as transportation, protection, or training. "Also like Virginia, it depended for labor in its early years mainly on white indentured servants. . . ."

8. **toleration** Originally, religious freedom granted by an established church to a religious minority. "Maryland's new religious statute guaranteed toleration to all Christians."

9. **squatter** A frontier farmer who illegally occupied land owned by others, or land not yet officially opened for settlement. "The newcomers, who frequently were 'squatters' without legal right to the soil . . . ."

10. **buffer** In politics, a small territory or state between two larger, antagonistic powers, established to minimize the possibility of conflict between them. "The English crown intended Georgia to serve chiefly as a buffer."

11. **melting pot** Popular American term for an ethnically diverse population that is presumed to be "melting" toward some common homogeneous national identity. "The hamlet of Savannah, like Charleston, was a melting-pot community."

PART II: CHECKING YOUR PROGRESS

A. True-False

Where the statement is true, circle **T**; where it is false, circle **F**.

1. T F England's politics and foreign policy in the sixteenth century were primarily shaped by its religious rivalry with Catholic Spain.

2. T F The earliest English colonization efforts experienced surprising success.

3. T F The defeat of the Spanish Armada was important to North American colonization because it enabled England to conquer Spain's New World empire.

4. T F Two groups eager to join colonization ventures were farmers driven off their lands by enclosure and disinherited younger sons of the upper-class gentry.

5. T F Originally, the primary purpose of the joint-stock Virginia Company was to guarantee the long-term welfare of the freeborn English settlers in the colony.

6. T F The survival rate of colonists in Jamestown's first two decades was very low, less than 20 percent.

7. T F Virginia's leaders promoted a policy of peaceful assimilation of the Indians, which resulted in frequent white-Indian intermarriage.

8. T F The Maryland colony was founded to establish a religious refuge for persecuted English Quakers.

9. T F From the time of its founding, South Carolina had close economic ties with the British West Indies.

10. T F The slave codes, eventually adopted throughout England's North American colonies, gradually developed from the model of Virginia's indentured servitude laws.

11. T F After considerable experimentation, South Carolina's plantation owners finally found in silk a successful product that they could export.

12. T F South Carolina prospered partly by selling African slaves in the West Indies.

13. T F   Compared with its neighbors Virginia and South Carolina, North Carolina was more democratic and individualistic in social outlook.

14. T F   Britain valued the Georgia colony primarily as a rich source of gold and timber.

15. T F   All the southern colonies eventually came to rely on staple-crop plantation agriculture for their economic prosperity.

B. Multiple Choice

Select the best answer and circle the corresponding letter.

1. After decades of religious turmoil, Protestantism finally gained permanent dominance in England after the succession to the throne of

    a. King Edward VI.
    b. Queen Mary I.
    c. Queen Elizabeth I.
    d. King James I.
    e. King Charles I.

2. England's first two North American colonies, which completely failed, were launched in

    a. Florida and Georgia.
    b. Newfoundland and North Carolina.
    c. Massachusetts and Maine.
    d. Bermuda and Barbados.
    e. New York and New Jersey.

3. Imperial England and English soldiers developed a contemptuous attitude toward natives partly through their earlier colonizing experiences in

    a. Canada.
    b. Spain.
    c. India.
    d. Ireland.
    e. the West Indies.

4. England's victory over the Spanish Armada gave it

    a. control of the Spanish colonies in the New World.
    b. naval dominance of the Atlantic Ocean and a vibrant sense of nationalism.
    c. a stable social order and economy.
    d. effective control of the African slave trade.
    e. the power to control and colonize Ireland.

5. At the time of its first colonization efforts, England was

    a. struggling under the political domination of Spain.
    b. enjoying a period of social and economic stability.
    c. experiencing increasing ethnic and religious diversity.
    d. undergoing sharp political conflicts between advocates of republicanism and the monarchy of Elizabeth I.
    e. undergoing rapid and disruptive economic and social transformations.

6. Many of the early Puritan settlers of America were

    a. displaced sailors from Liverpool and Bath.
    b. merchants and shopkeepers from the Midlands.
    c. urban laborers from Glasgow and Edinburgh.
    d. displaced farmers from eastern and western England.
    e. dissenting clergy from Canterbury and York.

7. England's first colony at Jamestown
    a. was an immediate economic success.
    b. was saved from failure by John Smith's leadership and by John Rolfe's introduction of tobacco.
    c. enjoyed the strong and continual support of King James I.
    d. depended on the introduction of African slave labor for its survival.
    e. was saved from near-starvation by generous food contributions from the Powhatan Indians.
8. Representative government was first introduced to the Americas in the colony of
    a. Bermuda.
    b. Maryland.
    c. North Carolina.
    d. Georgia.
    e. Virginia.
9. One important difference between the founding of the Virginia and Maryland colonies was that Virginia
    a. colonists were willing to come only if they could acquire their own land, while Maryland colonists were willing to work as tenants for feudal landlords.
    b. depended primarily on tobacco for its economy, while Maryland turned to rice cultivation.
    c. depended on African slave labor, while Maryland relied mainly on white indentured servitude.
    d. was founded as a strictly economic venture, while Maryland was intended partly to secure religious freedom for persecuted Roman Catholics.
    e. struggled to find effective leadership for several decades, while Lord Baltimore personally governed Maryland's early colonists.
10. After the Act of Toleration in 1649, Maryland provided religious freedom for
    a. Jews.
    b. atheists.
    c. Baptists and Quakers.
    d. those who denied the divinity of Jesus.
    e. Protestants and Catholics.
11. The primary reason that no new English colonies were founded between 1634 and 1670 was the
    a. obvious economic unprofitability of Virginia and Maryland.
    b. civil war in England.
    c. continuous naval conflicts between Spain and England that disrupted sea-lanes.
    d. English kings' increasing hostility to colonial ventures.
    e. inability of English capitalists to gather funds for investment in North America.
12. The early conflicts between English settlers and the Indians near Jamestown laid the basis for the
    a. intermarriage of white settlers and Indians.
    b. incorporation of Indians into the melting-pot of American culture.
    c. forced separation of the Indians into the separate territories of the reservation system.
    d. use of Indians as a slave-labor force on white plantations.
    e. romantic English image of Indians as noble savages.

13. After the defeat of the coastal Tuscarora and Yamasee Indians by North Carolinians in 1711–1715
    a. there were almost no Indians left east of the Mississippi River.
    b. the remaining southeastern Indian tribes formed an alliance to wage warfare against the whites.
    c. the powerful Creeks, Cherokees, and Iroquois remained in the Appalachian Mountains as a barrier against white settlement.
    d. the remaining coastal Indians migrated to the West Indies.
    e. North and South Carolinians began enslaving Africans rather than Indians.
14. Most of the early white settlers in North Carolina were
    a. religious dissenters and poor whites fleeing aristocratic Virginia.
    b. wealthy planters from the West Indies.
    c. the younger, ambitious sons of English gentry.
    d. ex-convicts and debtors released from English prisons.
    e. displaced English farmers who had been driven from their lands by enclosure.
15. The high-minded philanthropists who founded the Georgia colony were especially interested in the cause of
    a. women's rights.
    b. temperance.
    c. pacifism.
    d. religious and political freedom.
    e. prison reform.

C. Identification

Supply the correct identification for each numbered description.

1. _____ Nation where English Protestant rulers employed brutal tactics against the local Catholic population

2. _____ Island colony founded by Sir Walter Raleigh that mysteriously disappeared in the 1580s

3. _____ Naval invaders defeated by English sea dogs in 1588

4. _____ Forerunner of the modern corporation that enabled investors to pool financial capital for colonial and commercial ventures

5. _____ Name of two wars, fought in 1614 and 1644, between the English in Jamestown and the nearby Indian leader

6. _____ The harsh system of laws governing African labor, first developed in Barbados and later officially adopted by South Carolina in 1696

7. _____ The Virginia assembly that first established local representative self-government for English settlers in North America

8. _____ Penniless people obligated to engage in unpaid labor for a fixed number of years, usually in exchange for passage to the New World or other benefits

9. _____ Persecuted English religious minority for whom colonial Maryland was intended to be a refuge

10. _____ Poor farmers in North Carolina and elsewhere who occupied land and raised crops without gaining legal title to the soil

11. _____   Spain's North American colony from which Spanish intruders periodically threatened English settlers in Georgia and the Carolinas

12. _____   The primary staple crop of early Virginia, Maryland, and North Carolina

13. _____   The only southern colony with a slave majority

14. _____   The primary plantation crop of South Carolina

15. _____   A melting-pot town in early colonial Georgia

D. Matching People, Places, and Events

Match the person, place, or event in the left column with the proper description in the right column by inserting the correct letter on the blank line.

1. ___ Powhatan

2. ___ Walter Raleigh and Humphrey Gilbert

3. ___ Roanoke

4. ___ John Smith

5. ___ Virginia

6. ___ Maryland

7. ___ Lord De La Warr

8. ___ John Wesley

9. ___ Lord Baltimore

10. ___ South Carolina

11. ___ North Carolina

12. ___ Georgia

13. ___ James Oglethorpe

14. ___ Elizabeth I

15. ___ Jamestown

a. Colony originally founded as a haven for Roman Catholics

b. Indian leader who ruled tribes in the James River area of Virginia

c. Harsh military governor of Virginia who employed Irish tactics against the Indians

d. British founder of the Methodist Church who served for a time as a missionary in colonial Georgia

e. Colony originally founded as a refuge for debtors by philanthropists

f. Economically poorer colony that was called "a vale of humility between two mountains of conceit"

g. The unmarried ruler who established English Protestantism and fought the Catholic Spanish

h. The Catholic aristocrat who sought to build a sanctuary for his fellow believers

i. The failed lost colony founded by Sir Walter Raleigh

j. Riverbank site where Virginia Company settlers planted the first permanent English colony

k. Colony that established the House of Burgesses as first representative government in 1619

l. Virginia leader saved by Pocahantas,

m. Elizabethan courtiers who failed in their attempts to found New World colonies

n. Philanthropic soldier-statesman who founded the Georgia colony

o. Colony that turned to disease-resistant African slaves for labor in its extensive rice plantations

E. Putting Things in Order

Put the following events in correct order by numbering them from 1 to 5.

1. _____ A surprising naval victory by the English inspires a burst of national pride and paves the way for colonization.

2. _____ A Catholic aristocrat founds a colony as a haven for his fellow believers.

3. _____ Settlers from the West Indies found a colony on the North American mainland.

4. _____ An English colony is founded by philanthropists as a haven for imprisoned debtors.

5. _____ A company of investors launches a disaster-stricken but permanent English colony along a mosquito-infested river in Virginia.

F. Matching Cause and Effect

Match the historical cause in the left column with the proper effect in the right column by writing the correct letter on the blank line.

Cause

1. ___ The English victory over the Spanish Armada

2. ___ The English law of primogeniture

3. ___ The enclosing of English pastures and cropland

4. ___ Lord De La Warr's use of brutal Irish tactics in Virginia

5. ___ The English government's persecution of Roman Catholics

6. ___ The slave codes of England's Barbados colony

7. ___ John Smith's stern leadership in Virginia

8. ___ The English settlers' near-destruction of small Indian tribes

9. ___ The flight of poor farmers and religious dissenters from planter-run Virginia

10. ___ Georgia's unhealthy climate, restrictions on slavery, and vulnerability to Spanish attacks

Effect

a. Led to the two Anglo-Powhatan wars that virtually exterminated Virginia's Indian population

b. Enabled England to gain control of the North Atlantic sea-lanes

c. Forced gold-hungry colonists to work and saved them from total starvation

d. Led Lord Baltimore to establish the Maryland colony

e. Led to the founding of the independent-minded North Carolina colony

f. Led many younger sons of the gentry to seek their fortunes in exploration and colonization

g. Contributed to the formation of powerful Indian coalitions like the Iroquois and the Algonquians

h. Kept the buffer colony poor and largely unpopulated for a long time

i. Became the legal basis for slavery in North America

j.   Forced numerous laborers off the land and sent them looking for opportunities elsewhere

G. Developing Historical Skills

Understanding Historical Comparisons

To understand historical events, historians frequently compare one set of conditions with another so as to illuminate both similarities and differences. In this chapter, there are comparisons of English colonization in North America with (a) England's imperial activity in Ireland, (b) Spanish colonization, and (c) England's colonies in the West Indies. Examine these three comparisons, and then answer the following questions.

1.   What similarities developed between the English attitude toward the Irish and the English attitude toward Native Americans, and why?

2.   What characteristics of England after the victory over the Spanish Armada were similar to Spain's condition one century earlier?

3.   How was the sugar economy of the West Indies different from the tobacco economy of the Chesapeake?

H. Map Mastery

Map Discrimination

Using the maps and charts in Chapter 2, answer the following questions.

1.   *Sources of the Puritan "Great Migration" to New England, 1620–1650*: List any five of the English woolen district counties from which the Puritans came.

2.   *Early Maryland and Virginia*:

a.   The colony of Maryland was centered on what body of water?

b.   The *eastern* boundary of Lord Baltimore's original Maryland land grant was formed by what river and bay of the same name?

3. *Early Carolina and Georgia Settlements*:

    a. Which southern colony bordered on foreign, non-English territory?

    b. Which southern English colony had the smallest western frontier?

    c. In which colony was each of the following cities located: Charleston, Savannah, Newbern, Jamestown?

    d. It was exactly twice as many years between the formation of North Carolina and Georgia as between the formation of _____ and _____.

Map Challenge

1. Besides the James River, what shorter river defines the peninsula where Jamestown was located?

2. What river marked the border between the Virginia and Maryland colonies?

PART III: APPLYING WHAT YOU HAVE LEARNED

1. What was the primary purpose of the English settlement of Jamestown, and how successful were the colonists in achieving that goal in the first twenty years?

2. What features were common to all of England's southern colonies, and what features were peculiar to each one?

3. In what ways did the relationship between whites and Indians (Powhatans) in Virginia establish the pattern for later white-Indian relations across North America.

4. How did the search for a viable labor force affect the development of the southern colonies? Why did African slavery almost immediately become the dominant labor system in South Carolina, while only slowly taking firm hold in England's other southern colonies?

5. Which was the most important factor shaping the development of England's southern colonies in the seventeenth century: Indian relations, the one-crop plantation economy, or slavery? Explain and support your answer.

6. Compare and contrast the early colonial empires of Spain and England in terms of motives, economic foundations, and relations with Africans and Indians (see Chapter 1). What factors explain the similarities and differences in the two ventures?

CHAPTER 3

Settling the Northern Colonies, 1619–1700

PART I: REVIEWING THE CHAPTER

A. Checklist of Learning Objectives

After mastering this chapter, you should be able to:

1. Describe the Puritans and their beliefs, and explain why they left England for the New World.

2. Explain how the Puritans' theology shaped the government and society of the Massachusetts Bay Colony.

3. Explain how Massachusetts Bay's conflict with religious dissenters, as well as new economic opportunities, led to the expansion of New England into Rhode Island, Connecticut, and elsewhere.

4. Describe the conflict between colonists and Indians in New England and the effects of King Philip's War.

5. Summarize early New England attempts at intercolonial unity and the consequences of England's Glorious Revolution in America.

6. Describe the founding of New York and Pennsylvania, and explain why these two settlements as well as the other middle colonies became so ethnically, religiously, and politically diverse.

7. Describe the central features of the middle colonies, and explain how they differed from New England and the southern colonies.

B. Glossary

To build your social science vocabulary, familiarize yourself with the following terms.

1. **predestination** The Calvinist doctrine that God has foreordained some people to be saved and some to be damned. "Good works could not save those whom 'predestination' had marked for the infernal fires."

2. **elect** In Calvinist doctrine, those who have been chosen by God for salvation. "But neither could the elect count on their predetermined salvation. . . ."

3. **conversion** A religious turn to God, thought by Calvinists to involve an intense, identifiable personal experience of grace. "They constantly sought, in themselves and others, signs of 'conversion.' . . ."

4. **visible saints** In Calvinism, those who publicly proclaimed their experience of conversion and were expected to lead godly lives. "The most devout Puritans . . . believed that only 'visible saints' . . . should be admitted to church membership."

5. **calling** In Protestantism, the belief that saved individuals have a religious obligation to engage in worldly work. "Like John Winthrop, [the Puritans] believed in the doctrine of a 'calling' to do God's work on this earth."

6. **heresy** Departure from correct or officially defined belief. ". . . she eventually boasted that she had come by her beliefs through a direct revelation from God. This was even higher heresy."

7. **seditious** Concerning resistance to or rebellion against the government. "[His was] a seditious blow at the Puritan idea of government's very purpose."

8. **commonwealth** An organized civil government or social order united for a shared purpose. "They were allowed, in effect, to become semiautonomous commonwealths."

9. **autocratic** Absolute or dictatorial rule. "An autocratic spirit survived, and the aristocratic element gained strength. . . ."

10. **passive resistance** Nonviolent action or opposition to authority, often in accord with religious or moral beliefs. "As advocates of passive resistance, [the Quakers] would turn the other cheek and rebuild their meetinghouse on the site where their enemies had torn it down."

11. **asylum** A place of refuge and security, especially for the persecuted or unfortunate. "Eager to establish an asylum for his people. . . ."

12. **proprietary** Concerning exclusive legal ownership, as of colonies granted to individuals by the monarch. "Penn's new proprietary regime was unusually liberal. . . ."

13. **naturalization** The granting of citizenship to foreigners or immigrants. "No restrictions were placed on immigration, and naturalization was made easy."

14. **blue laws** Laws designed to restrict personal behavior in accord with a strict code of morality. "Even so, 'blue laws' prohibited 'ungodly revelers,' stage plays, playing cards, dice, games, and excessive hilarity."

15. **ethnic** Concerning diverse peoples or cultures, specifically those of non-Anglo-Saxon background. ". . . Pennsylvania attracted a rich mix of ethnic groups."

PART II: CHECKING YOUR PROGRESS

A. True-False

Where the statement is true, circle **T**; where it is false, circle **F**.

1. T F   The dominant form of the Protestant faith among New England's early colonists was Calvinism, as developed by the Geneva reformer John Calvin.

2. T F   The most fervent Puritans believed that the Church of England was corrupt because it did not restrict its membership to "visible saints" who had experienced conversion.

3. T F   The large, separatist Plymouth Colony of Pilgrims strongly influenced smaller Puritan Massachusetts Bay.

4. T F   Massachusetts Bay restricted the vote for elections to the General Court to adult male members of the Congregational Church.

5. T F   Roger Williams and Anne Hutchinson were both banished for organizing political rebellions against the Massachusetts Bay authorities.

6. T F   Rhode Island was the most religiously and politically tolerant of the New England colonies.

7. T F   The Wampanoag Indians of New England initially befriended the English colonists.

8. T F   After King Charles II was restored to the throne of England, the crown attempted to gain tighter control over its colonies, especially defiant Massachusetts.

9.   T   F   King Philip's War enabled New England's Indians to recover their numbers and morale.

10.   T   F   New York became the most democratic and economically equal of the middle colonies.

11.   T   F   Dutch New Netherland was conquered in 1664 by military expedition from the colony of New Sweden in Delaware.

12.   T   F   William Penn originally wanted his Pennsylvania colony to be settled exclusively by his fellow English Quakers.

13.   T   F   Later non-Quaker immigrants to Pennsylvania like the Scots-Irish welcomed the peaceful relations with the Indians established by William Penn's policies.

14.   T   F   The middle colonies' broad, fertile river valleys enabled them to develop a richer and more successful agricultural economy than that of New England.

15.   T   F   The middle colonies were characterized by tightly knit, ethically homogeneous communities that shared a common sense of religious purpose.

B. Multiple Choice

Select the best answer and circle the corresponding letter.

1.   The principal motivation shaping the earliest settlements in New England was

     a.   the desire for political freedom.
     b.   religious commitment and devotion.
     c.   economic opportunity and the chance for a better life.
     d.   a spirit of adventure and interest in exploring the New World.
     e.   a missionary zeal to convert the Indians to Calvinism.

2.   Compared with the Plymouth Colony, the Massachusetts Bay Colony was

     a.   dedicated to complete separation from the Church of England.
     b.   afflicted with corrupt and incompetent leaders.
     c.   more focused on religious rather than political liberty.
     d.   larger and more prosperous economically.
     e.   afflicted with incompetent leadership.

3.   One reason that the Massachusetts Bay Colony was *not* a true democracy is that

     a.   only church members could vote for the governor and the General Court.
     b.   political offices were dominated by the clergy.
     c.   people were not permitted to discuss issues freely in their own towns.
     d.   the governor and his assistants were appointed rather than elected.
     e.   the colony was ultimately under control of the English kings.

4.   The essential heresy that caused Anne Hutchinson to be convicted and banished from Massachusetts Bay was her declared belief that

     a.   the government of John Winthrop was corrupt and tyrannical.
     b.   the Puritan elect were just as sinful and those who had been "predestined" to damnation.
     c.   she had received a direct revelation from God that the saved did not need to obey either human or divine law.
     d.   the Bible did not teach that a personal conversion experience was necessary for salvation.
     e.   Calvin's doctrine that people were predestined to either heaven or hell violated fundamental human freedom.

5. Roger Williams based the religious freedom of his colony of Rhode Island on his belief that

    a. it really did not matter what religious beliefs people held, because all were more or less equal.

    b. the corrupt Massachusetts Bay Colony had proved that religious uniformity did not work.

    c. political democracy inevitably required freedom of speech and religion.

    d. God had created human beings fundamentally good and able to choose the right.

    e. civil government had no right to regulate religious behavior or individual conscience.

6. Which of the following New England settlements did *not* become a separate colony, but remained under the direct control of Massachusetts?

    a. Connecticut

    b. New Hampshire

    c. New Haven

    d. Maine

    e. Rhode Island

7. The Indian tribe that the Pilgrim colonists in New England first encountered were the

    a. Iroquois.

    b. Wampanoags.

    c. Narragansetts.

    d. Hurons.

    e. Powhatans.

8. King Philip's War represented

    a. the first serious military conflict between New England colonists and the English King.

    b. an example of the disastrous divisions among the Wampanoags, Pequots, and Narragansetts.

    c. the last major Indian effort to halt New Englanders' encroachment on their lands.

    d. a relatively minor conflict in terms of actual fighting and casualties.

    e. proof that the Puritans' missionary efforts among the Indians had been successful.

9. The primary value of the New England Confederation lay in

    a. restoring harmony between Rhode Island and the other New England colonies.

    b. promoting better relations between New England colonists and their Indian neighbors.

    c. enabling the smaller New England colonies to obtain equality with Massachusetts.

    d. providing the first small step on the road to intercolonial cooperation.

    e. defending colonial rights against increasing pressure from the English monarchy.

10. The event that sparked the collapse of the Dominion of New England was

    a. King Philip's War.

    b. the revocation of the Massachusetts Bay Colony's charter.

    c. Governor Andros's harsh attacks on colonial liberties.

    d. the Glorious Revolution in England.

    e. the Salem witch trials.

11. The Dutch Colony of New Netherland

    a. was harshly and undemocratically governed.

    b. contained little ethnic diversity.

    c. was developed as a haven for persecuted Dutch Calvinists.

    d. enjoyed prosperity and peace under the policies of the Dutch West India Company.

    e. represented the most ambitious colonial enterprise of the Dutch government.

12. The short-lived colony conquered by Dutch New Netherland in 1655 was

   a. New Jersey.
   b. New France.
   c. New England.
   d. Newfoundland.
   e. New Sweden.

13. William Penn's colony of Pennsylvania

   a. sought settlers primarily from England and Scotland.
   b. experienced continuing warfare with neighboring Indian tribes.
   c. actively sought settlers from Germany and other non-British countries.
   d. set up the Quaker religion as its tax-supported established church.
   e. made Penn himself a wealthy and powerful figure in the English government.

14. Besides Pennsylvania, Quakers were also heavily involved in the early settlement of both

   a. New Jersey and New York.
   b. New Jersey and Delaware.
   c. New Netherland and New York.
   d. Maryland and Delaware.
   e. Delaware and Rhode Island.

15. The middle colonies of New York, New Jersey, Pennsylvania, and Delaware

   a. depended almost entirely on industry rather than agriculture for their prosperity.
   b. had powerful established churches that suppressed religious dissenters.
   c. relied heavily on slave labor for their agriculture.
   d. fought frequent and bitter wars with the Indian tribes of the region.
   e. had more ethnic diversity than either New England or the southern colonies.

C. Identification

Supply the correct identification for each numbered description.

1. _____   Sixteenth-century religious reform movement begun by Martin Luther

2. _____   English Calvinists who sought a thorough cleansing of the Church of England while remaining officially within that church

3. _____   Radical Calvinists who considered the Church of England so corrupt that they broke with it and formed their own independent churches

4. _____   The shipboard agreement by the Pilgrim Fathers to establish a body politic and submit to majority rule

5. _____   The name eventually applied to the Puritans' established church in Massachusetts and several other New England colonies

6. _____   The elite English university where John Cotton and many other Puritan leaders of New England had been educated

7. _____   The two major nonfarming industries of Massachusetts Bay
   _____

8. _____   Anne Hutchinson's heretical belief that the truly saved need not obey human or divine law

9. _____   Common fate of Roger Williams and Anne Hutchinson after they were convicted of heresy in Massachusetts Bay

10. _____ Vicious war waged by English settlers and their Narragansett Indian allies that virtually annihilated a major Indian tribe in Connecticut

11. _____ A major pan-Indian uprising of 1675–1676 that destroyed many Puritan towns but ultimately represented a major defeat for New England's Indians

12. _____ English revolt of 1688–1689 that overthrew the Catholic King James II and also led to the overthrow of the Dominion of New England in America

13. _____ Vast feudal estates in the rich Hudson River valley that created an aristocratic elite in the New Netherland and later New York colony

14. _____ Collective term for the Pennsylvania statutes that prohibited the theater, cards, dice, and other activities and games deemed immoral.

15. _____ William Penn's "city of brotherly love" that became the most prosperous and tolerant urban center in England's North American colonies

D. Matching People, Places, and Events

Match the person, place or event in the left column with the proper description in the right column by inserting the correct letter on the blank line.

1. ___ Martin Luther

2. ___ John Calvin

3. ___ Massasoit

4. ___ Plymouth

5. ___ Massachusetts Bay Colony

6. ___ John Winthrop

7. ___ Baptists

8. ___ General Court

9. ___ Puritans

10. ___ Quakers

11. ___ Anne Hutchinson

12. ___ Roger Williams

13. ___ King Philip

14. ___ Peter Stuyvesant

15. ___ William Penn

a. Dominant religious group in Massachusetts Bay

b. Founder of the most tolerant and democratic of the middle colonies

c. Dissenting religious group first founded in Rhode Island by Roger Williams

d. Small colony that eventually merged into Massachusetts Bay

e. Religious dissenter convicted of the heresy of antinomianism

f. Indian leader who waged an unsuccessful war against New England's white colonists

g. German monk who began Protestant Reformation

h. Religious group persecuted in Massachusetts and New York but not in Pennsylvania

i. Representative assembly of Massachusetts Bay

j. Promoter of Massachusetts Bay as a holy "city upon a hill"

k. Conqueror of New Sweden who later lost New Netherland to the English

l.   Reformer whose religious ideas inspired English Puritans, Scotch Presbyterians, French Huguenots, and Dutch Reformed

m.   Wampanoag chieftain who befriended English colonists

n.   Colony whose government sought to enforce God's law on believers and unbelievers alike

o.   Radical founder of the most tolerant New England colony

E. Putting Things in Order

Put the following events in correct order by numbering them from 1 to 10.

1. _____   New England Confederation achieves a notable military success.

2. _____   English separatists migrate from Holland to America.

3. _____   Swedish colony on Delaware River is conquered by Dutch neighbor.

4. _____   Manhattan Island is acquired by non-English settlers.

5. _____   Protestant Reformation begins in Europe and England.

6. _____   Quaker son of an English admiral obtains a royal charter for a colony.

7. _____   Puritans bring a thousand immigrants and a charter to America.

8. _____   England conquers a colony on the Hudson River.

9. _____   Convicted Massachusetts Bay heretic founds a colony as a haven for dissenters.

10. _____   James II is overthrown in England, and Edmund Andros is overthrown in America.

F. Matching Cause and Effect

Match the historical cause in the left column with the proper effect in the right column by writing the correct letter on the blank line.

Cause	Effect
1. ___ Charles I's persecution of the Puritans	a. Led to overthrow of Andros's Dominion of New England
2. ___ Puritans' belief that their government was based on a covenant with God	b. Encouraged development of Pennsylvania, New York, and New Jersey as rich, grain-growing bread colonies
3. ___ Puritan persecution of religious dissenters like Roger Williams	
4. ___ The Glorious Revolution	c. Secured political control of New York for a few aristocratic families
5. ___ King Philip's War	

6. ___ The Dutch West India Company's search for quick profits

7. ___ Dutch and English creation of vast Hudson Valley estates

8. ___ The English government's persecution of Quakers

9. ___ William Penn's liberal religious and immigration policies

10. ___ The middle colonies' cultivation of broad, fertile river valleys

d. Spurred formation of the Massachusetts Bay Company and mass migration to New England

e. Encouraged large-scale foreign immigration to Pennsylvania

f. Led to restriction of political participation in colonial Massachusetts to visible saints

g. Spurred William Penn's founding of Pennsylvania

h. Meant that New Netherland was run as an authoritarian fur trading venture

i. Ended New England Indians' attempts to halt white expansion

j. Led to the founding of Rhode Island as a haven for unorthodox faiths

G. Developing Historical Skills

Using Quantitative Maps

Some maps, like *The Great English Migration*, present quantitative as well as geographical information. By making a few simple calculations, additional information and conclusions can be derived. Adding the figures on the map indicates that about 68,000 English people came to North America and the West Indies from about 1630 to 1642. Study the map and answer the following questions.

1. About what percentage of the total English migration went to New England? (Divide the figure for New England by the total number of immigrants.)

2. How many more English settlers went to the West Indies than to New England?

H. Map Mastery

Map Discrimination

Using the maps and charts in Chapter 3, answer the following questions.

1. *Seventeenth-Century New England Settlements*: Which New England colony was largely centered on a single river valley?

2. *Seventeenth-Century New England Settlements*: Which New England colony was made part of Massachusetts Bay in 1641 but separated from the Bay Colony in 1679?

3. *Seventeenth-Century New England Settlements*: When Roger Williams fled Massachusetts to found a new colony, in which direction did he go?

4. *The Stuart Dynasty in England*: Which was the only New England colony founded during the Restoration regime of Charles II?

5. *The Stuart Dynasty in England*: Which New England colony was not founded during the reigns of Charles I or Charles II?

6. *Early Settlements in the Middle Colonies, with Founding Dates*: The territory that was once New Sweden became part of which three English colonies?

Map Challenge

Using the map of *Seventeenth Century New England Settlements* and the related text, write an essay explaining why New England came to be politically and religiously dominated by Massachusetts Bay. Which one New England colony, even though founded by someone originally from the Bay Colony, most vigorously resisted Massachusetts' domination, and why?

PART III: APPLYING WHAT YOU HAVE LEARNED

1. Compare and contrast the New England and middle colonies in terms of motives for founding, religious and social composition, economic foundations, and political development.

2. How did the Puritans' distinctive religious outlook and church organization shape the politics, society, and culture of Massachusetts Bay and most of the other New England colonies?

3. "The dissent from Puritanism was as important in the formation of New England as Puritanism itself." How valid is this statement? Defend your answer.

4. Contrast Puritan New England's policies toward the Indians with the initial policies of the Quaker settlers in Pennsylvania. Why was Pennsylvania's Indian policy ultimately unsuccessful?

5. Describe and analyze the English government's relationship with New England and the middle colonies during the course of the seventeenth century. Is the term *benign neglect* an accurate description of English colonial policy?

6.   Discuss the development of religious and political freedom in Massachusetts, Rhode Island, New York, and Pennsylvania. How did the greater degree of such freedoms enjoyed by Rhode Island and Pennsylvania affect life in those colonies?

7.   What economic, social, and ethnic conditions typical of the early southern colonies (see Chapter 2) were generally absent in the New England and middle colonies? What characteristics did the middle colonies have that were not generally present in the South?

CHAPTER 4

American Life in the Seventeenth Century, 1607–1692

PART I: REVIEWING THE CHAPTER

A. Checklist of Learning Objectives

After mastering this chapter, you should be able to:

1. Describe the basic economy, demographics, and social structure and life of the seventeenth-century colonies.

2. Compare and contrast the different forms of society and ways of life of the southern colonies and New England.

3. Explain how the practice of indentured servitude failed to solve the colonial labor problem and why colonists then turned to African slavery.

4. Describe the character of slavery in the early English colonies and explain how a distinctive African American identity and culture emerged from the mingling of numerous African ethnic groups.

5. Summarize the unique New England way of life centered on family, town, and church, and describe the problems that afflicted this comfortable social order in the late seventeenth century.

6. Describe family life and the roles of women in both the southern and New England colonies, and indicate how these changed over the course of the seventeenth century.

B. Glossary

To build your social science vocabulary, familiarize yourself with the following terms.

1. **headright** The right to acquire a certain amount of land granted to the person who finances the passage of a laborer. "Masters—not servants themselves—thus reaped the benefits of landownership from the headright system."

2. **disfranchise** To take away the right to vote. "The Virginia Assembly in 1670 disfranchised most of the landless knockabouts. . . ."

3. **civil war** Any conflict between the citizens or inhabitants of the same country. "As this civil war in Virginia ground on. . . ."

4. **indentured servant** A laborer bound to unpaid service to a master for a fixed term, in exchange for benefits such as transportation, tools, and clothes. "There they boarded ship for America as indentured servants. . . ."

5. **tidewater** The territory adjoining water affected by tides—that is, near the seacoast or coastal rivers. "Bacon . . . had pitted the hard scrabble backcountry frontiersmen against the haughty gentry of the tidewater plantations."

6. **middle passage** That portion of a slave ship's journey in which slaves were carried from Africa to the Americas. "... the captives were herded aboard sweltering ships for the gruesome 'middle passage.'..."

7. **fertility** The ability to reproduce and bear abundant young. "The captive black population of the Chesapeake area soon began to grow not only through new imports but also through its own fertility...."

8. **menial** Fit for servants; humble or low. "But chiefly they performed the sweaty toil of clearing swamps, grubbing out trees, and other menial tasks."

9. **militia** A voluntary, nonprofessional armed force of citizens, usually called to military service only in emergencies. "[They] tried to march to Spanish Florida, only to be stopped by the local militia."

10. **hierarchy** A social group arranged in ranks or classes. "The rough equality ... was giving way to a hierarchy of wealth and status...."

11. **corporation** A private group or institution to which the government grants legal rights to carry on certain specified activities. "... the Massachusetts Puritans established Harvard College, today the oldest corporation in America...."

12. **jeremiad** A sermon or prophecy recounting wrongdoing, warning of doom, and calling for repentance. "Jeremiads continued to thunder from the pulpits...."

13. **lynching** The illegal execution of an accused person by mob action, without due process of law. "A hysterical 'witch-hunt' ensued, leading to the legal lynching in 1692 of twenty individuals...."

14. **hinterland** An inland region set back from a port, river, or seacoast. "... their accusers came largely from subsistence farming families in Salem's hinterland."

15. **social structure** The basic pattern of the distribution of status and wealth in a society. "... many settlers ... tried to re-create on a modified scale the social structure they had known in the Old World."

16. **blue blood** Of noble or upper-class descent. "... would-be American blue bloods resented the pretensions of the 'meaner sort.'..."

PART II: CHECKING YOUR PROGRESS

A. True-False

Where the statement is true, circle **T**; where it is false, circle **F**.

1. T F Life expectancy among the seventeenth-century settlers of Maryland and Virginia was about sixty years.

2. T F Because men greatly outnumbered women in the Chesapeake region, a fierce competition arose among men for scarce females to marry.

3. T F Pregnancies among unmarried young women were common in the seventeenth-century colonial South.

4. T F Chesapeake Bay tobacco planters responded to falling prices by cutting back production.

5. T F The headright system of land grants to those who brought laborers to America primarily benefited wealthy planters rather than the poor indentured servants.

6. T F   Most of the European immigrants who came to Virginia and Maryland in the seventeenth century were poor indentured servants.

7. T F   Bacon's Rebellion involved an alliance of white indentured servants with Virginia's Indians in an attack on the elite planter class.

8. T F   African slaves began to outnumber white indentured servants as the primary labor supply in the plantation colonies by the 1680s.

9. T F   Slaves brought to North America developed a culture that mixed African and American speech, religion, and patterns of life.

10. T F   Directly beneath the wealthy slaveowning planters, in the southern social structure, were the white indentured servants.

11. T F   New Englanders' long lives contributed to the general stability and order of their childrearing and family life.

12. T F   New England expansion was carried out primarily by independent pioneers and land speculators who bought up large plots and then sold them to individual farmers.

13. T F   The development of the Half-Way Covenant, in the 1660s, reflected both a decline in Puritan religious fervor and a broadening of religious participation.

14. T F   The Salem Witch Trials reflected the persecution of poor women by upper-class males and clergy.

15. T F   New Englanders' Calvinist heritage and stern, self-reliant character created a legacy of high idealism and reform that greatly affected later American society.

B. Multiple Choice

Select the best answer and circle the corresponding letter.

1. For most of their early history, the colonies of Maryland and Virginia
    a. provided a healthy environment for child rearing.
    b. contained far more men than women.
    c. had harsh laws punishing premarital sexual relations.
    d. encouraged the formation of stable and long-lasting marriages.
    e. tolerated interracial sexual relations.

2. The primary beneficiaries of the headright system were
    a. well-off planters who acquired land by paying the transatlantic passage for indentured servants.
    b. widows who acquired new husbands from England.
    c. indentured servants who were able to acquire their own land.
    d. English ship owners who transported new laborers across the Atlantic.
    e. backcountry settlers who gained reinforcements for their fights with the Indians.

3. The primary cause of Bacon's Rebellion was
    a. Governor Berkeley's harsh treatment of the Indians.
    b. the refusal of landlords to grant indentured servants their freedom.
    c. white settlers' resentment against the growing use of African slave labor.
    d. the persecution of the colonists by King Charles II.
    e. the poverty and discontent of many single young men unable to acquire land.

4.   African slavery became the prevalent form of labor in the 1680s when

    a.   Bacon's rebellion and rising wages in England made white indentured servants no longer a reliable labor force.

    b.   the first captives were brought from Africa to the New World.

    c.   blacks could be brought to the New World in safer and healthier condition.

    d.   the once-clear legal difference between a servant and a slave began to be blurred.

    e.   plantation owners discovered it was cheaper to buy slaves for life than replace white indentured servants every five years or so.

5.   Most of the slaves who eventually reached North America were originally

    a.   from southern and eastern Africa.

    b.   free servants who worked as household labor in African royal families.

    c.   captured by West African coastal tribes and sold to European slave merchants.

    d.   sold as slaves in the West Indies and then reshipped to North America.

    e.   brought to the New World in family groups.

6.   Political and economic power in the southern colonies was dominated by

    a.   urban professional classes such as lawyers and bankers.

    b.   small landowners.

    c.   the Anglican clergy

    d.   the English royal governors.

    e.   extended families of wealthy planters.

7.   Because there were few urban centers in the colonial South

    a.   good roads between the isolated plantations had to be constructed early on.

    b.   most southerners traveled regularly to England or the West Indies to enjoy more sophisticated forms of culture.

    c.   the rural church became the central focus of southern social and economic life.

    d.   there were almost no people of wealth and culture in the region.

    e.   a professional class of lawyers and financiers was slow to develop.

8.   The average colonial New England woman who did not die in childbirth could expect to

    a.   lose the majority of her children to death before adulthood.

    b.   outlive her husband by an average of fifteen years.

    c.   experience about ten pregnancies, occurring on average every two years from her twenties through menopause.

    d.   work regularly for pay outside the home besides care for her children.

    e.   be physically or mentally abused by her husband at some point in her life.

9.   In New England, elementary education

    a.   was mandatory for any town with more than fifty families.

    b.   failed to provide even basic literacy to the large majority of citizens.

    c.   was less widespread than in the South.

    d.   was oriented to preparing students for entering college.

    e.   was completely in the hands of the Puritan clergy.

10.   The Congregational Church of the Puritans contributed to

    a.   the development of basic ideas of democracy as expressed in the New England town meeting.

    b.   the extremely hierarchical character of New England life.

    c.   the increasing social harmony and unity displayed throughout the seventeenth century in New England towns.

    d.   the growing movement toward women's rights in New England.

    e.   a growing number of personal conversions among young New Englanders.

11. In contrast to the Chesapeake Bay colonists in the South, those in New England

    a.   had fewer women and more men in their population.
    b.   had shorter life expectancies.
    c.   practiced birth control as a means of preventing overpopulation.
    d.   provided no protections for women within the institution of marriage.
    e.   enjoyed longer lives and more stable families.

12. The focus of much of New England's politics, religion, and education was the institution of the

    a.   colonial legislature.
    b.   town.
    c.   militia company.
    d.   college.
    e.   commercial trading company.

13. The Half-Way Covenant provided

    a.   baptism, but not full communion, to people who had not had a conversion experience.
    b.   partial participation in politics to people who were not church members.
    c.   admission to communion, but not to voting membership in the church, for children aged twelve to seventeen.
    d.   partial participation in church affairs for women.
    e.   limited involvement in Massachusetts church councils to new frontier congregations.

14. Those people accused of being witches in Salem were generally

    a.   from the poorer and more uneducated segments of the town.
    b.   notorious for their deviation from the moral norms of the community.
    c.   outspoken opponents of the Puritan clergy.
    d.   from families associated with Salem's burgeoning market economy.
    e.   suspected of having Indian or African ancestry.

15. English settlers greatly altered the character of the New England environment by

    a.   raising wheat and oats rather than the corn grown by Indians.
    b.   burning the forests that the Indians had rigorously protected against fires.
    c.   beating trails through the woods as they pursued seasonal hunting and fishing.
    d.   building an extensive system of roads and canals.
    e.   their extensive introduction of livestock.

C. Identification

Supply the correct identification for each numbered description.

1. _____   Early Maryland and Virginia settlers had difficulty creating them and even more difficulty making them last

2. _____   The principal economic product of early Maryland and Virginia

3. _____   Immigrants who received passage to America in exchange for a fixed term of labor

4. _____   Maryland and Virginia's system of granting land to anyone who would pay trans-Atlantic passage for laborers

5. _____   Laws first passed in 1662 that made blacks and their children the lifelong property of their white masters

6. _____   New England colony that was home to most North American slave traders

7. _____   English company that lost its monopoly on the slave trade in 1698

8. _____ African American language that blended English with Yoruba, Ibo, and Hausa

9. _____ Site of northern slave revolt of 1712 that led to the deaths of nine whites and the execution of more than twenty blacks

10. _____ Shorthand term for the wealthy extended clans like the Fitzhughs, Lees, and Washingtons that dominated politics in the most populous colony

11. _____ Occupation of assisting in childbirth that was a virtual female monopoly in colonial New England

12. _____ The basic local political institution of New England, in which all freemen gathered to elect officials and debate local affairs

13. _____ Formula devised by Puritan ministers in 1662 to offer partial church membership to people who had not experienced conversion

14. _____ Late seventeenth-century judicial event that inflamed popular feelings, led to the deaths of twenty people, and weakened the Puritan clergy's prestige

15. _____ A form of Puritan sermon that scolded parishioners for declining piety and urged repentance and reform

D. Matching People, Places, and Events

Match the person, place, or event in the left column with the proper description in the right column by inserting the correct letter on the blank line.

1. ___ Chesapeake
2. ___ Indentured servants
3. ___ Nathaniel Bacon
4. ___ William Berkeley
5. ___ Royal African Company
6. ___ Middle passage
7. ___ Ringshout
8. ___ Stono River
9. ___ Gullah
10. ___ New England conscience
11. ___ Harvard
12. ___ William and Mary
13. ___ Half-Way Covenant
14. ___ Salem witch trials
15. ___ Leisler's Rebellion

a. Site of a 1739 South Carolina slave revolt

b. Helped erase the earlier Puritan distinction between the converted elect and other members of society

c. A bloody New York revolt of 1689–1691 that reflected class antagonism between rich landlords and aspiring merchants

d. Primary form of labor in early southern colonies until the 1680s

e. Term for the brutal slave journey from Africa to the Americas

f. Coastal African American language that blended elements of English with the African languages Yoruba, Ibo, and Hausa

g. West African religious rite, retained by African Americans, in which participants responded to the shouts of a preacher

h. Phenomena started by adolescent girls' accusations that ended with the deaths of twenty people

i. Virginia-Maryland bay area, site of the earliest colonial settlements

j.   The legacy of Puritan religion that inspired idealism and reform among later generations of Americans

k.   Colonial Virginia official who crushed rebels and wreaked cruel revenge

l.   The oldest college in the South, founded in 1693

m.   Organization whose loss of the slave trade monopoly in 1698 led to free-enterprise expansion of the business

n.   Agitator who led poor former indentured servants and frontiersmen on a rampage against Indians and colonial government

o.   The oldest college in America, originally based on the Puritan commitment to an educated ministry

E. Putting Things in Order

Put the following events in correct order by numbering them from 1 to 10.

1. _____   Legal lynching of twenty accused witches occurs.

2. _____   Royal slave trade monopoly ends.

3. _____   First colonial college is founded.

4. _____   Landless whites in Virginia lose the right to vote.

5. _____   Major rebellion by African Americans occurs in one of the middle colonies.

6. _____   Southern slaves in revolt try, but fail, to march to Spanish Florida.

7. _____   Partial church membership is opened to the unconverted.

8. _____   African slaves begin to replace white indentured labor on southern plantations.

9. _____   Poor Virginia whites revolt against governor and rich planters.

10. _____   First Africans arrive in Virginia.

F. Matching Cause and Effect

Match the historical cause in the left column with the proper effect in the right column by writing the correct letter on the blank line.

Cause		**Effect**
1. ___ The severe shortage of females in southern colonies	a.	Inspired passage of strict slave codes
	b.	Sparked Bacon's Rebellion
2. ___ Poor white males' anger at their inability to acquire land or start families	c.	Produced large number of unattached males and weak family structure

3. ___ Planters' fears of indentured servants' rebellion, coupled with rising wages in England

4. ___ The dramatic increase in colonial slave population after 1680s

5. ___ The growing proportion of female slaves in the Chesapeake region after 1720

6. ___ New Englanders' introduction of livestock and intensive agriculture

7. ___ The healthier climate and more equal male-female ratio in New England

8. ___ The decline of religious devotion and in number of conversions in New England

9. ___ Unsettled New England social conditions and anxieties about the decline of the Puritan religious heritage

10. ___ The rocky soil and harsh climate of New England

d. Thwarted success in agriculture but helped create the tough New England character

e. Inspired the Half-Way Covenant and jeremiad preaching

f. Reduced forests and damaged the soil

g. Produced high birthrates and a very stable family structure

h. Fostered stronger slave families and growth of slave population through natural reproduction of children

i. Underlay the Salem witchcraft persecutions

j. Caused southern planters to switch from indentured-servant labor to African slavery

G. Developing Historical Skills

Learning from Historical Documents

The illustrations on pp. 71 and 82 reproduce parts of two colonial documents: excerpts from an indentured servant's contract and some pages from a children's schoolbook, *The New England Primer*. By carefully examining these documents, you can learn much about early colonial culture and ideas. Answering the following questions will illustrate the kind of information that historical documents can provide.

1. What principal goals are the master and the indentured servant each seeking in the contract?

2. What do the potential problems that each side anticipates reveal about the nature of the relationship between masters and indentured servants?

3. How does the *New England Primer* directly link religious obligation with obedience to political authority and to parents?

4. Besides reading and writing, what other skill does the *Primer* instruct the teacher to develop in the child through sentences like this?

PART III: APPLYING WHAT YOU HAVE LEARNED

1. Why was the tobacco culture of early Maryland and Virginia so harsh and unstable. How did the environmental and demographic conditions of the Chesapeake region—especially rampant disease and the scarcity of women—affect the social and political life of the colonies?

2. What was the underlying cause of the expansion of African slavery in English North America?

3. Could the colonies' labor problem have been solved without slavery?

4. How did African Americans develop a culture that combined African and American elements? What were some of the features of that culture?

5. Compare and contrast the typical family conditions and ways of life of southern whites, African American slaves, and New Englanders in the seventeenth century.

6. How did the harsh climate and soil, stern religion, and tightly knit New England town shape the Yankee character?

7. In what ways were married colonial New England women second-class citizens, subjected to discrimination and control, and in what ways was their status and well-being protected by law and society. Is it fair to critically judge colonial gender relations by later standards of equality and rights?

8. How did the Salem witch episode reflect the tensions and changes in seventeenth-century New England life and thought?

9. In what ways was seventeenth-century colonial society already recognizably American in relation to issues of family life, social class, ethnicity, and religion, and in what ways did it still reflect Old World features—whether European or African?

CHAPTER 5

Colonial Society on the Eve of Revolution, 1700–1775

PART I: REVIEWING THE CHAPTER

A. Checklist of Learning Objectives

After mastering this chapter, you should be able to:

1.   Describe the demographic, ethnic, and social character of Britain's colonies in the eighteenth century, and indicate how colonial society had changed since the seventeenth century.

2.   Explain how the economic development of the colonies altered the patterns of social prestige and wealth, and brought growing class distinctions and class conflict to British North America.

3.   Identify the major religious denominations of the eighteenth-century colonies, and indicate their role in early American society.

4.   Explain the causes of the Great Awakening, and describe its effects on American religion, education, and politics.

5.   Describe the origins and development of education, culture, and journalism in the colonies.

6.   Describe the basic features of colonial politics, including the role of various official and informal political institutions.

7.   Indicate the key qualities of daily existence in eighteenth-century colonial America, including forms of socialization and recreation.

B. Glossary

To build your social science vocabulary, familiarize yourself with the following terms.

1.   **sect** A small religious group that has broken away from some larger mainstream church, often claiming superior or exclusive possession of religious truth. (A **denomination** is a branch of the church—usually Protestant—but makes no such exclusive claims.) "They belonged to several different Protestant sects. . . ."

2.   **agitators** Persons who seek to excite or persuade the public on some issue. "Already experienced colonizers and agitators in Ireland, the Scots-Irish proved to be superb frontiersmen. . . ."

3.   **stratification** The visible arrangement of society into a hierarchical pattern, with distinct social groups layered one on top of the other. ". . . colonial society . . . was beginning to show signs of stratification. . . ."

4.   **mobility** The capacity to pass readily from one social or economic condition to another. (Social mobility may be **upward**, from a lower status to higher, or **downward**, from higher status to lower.)". . . barriers to mobility . . . raised worries about the 'Europeanization' of America."

5.   **elite** A small, identifiable group at the top of a society or particular institution, usually possessing wealth, power, or special privileges. ". . . these elites now feathered their nests more finely."

6.   **almshouse** In the premodern era, a home for the poor, supported by charity or public funds. "Both Philadelphia and New York built almshouses in the 1730s. . . ."

7.   **gentry** Landowners of substantial property, social standing, and leisure, but not titled nobility. "Wealth was concentrated in the hands of the largest slaveowners, widening the gap between the prosperous gentry and the 'poor whites'. . . . "

8.   **tenant farmer** One who rents rather than owns land. ". . . the 'poor whites' . . . were increasingly forced to become tenant farmers."

9.   **penal code** The body of criminal laws specifying offenses and prescribing punishments. "But many convicts were the unfortunate victims . . . of a viciously unfair English penal code. . . ."

10. **veto** The executive power to prevent acts passed by the legislature from becoming law. "Thomas Jefferson, himself a slaveholder, assailed the British vetoes. . . ."

11. **profession** An occupation traditionally characterized by specialized skill, mastery of a body of knowledge, and publicly defined privileges and responsibilities. "Most honored of the professions was the Christian ministry."

12. **apprentice** A person who works under a master to acquire instruction and skill in a trade or profession. "Aspiring young doctors served for a while as apprentices to older practitioners. . . ."

13. **speculation** Buying land or anything else in the hope of profiting by an expected rise in price. "Commercial ventures and land speculation . . . were the surest avenues to speedy wealth."

14. **revival** In religion, a movement of renewed enthusiasm and commitment, often accompanied by special meetings or evangelical activity. "The stage was thus set for a rousing religious revival."

15. **secular** Belonging to the worldly sphere, as distinct from the specifically sacred or churchly. "A more secular approach was evident late in the eighteenth century. . . ."

PART II: CHECKING YOUR PROGRESS

A. True-False

Where the statement is true, circle **T**; where it is false, circle **F**.

1.   T   F   Most of the spectacular growth of the colonial population came from immigration rather than natural increase.

2.   T   F   The Scots-Irish were uprooted Scottish Protestants who largely settled in the Appalachian frontier and back country.

3.   T   F   Compared with the seventeenth-century colonies, the eighteenth-century colonies were becoming more socially equal and democratic.

4.   T   F   The lowest class of whites in the colonies consisted of the paupers and convicted criminals involuntarily shipped to America by British authorities.

5.   T   F   When some North American colonists attempted to curtail the transatlantic slave trade, their efforts were thwarted by British government vetoes.

6.   T   F   The most highly regarded professionals in the colonies were doctors and lawyers.

7.   T   F   Besides agriculture, the most important colonial economic activities were fishing, shipping, and ocean-going trade.

8.   T   F   The British government's passage of the Molasses Act and other economic regulations effectively ended American merchants' lucrative trade with the French West Indies.

9. T F   The clergy of the established Anglican Church in the South and New York had a reputation for serious theology and high ethical standards.

10. T F   The Great Awakening was a revival of fervent religion after a period of religious decline caused by clerical dullness and overintellectualism and lay liberalism in doctrine.

11. T F   Great Awakening revivalists like Jonathan Edwards and George Whitefield tried to replace the older Puritan ideas of conversion and salvation with more rational and less emotional beliefs.

12. T F   The Great Awakening was the first mass movement across the thirteen colonies to create a strong sense of common American identity and shared destiny.

13. T F   By the late eighteenth century, the nine American colleges were comparable to the best university education offered in Europe.

14. T F   The conviction of newspaper printer John Peter Zenger for seditious libel of a colonial governor stirred Americans' opposition to British censorship of the press.

15. T F   The central point of conflict in colonial politics was the relation between the democratically elected lower house of the assembly and the governors appointed by the king or colonial proprietor.

B. Multiple Choice

Select the best answer and circle the corresponding letter.

1. The primary reason for the spectacular growth of America's population in the eighteenth century was
    a.   the conquering of new territories.
    b.   the natural fertility of the population.
    c.   the increased importation of white indentured servants and black slaves.
    d.   new immigration from Europe.
    e.   increased longevity due to better diet and health care.

2. German settlement in the colonies was especially heavy in
    a.   Massachusetts.
    b.   Maryland.
    c.   New York.
    d.   Pennsylvania.
    e.   North Carolina.

3. Which of the following is *not* true of the colonial Scots-Irish?
    a.   They were not really Irish, but Scottish Presbyterians who had temporarily migrated to Ireland.
    b.   They tended to settle in the Appalachian frontier, mountains, and valleys from Pennsylvania southward.
    c.   They hated the British government and frequently rebelled against colonial authorities.
    d.   Their hostility to Indians and encroachment on Indian land often sparked frontier warfare.
    e.   They fervently practiced their Calvinist religion, which forbade dancing, gambling, and liquor consumption.

4. The two largest non-English white ethnic groups in the colonies were the
   a. French and the Dutch.
   b. Germans and the Scots-Irish.
   c. Arabs and the Jews.
   d. Welsh and the Irish.
   e. Swedes and the Germans.

5. One way in which Indians and Africans were similar to whites in eighteenth-century North America was they
   a. were committed to the Christian religion as their basic belief system.
   b. increasingly mingled and intermarried with people from beyond their original ethnic group or tribe.
   c. fundamentally disliked violence and looked to government to establish law and order.
   d. increasingly found greater opportunities for freedom and upward mobility.
   e. tended to prefer stable, homogenous communities.

6. Compared to the seventeenth century, American colonial society in the eighteenth century showed
   a. greater domination by small farmers and artisans.
   b. greater equality of wealth and status.
   c. greater gaps in wealth and status between rich and poor.
   d. greater opportunity for convicts and indentured servants to climb to the top.
   e. growing divisions by race and ethnicity rather than social class.

7. The most honored professional in colonial America was the
   a. lawyer.
   b. college professor.
   c. doctor.
   d. journalist.
   e. clergyman.

8. The primary source of livelihood for most colonial Americans was
   a. manufacturing.
   b. agriculture.
   c. lumbering.
   d. commerce and trade.
   e. fishing.

9. Which of the following was *not* among the generally small-scale manufacturing enterprises in colonial America?
   a. Carriage manufacturing
   b. Liquor distilling
   c. Beaver hat making
   d. Iron making
   e. Spinning and weaving

10. An unfortunate group of involuntary immigrants who ranked even below indentured servants on the American social scale were
   a. the younger sons of English gentry.
   b. French-Canadians forcibly removed from Quebec.
   c. convicts and paupers.
   d. prostitutes.
   e. impressed sailors and seamen.

11.   The triangular trade involved the sale of rum, molasses, and slaves among the ports of

   a.   Virginia, Canada, and Britain.
   b.   the West Indies, France, and South America.
   c.   New England, Britain, and Spain.
   d.   New England, Africa, and the West Indies.
   e.   South Carolina, the Mediterranean, and the Black Sea.

12.   The passage of increasing British restrictions on trade encouraged colonial merchants to

   a.   organize political resistance in the British Parliament.
   b.   find ways to smuggle and otherwise evade the law by trading with other countries.
   c.   turn to domestic trade within the colonies.
   d.   turn from trading to such other enterprises as fishing and manufacturing.
   e.   establish branch offices in London that were not covered by the restrictions.

13.   Besides offering rest, refreshment, and entertainment, colonial taverns served an important function as centers of

   a.   news and political opinion.
   b.   trade and business.
   c.   medicine and law.
   d.   religious revival.
   e.   dating and social relations with the opposite sex.

14.   The Anglican Church suffered in colonial America because of

   a.   its strict doctrines and hierarchical church order.
   b.   its poorly qualified clergy and close ties with British authorities.
   c.   its inability to adjust to conditions of life in New England.
   d.   its reputation for fostering fanatical revivalism.
   e.   the succession of corrupt and incompetent bishops who ran the church.

15.   The two denominations that enjoyed the status of established churches in various colonies were the

   a.   Quakers and Dutch Reformed.
   b.   Baptists and Lutherans.
   c.   Mennonites and Church of the Brethren.
   d.   Roman Catholics and Presbyterians.
   e.   Anglicans and Congregationalists.

16.   Among the many important results of the Great Awakening was that it

   a.   broke down sectional boundaries and created a greater sense of common American identity.
   b.   contributed to greater religious liberalism and toleration in the churches.
   c.   caused a decline in colonial concern for education.
   d.   moved Americans closer to a single religious outlook.
   e.   made Americans suspicious of eloquent preachers and traveling evangelists.

17.   A primary weapon used by colonial legislatures in their conflicts with royal governors was

   a.   extending the franchise to include almost all adult white citizens.
   b.   passing laws prohibiting the governors from owning land or industries.
   c.   voting them out of office.
   d.   using their power of the purse to withhold the governor's salary.
   e.   appealing over the heads of the governors to the British Parliament.

C. Identification

Supply the correct identification for each numbered description.

1. _____   Corruption of a German word used as a term for German immigrants in Pennsylvania

2. _____   Ethnic group that had already relocated once before immigrating to America and settling largely on the western frontier of the middle and southern colonies

3. _____   Rebellious movement of North Carolina frontiersmen against eastern domination that included future President Andrew Jackson

4. _____   Popular term for convicted criminals dumped on colonies by British authorities

5. _____   Dread disease that afflicted one out of every five colonial Americans, including George Washington

6. _____   Lucrative profession, especially prevalent in New England, that marketed its product to the Catholic nations of southern Europe

7. _____   Small but profitable trade route that linked New England, Africa, and the West Indies

8. _____   Popular colonial centers of recreation, gossip, and political debate

9. _____   Term for tax-supported condition of Congregational and Anglican churches, but not of Baptists, Quakers, and Roman Catholics

10. _____   Spectacular, emotional religious revival of the 1730s and 1740s

11. _____   Ministers who supported the Great Awakening against the old light clergy who rejected it

12. _____   Followers of a Dutch theologian who challenged traditional Calvinist doctrine by arguing for free will and the dispensation of divine grace beyond a few elect

13. _____   The case that established the precedent that true statements about public officials could not be prosecuted as libel

14. _____   The first American college not to be sponsored by a religious denomination, strongly supported by Benjamin Franklin

15. _____   Benjamin Franklin's highly popular collection of information, parables, and advice

D. Matching People, Places, and Events

Match the person, place, or event in the left column with the proper description in the right column by inserting the correct letter on the blank line.

1. ___ Philadelphia

2. ___ African Americans

3. ___ Scots-Irish

4. ___ Paxton Boys and Regulators

5. ___ Patrick Henry

a. Itinerant British evangelist who spread the Great Awakening throughout the colonies

b. Colonial printer whose case helped begin freedom of the press

6.   ___   Molasses Act

7.   ___   Anglican church

8.   ___   Jonathan Edwards

9.   ___   George Whitefield

10. ___   Phillis Wheatley

11. ___   Benjamin Franklin

12. ___   John Peter Zenger

13. ___   Quakers

14. ___   Baptists

15. ___   John Singleton Copley

c.   Colonial painter who studied and worked in Britain

d.   Leading city of the colonies; home of Benjamin Franklin

e.   Largest non-English group in the colonies

f.   Dominant religious group in colonial Pennsylvania, criticized by others for their attitudes toward Indians

g.   Former slave who became a poet at an early age

h.   Scots-Irish frontiersmen who protested against colonial elites of Pennsylvania and North Carolina

i.   Attempt by British authorities to squelch colonial trade with French West Indies

j.   Brilliant New England theologian who instigated the Great Awakening

k.   Group that settled the frontier, made whiskey, and hated the British and other governmental authorities

l.   Nonestablished religious group that benefited from the Great Awakening

m.   Author, scientist, printer; "the first civilized American"

n.   Eloquent lawyer-orator who argued in defense of colonial rights

o.   Established religion in southern colonies and New York; weakened by lackadaisical clergy and too-close ties with British crown

E. Putting Things in Order

Put the following events in correct order by numbering them 1 to 10.

1.   _____   Epochal freedom of the press case is settled.

2.   _____   First southern college to train Anglican clergy is founded.

3.   _____   Britain vetoes colonial effort to halt slave importation.

4.   _____   Scots-Irish protestors stage armed marches.

5.   _____   First medical attempts are made to prevent dreaded disease epidemics.

6.   _____   Parliament attempts to restrict colonial trade with French West Indies.

7. _____ Princeton College is founded to train new light ministers.

8. _____ An eloquent British preacher spreads evangelical religion through the colonies.

9. _____ Benjamin Franklin starts printing his most famous publication.

10. _____ A fiery, intellectual preacher sets off a powerful religious revival in New England.

F. Matching Cause and Effect

Match the historical cause in the left column with the proper effect in the right column by writing the correct letter on the blank line.

Cause	**Effect**
1. ___ The high natural fertility of the colonial population	a. Prompted colonial assemblies to withhold royal governors' salaries
2. ___ The heavy immigration of Germans, Scots-Irish, Africans, and others into the colonies	b. Created the conditions for the Great Awakening to erupt in the early eighteenth century
3. ___ The large profits made by merchants as military suppliers for imperial wars	c. Resulted in the development of a colonial melting pot, only one-half English by 1775
4. ___ American merchants' search for non-British markets	d. Was met by British attempts to restrict colonial trade, such as the Molasses Act
5. ___ Dry overintellectualism and loss of religious commitment	e. Increased the wealth of the eighteenth-century colonial elite
6. ___ The Great Awakening	f. Led to the increase of American population to one-third of England's in 1775
7. ___ The Zenger case	g. Forced the migration of colonial artists to Britain to study and pursue artistic careers
8. ___ The appointment of unpopular or incompetent royal governors to colonies	h. Marked the beginnings of freedom of printed political expression in the colonies
9. ___ Upper-class fear of democratic excesses by poor whites	i. Reinforced colonial property qualifications for voting
10. ___ The lack of artistic concerns, cultural tradition, and leisure in the colonies	j. Stimulated a fervent, emotional style of religion, denominational divisions, and a greater sense of intercolonial American identity

G. Developing Historical Skills

Learning from Map Comparison

By comparing two similar maps dealing with the same historical period, you can derive additional information about the relations between the two topics the maps emphasize. The map on p. 89 shows immigrant groups in 1775, and the map on p. 94 shows the colonial economy. By examining both maps, you can learn about the likely economic activities of various immigrant groups. Answer the following questions.

1.   To what extent were Scots-Irish immigrants involved in tobacco cultivation?

2.   What agricultural activities were most of the Dutch immigrants involved in?

3.   With what part of the agricultural economy were African American slaves most involved?

4.   Which major immigrant group may have had some involvement in the colonial iron industry?

H. Map Mastery

Map Discrimination

Using the maps and charts in Chapter 5, answer the following questions.

1.   Which section contained the fewest non-English minorities?

2.   The Scots-Irish were concentrated most heavily on the frontiers of which four colonies?

3.   In which colony were German and Swiss immigrants most heavily concentrated?

4.   Which colony contained the largest concentration of French immigrants?

5.   Which four colonies had the greatest concentration of tobacco growing?

6.   Which was the larger minority in the colonies: all the non-English white ethnic groups together or the African Americans?

7.   Which two social groups stood between the landowning farmers and the slaves in the colonial social pyramid?

8.   Which of the following religious groups were most heavily concentrated in the middle colonies: Lutherans, Dutch Reformed, Quakers, Baptists, or Roman Catholics?

9.   How many years after the Declaration of Independence in 1776 was the last church officially disestablished?

10. How many of the colonial colleges were originally founded by established denominations?

Map Challenge

Using the map on p. 89, write a brief essay in which you compare the ethnic mix in each of the following colonies: North Carolina, Virginia, Pennsylvania, New York, and Massachusetts.

PART III: APPLYING WHAT YOU HAVE LEARNED

1.   What factors contributed to the growing numbers and wealth of the American colonists in the eighteenth century?

2.   Describe the structure of colonial society in the eighteenth century. What developments tended to make society less equal and more hierarchical?

3.   What attitudes toward government and authority did eighteenth-century Americans most commonly display. Cite specific developments or events that reflect these outlooks.

4.   What were the causes and consequences of the Great Awakening? How was religious revival linked to the development of a sense of American uniqueness and identity?

5.   What features of colonial politics contributed to the development of popular democracy, and what kept political life from being more truly democratic?

6. What were Americans' essential attitudes toward education, professional learning, and higher forms of culture and science. Why were colonial newspapers and publications like Benjamin Franklin's *Poor Richard's Almanack* so popular?

7. Some historians claim that eighteenth-century American society was actually becoming more European than it had been in the previous century, while others contend that developments like the Great Awakening and the rise of colonial assemblies made the colonies truly American for the first time. Which of these interpretations is more persuasive, and why?

8. Compare and contrast the social structure and culture of the eighteenth century with that of the seventeenth century (see Chapter 4). In what ways was eighteenth-century society more complex and in what ways did it clearly continue earlier ideas and practices?

CHAPTER 6

The Duel for North America, 1608–1763

PART I: REVIEWING THE CHAPTER

A. Checklist of Learning Objectives

After mastering this chapter, you should be able to:

1. Explain what caused the great contest for North America between Britain and France, and why Britain won.

2. Describe France's colonial settlements and their expansion, and compare New France with Britain's colonies in North America.

3. Explain how Britain's colonists became embroiled in the home country's wars with France.

4. Describe the colonists' role in the Seven Years' War (French and Indian War), and indicate the consequences of the French defeat for Americans.

5. Indicate how and why the British victory in the Seven Years' War (French and Indian War) became one of the causes of the American Revolution.

B. Glossary

To build your social science vocabulary, familiarize yourself with the following terms.

1. **domestic** Concerning the internal affairs of a country. "It was convulsed . . . by foreign wars and domestic strife. . . ."

2. **minister** In politics, a person appointed by the head of state to take charge of some department or agency of government. "France blossomed . . . led by a series of brilliant ministers. . . ."

3. **autocratic** Marked by strict authoritarian rule, without consent or participation by the populace. "This royal regime was almost completely autocratic."

4. **peasant** A farmer or agricultural laborer, sometimes legally tied to the land and owing obligations to local nobles or gentry. "Landowning French peasants . . . had little economic motive to move."

5. *coureurs des bois* French-Canadian fur trappers; literally, "runners of the woods." "These colorful *coureurs des bois* . . . were also runners of risks. . . ."

6. *voyageurs* French-Canadian explorers, adventurers, and traders. "Singing, paddle-swinging French *voyageurs* also recruited Indians. . . ."

7. **flotilla** A fleet of boats, usually smaller vessels. "The Indian fur flotilla . . . numbered four hundred canoes."

8. **ecological** Concerning the relations between the biological organisms and their environment. ". . . they all but extinguished the beaver population in many areas, inflicting incalculable ecological damage."

9.   **mutinous** Concerning revolt by subordinate soldiers or seamen against their commanding officers. "But he failed to find the Mississippi delta, . . . and was murdered by his mutinous men."

10.   **strategic** Concerning the placement and planned movement of large-scale forces so as to gain political or military advantage in confrontation with the enemy. (By contrast, **tactical** refers to specific, variable, smaller-scale methods of waging conflict or achieving strategic objectives.) "Commanding the mouth of the Mississippi River, this strategic semitropical outpost also tapped the fur trade of the huge interior valley."

11.   **guerilla warfare** Unconventional combat waged by small military units using hit-and-run tactics. ". . . so the combatants waged a kind of primitive guerilla warfare."

12.   **sallies (sally)** In warfare, very rapid military movements, usually by small units, against an enemy force or position. "For their part the British colonists failed miserably in sallies against Quebec and Montreal. . . ."

13.   **siege** A military operation of surrounding and attacking a fortified place, often over a sustained period. "After a ten-hour siege he was forced to surrender. . . ."

14.   **regulars** Trained professional soldiers, as distinct from part-time militia or conscripts. ". . . they had fought bravely alongside the crack British regulars. . . ."

15.   **commissions** An official government certification granting a commanding rank in the armed forces. ". . . the British refused to recognize any American militia commission. . . ."

PART II: CHECKING YOUR PROGRESS

A. True-False

Where the statement is true, circle **T**; where it is false, circle **F**.

1.   T   F   French colonization was late developing because of the nation's internal religious and political conflicts.

2.   T   F   The French Empire in North America rested on an economic foundation of forestry and sugar production.

3.   T   F   Early imperial conflicts in North America often saw the French and their Indian allies engaging in guerrilla warfare against British frontier outposts.

4.   T   F   Colonists in British North America managed to avoid direct involvement in most of Britain's world wars until the French and Indian War.

5.   T   F   In the early seventeenth century, both France and England committed large regular forces to what they considered the crucial struggle for control of North America.

6.   T   F   George Washington's battle at Fort Necessity substantially resolved the issue of control of the Ohio Valley.

7.   T   F   The delegates to the Albany Congress demonstrated a strong desire to overcome differences among different colonies and to control their own affairs.

8.   T   F   William Pitt's successful strategy was to concentrate British forces and focus on capturing the French strongholds of Louisbourg, Quebec, and Montreal.

9.   T   F   British regular troops under General Braddock succeeded in capturing the key French forts in the Ohio Valley.

10. T F The French and Indian War left France with only Louisiana as a remnant of its once-mighty North American empire.

11. T F American soldiers gained new respect for British military men after the British success against the French.

12. T F The American colonists enthusiastically united in patriotic support of the British cause against the French.

13. T F The removal of the French threat made American colonists more secure and therefore less reliant on the mother country for protection.

14. T F A British commander used the biological warfare tactic of distributing blankets infected with smallpox to suppress Pontiac's Indian uprising.

15. T F The British government's attempt to prohibit colonial expansion across the Appalachian Mountains aroused colonial anger and defiance of the law.

B. Multiple Choice

Select the best answer and circle the corresponding letter.

1. Compared with the English colonies in North America, New France was
   a. more wealthy and successful.
   b. better able to maintain consistently friendly relations with the Indians.
   c. more heavily populated.
   d. more autocratically governed.
   e. more divided by serious religious conflict.

2. The expansion of New France occurred especially
   a. in the interior mountain areas.
   b. into the Canadian Pacific West.
   c. into areas already occupied by English settlers.
   d. to the north of the original St. Lawrence River settlement, around Hudson's Bay.
   e. along the paths of North America's interior lakes and rivers.

3. Colonial Americans were unhappy about the peace treaty of 1748 following the War of Jenkins's Ear because
   a. it refused to acknowledge the great colonial contribution to British victory.
   b. it returned the Louisbourg fortress they had captured back to France.
   c. it created further conflicts with Spain.
   d. it failed to deal with the issue of Indian attacks on the frontier.
   e. they thought the treaty was grossly disproportionate to the war's trivial cause.

4. The original cause of the French and Indian War was
   a. conflict in Europe between Britain and France.
   b. British removal of the Acadian French settlers from Nova Scotia.
   c. British seizure of Indian lands on the shores of Lake Ontario and Lake Erie.
   d. a French attack on George Washington's Virginia headquarters.
   e. competition between French and English colonists for land in the Ohio River valley.

5. The French and Indian War eventually became part of the larger world conflict known as
   a. the Seven Years' War.
   b. the War of Jenkins's Ear.
   c. the War of the Austrian Succession.
   d. King George's War.
   e. the American Revolution.

6. Benjamin Franklin's attempt to create intercolonial unity at the Albany Congress resulted in

    a. a permanent cooperative organization of the colonies.
    b. rejection of the congress's proposal for colonial home rule both by London and by the individual colonies.
    c. a sharp increase in Indian attacks on colonial settlements.
    d. a growing colonial sympathy with France in the war against Britain.
    e. the emergence of New York as the most politically influential of the colonies.

7. The British forces suffered crushing early defeats in the French and Indian War under the overall command of

    a. General Braddock.
    b. General Washington.
    c. General Wolfe.
    d. General Montcalm.
    e. Admiral Jenkins.

8. The fundamental flaw in British strategy before William Pitt gained control of the London government was it

    a. devoted all its energy to winning naval victories, while ignoring the war on the land.
    b. failed to elicit the full support and cooperation of its Indian allies.
    c. tried to attack numerous French wilderness forts simultaneously, instead of concentrating on the key French fortresses.
    d. refused to give sufficient forces to its best colonial general, George Washington.
    e. concentrated on the St. Lawrence River valley rather than attacking the French in the more vulnerable Mississippi River valley.

9. The decisive event in the French-British contest for North America was the

    a. British capture of Fort Duquesne.
    b. British victory in the Battle of Quebec.
    c. American capture of the Louisbourg fortress.
    d. British attack on the French West Indies.
    e. defeat of the Indian leader Pontiac through the distribution of smallpox-infected blankets.

10. Among the factors that tended to promote British colonists' intercolonial unity during the French and Indian War was

    a. their religious unity.
    b. their common language and shared wartime experience.
    c. their ethnic and social harmony.
    d. improved transportation and settlement of boundary disputes.
    e. their desire to seize French land.

11. The French and Indian War weakened interior Indian peoples like the Iroquois and Creeks by

    a. establishing new American settlements on their territory.
    b. eliminating their most effective leaders.
    c. ending their hopes for diplomatic recognition in Europe.
    d. giving control of the Great Lakes to the British colonists.
    e. removing their French and Spanish allies from Canada and Florida.

12. Perhaps the most enduring result of France's years of colonial rule in North America was

    a. a permanent French-Canadian minority in Quebec in Canada.
    b. continuing warfare into the nineteenth century between Britain and France over North America.
    c. the legal recognition of Roman Catholicism as a minority religion in all the British colonies.
    d. the creation of a rich tradition of French cuisine and fashion in North America.
    e. support for the French Revolution by Britain's former North American colonists.

13. The British Proclamation of 1763
    a. was welcomed by most American colonists.
    b. angered colonists who thought that it deprived them of the fruits of victory.
    c. was aimed at further suppressing the French population of Canada.
    d. halted American westward settlement for several years.
    e. encouraged Daniel Boone and his followers to cross the Appalachians into Kentucky.
14. The French and Indian War created conflict between the British and the American military because
    a. the American soldiers had failed to support the British military effort.
    b. the British regulars had carried the brunt of the fighting.
    c. the Americans opposed the forced resettlement of French Acadians ("Cajuns") to Louisiana.
    d. American soldiers refused to accept orders from British officers.
    e. British officers treated the American colonial militia with contempt.
15. The most significant effect on the colonists of the French defeat in North America was
    a. to increase their gratitude to Britain for defending them in the war.
    b. to create new threats to colonial expansion from Spain and the Indians.
    c. to reduce the colonies' reliance on Britain for protection and increase their sense of independence.
    d. to focus colonial energies on trade.
    e. the creation of a strong intercolonial political organization.

C. Identification

Supply the correct identification for each numbered description.

1. _____   French Protestants who were granted toleration by the Edict of Nantes in 1598 but not permitted to settle in New France

2. _____   Absolute French monarch who reigned for seventy-two years

3. _____   Animal whose pelt provided great profits for the French empire and enhanced European fashion at enormous ecological cost

4. _____   Catholic religious order that explored the North American interior and sought to protect and convert the Indians

5. _____   Far-running, high-living French fur trappers

6. _____   Part of a certain British naval officer's anatomy that set off an imperial war with Spain

7. _____   Strategic French fortress conquered by New England settlers, handed back to the French in 1748, and finally conquered again by the British in 1759

8. _____   Inland river territory, scene of fierce competition between the French and land-speculating English colonists

9. _____   Bloodiest European theater of the Seven Years' War, where Frederick the Great's troops drained French strength away from North America

10. _____   Unification effort that Benjamin Franklin nearly led to success by his eloquent leadership and cartoon artistry

11. _____   Military aide to British General Braddock who defended the frontier after Braddock's defeat

12. _____   Fortress boldly and successfully assaulted by General Wolfe, spelling doom for New France

13. _____   Prussian king whose defeats of the French and others in Germany provided a key to the British victory in the Seven Years' War

14. _____   Allies of the French against the British, who continued to fight under Pontiac even after the peace settlement in 1763

15. _____   The larger European struggle of which the French and Indian War was part

D. Matching People, Places, and Events

Match the person, place, or event in the left column with the proper description in the right column by inserting the correct letter on the blank line.

1. ___ Samuel de Champlain

2. ___ Robert de la Salle

3. ___ Albany

4. ___ War of Austrian Succession

5. ___ Fort Duquesne

6. ___ George Washington

7. ___ Benjamin Franklin

8. ___ General Braddock

9. ___ William Pitt

10. ___ Plains of Abraham

11. ___ Seven Years' War

12. ___ Pontiac

13. ___ Proclamation of 1763

14. ___ New Orleans

15. ___ Acadians (Cajuns)

a. Advocate of colonial unity at a 1754 meeting in upstate New York

b. British document that aroused colonial anger but failed to stop frontier expansion

c. French colonists in Nova Scotia brutally uprooted by the victorious British and shipped to Louisiana

d. Conflict that started with the War of Jenkins's Ear and ended with the return of Louisbourg to France

e. Strategic French outpost at the mouth of the Mississippi

f. Indian leader whose frontier uprising caused the British to attempt to limit colonial expansion

g. Blundering British officer whose defeat gave the advantage to the French and Indians in the early stages of their war

h. The Father of New France, who established a crucial alliance with the Huron Indians

i. Site of the death of Generals Wolfe and Montcalm, where France's New World empire also perished

j. Strategic French stronghold; later renamed after a great British statesman

k. Militia commander whose frontier skirmish in Pennsylvania touched off a world war

l.   Site of a meeting that proposed greater unity and home rule among Britain's North American colonies

m.   Conflict that began with George Washington's skirmish in Ohio and ended with the loss of France's North American empire

n.   French empire builder who explored the Mississippi Basin and named it after his monarch

o.   Splendid British orator and organizer of the winning strategy against the French in North America

E. Putting Things in Order

Put the following events in correct order by numbering them from 1 to 10.

1. _____   A Virginia militia commander attempts an unsuccessful invasion of the Ohio Valley.

2. _____   The Great Commoner takes command of the British government and its war effort.

3. _____   Toleration of French Huguenots brings religious peace to France.

4. _____   New France is founded, one year after Jamestown.

5. _____   Britain issues a proclamation to prohibit colonial expansion and thereby prevent another Indian war.

6. _____   The second world war between France and Britain ends in British victory and the acquisition of Acadia.

7. _____   British victory on the Plains of Abraham seals the fate of New France.

8. _____   Return of Louisbourg fortress at the end of King George's War angers colonial New Englanders

9. _____   War begins badly for the British when Braddock fails to take Fort Duquesne.

10. _____   A great empire builder explores Louisiana and claims it for the French king.

F. Matching Cause and Effect

Match the historical cause in the left column with the proper effect in the right column by writing the correct letter on the blank line.

Cause	Effect
1. ___ The French fur trade	a. Resulted in decisive French defeat and British domination of North America
2. ___ The four world wars between 1688 and 1763	

3. ___   Competition for land and furs in the Ohio Valley

4. ___   The summoning of the Albany Congress by the British

5. ___   William Pitt's assumption of control of British government and strategy

6. ___   Wolfe's victory over Montcalm at Quebec

7. ___   The colonial militia's military success in the French and Indian War

8. ___   Colonial American smuggling and trading with French enemy

9. ___   British issuance of the Proclamation of 1763

10. ___   Braddock's defeat at Fort Duquesne

b.   Prompted widespread Indian assaults on the weakly defended colonial frontier

c.   Led to Washington's expedition and battle with the French at Fort Necessity

d.   Heightened colonial anger and encouraged illegal westward expansion

e.   Increased American military confidence and resentment of British redcoats

f.   Decimated beaver populations while spreading the French empire

g.   Were echoed by four small wars between French and British subjects in North America

h.   Represented the first major attempt at intercolonial unity

i.   Increased British government's disdain for colonial Americans and raised doubts about their loyalty to the empire

j.   Ended a string of defeats and turned the French and Indian War in Britain's favor

G. Developing Historical Skills

Using a Map to Understand the Text

Reading maps frequently aids in understanding a point being made in the text—especially when it involves geography or strategy. On p.116, the text emphasizes that the British did not turn the tide in the French and Indian War until Pitt altered strategy to concentrate on the strategic points of Louisbourg, Montreal, and Quebec. Examining the map *Events of 1755–1760* helps you to understand why this was so. Answer the following questions.

1.   Why is Quebec more important than, say, Fort Duquesne in relation to the St. Lawrence River and the Atlantic Ocean?

2.   Why was it essential to capture Louisbourg before attacking Quebec?

3. What was the strategic situation of remaining French forces in the Great Lakes area once Montreal and Quebec were captured?

H. Map Mastery

Map Discrimination

Using the maps and charts in Chapter 6, answer the following questions.

1. *France's American Empire at the Greatest Extent, 1700*: Around which great river valley was New France first colonized?

2. *France's American Empire at the Greatest Extent, 1700*: Which French colonial settlement on the Great Lakes linked the St. Lawrence and Mississippi river basins?

3. *Fur-Trading Posts*: Along which river, besides the Mississippi, were the greatest number of French fur-trading posts located?

4. *The Nine World Wars*: How many years of peace did Britain and France enjoy between France's loss of Acadia in the War of Spanish Succession and the beginning of the War of Austrian Succession?

5. *Scenes of the French Wars*: The attacks on Schenectady and Deerfield occurred during attacks from which French Canadian city?

6. *The Ohio Country, 1753–1754*: Fort Duquesne was located at the intersection of which two rivers (which unite at that point to form a third river)?

7. *Events of 1755–1760*: Which French Canadian stronghold did not finally fall until a year after Wolfe's defeat of Montcalm on the Plains of Abraham at Quebec?

8. *North America Before 1754/After 1763*: In the peace treaty of 1763, which nation besides Britain acquired North American territory from France?

9. *North America Before 1754/After 1763*: Which North American territory, owned by Spain before 1754, was acquired by Britain in the peace of 1763?

Map Challenge

Using the maps in this chapter, write a brief essay explaining why the St. Lawrence River valley was the strategic key to control of the whole center of North America.

PART III: APPLYING WHAT YOU HAVE LEARNED

1. Compare France's colonizing efforts in the New World with Spain's and England's colonies (see especially Chapters 1 and 2). What factors explain France's relatively weak impact on the New World compared with that of England's and Spain's?

2. In what ways were the American colonists involved in the home country's struggle with France?

3. How did French relations with the Indians compare with the Indian policies of Britain and Spain?

4. Why did most Indian peoples fight with the French against Britain and its American colonists in the French and Indian War?

5. Explain why Britain's success in defeating the French empire led to failures in dealing with its colonial subjects.

6. What did the French and Indian War reveal about Britain's fundamental attitudes toward its North American colonies. How did the British view of the colonists differ from the way the colonists understood themselves and their identity?

7. When the Seven Years' War (French and Indian War) began, most American colonists were extremely proud and happy to be British citizens, part of the world's greatest empire. When it ended many of them no longer felt that way, even though the British Empire was more powerful than ever. Why?

CHAPTER 7

The Road to Revolution, 1763–1775

PART I: REVIEWING THE CHAPTER

A. Checklist of Learning Objectives

After mastering this chapter, you should be able to:

1. Explain the ideas of republicanism and radical Whiggery that Britain's American colonists had adopted by the eighteenth century.

2. Describe the theory and practice of mercantilism, and explain why Americans resented it.

3. Explain why Britain adopted policies of tighter political control and higher taxation of Americans after 1763 and how these policies sparked fierce colonial resentment.

4. Describe the first major new British taxes on the colonies and how colonial resistance forced repeal of all taxes, except the tax on tea, by 1770.

5. Explain how colonial agitators kept resistance alive from 1770–1773.

6. Indicate why the forcible importation of taxable British tea sparked the Boston Tea Party, the Intolerable Acts, and the outbreak of conflict between Britain and the colonists.

7. Assess the balance of forces between the British and the American rebels as the two sides prepared for war.

B. Glossary

To build your social science vocabulary, familiarize yourself with the following terms.

1. **patronage** A system in which benefits, including jobs, money, or protection are granted in exchange for political support. "The Whigs mounted withering attacks on the use of patronage and bribes by the king's ministers. . . ."

2. **mercantilism** The economic theory that all parts of a nation's or empire's economy should be coordinated for the good of the whole state; hence, that colonial economic welfare should be subordinated to that of the imperial power. "The British authorities nevertheless embraced a theory called mercantilism. . . ."

3. **depreciate** To decrease in value, as in the decline of the purchasing power of money. ". . . dire financial need forced many of the colonies to issue paper money, which swiftly depreciated."

4. **veto** The constitutional right of a ruler or executive to block legislation passed by another unit of government. "This royal veto was used rather sparingly. . . ."

5. **monopoly** The complete control of a product or sphere of economic activity by a single producer or business. "Virginia tobacco planters enjoyed a monopoly in the British market. . . ."

6. **admiralty courts** In British law, special administrative courts designed to handle maritime cases without a jury. "Both the Sugar Act and the Stamp Act provided for trying offenders in the hated admiralty courts. . . ."

7. **virtual representation** The political theory that a class of persons is represented in a lawmaking body without direct vote. "Elaborating the theory of 'virtual representation,' Grenville claimed that every member of Parliament represented all British subjects, even . . . Americans. . . ."

8. **nonimportation agreement** Pledges to boycott, or decline to purchase, certain goods from abroad. "More effective than the congress was the widespread adoption of nonimportation agreements. . . ."

9. **mulatto** A person of mixed African and European ancestry. ". . . Crispus Attucks [was] described . . . as a powerfully built runaway 'mulatto.'. . . "

10. **duty (duties)** A customs tax on the export or import of goods. ". . . finally persuaded Parliament to repeal the Townshend revenue duties."

11. **propaganda (propagandist)** A systematic program or particular materials designed to promote certain ideas; sometimes but not always the term is used negatively, implying the use of manipulative or deceptive means. (A propagandist is one who engages in such practices.) "Resistance was further kindled by a master propagandist and engineer of rebellion, Samuel Adams of Boston. . . ."

12. **boycott** An organized refusal to deal with some person, organization, or product. "The Association called for a *complete* boycott of British goods. . . ."

13. **inflation** An increase in the supply of currency relative to the goods available, leading to a decline in the purchasing power of money. "Inflation of the currency inevitably skyrocketed prices."

14. **desert** To leave official government or military service without permission. ". . . hundreds of anxious husbands and fathers deserted."

PART II: CHECKING YOUR PROGRESS

A. True-False

Where the statement is true, circle **T**; where it is false, circle **F**.

1. T   F   The republican idea of a just society, in which selfish interests were subordinated to the common good, took deep root in Britain's North American colonies.

2. T   F   The theory of mercantilism held that colonies existed primarily to provide the mother country with raw materials as well as a market for exports.

3. T   F   British mercantilism prohibited the colonies from printing their own paper money.

4. T   F   In practice, British mercantilism provided the colonies with substantial economic benefits such as military protection and guaranteed markets for certain goods.

5. T   F   The fundamental motive behind the steep new taxes in the 1760s was to repay the large debt that Britain had incurred in defending its North American colonies.

6. T   F   Americans generally accepted the right of Parliament to tax the colonies to provide money for defense, but denied its right to legislate about colonial affairs.

7. T   F   When Americans first cried "no taxation without representation," what they wanted was to have their own representatives elected to the British Parliament.

8. T   F   The colonies finally forced repeal of the Stamp Act by organizing political protests and enforcing nonimportation agreements against British goods.

9. T   F   The new British Townshend Acts were not direct taxes, but rather required colonists to shelter and feed British troops in their homes.

10. T   F   The Boston Massacre provoked colonial outrage because the British troops suddenly opened fire on peaceful Boston citizens without any provocation.

11. T   F   After the repeal of the Townshend Act, the spirit of colonial resistance was kept alive largely by agitators like Samuel Adams and his Committees of Correspondence.

12. T   F   Even though the Quebec Act was not really part of the Intolerable Acts, the colonists thought it especially oppressive because of their fear that it would expand Roman Catholicism.

13. T   F   The First Continental Congress proclaimed that the colonies would declare independence from Britain unless their grievances were redressed.

14. T   F   One fundamental American asset in the impending war with Britain was an extensive stockpile of military weapons and supplies.

15. T   F   A key British advantage was that they did not have to defeat all the rebellious American forces, but only fight to a draw in order to crush the Revolution.

B. Multiple Choice

Select the best answer and circle the corresponding letter.

1. The British theory of mercantilism, by which the colonies were governed, held that
    a. a nation's economy should be entirely shaped by free market forces, without government interference.
    b. the colonies should develop by becoming as economically self-sufficient as possible.
    c. the colonial economy should be carefully controlled to serve the home country's needs.
    d. colonists could develop economic growth by trading with whatever country offered the best profits.
    e. the mother country and the colonies should each specialize in producing goods where they had a comparative economic advantage.

2. One of the ways in which mercantilism harmed the colonial economy was by
    a. prohibiting colonial merchants from owning and operating their own ships.
    b. inhibiting the development of banking and paper currency in the colonies.
    c. forcing the colonists to fall into debt through the purchase of goods on credit.
    d. forcing Virginia tobacco planters to sell their product only in Britain.
    e. taxing colonial goods at a higher rate than the same goods produced in Britain.

3. The mobilization of nonimportation policies against the Stamp Act was politically important because it
    a. aroused the first French support for the American cause.
    b. aroused revolutionary fervor among many ordinary American men and women.
    c. reinforced the completely nonviolent character of the anti-British movement.
    d. helped stimulate the development of colonial manufacturing.
    e. crippled the British shipping industry.

4. When British officials decided to enforce the East India Company's tea monopoly and the three-pence tax on tea,

    a. they were successful in landing the tea everywhere except Boston.
    b. colonists were outraged because their favorite beverage would cost more than ever before.
    c. the colonists persuaded friendly Indian tribes to dump the tea into Boston harbor.
    d. colonists were outraged because they saw it as a trick to undermine their principled resistance to the tax.
    e. the nonimportation agreements required Americans to switch to other beverages.

5. The most intolerable of the Intolerable Acts that the British imposed as punishment for the Boston Tea Party were

    a. the Quebec Act permitting Catholic expansion and overturning anti-Catholic Massachusetts laws.
    b. the laws undermining the Massachusetts colonial charter and restricting town meetings.
    c. the law re-asserting Parliament's right to tax the colonies and doubling the tax on tea.
    d. the law ending colonial self-governance and imposing martial law on Massachusetts.
    e. closing the port of Boston and the Quartering Act lodging British soldiers in private homes.

6. American colonists especially resented the Townshend Acts because

    a. they strongly disliked the British minister, "Champagne Charley" Townshend, who proposed them.
    b. the revenues from the taxation would go to support British officials and judges in America.
    c. they called for the establishment of the Anglican church throughout the colonies.
    d. the taxes were to be imposed directly by the king without an act of Parliament.
    e. the administration of the tax laws was so corrupt.

7. The passage of the Quebec Act aroused intense American fears because it

    a. put the French language on an equal standing with English throughout the colonies.
    b. involved stationing British troops throughout the colonies.
    c. seemed likely to stir up ethnic divisions within the thirteen colonies south of Canada.
    d. threatened to make Canada the dominant British colony in North America.
    e. extended Catholic jurisdiction and a non-jury judicial system into the English-speaking Ohio country.

8. The most important action the First Continental Congress took to protest the Intolerable Acts was

    a. forming the Association to impose a complete boycott of all British goods.
    b. organizing a colonial militia to prepare for military resistance.
    c. forming Committees of Correspondence to communicate among all the colonies and develop political opposition to British rule.
    d. sending petitions to the British Parliament demanding repeal of the laws.
    e. adopting a provisional declaration of independence, which would go into effect if the law were not repealed.

9. The event that precipitated the first real shooting between the British army and American colonists was the

    a. British attempt to seize Bunker Hill and the Old North Church.
    b. British attempt to seize colonial supplies and leaders at Lexington and Concord.
    c. Boston Tea Party.
    d. Boston Massacre.
    e. American burning of a British tea ship at Annapolis, Maryland.

10.   The British parliamentary government at the time of the American Revolution was headed by
      a.   William Pitt.
      b.   "Champagne Charley" Townshend.
      c.   Edmund Burke.
      d.   Lord North.
      e.   Thomas Hutchinson.
11.   At the time of the American Revolution, the population of Britain was approximately _____ _____ than the population of the thirteen American colonies.
      a.   five times larger
      b.   one-third smaller
      c.   ten times larger
      d.   three times larger
      e.   one-tenth smaller
12.   The British political party that was generally more sympathetic to the American cause was the
      a.   Tory Party.
      b.   Labour Party.
      c.   Country Party.
      d.   Whig Party.
      e.   Liberal Party.
13.   One of the advantages the British enjoyed in the impending conflict with the colonies was
      a.   a determined and politically effective government.
      b.   the ability to enlist foreign soldiers, Loyalists, and Native Americans in their military forces.
      c.   a highly motivated and efficiently run military force in America.
      d.   the concentration of colonial resistance in a few urban centers.
      e.   the strong backing of the other European great powers.
14.   One of the advantages the colonists enjoyed in the impending conflict with Britain was
      a.   fighting defensively on a large, agriculturally self-sufficient continent.
      b.   a well-organized and effective political leadership.
      c.   a strong sense of unity among the various colonies.
      d.   the fact that nearly all Americans owned their own firearms.
      e.   a small but effective navy that could harass British shipping.
15.   In the Revolutionary War, African Americans
      a.   unanimously supported the American patriot cause.
      b.   were generally neutral between the British and American forces.
      c.   were used only as servants and manual labor by the American army.
      d.   took the opportunity to stage substantial slave revolts.
      e.   fought in both the American patriot and British loyalist military forces.

C. Identification

Supply the correct identification for each numbered description.

1.   _____   The basic economic and political theory by which seventeenth- and eighteenth-century European powers governed their overseas colonies

2.   _____   The early modern political theory, modeled on ancient Greek and Roman ideas, that a just and stable society required citizens to subordinate their individual interests to support the common good

3. _____   The eighteenth-century British political theorists, popular in the colonies, who argued that centralized government power inevitably led to political corruption and destruction of individual rights and liberties

4. _____   The first law, passed in 1764, that aimed specifically to raise revenue in the colonies for benefit of the British crown

5. _____   British governmental theory that Parliament spoke for all British subjects, including Americans, even if they did not vote for its members

6. _____   The effective form of organized colonial resistance against the Stamp Act, which made homespun clothing fashionable

7. _____   The product taxed under the Townshend Acts that generated the greatest colonial resistance

8. _____   Underground networks of communication and propaganda, initiated by Samuel Adams, that sustained colonial resistance even when public anger died down from 1770–1773

9. _____   A spectacular protest by men disguised as Indians that actually destroyed large quantities of a valuable product and provoked fierce governmental repression

10. _____   Religion that was granted toleration in the trans-Allegheny West by the Quebec Act, arousing deep colonial hostility

11. _____   German mercenaries hired by George III to fight the American revolutionaries

12. _____   Paper currency authorized by Congress to finance the Revolution depreciated to near worthlessness

13. _____   Effective organization created by the First Continental Congress to provide a total, unified boycott of all British goods

14. _____   Rapidly mobilized colonial militiamen whose refusal to disperse sparked the first battle of the Revolution

15. _____   Popular term for British regular troops, scorned as "lobster backs" and "bloody backs" by Bostonians and other colonials

D. Matching People, Places, and Events

Match the person, place, or event in the left column with the proper description in the right column by inserting the correct letter on the blank line.

1. ___   John Adams

2. ___   George Grenville

3. ___   Stamp Act

4. ___   Sons and Daughters of Liberty

5. ___   "Champagne Charley" Townshend

6. ___   Crispus Attucks

7. ___   George III

8. ___   Samuel Adams

9. ___   Boston Tea Party

a. British minister who raised a storm of protest by passing the Stamp Act

b. Legislation passed in 1765, but repealed the next year, after colonial resistance made it impossible to enforce

c. The organization created by the First Continental Congress to enforce a total boycott of all British goods in America

10. ___ Intolerable Acts

11. ___ Thomas Hutchinson

12. ___ The Association

13. ___ Marquis de Lafayette

14. ___ Baron von Steuben

15. ___ Quartering Act

d. Legislation that required colonists to feed and shelter British troops; disobeyed in New York and elsewhere

e. Nineteen-year-old major general in the Revolutionary army

f. Massachusetts leader who successfully opposed compromise and promoted colonial rights in the First Continental Congress

g. Minister whose clever attempt to impose import taxes nearly succeeded, but eventually brewed trouble for Britain

h. Zealous defender of the common people's rights and organizer of underground propaganda committees

i. Harsh measures of retaliation for a tea party, including the Boston Port Act closing that city's harbor

j. Stubborn ruler, lustful for power, who promoted harsh ministers like Lord North

k. Alleged leader of radical protesters killed in Boston Massacre

l. Organizational genius who turned raw colonial recruits into tough professional soldiers

m. Male and female organizations that enforced the nonimportation agreements, sometimes by coercive means

n. British governor of Massachusetts whose stubborn policies helped provoke the Boston Tea Party

o. Event organized by men disguised as Indians to sabotage British support of a British East India Company monopoly

E. Putting Things in Order

Put the following events in correct order by numbering them from 1 to 10.

1. _____ Britain attempts to gain revenue by a tax on papers and documents, creating a colonial uproar.

2. _____ Britain closes the port of Boston and opens the western frontier to Catholicism.

3. _____   Crispus Attucks leads a crowd in an attack on British troops, and eleven people are killed.

4. _____   Colonial Minute Men fire "the shot heard around the world" in the first battle of the Revolution.

5. _____   A British minister cleverly attempts to gain revenue and dampen colonial protest by imposing an import tax only on certain specialized products.

6. _____   A British agency is established with broad but generally ineffective power over colonial commerce.

7. _____   Samuel Adams and others organize revolutionary cells of communication and agitation across the colonies.

8. _____   Parliament repeals a direct tax in response to colonial protest but declares that it has the right to tax colonies.

9. _____   A band of men disguised as Indians dumps the rich cargo of the British East India Company into Boston Harbor, provoking a harsh British response.

10. _____   First acts are passed by Parliament to regulate colonial trade based on mercantilist principles.

F. Matching Cause and Effect

Match the historical cause in the left column with the proper effect in the right column by writing the correct letter on the blank line.

Cause

1. ____ America's distance from Britain and the growth of colonial self-government

2. ____ British mercantilism

3. ____ The large British debt incurred defending the colonies in the French and Indian War

4. ____ Passage of the Stamp Act

5. ____ British troops sent to enforce order in Boston

6. ____ The British government's attempt to maintain the East India Company's tea monopoly

7. ____ The Boston Tea Party

8. ____ The Intolerable Acts

9. ____ A British attempt to seize the colonial militia's gunpowder supplies

10. ____ The Continental Congress's reluctance to tax Americans for war

Effect

a. Prompted the summoning of the First Continental Congress

b. Led Grenville to propose the Sugar Act, Quartering Act, and Stamp Act

c. Precipitated the Battle of Lexington and Concord

d. Fired on colonial citizens in the Boston Massacre

e. Prompted passage of the Intolerable Acts, including the Boston Port Act

f. Resulted in the printing of large amounts of paper currency and skyrocketing inflation

g. Enforced restrictions on colonial manufacturing, trade, and paper currency

h. Led to gradual development of a colonial sense of independence years before the Revolution

i. Spurred patriots to stage Boston Tea Party

j.   Was greeted in the colonies by the nonimportation agreements, the Stamp Act Congress, and the forced resignation of stamp agents

G. Developing Historical Skills

Interpreting Historical Illustrations

Contemporary illustrations of historical events may not only give us information about those events but tell us something about the attitude and intention of those who made the illustrations. The caption to the engraving of the Boston Massacre by Paul Revere (p. 133) observes that it is "both art and propaganda." Drawing on the account of the massacre in the text (pp. 132–133) enables you to see the ways in which Revere's engraving combines factual information with a political point of view. Answer the following questions.

1.   What parts of the encounter between the British redcoats and the colonists does the engraving entirely leave out?

2.   The text says that the British troops fired "without orders." How does the engraving suggest the opposite?

3.   How does Revere's presentation of the colonial victims seem especially designed to inflame the feelings of the viewer?

PART III: APPLYING WHAT YOU HAVE LEARNED

1.   What central political ideas had colonial Americans developed by the eighteenth century that made them deeply suspicious of centralized authority and fervent in defense of their rights?

2.   How and why did the Americans and the British differ in their views of taxation and of the relationship of colonies to the empire?

3.   What was the theory and practice of mercantilism? Was mercantilism actually as economically oppressive as the colonists came to believe? Were the psychological effects of colonial dependence less or more important than the economic ones?

4.   Prior to the outbreak of violence in 1775, what essentially nonviolent methods did the colonists use in their struggle with British authorities? Were these methods effective in achieving colonial goals? How did the British respond to them?

5.   What advantages and disadvantages did the American rebels and the British each possess as the war began? What did each side do to mobilize its resources most effectively?

6. At various times during the decade from 1765–1775, the British government backed down and sought compromise with the American colonies. Why did it react so differently, and harshly, after the Boston Tea Party? Was there any possibility that the Empire could have been repaired after the imposition of the Intolerable Acts?

7. Could the American people have won their independence without George Washington and the small, professional Continental Army? Why have the myths of the militiamen and the part-time citizen-soldiers (Minute Men) loomed almost larger in American memories of the Revolutionary War than memories of Washington's trained professional military?

8. Was the American Revolution inevitable? Or could the thirteen colonies have remained attached to Britain for many years and then peacefully achieved their independence as the British colonies of Canada and Australia later did? How would the meaning of America have been different without this violent revolt from the home country?

CHAPTER 8

America Secedes from the Empire, 1775–1783

PART I: REVIEWING THE CHAPTER

A. Checklist of Learning Objectives

After mastering this chapter, you should be able to:

1. Explain how American colonists could continue to proclaim their loyalty to the British crown even while they engaged in major military hostilities with Britain after April 1775.

2. Explain why Thomas Paine's *Common Sense* finally inspired Americans to declare their independence in the summer of 1776, and outline the principal ideas of republicanism that Paine and other American revolutionary leaders promoted.

3. Explain both the specific political grievances and the universal ideals and principles that Jefferson's Declaration of Independence used to justify America's separation from Britain.

4. Show why the American Revolution should be understood as a civil war between Americans as well as a war with Britain, and describe the motivations and treatment of the Loyalists.

5. Describe how Britain's original strategic plan to crush the Revolution was foiled, especially by the Battle of Saratoga.

6. Describe the fundamental military strategy that Washington and his generals, especially Nathanael Greene, adopted, and why it proved successful.

7. Describe the key role of the French alliance in winning American independence, including the final victory at Yorktown.

8. Describe the terms of the Treaty of Paris, and explain why America was able to achieve a diplomatic victory that far exceeded its military and economic strength.

B. Glossary

To build your social science vocabulary, familiarize yourself with the following terms.

1. **mercenary** A professional soldier who serves in a foreign army for pay. ". . . the Americans called all the European mercenaries Hessians."

2. **indictment** A formal written accusation charging someone with a crime. "The overdrawn bill of indictment included imposing taxes without consent. . . ."

3. **dictatorship** A form of government characterized by absolute state power and unlimited, arbitrary control by the ruler or rulers. "The [charges] included . . . establishing a military dictatorship. . . ."

4. **neutral** A nation or person not taking sides in a war. "Many colonists were apathetic or neutral. . . ."

5. **civilian** A citizen not in military service. "The opposing forces contended . . . for the allegiance . . . of the civilian population."

6. **traitor** One who betrays a country by aiding an enemy. ". . . they regarded their opponents, not themselves, as traitors."

7. **confiscate** To seize private property for public use, often as a penalty. "The estates of many of the fugitives were confiscated. . . ."

8. **envoy** A messenger or agent sent by a government on official business. "Benjamin Franklin, recently sent to Paris as an envoy, truthfully jested that Howe had not captured Philadelphia. . . ."

9. **rabble** A mass of disorderly and crude common people. "This rabble was nevertheless whipped into a professional army. . . ."

10. **blockade** The isolation of a place by hostile ships or troops, preventing the movement of people or goods. "Now the French had powerful fleets. . . in a position to jeopardize Britain's blockade and lines of supply."

11. **privateer** A private vessel temporarily authorized to capture or plunder enemy ships in wartime. "More numerous and damaging than ships of the regular American navy were swift privateers."

12. **graft** Taking advantage of one's official position to gain money or property by illegal means. "It had the unfortunate effect of . . . involving Americans, including Benedict Arnold, in speculation and graft."

PART II: CHECKING YOUR PROGRESS

A. True-False

Where the statement is true, circle **T**; where it is false, circle **F**.

1. T F George Washington was chosen commander of the American army primarily because of his military abilities and experience.

2. T F Following the Battle of Bunker Hill, King George made one last attempt at reconciliation with his American subjects and their Continental Congress.

3. T F The American invasion of Canada in 1775 was based in part on the false belief that oppressed French Canadians would rise up in revolt and join the thirteen colonies in revolt.

4. T F Tom Paine's *Common Sense* was most important because it advocated not only American independence but a republican form of government based on consent of the people.

5. T F The Declaration of Independence justified American independence not on the basis of the historic rights of Englishmen, but on the basis of the universal natural rights of all humankind.

6. T F The Declaration of Independence made the colonists seditious rebels against the king and enabled them to seek foreign assistance for their cause.

7. T F The Loyalists considered the Patriots to be the traitors to their country (Britain) and themselves to be the true patriots.

8. T F Most Loyalists were executed or driven from the country after the Patriot victory.

9. T F The Loyalists were strongest in New England and Virginia.

10. T F The most critical result of General Burgoyne's defeat at Saratoga in 1777 was that it led to the American alliance with France.

11. T   F   Americans' enlightened revolutionary idealism made them believe that the rule of law and free commercial trade, not traditional power politics, should be the basis of all international relations.

12. T   F   By using delay and strategic retreat, General Nathanael Greene successfully thwarted the British attempt to crush the Revolution in the South 1780–1781.

13. T   F   At Yorktown, the Americans finally showed that they could win an important battle without French assistance.

14. T   F   American diplomats in Paris were successful in guaranteeing American political independence but failed to gain the territorial concessions they wanted.

15. T   F   Although Britain lost its North American colonies in the Revolutionary War, it gained strategic and military dividends that paid off in the much larger wars with Napoleon for control of Europe.

B. Multiple Choice

Select the best answer and circle the corresponding letter.

1. During the initial period of fighting between April 1775 and July 1776, the colonists constantly insisted that their goal was
    a. the removal of all British troops from America.
    b. to restore their rights within the British Empire.
    c. complete independence from Britain.
    d. to end the arbitrary power of King George III to impose taxes on them.
    e. local autonomy and self-rule within the wider British empire.

2. George Washington proved to be an especially effective commander of American forces in the Revolution because
    a. he was able to rally previously skeptical New Englanders to the Patriot cause.
    b. of his exceptionally brilliant military mind.
    c. of his eloquence in defining the political goals for which Americans fought.
    d. his humble background inspired the ordinary soldiers in the Revolutionary army.
    e. of his integrity, courage, and moral forcefulness.

3. The bold American military strategy that narrowly failed in December 1775 involved a/an
    a. two-pronged attack on British forces in New Jersey.
    b. invasion of Canada by generals Arnold and Montgomery.
    c. attack on British forts in the Ohio country.
    d. naval assault on British warships in Boston harbor.
    e. attempt to divide British forces by conquering and controlling the Hudson Valley.

4. Many of the German Hessian soldiers hired by King George III to fight for the British
    a. hated the American revolutionaries and their cause.
    b. helped draw in the Prussian King Frederick II as a British ally.
    c. were ineffective in battle against American militiamen.
    d. had little loyalty to the British cause and ended up deserting.
    e. helped recruit the numerous Germans in Pennsylvania to the Loyalist cause.

5. Thomas Paine's appeal for a new republican form of government attracted many Americans because

    a. they believed that social class differences promoted by monarchy were wrong.
    b. they expected that it would encourage an alliance with republican France.
    c. they were impressed that Paine was drawing on the best classical ideas from Plato's *Republic.*
    d. they were fearful that wealthy southern planters like Washington wanted to establish nobility in America.
    e. their own experience with local and colonial self-governance had prepared them for the idea that they did not need a monarch.

6. The Declaration of Independence's proclamation that all governments everywhere should be based on universal human rights and consent of the people soon had an impact on

    a. the movement to abolish the British monarchy.
    b. the French Revolution and its Declaration of the Rights of Man.
    c. Thomas Jefferson's decision to emancipate his own slaves.
    d. the first attempts to create an international organization comparable to the United Nations.
    e. political philosophers like Edmund Burke and Voltaire.

7. Which of the following was *not* among the groups that produced large numbers of Loyalists?

    a. Conservative and well-off Americans
    b. Recent immigrants from Scotland and Ireland
    c. Presbyterians and Congregationalists
    d. African Americans
    e. Members of the Anglican and Quaker churches

8. Besides George Washington, the most militarily brilliant and effective American officer in the early campaigns of 1776 and 1777 was General

    a. Nathanael Greene.
    b. Baron von Steuben.
    c. Benedict Arnold.
    d. William Howe.
    e. John Burgoyne.

9. The Battle of Saratoga was a key turning point of the War for Independence because it

    a. prevented the British from keeping control of the key port of New York City.
    b. demonstrated that the Americans could fight more than guerrilla wars.
    c. displayed George Washington's brilliance as military strategist.
    d. effectively destroyed British military power in the middle colonies.
    e. foiled the British attempt to isolate New England and it brought French assistance to the Revolutionary cause.

10. In his successful negotiation of a military alliance with France, Benjamin Franklin attempted to personally represent

    a. the power of the new, continent-wide American republic.
    b. the American ideals of homespun simplicity and democratic social order.
    c. his knowledge and status as a leading scientist on both sides of the Atlantic.
    d. his skill as a political propagandist and coiner of wise, clever sayings.
    e. the elegant polish and sophisticated manner that would impress the French court.

11. The British relied on the numerous Loyalists to aid them in fighting the Patriots especially in
    a. Rhode Island and the rest of New England.
    b. the western Illinois country.
    c. the warfare at sea.
    d. the Carolinas.
    e. Canada.

12. Most of the Six Nations of the Iroquois under Joseph Brant fought for Britain against the American revolutionaries because
    a. they disagreed with the principles of the Declaration of Independence.
    b. they believed that a victorious Britain would contain westward American expansion.
    c. they were paid as mercenary soldiers by the British government.
    d. they hoped to drive the American colonists off the North American continent.
    e. the British promised them their own independent nation in upstate New York.

13. The British defeat at Yorktown was brought about by George Washington's veteran Continental Army and the
    a. French navy under Admiral de Grasse.
    b. American navy under John Paul Jones.
    c. American militia under George Rogers Clark.
    d. Armed Neutrality under Catherine the Great.
    e. local Virginia militia.

14. In the peace negotiations at Paris, the French wanted the new American republic to
    a. be divided into three smaller nations.
    b. negotiate a separate peace with Britain.
    c. guarantee that they would not spread revolutionary ideas in France.
    d. help France regain Quebec from the British.
    e. be confined to the territory east of the Appalachian Mountains.

15. The British yielded the Americans a generous peace treaty that included the western territories primarily because of the
    a. desire of the weak Whig ministry in London for friendly future relations with the United States.
    b. threat of further war with France.
    c. military power of the United States.
    d. willingness of the Americans to yield on other issues like trade and fishing rights.
    e. Americans were willing to guarantee British control of Canada.

C. Identification

Supply the correct identification for each numbered description.

1. _____ The body that chose George Washington commander of the Continental Army

2. _____ The British colony that Americans invaded in 1775 in hopes of adding it to the rebellious thirteen

3. _____ The inflammatory pamphlet that demanded independence and heaped scorn on "the Royal Brute of Great Britain"

4. _____ The document that provided a passionate explanation and justification of Richard Henry Lee's official resolution passed by Congress on July 2, 1776

5. _____ Another name for the American Tories

6. _____ One of George Washington's most brilliant military victories, when he surprised the British and Hessians the day after Christmas, 1776

7. _____ Pennsylvania valley where Washington's army nearly starved and froze to death in the winter of 1777–1778

8. _____ The river valley that was the focus of Britain's early military strategy and the scene of Burgoyne's surrender at Saratoga in 1777

9. _____ Term for the alliance of Catherine the Great of Russia and other European powers who did not declare war but assumed a hostile neutrality toward Britain

10. _____ English translation of the new American republic's official motto, *novus ordo seculorum*

11. _____ Self-denying document drafted by Congress in 1776 to guide American diplomacy that specified no political or military alliances but only commercial relations

12. _____ Legalized pirates, more than a thousand strong, who inflicted heavy damage on British shipping

13. _____ British political party that replaced Lord North's Tories in 1782 and made a generous treaty with the United States

14. _____ The key American fort on the Hudson River that General Benedict Arnoldattempted to hand over to the British

15. _____ Treaty between the United States and the Iroquois that represented the first Indian treaty ever signed by the new nation.

D. Matching People, Places, and Events

Match the person, place, or event in the left column with the proper description in the right column by inserting the correct letter on the blank line.

1. ___ George Washington
2. ___ Bunker Hill
3. ___ Benedict Arnold
4. ___ Thomas Paine
5. ___ Richard Henry Lee
6. ___ Thomas Jefferson
7. ___ Nathanael Greene
8. ___ General Burgoyne
9. ___ General Howe
10. ___ Benjamin Franklin
11. ___ George Rogers Clark
12. ___ John Paul Jones
13. ___ Saratoga
14. ___ Yorktown
15. ___ Joseph Brant

a. British general who chose to enjoy himself in New York and Philadelphia rather than vigorously pursue the American enemy

b. Brilliant American general who invaded Canada, foiled Burgoyne's invasion, and then betrayed his country in 1780

c. American naval commander who successfully harassed British shipping

d. Author of an explanatory indictment, signed on July 4, 1776, that accused George III of establishing a military dictatorship

e. Shrewd and calculatingly homespun American diplomat who forged the alliance with France and later secured a generous peace treaty

    f.   Mohawk chief who led many Iroquois to fight with Britain against American revolutionaries

    g.   The decisive early battle of the American Revolution that led to the alliance with France

    h.   Military engagement that led King George III officially to declare the colonists in revolt

    i.   Brilliant "Fighting Quaker" whose strategy of retreat and delay finally defeated the British in the Carolinas

    j.   A wealthy Virginian of great character and leadership abilities who served his country without pay

    k.   The British defeat that led to the fall of North's government and the end of the war

    l.   Leader whose small force conquered key British forts in the West

    m.   A radical British immigrant who put an end to American toasts to King George

    n.   Fiery Virginian and author of the official resolution of July 2, 1776, formally authorizing the colonies' independence

    o.   Blundering British general whose slow progress south from Canada ended in disaster at Saratoga

E. Putting Things in Order

Put the following events in correct order by numbering them from 1 to 6.

1. _____   Lord North's military collapses, and Britain's Whigs take power, ready to make peace.

2. _____   Thomas Jefferson writes an eloquent justification of Richard Henry Lee's resolution.

3. _____   Burgoyne and Howe are defeated both by the generalship of Washington and Arnold and by their own blundering.

4. _____   The Treaty of Paris is signed, guaranteeing American independence.

5. _____   The British launch a frontal attack on entrenched American forces near Boston and suffer drastic losses in their victory.

6. _____   Washington's army and the French navy trap General Cornwallis, spelling the end for the British.

F. Matching Cause and Effect

Match the historical cause in the left column with the proper effect in the right column by writing the correct letter on the blank line.

Cause	Effect
1. ___ The Battle of Bunker Hill	a. Led to American acquisition of the West up to the Mississippi River
2. ___ Thomas Paine's *Common Sense*	b. Caused King George to proclaim the colonies in revolt and import Hessian troops to crush them
3. ___ Jefferson's Declaration of Independence	c. Led to a favorable peace treaty for the United States and the end of French schemes for a smaller, weaker America
4. ___ The Patriot militia's political education and recruitment	
5. ___ The blundering of Burgoyne and Howe and the superb military strategy of Arnold and Washington	d. Caused the British to begin peace negotiations in Paris
6. ___ The Battle of Saratoga	e. Inspired universal awareness of the American Revolution as a fight for the belief that "all men are created equal"
7. ___ Clark's military conquests and Jay's diplomacy	f. Caused the British defeat at Yorktown and the collapse of North's Tory government
8. ___ The trapping of Cornwallis between Washington's army and de Grasse's navy	g. Led to the failure of Britain's grand strategy and the crucial American victory at Saratoga
9. ___ The collapse of the North ministry and the Whig takeover of the British government	h. Made France willing to become an ally of the United States
10. ___ Jay's secret and separate negotiations with Britain	i. Stirred growing colonial support for declaring independence from Britain
	j. Won neutral or apathetic Americans over to the Patriot cause

G. Developing Historical Skills

Distinguishing Historical Fact and Historical Meaning

Some historical events can be understood as simple facts requiring little explanation. But other historical events have meaning only when their significance is analyzed. The text contains examples of both kinds of historical events. Comparing them will help sort out the difference between the two.

Indicate which of these pairs of historical events is (a) a simple factual event requiring little explanation and which is (b) an event whose meaning needs to be interpreted in order to be understood. In each case, list the meaning the text gives to the second kind of event.

1. The British burning of Falmouth (Portland), Maine, and King George's proclamation that the colonies were in rebellion

2. Tom Paine's *Common Sense* and the death of General Richard Montgomery

3. Richard Henry Lee's resolution of July 2, 1776, and Thomas Jefferson's Declaration of Independence

H. Map Mastery

Map Discrimination

Using the maps and charts in Chapter 8, answer the following questions.

1. *Revolution in the North, 1775–1776*: Which two British strong points in Canada did the American generals Arnold and Montgomery attack in 1775?

2. *New York-Pennsylvania Theater, 1777–1778*: When Washington recrossed the Delaware River before the Battle of Trenton on December 26, 1776, which state did he come from, and which state did he go to?

3. *New York-Pennsylvania Theater, 1777–1778*: Which of the three British generals who were supposed to meet near Albany, New York, moved in the opposite direction and failed to get to the appointed gathering?

4. *Britain Against the World*: Besides France, which two European nations directly declared war on Britain during the American Revolution?

5. *War in the South, 1780–1781*: Name three cities in the South occupied at one time or another by General Cornwallis.

6. *George Rogers Clark's Campaign, 1778–1779*: Which river did George Rogers Clark move down as he went to conquer western forts from the British?

7. *George Rogers Clark's Campaign, 1778–1779*: Which three British posts did Clark capture?

Map Challenge

Using the maps of *The Revolution in the North* and *New York-Pennsylvania Theater, 1777–1778* as a basis, write a brief essay explaining why control of the Hudson River–Lake Champlain Valley was strategically crucial to both the British and the Americans in the Revolutionary War.

PART III: APPLYING WHAT YOU HAVE LEARNED

1. Why were Americans so long reluctant to break with Britain. How does the Declaration of Independence explain "the causes that impel them to separation" (see Appendix)?

2. Why was the Battle of Saratoga such a key battle in the Revolutionary War? Did Saratoga put the Americans on a clear path to victory, or only prevent them from being quickly defeated?

3. Why did Tom Paine's radical vision of republican virtue and the rights of the people appeal to so many Americans at the time of independence? Why did more conservative Patriots develop a different vision of America's republican future?

4. In what ways was the Revolution a civil war among Americans as well as a fight between Britain and those Americans seeking independence? Why have the Loyalists generally been forgotten in the story of America's beginnings?

5. How did the idealism and self-evident truths of the Declaration of Independence shape Americans' outlook and conduct during the Revolutionary War, including their attempt to establish entirely new principles of international relations?

6. Argue for and against: Even though it was necessary to achieve American independence, the American alliance with the reactionary French monarchy violated revolutionary ideals and demonstrated their impracticality as a basis for international relations.

7. Argue for and against: Washington was a great general not so much because of his victories but because of his brilliant strategic retreats.

8. In what ways did the principles of the American Revolution and the Declaration of Independence emerge from the practical historical experience of the American people, and in what ways did it reflect the abstract Enlightenment beliefs in a new age of progress, liberty, and human rights?

CHAPTER 9

The Confederation and the Constitution, 1776–1790

PART I: REVIEWING THE CHAPTER

A. Checklist of Learning Objectives

After mastering this chapter, you should be able to:

1. Explain the broad movement toward social and political equality that flourished after the Revolution and indicate why certain social and racial inequalities remained in place.

2. Describe the government of the Articles of Confederation and summarize its achievements and failures.

3. Explain the crucial role of Shays's Rebellion in sparking the movement for a new Constitution.

4. Describe the basic ideas and goals of the Founding Fathers in the Philadelphia Constitutional Convention and how they incorporated their fundamental principles into the Constitution.

5. Understand the central concerns that motivated the antifederalists, and indicate their social, economic, and political differences with the federalists.

6. Describe the issues at stake in the political fight over ratification of the Constitution between federalists and antifederalists, and explain why the federalists won.

7. Explain how the new government, set up by the Constitution, represented a conservative reaction to the American Revolution, yet at the same time, institutionalized the Revolution's central radical principles of popular government and individual liberty.

B. Glossary

To build your social science vocabulary, familiarize yourself with the following terms.

1. **disestablish** To separate an official state church from its connection with the government. "... the Protestant Episcopal church ... was everywhere disestablished."

2. **emancipation** Setting free from servitude or slavery. "Several northern states ... provided for the gradual emancipation of blacks."

3. **chattel** An article of personal or movable property; hence a term applied to slaves, since they were considered the personal property of their owners. "... a few idealistic masters freed their human chattels."

4. **abolitionist** An advocate of the end of slavery. "In this ... were to be found the first frail sprouts of the later abolitionist movement."

5. **ratification** The official confirmation or validation of a provisional governing document or act (such as a constitution) by authoritative approval. "Massachusetts ... submitted the final draft directly to the people for ratification."

6. **bill of rights** A document guaranteeing certain fundamental freedoms assumed to be central to society. "Most of these documents included bills of rights. . . ."

7. **speculators (speculation)** Those who buy property, goods, or financial instruments not primarily to use them, but in anticipation of profitable resale after a general rise in value. "States seized control of former crown lands . . . although rich speculators had their day."

8. **township** In America, a surveyed territory six miles square; the term also refers to a unit of local government, smaller than a county, that is often based on these survey units. "The sixteenth section of each township was set aside to be sold for the benefit of the public schools. . . ."

9. **territory** In American government, an organized political entity not yet enjoying the full and equal status of a state. ". . . when a territory could boast sixty thousand inhabitants, it might be admitted by Congress as a state. . . ."

10. **annex** To incorporate a smaller territory or political unit into a larger one. "They . . . sought to annex that rebellious area to Britain."

11. **requisition** A demand for something issued on the basis of public authority. "The requisition system of raising money was breaking down. . . ."

12. **foreclosure** Seizing private, mortgaged property from the owner because the legal payments on the loan have not been kept up. ". . . Revolutionary war veterans were losing their farms through mortgage foreclosures."

13. **quorum** The minimum number of persons who must be present in a group before it can conduct valid business. "A quorum of the fifty-five emissaries from twelve states finally convened at Philadelphia. . . ."

14. **anarchy** The theory that formal government is unnecessary and wrong in principle; the term is also used generally for lawlessness or antigovernmental disorder. "Delegates were determined to preserve the union [and] forestall anarchy. . . ."

15. **bicameral, unicameral** Referring to a legislative body with two houses (bicameral) or one (unicameral). ". . . representation in both houses of a bicameral Congress should be based on population. . . ." "This provided for equal representation in a unicameral Congress. . . ."

PART II: CHECKING YOUR PROGRESS

A. True-False

Where the statement is true, circle **T**; where it is false, circle **F**.

1. T   F   The American Revolution created a substantial, though not radical, push in the direction of social and political equality.

2. T   F   The movement toward the separation of church and state in America was greatly accelerated by the disestablishment of the Anglican church in Virginia.

3. T   F   The abolition of slavery in the North after the Revolution led to a strong movement for equal rights for free blacks.

4. T   F   The Revolutionary ideal of republican motherhood emphasized the central role of women in raising the selfless, virtuous citizens necessary to sustain self-government.

5. T   F   The state governments, established after the Revolution, created strong judicial and legislative branches of government as a check against popular misrule.

6.   T   F   Speculation, profiteering, and inflation weakened the economy and spurred social discontent during the years under the Articles of Confederation (1781–1787).

7.   T   F   The greatest failure of the national government, under the Articles of Confederation, was its inability to deal with the issue of western lands.

8.   T   F   The U.S. Congress, under the Articles of Confederation, was extremely weak because it had no power to regulate commerce or impose taxes on the states.

9.   T   F   The Northwest Ordinance, passed under the Articles of Confederation, established the western territories as permanent colonies of the federal government.

10.   T   F   Shays's Rebellion significantly strengthened the movement for a stronger central government by raising fears that the United States was falling into anarchy and mobocracy.

11.   T   F   The states sent their delegates to Philadelphia in 1787 for the purpose of discarding the Articles of Confederation and writing a new Constitution with a strong central government.

12.   T   F   The delegates to the Constitutional Convention were a mix of wealthy landowners and merchants with poorer farmers, artisans, and laborers.

13.   T   F   The Great Compromise between large and small states at the convention resulted in a House of Representatives based on population and a Senate with equal representation from all states.

14.   T   F   The antifederalists opposed the Constitution, partly because they thought it gave too much power to the states and not enough to Congress.

15.   T   F   The federalists used tough political maneuvering and the promise of a bill of rights to win a narrow ratification of the Constitution in key states.

B. Multiple Choice

Select the best answer and circle the corresponding letter.

1.   Among the important social changes brought about by the American Revolution was
    a.   the abolition of slavery everywhere except in South Carolina and Georgia.
    b.   a strong movement toward equality of property.
    c.   an army where the soldiers elected their own officers.
    d.   full equality and voting rights for women.
    e.   the increasing separation of church and state.

2.   A major new political innovation that emerged in the Revolutionary era was the
    a.   election of legislative representatives capable of voting on taxation.
    b.   shifting of power from the legislative to the executive branch of government.
    c.   idea of a written constitution drafted by a convention and ratified by direct vote of the people.
    d.   extension of voting rights to indentured servants.
    e.   direct election of judges by the people.

3. Despite the Revolution's emphasis on human rights and equality, the Founding Fathers failed to abolish slavery because
    a. they saw it as necessary to maintain American power.
    b. they feared black rebellion if slavery were removed.
    c. of their fear that a fight over slavery would destroy fragile national unity.
    d. almost none of them believed that slavery was wrong.
    e. many of them felt guilty about interracial sexual liaisons with their slaves.

4. The ideal of republican motherhood that emerged from the American Revolution held that
    a. women should be rewarded politically for having helped establish the American republic.
    b. women had a special responsibility to cultivate the civic virtues of republicanism in their children.
    c. the government should establish social services to help mothers raise their children.
    d. mothers should be granted full political and economic rights in the American republic.
    e. mothers had a responsibility to teach principles of equality to their daughters as well as sons.

5. The fundamental difference between ordinary laws and a constitution that emerged from the American Revolution was that ordinary laws
    a. described specific illegal acts, while a constitution granted positive rights.
    b. addressed economic questions, while a constitution addressed the distribution of political power.
    c. could be passed and repealed by legislatures, while a constitution was a fundamental law ratified by the people and superior to all legislation.
    d. applied to the states; a constitution was a document of the federal government.
    e. were approved by the people, while a constitution emerged from the decisions of judges.

6. One way that American independence actually harmed the nation's economic fortunes was by
    a. ending British trade and investment in America.
    b. abolishing the stable currency system that had existed under the empire.
    c. creating too much taxation and regulation by the federal government in Philadelphia.
    d. weakening the manufacturing efforts begun under the British.
    e. cutting off American trade with the British empire.

7. Attempts to establish strong governments in post-Revolutionary America were seriously hindered by the
    a. lack of strong leadership available in the new nation.
    b. revolutionary ideology that preached natural rights and suspicion of all governmental authority.
    c. hostility of the clergy toward the idea of separation of church and state.
    d. fear that a strong government would suppress economic development.
    e. seizure of power by dangerous demagogues like Daniel Shays.

8. The first U.S. government of the Articles of Confederation was finally approved when
    a. George Washington insisted that he needed a single ruling authority to deal with.
    b. land-rich states like Virginia and New York agreed to hand over their lands to the new government for the common benefit.
    c. Congress abandoned the principle that each state had one vote regardless of size.
    d. the economy was plunged into severe depression that required drastic action.
    e. Britain refused to honor the Peace of Paris by holding onto its forts in the West.

9.   The greatest weakness of the government under the Articles of Confederation was that

   a.   it was unable to deal with the issue of western lands.
   b.   it was still too subservient to America's ally, France.
   c.   it had no power to establish relations with foreign governments.
   d.   there was no judicial branch to balance the legislative and executive branches.
   e.   it had no power to regulate commerce or collect taxes from the sovereign states.

10.   The Northwest Ordinance of 1787 provided that

   a.   the states should retain permanent control of their western lands.
   b.   money from the sale of western lands should be used to promote manufacturing.
   c.   after sufficient population growth, western territories could be organized and then join the union as states.
   d.   the settlers in the northwest could vote on whether or not they should have slavery.
   e.   the Old Northwest states should have permanent access to the Great Lakes water.

11.   Shays's Rebellion contributed greatly to the movement for a new constitution by

   a.   revealing that Revolutionary War veterans like Shays wanted a more powerful federal government.
   b.   raising the fear of anarchy and disorder among wealthy conservatives.
   c.   raising the prospect of British or French interference in American domestic affairs.
   d.   showing that state legislatures could effectively resist the demands of radical farmers.
   e.   proving that America needed a stronger military to crush domestic rebellions.

12.   Besides George Washington, the most influential delegates to the Constitutional Convention were

   a.   John Jay, Thomas Jefferson, and John Hancock.
   b.   Samuel Adams, Patrick Henry, and Thomas Paine.
   c.   John Adams, Abigail Adams, and Gouverneur Morris.
   d.   Benjamin Franklin, James Madison, and Alexander Hamilton.
   e.   Daniel Shays, Richard Henry Lee, and John Marshall.

13.   The Great Compromise, finally agreed to by the Constitutional Convention, provided that

   a.   the House of Representatives would be elected by the people and the Senate by the state legislatures.
   b.   the large states would be taxed on the basis of population and the small states on the basis of territory.
   c.   there would be separation of powers between the executive and legislative branches of government.
   d.   there would be representation by population in the House of Representatives but equal representation of all states in the Senate.
   e.   slavery would continue to be permitted in the South but not in the North.

14.   Antifederalists generally found their greatest support among

   a.   residents of small states like Delaware and New Jersey.
   b.   the commercial areas of the eastern seaboard.
   c.   former Loyalists and others who disliked American Revolutionary ideals.
   d.   the wealthy and well educated.
   e.   the poorer debtors and farmers.

15.   The crucial federalist successes in the fight for ratification occurred in the states of

   a.   Georgia, Maryland, and Delaware.
   b.   Massachusetts, Virginia, and New York.
   c.   Pennsylvania, North Carolina, and Rhode Island.
   d.   Connecticut, South Carolina, and New Hampshire.
   e.   Kentucky, Tennessee, and Vermont.

C. Identification

Supply the correct identification for each numbered description.

1. _____ New name for the Anglican Church after it was disestablished and de-Anglicized in Virginia and elsewhere

2. _____ The idea that American women had a special responsibility to cultivate civic virtue in their children

3. _____ A type of special assembly, originally developed in Massachusetts, for drawing up a fundamental law that would be superior to ordinary law

4. _____ The first constitutional government of the United States

5. _____ The territory north of the Ohio River and east of the Mississippi River that came to be governed by the Confederation's acts of 1785 and 1787

6. _____ In the new Northwest territories, six-mile by six-mile square areas consisting of thirty-six sections, one of which was set aside for public schools

7. _____ The status of a western area under the Northwest Ordinance after it established an organized government but before it became a state

8. _____ A failed revolt in 1786 by poor debtor farmers that raised fears of mobocracy

9. _____ The large-state plan proposed to the Constitutional Convention by which representation both houses of the federal legislature would be based on population

10. _____ The small-state plan proposed to the Constitutional Convention by which every state would have completely equal representation in a unicameral legislature

11. _____ The Constitutional compromise between North and South that resulted in each slave being counted as 60 percent of a free person for purposes of representation in Congress

12. _____ The opponents of the Constitution who argued against creating such a strong central government

13. _____ A masterly series of pro-Constitution articles printed in New York by Jay, Madison, and Hamilton

14. _____ The official under the new Constitution who would be commander-in-chief of the armed forces, appoint judges and other officials, and have the power to veto legislation

15. _____ A list of guarantees that federalists promised to add to the Constitution in order to win ratification

D. Matching People, Places, and Events

Match the person, place, or event in the left column with the proper description in the right column by inserting the correct letter on the blank line.

1. ____ Society of the Cincinnati

2. ____ Virginia Statute for Religious Freedom

3. ____ Articles of Confederation

a. Group that failed to block the central government they feared but did force the promise of a bill of rights

4. ____ Northwest Ordinance of 1787

5. ____ Benjamin Franklin

6. ____ Daniel Shays

7. ____ George Washington

8. ____ James Madison

9. ____ federalists

10. ____ antifederalists

11. ____ Patrick Henry

12. ____ Alexander Hamilton

13. ____ John Jay

14. ____ Samuel Adams

15. ____ *The Federalist*

b. Father of the Constitution and author of *Federalist* No. 10

c. An exclusive order of military officers that aroused strong democratic opposition

d. Wealthy conservatives devoted to republicanism who engineered a nonviolent political transformation

e. Legislation passed by an alliance of Jefferson and the Baptists that disestablished the Anglican church

f. Revolutionary War veteran who led poor farmers in a revolt that failed but had far-reaching consequences

g. Revered elder statesman whose prestige in the Constitutional Convention helped facilitate the Great Compromise

h. Brilliant book of essays by Madison, Hamilton, and Jay that helped sway critical support for the Constitution in New York

i. Frustrated foreign affairs secretary under the Articles; one of the three authors of *The Federalist*

j. Legislation that provided for the orderly transformation of western territories into states

k. Leading Massachusetts radical during the American Revolution who led the opposition to the Constitution in his state in 1787

l. Virginia antifederalist leader who thought the Constitution spelled the end of liberty and equality

m. Unanimously elected chairman of the secret convention of demi-gods

n. Young New Yorker who argued eloquently for the Constitution even though he favored an even stronger central government

o. Original American governmental charter of 1781 that was put out of business by the Constitution

E. Putting Things in Order

Put the following events in correct order by numbering them from 1 to 5.

1. _____ Fifty-five demi-gods meet secretly in Philadelphia to draft a new charter of government.

2. _____ The first American national government, more a league of states than a real government, goes into effect.

3. _____ At the request of Congress, the states draft new constitutions based on the authority of the people.

4. _____ The Constitution is ratified by the nine states necessary to put it into effect.

5. _____ Debtor farmers fail in a rebellion, setting off conservative fears and demands for a stronger government to control anarchy.

F. Matching Cause and Effect

Match the historical cause in the left column with the proper effect in the right column by writing the correct letter on the blank line.

Cause	**Effect**
1. ___ The American Revolution	a. Forced acceptance of the Three-Fifths Compromise, counting each slave as three-fifths of a person for purposes of representation
2. ___ Agreement among states to give up western land claims	b. Made the federalists promise to add a bill of rights to the Constitution
3. ___ The weakness of the Articles of Confederation	c. Nearly bankrupted the national government and invited assaults on American interests by foreign powers
4. ___ Shays's Rebellion	d. Laid the basis for the Virginia Statute for Religious Freedom and the separation of church and state
5. ___ The conflict in the Constitutional Convention between large and small states	e. Brought about somewhat greater social and economic equality and the virtual end of slavery in the North
6. ___ The North-South conflict in the Constitutional Convention over counting slaves for representation	f. Finally brought New York to ratify the Constitution by a narrow margin
7. ___ A meeting in Annapolis to discuss revising the Articles of Confederation	g. Issued a call to Congress for a special convention to revise the Articles of Confederation
8. ___ Antifederalist fears that the Constitution would destroy liberties	h. Forced the adoption of the Great Compromise, which required a bicameral legislature with two different bases of representation
9. ___ *The Federalist* and fears that New York would be left out of the Union	
10. ___ The disestablishment of the Anglican Church	

        i.   Scared conservatives and made them determined to strengthen the central government against debtors

        j.   Made possible the approval of the Articles of Confederation and the passage of two important laws governing western lands

G. Developing Historical Skills

Interpreting a Chart

Analyzing a chart in more detail can enhance understanding of the historical information in the text and add further information. The chart on p. 192 provides information on the voting for ratification of the Constitution in the states. Answer the following questions.

1.   Look carefully at the vote in the five most populous states. What conclusions can you draw about the relation between population and support for ratification?

2.   Look at the vote in the five least populous states. In what ways would the figures support your conclusion about the relation between population and support for ratification in #1? How would the results in New Hampshire and Rhode Island partially qualify that conclusion?

3.   Look at the relation between region and date of ratification. Which region—New England, the Middle Atlantic States, or the South—had only one state ratify after January of 1788? Which region had only one state ratify before April of 1788? In which region was opinion more evenly divided?

4.   The text indicates that four states—Pennsylvania, Massachusetts, Virginia, and New York—were the keys to ratification. How many total delegates would have had to switch sides in order for all of those states to have opposed ratification? (Remember that each change subtracts from one side and adds to the other.)

H. Map Mastery

Map Discrimination

Using the maps and charts in Chapter 9, answer the following questions.

1.   *Western Land Cessions to the United States*: Which two of the thirteen states had the largest western land claims?

2.   *Western Land Cessions to the United States*: Which states had claims in the area that became the Old Northwest Territory?

3.   *Surveying the Old Northwest*: How many square miles were there in each township established by the Land Ordinance of 1785?

4.   *Main Centers of British and Spanish Influence After 1783*: Which nation exercised the greatest foreign influence in the American Southwest from 1783 to 1787?

5.   *Strengthening the Central Government*: Of the measures that strengthened the central government under the Constitution, as compared with the Articles of Confederation, how many dealt with economic matters?

6.   *Ratification of the Constitution*: In which three states was there no opposition to the Constitution?

7.   *Ratification of the Constitution*: In which state was there only slender opposition?

8.   *Ratification of the Constitution*: In which four states was support for the Constitution strong—by a ratio of two to one or three to one—but not overwhelming?

9. *Ratification of the Constitution*: In which five states was the Constitution ratified by very slender margins?

10. *Ratification of the Constitution*: Of the top five states in population, how many had extremely narrow votes in favor of the Constitution (less than twenty votes difference)?

11. *The Struggle Over Ratification*: The map shows that western frontier residents were generally antifederalist. In which two large states, though, was western opinion divided over, or even inclined to favor, adoption of the Constitution?

Map Challenge

Using the map of *The Struggle over Ratification*, write a brief essay describing how the factors of (a) nearness to the commercial seacoast and (b) size of state influenced profederalist or antifederalist views. Indicate which states were exceptions to the general pattern.

PART III: APPLYING WHAT YOU HAVE LEARNED

1. What changes in American society did the revolutionary American ideas of natural human rights, equality, and freedom from governmental tyranny bring about in the years immediately following the successful American Revolution?

2. Why did neither the Revolution nor the Constitution bring an end to the greatest contradiction of American Revolutionary principles—human slavery? Does the post-Revolutionary abolition of slavery in the North but not the South show the strength of the Revolution's proclamation of human rights, or demonstrate its weakness?

3. What were the strengths and weaknesses of the Articles of Confederation? Were the social problems of the 1780s really due to the national government's failings, or were they simply the natural aftermath of the Revolutionary War and separation from Britain?

4. What really motivated the leaders who called the Constitutional Convention and worked out the essential compromises in the Constitution?

5. Who were the federalists and the antifederalists, what were the issues that divided them, and why did the federalists win?

6. Should the Constitution be seen as a conservative reaction to the Revolution, an enshrinement of revolutionary principles, or both? What was most truly original about the Constitution?

7. In Chapters 4 and 5, the basic structure of early American society and economy was described. How was that structure changed by the political developments during the period after the Revolution? How did the Constitution itself reflect American attitudes toward liberty, equality, power, and property (including slave property)?

8.   The greatest concession that federalist supporters of the Constitution made to antifederalist opponents was to promise to add a bill of rights as soon as the Constitution was ratified. Should the antifederalists therefore be honored as founding fathers of American liberty? How would the Constitution have been viewed if the first ten amendments (the Bill of Rights) had not been added?

9.   Americans have traditionally revered the Constitution, and viewed its writers as demigods. Does the historical account of the actual initiation, writing, and ratification of the Constitution confirm or detract from that view. Why or why not?

CHAPTER 10

Launching the New Ship of State, 1789–1800

PART I: REVIEWING THE CHAPTER

A. Checklist of Learning Objectives

After mastering this chapter, you should be able to:

1. State why George Washington was pivotal to inaugurating the new federal government.

2. Describe the methods and policies Alexander Hamilton used to put the federal government on a sound financial footing.

3. Explain how the conflict between Hamilton and Jefferson led to the emergence of the first political parties.

4. Describe the polarizing effects of the French Revolution on American foreign and domestic policy and politics from 1790 to 1800.

5. Explain the rationale for Washington's neutrality policies, including the conciliatory Jay's Treaty and why the treaty provoked Jeffersonian outrage.

6. Describe the causes of the undeclared war with France, and explain Adams's decision to seek peace rather than declare war.

7. Describe the poisonous political atmosphere that produced the Alien and Sedition Acts and the Kentucky and Virginia resolutions.

8. Describe the contrasting membership and principles of the Hamiltonian Federalists and the Jeffersonian Republicans, and how they laid the foundations of the American political party system.

B. Glossary

To build your social science vocabulary, familiarize yourself with the following terms.

1. **census** An official count of population; in the United States, the federal census occurs every ten years. ". . . the first official census of 1790 recorded almost 4 million people."

2. **public debt** The money owed by a government to individual or institutional creditors, also called the national debt. ". . . the public debt, with interest heavily in arrears, was mountainous."

3. **cabinet** The body of official advisers to the head of a government; in the United States, it consists of the heads of the major executive departments as designated by Congress. "The Constitution does not mention a cabinet. . . ."

4. **circuit court** A court that hears cases in several designated locations rather than a single place; originally, in the United States, the higher courts of appeals were all circuit courts, and are still designated as such even though they no longer migrate. "The act organized . . . federal district and circuit courts. . . ."

5. **fiscal** Concerning public finances—expenditures and revenues. "His plan was to shape the fiscal policies of the administration. . . ."

6. **assumption** In finance, the appropriation or taking on of monetary obligations not originally one's own. "The secretary made a convincing case for 'assumption.' "

7. **excise** A tax on the manufacture, sale, or consumption of certain products. "Hamilton . . . secured from Congress an excise tax on a few domestic items, notably whiskey."

8. **stock** The shares of capital ownership gained from investing in a corporate enterprise; the term also refers to the certificates representing such shares. "Stock was thrown open to public sale."

9. **medium of exchange** Any item, metallic, paper, or otherwise, used as money. "They regarded [whiskey] as a . . . medium of exchange."

10. **despotism** Arbitrary or tyrannical rule. "The American people, loving liberty and deploring despotism, cheered."

11. **impress** To force people or property into public service without choice; to conscript. "They . . . impressed scores of seamen into service on British vessels. . . ."

12. **assimilation** The merging of diverse cultures or peoples into one; especially, the merging of a smaller or minority community into a larger one. "The drastic new law violated the traditional American policy of open-door hospitality and speedy assimilation."

13. **witch-hunt** An investigation carried on with much publicity, supposedly to uncover dangerous activity but actually intended to weaken the political opposition by presuming guilt from the outset. "Anti-French hysteria played directly into the hands of witch-hunting conservatives."

14. **compact** An agreement or covenant between states to perform some legal act. "Both Jefferson and Madison stressed the compact theory. . . ."

15. **nullification** In American politics, the assertion that a state may legally invalidate a federal act deemed inconsistent with its rights or sovereignty. "[The] resolutions concluded that . . . 'nullification' was the 'rightful remedy.' "

PART II: CHECKING YOUR PROGRESS

A. True-False

Where the statement is true, circle **T**; where it is false, circle **F**.

1. T   F   The primary force threatening American national security and unity in the 1790s were the international wars set off by the French Revolution.

2. T   F   The passage of the first ten amendments to the Constitution demonstrated the Federalist determination to develop a powerful central government even if it threatened minority rights.

3. T   F   Hamilton's basic purpose in all his financial measures was to strengthen the federal government by building up a larger national debt.

4. T   F   A political deal between Jefferson and Hamilton involved obtaining Virginia's support for assumption of state debts in exchange for locating the District of Columbia along the Potomac River by Virginia.

5. T   F   Hamilton financed his large national debt by revenues from tariffs and excise taxes on products such as whiskey.

6. T F   In the battle over the Bank of the United States, Jefferson favored a loose construction of the Constitution, and Hamilton favored a strict construction.

7. T F   The first political rebellion against the new United States government was by frontier whiskey distillers who hated Hamilton's excise tax on alcohol.

8. T F   The first American political parties grew mainly out of the debate over Hamilton's fiscal policies and U.S. foreign policy toward Europe.

9. T F   Jefferson and his Republican Party followers turned against the French Revolution when it turned radically violent in the Reign of Terror.

10. T F   President Washington believed that America was so powerful that it could afford to stay neutral in the great revolutionary wars between Britain and France.

11. T F   John Jay's unpopular treaty with Britain stirred outrage among many Americans and fueled the rise of Jefferson's Republican Party.

12. T F   Adams decided to seek a negotiated peace with France in order to unite his Federalist party and enhance his own popularity with the public.

13. T F   The Alien Laws were a reasonable Federalist attempt to limit uncontrolled immigration into the United States and protect dangerous French revolutionaries from weakening American national security.

14. T F   Jeffersonian Republicans believed that the common people were not to be trusted and had to be led by those who were wealthier and better educated.

15. T F   The Jeffersonian Republicans generally sympathized with Britain in foreign policy, while the Hamiltonian Federalists sympathized with France and the French Revolution.

B. Multiple Choice

Select the best answer and circle the corresponding letter.

1. A key addition to the new federal government that had been demanded by many critics of the Constitution and others in the ratifying states was
   a. a cabinet to advise the president.
   b. a written bill of rights to guarantee liberty.
   c. a supreme court.
   d. federal assumption of state debts.
   e. a federal district where the capital would be located.

2. The influential Founder and member of Congress who personally wrote the Bill of Rights was
   a. George Washington.
   b. Thomas Jefferson.
   c. John Marshall.
   d. Alexander Hamilton.
   e. James Madison.

3. The Bill of Rights is the name given to provisions whose actual legal form consists of
   a. an executive proclamation of President George Washington.
   b. Article II, Section 3 of the U.S. Constitution.
   c. a set of rulings issued by the Supreme Court.
   d. the first ten amendments to the Constitution of the United States.
   e. the common law rights inherited from the English Magna Carta.

4.   The Ninth and Tenth Amendments partly reversed the federalist momentum of the Constitution by declaring that

    a.   the federal government had no power to restrict the action of local governments.

    b.   the powers of the presidency did not extend to foreign policy.

    c.   all rights not mentioned in the federal Constitution were retained by the states or by the people themselves.

    d.   the Supreme Court had no power to rule in cases affecting property rights.

    e.   the states themselves were not bound by the guarantees in the bill of rights.

5.   Hamilton's first financial policies were intended to

    a.   finance the new government through the sale of western lands.

    b.   fund the national debt and to have the federal government assume the debts owed by the states.

    c.   repudiate the debts accumulated by the government of the Articles of Confederation.

    d.   insure that low federal taxes would spur economic growth.

    e.   guarantee that the dollar would become a sound and respected international currency.

6.   The deep disagreement between Hamilton and Jefferson over the proposed Bank of the United States was over whether

    a.   the Constitution granted the federal government the power to establish such a bank.

    b.   it would be economically wise to create a bank-guaranteed national currency.

    c.   the bank should be under the control of the federal government or the states.

    d.   such a Bank violated the Bill of Rights.

    e.   the Bank should be a private institution or an agency of the federal government.

7.   The first American political parties developed primarily because of

    a.   the sectional division over slavery.

    b.   the Founders' belief that organized political opposition was a necessary part of good government.

    c.   the antifederalists' continuing hostility to the legitimacy of the new federal Constitution.

    d.   patriotic opposition to foreign intervention in American domestic affairs.

    e.   the opposition of Thomas Jefferson and his followers to Hamilton's financial policies and enhancement of federal government power.

8.   The Whiskey Rebellion proved to be most significant in the long run because it

    a.   showed that the tariff was a more effective producer of revenue than the excise tax.

    b.   showed that the new federal government would use force if necessary to uphold its authority.

    c.   demonstrated that the American military could suppress a powerful domestic rebellion.

    d.   showed the strength of continuing antifederalist hostility to the new constitutional government.

    e.   showed that Americans would not tolerate federal taxation of their alcohol, tobacco, and firearms.

9.   Regarding the French Revolution, most Jeffersonian Democratic-Republicans believed that

    a.   even the extreme violence of the Reign of Terror was regrettable but necessary.

    b.   the overthrow of the king was necessary, but the Reign of Terror went much too far.

    c.   the Revolution should be supported by American military aid if necessary.

    d.   the French Revolution represented a complete distortion of American Revolutionary ideals of liberty.

    e.   its political goals were valid but its atheistic attack on Christianity was unjustified.

10. President Washington's foreign policy rested on the firm conviction that
    a. there should be an end to European colonialism in the Americas.
    b. the United States could enhance its power by mediating between warring Britain and France.
    c. America needed to adhere firmly to its Revolutionary alliance with France.
    d. America ought to enter the French-British war only if its own republican ideals were at stake.
    e. the United States was too militarily weak and political disunited to become involved in European wars.

11. In the 1790s, the powerful Miami Indians led by Little Turtle battled with the U.S. Army for control of
    a. Lake Erie and Lake Huron.
    b. the Ohio territory.
    c. Kentucky.
    d. hunting rights west of the Appalachians.
    e. Florida.

12. George Washington's successor, John Adams, was politically crippled by
    a. Washington's refusal to give him his whole-hearted endorsement.
    b. the political hostility directed at his assertive wife, Abigail Adams.
    c. the attacks and plots by enemies within his own Federalist party, including Hamilton.
    d. his ignorance and weakness in managing foreign and military affairs.
    e. his support for the unpopular Alien and Sedition Acts.

13. The United States became involved in an undeclared war with France in 1797 because of
    a. fierce American opposition to the concessions of Jay's Treaty.
    b. American anger at attempted French bribery of American diplomats in the XYZ Affair.
    c. French interference with American shipping and freedom of the seas.
    d. President Adams's sympathy with Britain and hostility to Revolutionary France.
    e. France's refusal to sell New Orleans and Louisiana.

14. Thomas Jefferson and the Republican Party essentially believed that the whole future of American society rested on an essential foundation of
    a. wealthy planters and merchants.
    b. international trade and westward expansion.
    c. free, white, educated, small landowning farmers.
    d. evangelical Protestants and learned scientists and technicians.
    e. a political coalition of whites and African Americans.

15. The Federalists essentially believed that
    a. most governmental power should be retained by the states or by the people themselves.
    b. the federal government should provide no special aid to private business.
    c. the common people could, if educated, participate in government affairs.
    d. the United States should have a powerful central government controlled by the wealthy and well educated.
    e. the United States should isolate itself from Europe and turn toward westward expansion.

C. Identification

Supply the correct identification for each numbered description.

1. _____   The body of advisers to the president, not mentioned in the Constitution, that George Washington established as an important part of the new federal government

2. _____   The first ten amendments to the United States Constitution that protected individual liberties

3. _____   The cabinet office in Washington's administration headed by a brilliant young West Indian immigrant who distrusted the people

4. _____   Alexander Hamilton's policy of paying off all federal bonds at face value in order to strengthen the national credit

5. _____   Hamilton's policy of having the federal government pay the financial obligations of the states

6. _____   Federally chartered financial institution set up by Alexander Hamilton and vehemently opposed by Thomas Jefferson

7. _____   Political organizations, not envisioned in the Constitution, and considered dangerous to national unity by most of the Founders

8. _____   Political and social upheaval supported by most Americans during its moderate beginnings in 1789, but the cause of bitter divisions after it took a radical turn in 1792

9. _____   Declaration by President Washington in 1793 that announced America's policy with respect to the French Revolutionary wars between Britain and France

10. _____   Treaty following Miami Indians' defeat in the Battle of Fallen Timbers that ceded Ohio to the United States but gave Indians limited sovereignty

11. _____   International agreement, signed in 1794, whose terms favoring Britain outraged Jeffersonian Republicans

12. _____   Scandal in which three French secret agents attempted to bribe U.S. diplomats, outraging the American public and causing the undeclared war with France

13. _____   Law passed by Federalists during the undeclared French war that made it a criminal offense to criticize or defame government officials, including the president

14. _____   The peace treaty courageously signed by President John Adams that ended the undeclared war with France as well as the official French-American alliance

15. _____   The doctrine, proclaimed in the Thomas Jefferson's Kentucky resolution, that a state can block a federal law it considers unconstitutional

D. Matching People, Places, and Events

Match the person, place, or event in the left column with the proper description in the right column by inserting the correct letter on the blank line.

1. ____ John Adams

2. ____ Alexander Hamilton

3. ____ Thomas Jefferson

4. ____ James Madison

5. ____ Supreme Court

6. ____ Funding and assumption

7. ____ Bank of the United States

8. ____ Whiskey Rebellion

9. ____ Federalists

10. ____ Republicans

11. ____ XYZ

12. ____ Battle of Fallen Timbers

13. ____ Alien and Sedition Acts

14. ____ Bill of Rights

15. ____ Washington's Farewell Address

a. A protest by poor western farmers that was firmly suppressed by Washington and Hamilton's army

b. Body organized by the Judiciary Act of 1789 and first headed by John Jay

c. Brilliant administrator and financial wizard whose career was plagued by doubts about his character and his beliefs concerning popular government

d. Political party that believed in the common people, no government aid for business, and a pro-French foreign policy

e. The second president of the United States, whose Federalist enemies and political weaknesses undermined his administration

f. Skillful politician-scholar who drafted the Bill of Rights and moved it through the First Congress

g. Institution established by Hamilton to create a stable currency and bitterly opposed by states' rights advocates

h. Hamilton's aggressive financial policies of paying off all federal bonds and taking on all state debts

i. Harsh and probably unconstitutional laws aimed at radical immigrants and Jeffersonian writers

j. General Anthony Wayne's victory over the Miami Indians that brought Ohio territory under American control

k. Message telling America that it should avoid unnecessary foreign entanglements—a reflection of the foreign policy of its author

l. Secret code names for three French agents who attempted to extract bribes from American diplomats in 1797

m. Washington's secretary of state and the organizer of a political party opposed to Hamilton's policies

n. Ten constitutional amendments designed to protect American liberties

o. Political party that believed in a strong government run by the wealthy, government aid to business, and a pro-British foreign policy

E. Putting Things in Order

Put the following events in correct order by numbering them from 1 to 5.

1. _____   Revolutionary turmoil in France causes the U.S. president to urge Americans to stay out of foreign quarrels.

2. _____   Envoys sent to make peace in France are insulted by bribe demands from three mysterious French agents.

3. _____   First ten amendments to the Constitution are adopted.

4. _____   Western farmers revolt against a Hamiltonian tax and are harshly suppressed.

5. _____   Jefferson organizes a political party in opposition to Hamilton's financial policies.

F. Matching Cause and Effect

Match the historical cause in the left column with the proper effect in the right column by writing the correct letter on the blank line.

Cause	**Effect**
1. ___ The need to gain support of wealthy groups for the federal government	a. Led to the formation of the first two American political parties
2. ___ Passage of the Bill of Rights	b. Caused the Whiskey Rebellion
3. ___ The need for federal revenues to finance Hamilton's ambitious policies	c. Led Hamilton to promote the fiscal policies of funding and assumption
4. ___ Hamilton's excise tax on western farmers' products	d. Guaranteed basic liberties and indicated some swing away from Federalist centralizing
5. ___ Clashes between Hamilton and Jefferson over fiscal policy and foreign affairs	e. Led to imposition of the first tariff in 1789 and the excise tax on whiskey in 1791
6. ___ The French Revolution	f. Aroused Jeffersonian Republican outrage at the Washington administration's pro-British policies
7. ___ The danger of war with Britain	
8. ___ Jay's Treaty	
9. ___ The XYZ Affair	

10.   ___   The Federalist fear of radical French immigrants

g.   Created bitter divisions in America between anti-Revolution Federalists and pro-Revolution Republicans

h.   Caused an undeclared war with France

i.   Led Washington to support Jay's Treaty

j.   Caused passage of the Alien Acts

G. Developing Historical Skills

Reading for Main Idea and Supporting Details

Any historical generalization must be backed up by supporting details and historical facts. For example, the text states that "the key figure in the new government was smooth-faced Alexander Hamilton ..." (p. 202). This generalization is then supported by details and facts showing Hamilton's importance, such as his policy of funding and assumption, his customs and excise taxes, and his establishment of the Bank of the United States.

List at least two supporting details or facts that support each of the following general assertions in the text.

1.   "President Washington's far-visioned policy of neutrality was sorely tried by the British" (p. 211).

2.   "True to Washington's policy of steering clear of war at all costs, [President Adams] tried again to reach an agreement with the French. . . " (p. 215).

3.   "Exulting Federalists had meanwhile capitalized on the anti-French frenzy to drive through Congress in 1798 a sheaf of laws designed to muffle or minimalize their Jeffersonian foes" (p. 217).

4.   "Resentful Jeffersonians naturally refused to take the Alien and Sedition Laws lying down" (p. 218).

5.   "As the presidential contest of 1800 approached, the differences between Federalists and Democratic-Republicans were sharply etched" (p. 219).

a.   Indicate two clear differences between the parties.

PART III: APPLYING WHAT YOU HAVE LEARNED

1. What were the most important steps that George Washington took to establish the authority and prestige of the new federal government under the Constitution?

2. Explain the purpose and significance of the Bill of Rights. Did these Ten Amendments significantly weaken the authority of the federal government, or actually enhance it?

3. What were Hamilton's basic economic and political goals, and how did he attempt to achieve them?

4. What were the philosophical and political disagreements between Hamilton and Jefferson that led to the creation of the first American political parties?

5. What were the basic goals of Washington's and Adams's foreign policies, and how successful were they in achieving them?

6. How did divisions over foreign policy, especially the French Revolution, poison American politics and threaten the fledgling nation's unity in the 1790s?

7. In foreign policy, the Federalists believed that the United States needed to build a powerful national state to gain equality with the great powers of Europe, while the Republicans believed the country should isolate itself from Europe and turn toward the West. What were the strengths and weaknesses of each policy, and why was the Republicans' view generally favored by most Americans in the 1800s?

8. Although Federalists and Republicans engaged in extremely bitter political struggles during this period, they both retained their commitment to the American experiment, and in 1800, power was peacefully handed from Federalists to Republicans. What shared beliefs and experiences enabled them to keep the nation together, despite their deep disagreements? Was there ever a serious danger that the new federal government could have collapsed in civil war?

CHAPTER 11

The Triumphs and Travails of the Jeffersonian Republic, 1800–1812

PART I: REVIEWING THE CHAPTER

A. Checklist of Learning Objectives

After mastering this chapter, you should be able to:

1. Explain how Jefferson's idealistic Revolution of 1800 proved to be more moderate and practical once he began exercising presidential power.

2. Describe the conflicts between Federalists and Republicans over the judiciary and how John Marshall turned the Supreme Court into a bastion of conservative, federalist power to balance the rise of Jeffersonian democracy

3. Describe Jefferson's basic foreign-policy goals and how he attempted to achieve them.

4. Analyze the causes and effects of the Louisiana Purchase.

5. Describe how America was gradually drawn into the turbulent international crisis of the Napoleonic Wars.

6. Describe the original goal of Jefferson's embargo, and explain why it failed.

7. Explain why President Madison became convinced that a new war with Britain was necessary to maintain America's experiment in republican government.

B. Glossary

To build your social science vocabulary, familiarize yourself with the following terms.

1. **lame duck** A political official during the time he or she remains in office after a defeat or inability to seek another term, and whose power is therefore diminished. "This body was controlled for several more months by the lame-duck Federalists. . . ."

2. **commission** The official legal authorization appointing a person to a public office or military position, describing the nature of the duty, term of office, chain of command, and so on. "When Marbury learned that his commission was being shelved by the new secretary of state, James Madison, he sued for its delivery."

3. **writ** A formal legal document ordering or prohibiting some act. ". . . his Jeffersonian rivals . . . would hardly enforce a writ to deliver the commission. . . ."

4. **impeachment** The charging of a public official with major misconduct, with the penalty of removal from office if convicted of the charge. "Jefferson urged the impeachment of an arrogant and tart-tongued Supreme Court justice. . . ."

5. **pacifist** Characterized by principled opposition to all war and belief in nonviolent solutions to conflict. "A challenge was thus thrown squarely into the face of Jefferson—the non-interventionist, the pacifist. . . ."

6. **consulate (consul)** A place where a government representative is stationed in a foreign country, but not the main headquarters of diplomatic representation headed by an ambassador (the embassy). "The pasha of Tripoli . . . informally declared war on the United States by cutting down the flagstaff of the American consulate."

7. **cede** To yield or grant something, often upon request or under pressure. (Anything ceded is a *cession*.) "Napoleon Bonaparte induced the king of Spain to cede to France . . . the immense trans-Mississippi region. . . ."

8. **precedent** In law and government, a decision or action that establishes a sanctioned rule for determining similar cases in the future. "At the same time, the transfer established valuable precedents for future expansion. . . ."

9. **secession** The withdrawal, by legal or illegal means, of one portion of a political entity from the government to which it has been bound. "Burr joined with a group of Federalist extremists to plot the secession of New England and New York."

10. **conscription** Compulsory enrollment of civilians into the armed forces; a draft. "Impressment . . . was a crude form of conscription. . . ."

11. **broadside** The simultaneous firing of all guns on one side of a ship. "The British warship thereupon fired three devastating broadsides. . . ."

12. **embargo** A government order prohibiting commerce in or out of a port; an embargo may be applied to all goods or only to designated goods. "The hated embargo was not continued long enough or tightly enough to achieve the desired result. . . ."

PART II: CHECKING YOUR PROGRESS

A. True-False

Where the statement is true, circle **T**, where it is false, circle **F**.

1. T F In the campaign of 1800, the Federalists criticized Jefferson's governmental ideas but avoided attacking him personally.

2. T F An unexpected deadlock with Aaron Burr meant that Jefferson had to be elected by the House of Representatives.

3. T F As president, Jefferson attempted to exemplify his principles of democracy and equality by reducing formality and hierarchy in official Washington.

4. T F To carry out his Revolution of 1800, Jefferson directly overturned the Federalist tariff and Bank of the United States.

5. T F The case of *Marbury* v. *Madison* established the principle that the president could appoint but not remove Supreme Court justices.

6. T F Jefferson cut the size of the United States Army to twenty-five hundred men because he believed that a large standing army posed a danger of dictatorship and could embroil the nation in unnecessary foreign wars.

7. T F Jefferson's envoys to Paris initially intended to buy only New Orleans and the immediate vicinity.

8. T F Jefferson's deepest doubt about the Louisiana Purchase was that the price of $15 million was too high.

9. T F   Lewis and Clark's Corps of Discovery developed a rich scientific knowledge of the West and discovered an overland American route to the Pacific.

10. T F   Former vice president Aaron Burr's conspiracies to break apart the United States demonstrated the fragility of the American government's control of the trans-Appalachian West.

11. T F   The British precipitated a crisis with the United States by blockading American ports in order to prevent trade with Napoleon's continental Europe.

12. T F   After the *Chesapeake* affair, Jefferson could easily have declared war on Britain with the enthusiastic support of both Federalists and Republicans.

13. T F   Instead of forcing Britain and France to respect American rights, as Jefferson hoped, the embargo crippled the American economy.

14. T F   The Shawnee leaders Tecumseh and Tenskwatawa successfully organized a great Indian confederacy aimed at stemming white expansion and reviving Indian culture.

15. T F   New Englanders initially supported the War of 1812 in order to stop the widespread British practice of impressing American sailors into the British navy.

B. Multiple Choice

Select the best answer and circle the corresponding letter.

1. The most revolutionary development in the critical election of 1800 turned out to be
    a. the nasty campaign smears against Jefferson.
    b. Jefferson's radical proposals for overturning the existing political system.
    c. the peaceful transition of power from one political party to its opponent.
    d. the electoral stalemate between Jefferson and his running mate, Burr.
    e. the massive grass-roots mobilization of voters by Jefferson's Republican Party.
2. One Federalist policy that Jefferson quickly overturned was
    a. funding and assumption.
    b. the excise tax.
    c. the Bank of the United States.
    d. the protective tariff.
    e. the Judiciary Act.
3. The case of *Marbury* v. *Madison* established the principle that
    a. the president, Congress, and the Supreme Court are equal branches of government.
    b. federal laws take precedence over state legislation.
    c. the president has the right to appoint the federal judiciary.
    d. the Supreme Court is the final court of appeal in the federal judiciary.
    e. the Supreme Court has the final right to determine the constitutionality of legislation.
4. Jefferson was forced to reverse his strong opposition to maintaining any substantial American military because of
    a. growing French intervention in Santo Domingo and Louisiana.
    b. the plunder and blackmailing of American shipping by North African states.
    c. the threat to America posed by the British-French wars.
    d. the charge by his Federalist opponents that his dislike of the military was unpatriotic.
    e. the spreading Indian attacks in the West.

5. Jefferson's greatest concern about purchasing Louisiana was

    a. whether it was in America's interest to acquire such a vast territory.
    b. whether the cost was excessive for his frugal, small-government philosophy.
    c. how the existing French residents of Louisiana could be assimilated into the United States.
    d. how to defend and govern the territory once it was part of the United States.
    e. whether the purchase was permissible under the Constitution.

6. The greatest political beneficiary of the Louisiana Purchase was

    a. Thomas Jefferson.
    b. Aaron Burr.
    c. the Federalist party.
    d. Napoleon.
    e. the American military.

7. Although greatly weakened after Jefferson's election, the Federalist party's philosophy continued to have great influence through

    a. the propaganda efforts of Federalist agitators.
    b. the Federalist control of the U.S. Senate.
    c. the Federalist Supreme Court rulings of John Marshall.
    d. Federalist sympathies within the U.S. army and navy.
    e. Federalist teachers and textbooks in the public schools.

8. The Republicans' failure to impeach Supreme Court Justice Samuel Chase established the principle that

    a. the deliberations of Supreme Court justices were absolutely confidential.
    b. presidents could appoint but not remove Supreme Court justices.
    c. impeachment should not be used as a political weapon to overturn Supreme Court decisions.
    d. the constitutional power of impeachment was almost impossible to carry out.
    e. the Supreme Court was one of three equal branches of the federal government.

9. Jefferson military policy and budgets were centered on

    a. a large naval force that could compete with the British navy.
    b. several hundred small gunboats that could protect American shores without provoking international wars.
    c. a strong system of forts along the coast and across the frontier West.
    d. effectively training and equipping the state militias so they could be called into service if needed.
    e. expanding the military academy at West Point and developing a substantial corps of professionally trained officers.

10. A key event that forced Napoleon to abandon his dreams of a French New World empire and instead sell Louisiana to the United States was

    a. a successful slave revolt that overthrew French rule in Santo Domingo.
    b. the widespread Spanish rebellion against French imperial rule.
    c. his army's defeat and retreat amidst the winter snows of Russia.
    d. the growing American military threat to seize New Orleans by force.
    e. the failed rebellion of the French population in Canada against British rule.

11. Which of the following was *not* among the consequences of the Louisiana Purchase?

    a. The geographical and scientific discoveries of the Lewis and Clark expedition
    b. The weakening of the power of the presidency in foreign affairs
    c. The precedent of incorporating foreign territory and populations into the United States through peaceful purchase
    d. The pursuit of isolationism as America's primary foreign policy outlook
    e. The opportunity of westward expansion and growth of the United States as a great power

12. Jefferson's Embargo Act provided that

    a. America would not trade with Britain until it ended impressment.
    b. American goods could be carried only in American ships.
    c. America would sell no military supplies to either warring nation, Britain or France.
    d. America would trade only with the neutral nations of Europe.
    e. America would prohibit all foreign trade.

13. A crucial foreign policy goal for many war hawks in the War of 1812 was the

    a. end of all Spanish colonization in the Americas.
    b. capture and annexation of Canada.
    c. conquest and settlement of Texas.
    d. destruction of the British navy.
    e. conquest of Spanish Florida.

14. Besides creating a pan-Indian military alliance against white expansion, Tecumseh and Tenskwatawa (the Prophet) urged American Indians to

    a. resist the whites' culture and alcohol and revive traditional Indian cultures.
    b. demonstrate their legal ownership of the lands that whites were intruding upon.
    c. adopt the whites' culture and technology as a way of resisting their further expansion.
    d. declare independence and form an alliance with Spain.
    e. abandon their tribes and develop a single Indian language and government.

15. President Madison's primary goal in asking Congress to declare war against Britain in 1812 was to

    a. restore confidence in America's republican experiment by fighting against British disrespect for American rights.
    b. halt Tecumseh's successful Indian revolt and alliance with the British.
    c. conquer Canada and incorporate it into the United States.
    d. end the British practice of impressing American seamen into the British navy.
    e. reinforce the Republican party's patriotism and undermine Federalist power in New England.

C. Identification

Supply the correct identification for each numbered description.

1. _____   Hamiltonian economic measure repealed by Jefferson and Gallatin

2. _____   Term applied by historians to suggest the dramatic, unprecedented change that took place when the Republican Thomas Jefferson defeated the incumbent Federalist John Adams for the presidency

3. _____   Derogatory Republican term for Federalist judges appointed during the last hours of his term by President Adams

4. _____   Precedent-setting Supreme Court case in which Marshall declared part of the Judiciary Act of 1789 unconstitutional

5. _____   The principle, established by Chief Justice Marshall in a famous case, that the Supreme Court can declare laws unconstitutional

6. _____   Action voted by the House of Representatives against Supreme Court Justice Samuel Chase

7. _____   Branch of military service that Jefferson considered least threatening to liberty and most necessary to suppressing the Barbary States

8. _____ Sugar-rich island where Toussaint L'Ouverture's slave rebellion disrupted Napoleon's dreams of a vast New World empire

9. _____ Territory beyond the boundaries of the Louisiana Purchase, along the Columbia River, explored by Lewis and Clark

10. _____ Price paid by the United States for the Louisiana Purchase

11. _____ American ship fired on by British in 1807, nearly leading to war between the two countries

12. _____ Jefferson's policy of forbidding the shipment of any goods in or out of the United States

13. _____ Militantly nationalistic western congressmen eager for hostilities with the Indians, Canadians, and British

14. _____ Battle in 1811, where General William Henry Harrison defeated the Indian forces led by Tenskwatawa (the Prophet), brother of the charismatic Shawnee chief Tecumseh

15. _____ Derisive Federalist name for the War of 1812 that blamed it on the Republican president

D. Matching People, Places, and Events

Match the person, place, or event in the left column with the proper description in the right column by inserting the correct letter on the blank line.

1. ___ Thomas Jefferson

2. ___ Albert Gallatin

3. ___ John Marshall

4. ___ _Marbury_ v. _Madison_

5. ___ Samuel Chase

6. ___ Sally Hemings

7. ___ Napoleon Bonaparte

8. ___ Robert Livingston

9. ___ Toussaint L'Ouverture

10. ___ William Clark

11. ___ Aaron Burr

12. ___ Sacajawea

13. ___ James Wilkinson

14. ___ Tecumseh

15. ___ William Henry Harrison

a. Former vice-president, killer of Alexander Hamilton, and plotter of mysterious secessionist schemes

b. Military leader who defeated Tecumseh's brother, "the Prophet," at the Battle of Tippecanoe

c. Swiss-born treasury secretary who disliked national debt but kept most Hamiltonian economic measures in effect

d. American minister to Paris who joined James Monroe in making a magnificent real estate deal

e. Strong believer in strict construction, weak government, and antimilitarism who was forced to modify some of his principles in office

f. Shawnee leader who organized a major Indian confederation against U.S. expansion

g. Federalist Supreme Court justice impeached by the House in 1804 but acquitted by the Senate

h. Shoshoni Indian who provided valuable guidance and assistance to Lewis and Clark as they crossed the Rocky Mountains.

i. Young army officer who joined Jefferson's personal secretary in exploring the Louisiana Purchase and Oregon country

j. Traitorous military governor of Louisiana who joined Aaron Burr's conspiracy to break off parts of the southwest from the United States

k. Ruling based on a midnight judge case that established the right of the Supreme Court to declare laws unconstitutional

l. One of Thomas Jefferson's slaves at Monticello, whose affair with Jefferson has been confirmed by modern DNA evidence

m. Gifted black revolutionary whose successful slave revolution indirectly led to Napoleon's sale of Louisiana

n. French ruler who acquired Louisiana from Spain only to sell it to the United States

o. Federalist Supreme Court justice whose brilliant legal efforts established the principle of judicial review

E. Putting Things in Order

Put the following events in correct order by numbering them from 1 to 5.

1. ____ Rather than declare war after a British attack on an American ship, Jefferson imposes a ban on all American trade.

2. ____ President Adams appoints a host of midnight judges just before leaving office, outraging Republicans.

3. ____ The foreign difficulties of a French dictator lead him to offer a fabulous real estate bargain to the United States.

4. ____ After four years of naval war, the Barbary state of Tripoli signs a peace treaty with the United States.

5. ____ A deceitful French dictator and aggressive western Congressmen maneuver a reluctant president into a war with Britain.

F. Matching Cause and Effect

Match the historical cause in the left column with the proper effect in the right column by writing the correct letter on the blank line.

Cause	Effect
1. ____ Jefferson's moderation and continuation of many Federalist policies	a. Made operational the isolationist principles of Washington's Farewell Address

2. ___ Adams's appointment of midnight judges

3. ___ Marshall's ruling in *Marbury* v. *Madison*

4. ___ The Barbary pirates' attacks on American shipping

5. ___ France's acquisition of Louisiana from Spain

6. ___ Napoleon's foreign troubles with Britain and Santo Domingo

7. ___ The Louisiana Purchase

8. ___ British impressment of American sailors and anger at American harboring of British deserters

9. ___ French compliance with Macon's Bill No. 2

10. ___ Western war hawks' fervor for acquiring Canada and removing resisting Indians

b. Aroused Jeffersonian hostility to the Federalist judiciary and led to repeal of the Judiciary Act of 1801

c. Forced Madison to declare a policy of nonimportation that accelerated the drift toward war

d. Led to an aggressive and deadly assault on the American ship *Chesapeake*

e. Created stability and continuity in the transition of power from one party to another

f. Caused Harrison's and Jackson's military ventures and contributed to the declaration of war in 1812

g. Established the principle of judicial review of laws by the Supreme Court

h. Made Americans eager to purchase New Orleans in order to protect their Mississippi River shipping

i. Led to a surprise offer to sell Louisiana to the United States for $15 million

j. Forced a reluctant Jefferson to send the U.S. Navy into military action

G. Developing Historical Skills

Reading an Election Map: Reading an election map carefully yields additional information about voting patterns and political alignments. Using the map of the *Presidential Election of 1800*, answer the following questions.

1. How many electoral votes did Adams get from the five New England states?

2. Which was the only state north of Virginia that went completely for Jefferson?

3. How many electoral votes were there in the three states that divided between Adams and Jefferson?

4.   The text records the final electoral vote as 73 for Jefferson to 65 for Adams and notes that Jefferson carried New York only by a very slender margin. If Adams had carried New York, what would the electoral result have been?

PART III: APPLYING WHAT YOU HAVE LEARNED

1.   Is the phrase "Revolution of 1800" really justified when applied to Jefferson's victory over Adams in the election of that year? Did Jefferson's general moderation once in office reflect a loss of his more radical republican convictions, or simply a practical adjustment to the realities of presidential leadership?

2.   How did the conflict between Federalists and Republicans over the judiciary lead to a balance of power among political interests and different branches of government? Is it accurate to say that the Federalist Party continued to shape America for decades through the agency of John Marshall's Supreme Court?

3.   What were the political and economic consequences of the Louisiana Purchase?

4.   Argue for and against: the Louisiana Purchase made possible both the success of nineteenth-century American democracy as well as America's dangerous conviction that it could turn inward in isolation from the world.

5.   What was the essential idea behind Jefferson's imposition of the embargo? Was the plan for peaceful coercion of the European great powers simply fantastic from the start, or might it have actually succeeded as an alternative to war under somewhat different conditions?

6.   What were the real causes of the War of 1812? Was the declaration of war a mistake, or the result of President Madison's genuine fear that the American republican experiment could fail?

7.   Which event had the greatest impact on American society in the early decades of the nineteenth century: Jefferson's Republican party victory in the Revolution of 1800, the Louisiana Purchase, or the defeat of Tecumseh's Indian confederacy—the last major effort to unite all American Indians in opposition to U.S. expansion. Explain your answer.

8.   Thomas Jefferson prided himself on the principles of democracy, local self-rule, and limited government. How effectively did he and his friend and successor Madison transform those principles into policy. Could it be argued that Jefferson ironically laid the foundations for an imperial United States and a powerful federal government?

CHAPTER 12

The Second War for Independence and the Upsurge of Nationalism, 1812–1824

PART I: REVIEWING THE CHAPTER

A. Checklist of Learning Objectives

After mastering this chapter, you should be able to:

1. Explain why the War of 1812 was so politically divisive and poorly fought by the United States.

2. Describe the crucial military developments of the War of 1812, and explain why Americans experienced more success on water than on land.

3. Identify the terms of the Treaty of Ghent, and outline the short-term and long-term results of the War of 1812.

4. Describe and explain the burst of American nationalism that followed the War of 1812.

5. Describe the major political and economic developments of the period, including the death of the Federalist Party, the so-called Era of Good Feelings, and the economic depression that followed the Panic of 1819.

6. Describe the furious conflict over slavery that arose in 1819, and indicate how the Missouri Compromise at least temporarily resolved it.

7. Indicate how John Marshall's Supreme Court promoted the spirit of nationalism through its rulings in favor of federal power.

8. Describe the Monroe Doctrine and explain its real and symbolic significance for American foreign policy and for relations with the new Latin American republics.

B. Glossary

To build your social science vocabulary, familiarize yourself with the following terms.

1. **regiment** In earlier American military organization, a medium-sized military unit, larger than a company and smaller than a brigade or division. "Among the defenders were two Louisiana regiments of free black volunteers. . . ."

2. **mediation** An intervention, usually by consent of the parties, to aid in *voluntarily* settling differences between groups or nations by offering possible compromise solutions. (**Arbitration** involves a *mandatory* settlement determined by a third party.) "Tsar Alexander I of Russia . . . proposed mediation between the clashing Anglo-Saxon cousins in 1812."

3. **armistice** A temporary stopping of warfare by mutual agreement, sometimes in preparation for an actual peace negotiation between the parties. "The Treaty of Ghent, signed on Christmas Eve in 1814, was essentially an armistice."

4. **dynasty** A succession of rulers in the same family line; by extension, any system of succession in power by those closely connected to one another. "This last clause was aimed at the much-resented 'Virginia Dynasty.' . . ."

5. **reaction (reactionary)** In politics, extreme conservatism, looking to restore the political or social conditions of some earlier time. ". . . the Old World took the rutted road back to conservatism, illiberalism, and reaction."

6. **protection (protective)** In economics, the policy of stimulating or preserving domestic producers by placing barriers against imported goods, often through high tariffs. "The infant industries bawled lustily for protection."

7. **raw materials** Products in their natural, unmanufactured state. "Through these new arteries of transportation would flow foodstuffs and raw materials. . . ."

8. **internal improvements** The basic public works, such as roads and canals, that create the infrastructure for economic development. "Congress voted . . . for internal improvements."

9. **intrastate** Something existing wholly within a single state of the United States. (**Interstate** refers to movement between two or more states.) "Jeffersonian Republicans . . . choked on the idea of direct federal support of intrastate internal improvements."

10. **depression** In economics, a severe and very prolonged period of declining economic activity, high unemployment, and low wages and prices. "It brought deflation, depression, [and] bankruptcies. . . ."

11. **boom** In economics, a period of sudden, spectacular expansion of business activity, high employment, and rising prices. "The western boom was stimulated by additional developments."

12. **wildcat bank** An unregulated, unstable, speculative bank that issues paper bank notes without sufficient capital to back them. "Finally, the West demanded cheap money, issued by its own 'wildcat' banks. . . ."

13. **peculiar institution** Widely used nineteenth-century euphemistic term for the institution of American black slavery. "If Congress could abolish the 'peculiar institution' in Missouri, might it not attempt to do likewise in the older states of the South?"

14. **demagogic (demagogue)** Concerning a leader who stirs up the common people by appeals to raw emotion and prejudice, often for selfish or irrational ends. ". . . Marshall's decisions bolstered judicial barriers against democratic or demagogic attacks on property rights."

15. **contract** In law, an agreement in which each of two or more parties binds themselves to perform some act in exchange for what the other party similarly pledges to do. ". . . the legislative grant was a contract . . . and the Constitution forbids state laws 'impairing' contracts."

PART II: CHECKING YOUR PROGRESS

A. True-False

Where the statement is true, circle **T**; where it is false, circle **F**.

1. T   F   The Americans developed a brilliant strategy for conquering Canada that failed only when the British successfully defended Fort Michilimackinac on Lake Michigan.

2. T   F   Two bungling American military commanders in the War of 1812 were Oliver Hazard Perry and William Henry Harrison.

3.   T   F   After defeating Napoleon in 1814, Britain began sending thousands of crack veteran troops to North America in order to crush the upstart United States.

4.   T   F   New Englanders opposed the War of 1812 because they believed that Canada should be acquired by peaceful negotiation rather than war.

5.   T   F   The most effective branch of the American military in the War of 1812 proved to be the U.S. Army.

6.   T   F   The most humiliating American defeat of the War of 1812 occurred when the British captured and burned the city of Baltimore.

7.   T   F   Andrew Jackson's victory at the Battle of New Orleans enabled the United States to resist British demands and achieve at favorable peace settlement in the Treaty of Ghent.

8.   T   F   The British agreed to a status quo peace treaty at Ghent largely because they were tired of war and worried about a potentially dangerous France.

9.   T   F   The Hartford Convention's flirtation with secession during the War of 1812 left a taint of treason that contributed to the death of the Federalist party.

10.   T   F   Even though the War of 1812 was a military and diplomatic draw, it set off a burst of patriotic enthusiasm and heightened nationalism in the United States.

11.   T   F   Because of its wildcat banking practices and land speculation, the West was hit especially hard in the panic of 1819.

12.   T   F   The Missouri Compromise admitted Missouri to the Union as a free state, in exchange for the admission of Louisiana as a slave state.

13.   T   F   John Marshall's Supreme Court rulings generally defended the power of the federal government against the power of the states.

14.   T   F   Secretary of State John Quincy Adams successfully acquired both Oregon and Florida for the United States.

15.   T   F   Newly independent Latin Americans were thankful to the United States for the Monroe Doctrine, which declared that there could be no more European colonialism in the Americas.

B. Multiple Choice

Select the best answer and circle the corresponding letter.

1.   The greatest American military successes of the War of 1812 came in the
    a.   land invasions of Canada.
    b.   Chesapeake campaign fought around Washington and Baltimore.
    c.   naval battles on the Great Lakes and elsewhere.
    d.   defense of Fort Michilimackinac on Lake Michigan
    e.   raids on British forces in North Africa.

2.   Two prominent American military heroes during the War of 1812 were
    a.   Tecumseh and Henry Clay.
    b.   James Madison and Stephen Decatur.
    c.   Thomas Macdonough and Francis Scott Key.
    d.   Isaac Brock and John Quincy Adams.
    e.   Oliver Hazard Perry and Andrew Jackson.

3. Even though the victory in the Battle of New Orleans provided a large boost to American morale, it proved essentially meaningless because

    a.   General Jackson was unable to pursue and destroy the British army after his victory.
    b.   the British continued their guerrilla attacks on the Mississippi Valley region.
    c.   the peace treaty had been signed several weeks before.
    d.   the British navy retained control of the shipping lanes around New Orleans.
    e.   the United States had failed in its primary objective of conquering Canada.

4. The terms of the Treaty of Ghent ending the War of 1812 provided that

    a.   there would be a buffer Indian state between the United States and Canada.
    b.   Britain would stop the impressment of American sailors.
    c.   the United States would acquire western Florida in exchange for guaranteeing British control of Canada.
    d.   the two sides would stop fighting and return to the status quo before the war.
    e.   both the United States and Britain would guarantee the independence of Canada.

5. One significant domestic consequence of the War of 1812 was

    a.   a weakening of respect for American naval forces.
    b.   an increased threat from Indians in the West.
    c.   the revival of the Federalists as a threat to the politically weakened President Madison.
    d.   a decline of nationalism and a growth of sectionalism.
    e.   an increase in domestic manufacturing and economic independence.

6. One significant international consequence of the War of 1812 was

    a.   a growth of good relations between the United States and Britain.
    b.   a growth of Canadian patriotism and nationalism.
    c.   the spread of American ideals of liberty to much of western Europe.
    d.   increased American attention to the threat of attack from European nations.
    e.   an American turn toward seeking continental European allies such as France or Prussia.

7. The Era of Good Feelings was sharply disrupted by the

    a.   bitter political battles over the Tariff of 1816 and Henry Clay's American System.
    b.   renewal of international tensions with Britain over Canada and the Monroe Doctrine.
    c.   panic of 1819 and the battle over slavery in Missouri.
    d.   nasty presidential campaign of 1820.
    e.   war with the North African Barbary Coast states.

8. The new nationalistic feeling right after the War of 1812 was evident in all of the following *except*

    a.   the development of a distinctive national literature.
    b.   an increased emphasis on economic independence.
    c.   the addition of significant new territory to the United States.
    d.   a new pride in the American army and navy.
    e.   the cry for the development of a better national transportation system.

9. Besides admitting Missouri as a slave state and Maine as a free state, the Missouri Compromise provided that

    a.   slavery would not be permitted anywhere in the Louisiana Purchase territory north of the southern boundary of Missouri, except in Missouri itself.
    b.   the number of proslavery and antislavery members of the House of Representatives would be kept permanently equal.
    c.   the international slave trade would be permanently ended.
    d.   slavery would be gradually ended in the District of Columbia.
    e.   the United States would promote the settlement of free blacks in Liberia.

10. In the case of *Dartmouth College* v. *Woodward*, John Marshall's Supreme Court held that
    a. the Supreme Court had the power to decide on the constitutionality of state laws.
    b. private colleges, and not the state, had the right to set rules and regulations for their students and faculty.
    c. only Congress and not the states could regulate interstate commerce.
    d. only the federal government and not the states could charter educational and other nonprofit institutions.
    e. the states could not violate the charter of a private, nonprofit corporation like Dartmouth College once it had been granted.

11. One of the key components of the sectional Missouri Compromise negotiated by Henry Clay was
    a. a guarantee that there would always be an equal number of slave and free states.
    b. a congressional prohibition on slavery in the Louisiana territory north of the southern boundary of Missouri.
    c. the admission of Missouri as a slave state and Iowa as a free state.
    d. a guarantee that no new slave territories could be added to the United States.
    e. prohibition of the international slave trade and restrictions on slave trading with the United States.

12. Andrew Jackson's invasion of Florida led to permanent acquisition of that territory after
    a. President Monroe ordered him to seize all Spanish military posts in the area.
    b. the United States declared its rights under the Monroe Doctrine.
    c. President Monroe's cabinet endorsed Jackson's action and declared war on Spain.
    d. Secretary of State Adams pressured Spain to cede the area to the United States.
    e. Spain agreed to trade Florida in exchange for American guarantees of Spanish ownership of California.

13. The original impetus for declaring the Monroe Doctrine came from
    a. a British proposal that America join Britain in guaranteeing the independence of the Latin American republics.
    b. the growing British threat to intervene in Latin America.
    c. the American desire to gain new territory in the Caribbean and Central America.
    d. the Austrian Prince Metternich's plans to establish new European colonies in the Americas.
    e. Spain's crushing of the new Latin American republics' independence.

14. As proclaimed by Monroe in his message of 1823, the Monroe Doctrine asserted that
    a. only the United States had a right to intervene to promote democracy in Latin America.
    b. the British and Americans would act together to prevent further Russian expansion on the Pacific coast.
    c. the United States would not tolerate further European intervention or colonization in the Americas.
    d. the United States would support the Greeks in their fight for independence against Turkey.
    e. the United States and the new Latin American republics would resist British attempts to control American trade.

15. The immediate effect of the Monroe Doctrine at the time it was issued was
    a. a rise in tension between the United States and the major European powers.
    b. very small.
    c. a close alliance between the United States and the Latin American republics.
    d. a series of clashes between the American and British navies.
    e. a declaration by Russia that it would not attempt to colonize Oregon and California.

C. Identification

Supply the correct identification for each numbered description.

1. _____ One of the Great Lakes where Oliver H. Perry captured a large British fleet

2. _____ Stirring patriotic song written by Francis Scott Key while being held aboard a British ship in Baltimore harbor

3. _____ Andrew Jackson's stunning victory over invading British forces that occurred after the peace Treaty of Ghent had already been signed

4. _____ Gathering of antiwar New England Federalists whose flirtation with secession stirred outrage and contributed to the death of the Federalist party

5. _____ Post-War of 1812 treaty between Britain and the United States that limited the naval arms race on the Great Lakes

6. _____ Highly intellectual magazine that reflected the post-1815 spirit of American nationalism

7. _____ Henry Clay's ambitious nationalistic proposal for a federal banking system, higher tariffs, and internal improvements to help develop American manufacturing and trade

8. _____ Somewhat inappropriate term applied to the two Monroe administrations, suggesting that this period lacked major conflicts

9. _____ Once-prominent political party that effectively died by 1820

10. _____ Major water transportation route financed and built by New York State after President Madison vetoed federal funding

11. _____ Line designated as the future boundary between free and slave territories under the Missouri Compromise

12. _____ Supreme Court ruling that defended federal power by denying a state the right to tax a federal bank

13. _____ Supreme Court case in which Daniel Webster successfully argued that a state could not change the legal charter of a private college once granted

14. _____ Northwestern territory occupied jointly by Britain and the United States under the Anglo-American Convention of 1818

15. _____ A presidential foreign-policy proclamation that grandly warned European nations against colonization or interference in the Americas, even though the United States could not really enforce such a decree

D. Matching People, Places, and Events

Match the person, place, or event in the left column with the proper description in the right column by inserting the correct letter on the blank line.

1. ____ Stephen Decatur

2. ____ Treaty of Ghent

3. ____ Rush-Bagot agreement

4. ____ Hartford Convention

a. Admitted one slave and one free state to the Union, and fixed the boundary between slave and free territories

5. ____ Henry Clay

6. ____ James Monroe

7. ____ Washington Irving

8. ____ Missouri Compromise

9. ____ John Marshall

10. ____ John Quincy Adams

11. ____ George Canning

12. ____ Andrew Jackson

13. ____ Daniel Webster

14. ____ Russo-American Treaty of 1824

15. ____ Tsar Alexander I

b. Military commander who exceeded his government's instructions during an invasion of Spanish territory

c. The leading voice promoting nationalism and greater federal power in the United States Senate during the 1820s

d. Aristocratic Federalist jurist whose rulings bolstered national power against the states

e. Eloquent Kentucky spokesman for the American System and key architect of the Missouri Compromise in the U.S. Senate

f. Nationalistic secretary of state who promoted American interests against Spain and Britain

g. Agreement between the United States and one of the European great powers that fixed the southern boundary of that nation's colony of Alaska.

h. American naval hero of the War of 1812 who said, ". . . our country, right or wrong!"

i. One of the first nationalistic American writers to achieve literary recognition in Europe

j. British foreign secretary whose proposal for a joint British-American declaration led to the unilaterally declared Monroe Doctrine

k. Gathering of antiwar delegates in New England that ended up being accused of treason

l. President whose personal popularity contributed to the Era of Good Feelings

m. Agreement that simply stopped fighting and left most of the war issues unresolved

n. 1817 agreement that limited American and British naval forces on the Great Lakes

o. Russian ruler whose mediation proposal led to negotiations ending the War of 1812

E. Putting Things in Order

Put the following events in correct order by numbering them from 1 to 6.

1. _____ A battle over extending slavery finally results in two new states and an agreement on how to handle slavery in the territories.

2. _____ A major water route is completed across New York State.

3. _____ Infant American manufacturers successfully press Congress to raise barriers against foreign imports.

4. _____ Rather than follow a British diplomatic lead, President Monroe and Secretary Adams announce a bold new policy for the Western Hemisphere.

5. _____ Spain cedes Florida to the United States.

6. _____ An unpopular war ends in an ambivalent compromise that settles none of the key contested issues.

F. Matching Cause and Effect

Match the historical cause in the left column with the proper effect in the right column by writing the correct letter on the blank line.

Cause

1. ___ American lack of military preparation and poor strategy

2. ___ Oliver H. Perry's and Thomas Macdonough's naval successes

3. ___ Tsar Alexander I's mediation proposal

4. ___ The Hartford Convention

5. ___ Canadians' successful defense of their homeland in the War of 1812

6. ___ The Rush-Bagot agreement

7. ___ The rising nationalistic economic spirit after the War of 1812

8. ___ The disappearance of the Federalists and President Monroe's appeals to New England

9. ___ Overspeculation in western lands

10. ___ Cheap land and increasing westward migration

11. ___ The deadlock between North and South over the future of slavery in Missouri

12. ___ The Missouri Compromise

13. ___ John Marshall's Supreme Court rulings

Effect

a. Inspired a new sense of Canadian nationalism

b. Contributed to the death of the Federalist party and the impression that New Englanders were disloyal

c. Produced a series of badly failed attempts to conquer Canada

d. Reduced armaments along the border between the United States and Canada and laid the groundwork for "the longest unfortified boundary in the world"

e. Caused the economy to collapse in the panic of 1819

f. Angered Britain and other European nations but had little effect in Latin America

g. Fueled demands in Congress for transportation improvements and the removal of the Native Americans

h. Upheld the power of the federal government against the states

i. Created a temporary one-party system and an "Era of Good Feelings"

14. ___ The rise of European reactionary powers and the loss of Spain's colonial empire

15. ___ The Monroe Doctrine

j. Produced the Missouri Compromise, which admitted two states and drew a line between slave and free territories

k. Aroused American and British fears of European intervention in Latin America

l. Aroused southern fears for the long-term future of slavery

m. Inspired a new Bank of the United States and the protectionist Tariff of 1816

n. Eventually led to the beginnings of peace negotiations at Ghent

o. Reversed a string of American defeats and prevented a British-Canadian invasion from the north

G. Developing Historical Skills

Categorizing Historical Information

Historical events and information are usually presented in chronological order. But it is often useful to organize them into topical or other categories. The central idea of this chapter is the rise of American nationalism in the period 1815–1824. Among the major subdivisions of this general idea would be the following:

a. Economic nationalism

b. Political nationalism and unity

c. Judicial nationalism

d. Foreign-policy nationalism

Indicate under which of these categories each of the following facts or events from the chapter should be located.

1. Andrew Jackson's invasion of Florida

2. *Dartmouth College* v. *Woodward*

3. The Tariff of 1816

4. John Quincy Adams's rejection of British Foreign Minister Canning's proposed joint British-American statement

5.   Clay's American System

6.   President Monroe's tour of New England

7.   Daniel Webster's speeches

8.   The election of 1820

H. Map Mastery

Map Discrimination

Using the maps and charts in Chapter 12, answer the following questions.

1.   *The Three U.S. Invasions of 1812/Campaigns of 1813*: Near which two Great Lakes were the major battles related to the American invasions of Canada fought?

2.   *Presidential Election of 1812*: What were the only two states that voted in part contrary to the general trend of their section (that is, North vs. South)?

3.   *The Missouri Compromise and Slavery, 1820–1821*: After the Missouri Compromise of 1820, only two organized territories of the United States remained eligible to join the Union as slave states. Which were they?

4.   *The Missouri Compromise and Slavery, 1820–1821*: As of 1821, how many slave states had been carved out of the territory of the Louisiana Purchase?

5.   *The Missouri Compromise and Slavery, 1820–1821*: After Maine was admitted as a free state in 1820, how many organized territories were there north of the line 36° 30′—that is, the border between the slave and free territories?

6. *The Missouri Compromise and Slavery, 1820–1821*: As of 1821, which five slave states were north of the line of 36° 30′ that was intended to be the future northern limit of slavery?

7. *The U.S.-British Boundary Settlement, 1818:* Under the British-American boundary settlement of 1818, which nation gained the most territory (compared with the natural Missouri River watershed boundary)?

8. *The Southeast, 1810–1819*: Which organized American territory lay immediately north of West Florida at this time?

Map Challenge

Using the map of *The Missouri Compromise and Slavery, 1820–1821*, write a brief essay explaining how the Missouri Compromise related both to the existing territorial status of slavery and to its possible future expansion to the West. (Recall that the Compromise set 36° 30′ as the northern boundary of any future slave territory.)

PART III: APPLYING WHAT YOU HAVE LEARNED

1. Was the largely failed American military effort in the War of 1812 primarily a result of a flawed military strategy or of the deep political divisions and disagreements about the purposes of the war?

2. How did the divisive, demoralizing, and inconclusive War of 1812 nevertheless produce a dramatic outburst of American patriotism and nationalism in its aftermath?

3. What were the most important signs of the new American nationalism that developed in the period 1815–1824?

4. Why did the issue of admitting Missouri to the Union precipitate a major national crisis? Why did the North and South each agree to the terms of the Missouri Compromise?

5. Did the dramatic crisis over slavery in the Missouri Territory reveal the underlying weakness of American nationalism in 1819–1820, or did the resulting Missouri Compromise essentially demonstrate nationalistic Americans' strong desire to maintain national unity?

6. What part did the growing expansion into the West play in such crucial issues of the period as the tariff, internal improvements, and the controversy over slavery?

7. How did John Marshall's Supreme Court reflect the nationalistic spirit of the 1810s–1820s. In what ways did Marshall's conservative determination to uphold and expand the power of the federal government run contrary to the general American political direction of the time?

8. How did American nationalism display itself in foreign policy, particularly in the Florida crisis and in American policy toward Europe and the Western Hemisphere?

9. Was America's essential foreign policy goal in the period 1812–1824 an essentially defensive one designed to protect its still-fragile republican experiment against the dangers from reactionary European great powers and to isolate itself from European quarrels? Or was it a more aggressive, expansionist policy designed to guarantee that the United States would be the dominant power in all of North Americas, and possibly in Latin America as well?

10. Was the Monroe Doctrine fundamentally consistent with the isolationist principles established by George Washington in his Neutrality Proclamation and Farewell Address (see Chapter 10)?

CHAPTER 13

The Rise of a Mass Democracy, 1824–1840

PART I: REVIEWING THE CHAPTER

A. Checklist of Learning Objectives

After mastering this chapter, you should be able to:

1. Describe and explain the growth of Mass Democracy in the 1820s.

2. Indicate how the alleged corrupt bargain of 1824 and Adams' unpopular presidency set the stage for Jackson's election in 1828.

3. Analyze the celebration of Jackson's victory in 1828 as a triumph of the New Democracy over the more restrictive and elitist politics of the early Republic.

4. Describe the political innovations of the 1830s, especially the rise of mass parties, Jackson's use of the presidency to stir up public opinion, and indicate their significance for American politics and society.

5. Describe Jackson's policies of westward expansion, his relations with the new Republic of Texas, and his harsh removal of the southeastern Indian nations on the Trail of Tears.

6. Explain Jackson's economic and political motives for waging the bitter Bank War, and show how Jacksonian economics crippled his successor Van Buren after the Panic of 1837.

7. Describe the different ways that each of the new mass political parties, Democrats and Whigs, promoted the democratic ideals of liberty and equality among their constituencies.

B. Glossary

To build your social science vocabulary, familiarize yourself with the following terms.

1. **deference** The yielding of one's opinion to the judgment of someone else, usually of higher social standing. "The deference, apathy, and virtually nonexistent party organizations of the Era of Good Feelings yielded to the boisterous democracy. . . ."

2. **puritanical** Extremely or excessively strict in matters of morals or religion. "The only candidate left was the puritanical Adams. . . ."

3. **mudslinging** Malicious, unscrupulous attacks against an opponent. "Mudslinging reached new lows in 1828. . . ."

4. **spoils** Public offices or other favors given as a reward for political support. "Under Jackson the spoils system . . . was introduced on a large scale."

5. **denominations** In American religion, the major branches of Christianity, organized into distinct church structures, such as Presbyterians, Baptists, Disciples of Christ, etc. ". . . many denominations sent missionaries into Indian villages."

6. **evangelical** In American religion, those believers and groups, usually Protestant, who emphasize personal salvation, individual conversion experiences, voluntary commitment, and the authority of Scripture. "The Anti-Masons attracted support from many evangelical Protestant groups. . . ."

7. **hard money** Metal money or coins, as distinguished from paper money. (The term also came to mean reliable or secure money that maintained or increased its purchasing power over time. **Soft money**, or paper money, was assumed to be inflationary and to lose value.) ". . . a decree that required all public lands to be purchased with 'hard' . . . money."

8. **usurpation** The act of seizing, occupying, or enjoying the place, power, or functions of someone without legal right. "Hatred of Jackson and his 'executive usurpation' was its only apparent cement in its formative days."

9. **favorite sons** In American politics, presidential candidates who are nominated by their own state, primarily out of local loyalty, without expectation of winning. "Their long-shot strategy was instead to run several prominent 'favorite sons' . . . and hope to scatter the vote so that no candidate could win a majority."

10. **machine** A hierarchical political organization, often controlled through patronage or spoils, where professional politicians can deliver large blocs of voters to preferred candidates. "As a machine-made candidate, he incurred the resentment of many Democrats. . . ."

11. **temperance** Campaigns for voluntary commitment to moderation or total abstinence in the consumption of liquor. (Prohibition involved instead *forcible* legal bans on the production or consumption of alcohol.) ". . . the Arkansas Indians dubbed him 'Big Drunk.' He subsequently took the pledge of temperance."

12. **populist** A political program or style focused on the common people, and attacking perspectives and policies associated with the well-off, well-born, or well-educated. (The Populist Party was a specific third-party organization of the 1890s.) "The first was the triumph of a populist democratic style."

13. **divine right** The belief that government or rulers are directly established by God. ". . . America was now bowing to the divine right of the people."

PART II: CHECKING YOUR PROGRESS

A. True-False

Where the statement is true, circle **T**; where it is false, circle **F**.

1. T   F   The last election based on the old elitist political system was the four-way presidential campaign of 1824 involving Jackson, Clay, Crawford, and John Quincy Adams.

2. T   F   Henry Clay disproved the charge of a corrupt bargain between himself and President Adams by refusing to accept any favors from the new administration.

3. T   F   President Adams lost public support by promoting strong nationalistic principles in a time of growing support for sectionalism and states' rights.

4. T   F   Andrew Jackson became a great popular hero as president because he continued to live the same life of frontier toughness and simplicity as his followers.

5. T   F   The election campaign of 1828 was notable for the well-formulated debates between Andrew Jackson and President Adams on the issues of the tariff and removal of the barriers to political equality and democracy.

6.   T F   Jackson's victory in 1828 represented the triumph of the West and the common people over the older elitist political system.

7.   T F   The Jacksonians practiced their belief that because all citizens were equal, anyone could hold public positions without particular qualifications.

8.   T F   South Carolina's fierce opposition to the Tariff of Abominations reflected an underlying fear that enhanced federal power might be turned against the institution of slavery.

9.   T F   Andrew Jackson used mediation and compromise rather than threats of force to persuade South Carolina to back away from its nullification of the tariff laws.

10. T F   The powerful Cherokees of the southeastern United States fiercely resisted white efforts to alter their traditional culture and way of life.

11. T F   When the Supreme Court ruled against the state of Georgia and in favor of southeastern Indians' rights, Jackson defied the Supreme Court's rulings and ordered the Cherokees and other southeastern tribes forcibly removed to Oklahoma.

12. T F   Jackson successfully used his veto of the bill to recharter the wealthy Bank of the United States to politically mobilize the common people of the West against the financial elite of the East.

13. T F   The Whig party was united by its principles of states' rights, western expansionism, and opposition to the role of evangelical Christianity in politics.

14. T F   A primary source of tension between settlers in Texas and the Mexican government was Mexico's abolition of slavery and prohibition of slave importation.

15. T F   William Henry Harrison's background as an ordinary frontiersman born in a log cabin enabled Whigs to match and exceed the Democrats' appeal to the common man in the campaign of 1840.

B. Multiple Choice

Select the best answer and circle the corresponding letter.

1. The Jacksonian charge that John Quincy Adams won the presidency through a corrupt bargain arose because
   a. William Crawford threw his electoral votes to Adams in exchange for a seat in the Senate.
   b. members of the House of Representatives claimed that they had been bribed to vote for Adams.
   c. Adams ended his previous opposition to Henry Clay's American System.
   d. Jackson discovered that there had been vote fraud in several pro-Adams states.
   e. after Henry Clay threw his support to Adams, he was appointed secretary of state.

2. Which of the following was *not* among the factors that made John Quincy Adams's presidency a political failure?
   a. Adams's attempts to treat Indians fairly.
   b. Adams's involvement with corrupt machine deals and politicians.
   c. Adams's stubborn and prickly personality.
   d. Adams's support for national roads, a national university, and an astronomical observatory.
   e. Adams's hostility to western land speculation and unlimited expansionism.

3.   Andrew Jackson's strong appeal to the common people arose partly because

   a.   Americans finally understood the ideas of the Declaration of Independence.
   b.   many citizens were tired of the partisan fights between Republicans and Federalists.
   c.   he had risen from the masses and reflected many of their prejudices in his personal attitudes and outlook.
   d.   farmer and labor organizations aroused populist opposition to elitist politics.
   e.   he was skilled at appealing to the public's evangelical religion and fervent patriotism.

4.   One political development that demonstrated the power of the new popular democratic movement in politics was

   a.   the rise of the caucus system of presidential nominations.
   b.   the use of party loyalty as the primary qualification for appointing people to public office.
   c.   extensive public speaking tours by presidential candidates.
   d.   the strong support for public schools and a national university.
   e.   the vigorous campaign to abolish the electoral college.

5.   Andrew Jackson's fundamental approach during the South Carolina nullification crisis was to

   a.   acknowledge the injustice of the high Tariff of Abominations and seek to lower it.
   b.   seek to strengthen South Carolina unionists while politically isolating the nullifiers.
   c.   join hands with Henry Clay in attempting to find a compromise solution.
   d.   attempt to change the focus of attention from the tariff to slavery.
   e.   mobilize a sizable military force and threaten to hang the nullifiers.

6.   Under the surface of the South's strong opposition to the Tariff of Abominations was

   a.   a desire to develop its own textile industry.
   b.   competition between southern cotton growers and midwestern grain farmers.
   c.   a strong preference for British manufactured goods over American-produced goods.
   d.   a fear of growing federal power that might interfere with slavery.
   e.   a belief that the high tariff would foster immigration and urbanization.

7.   Some southeastern Indian tribes like the Cherokees were notable for their

   a.   effectiveness in warfare against encroaching whites.
   b.   development of effective agricultural, educational, and political institutions.
   c.   success in persuading President Jackson to support their cause.
   d.   adherence to traditional Native American cultural and religious values.
   e.   consistent opposition to slavery and racism.

8.   In promoting his policy of Indian removal, President Andrew Jackson

   a.   defied rulings of the U.S. Supreme Court that favored the Cherokees.
   b.   admitted that the action would destroy Native American culture and society.
   c.   acted against the advice of his cabinet and his military commanders in the Southeast.
   d.   tried to split the Cherokees apart from their allies such as the Creeks and Seminoles.
   e.   was convinced that the Indians would better thrive in Oklahoma.

9.   Jackson's veto of the Bank of the United States recharter bill represented a(n)

   a.   response to Europeans investors' lack of faith in the dollar.
   b.   attempt to assure bankers and creditors that the federal government had their interests at heart.
   c.   concession to Henry Clay and his National Republican followers.
   d.   gain for sound banking and a financially stable currency system.
   e.   bold assertion of presidential power on behalf of western farmers and other debtors.

10. One important result of President Jackson's destruction of the Bank of the United States was

    a. a successful economy to hand on to his successor, Van Buren.
    b. a sounder financial system founded upon thousands of locally controlled banks.
    c. the American banking system's dependence on European investment and control.
    d. the lack of a stable banking system to finance the era of rapid industrialization.
    e. Jackson's equally successful attack on the secretive and elitist Masons.

11. Among the political innovations that first appeared in the election of 1832 were

    a. political parties and direct popular voting for president.
    b. newspaper endorsements and public financing of presidential campaigns.
    c. nomination by congressional caucus and voting by the Electoral College.
    d. third-party campaigning, national conventions, and party platforms.
    e. secret ballots and the prohibition on liquor in polling places.

12. In the immediate aftermath of the successful Texas Revolution

    a. Texas petitioned to join the United States but was refused admission.
    b. Texas joined the United States as a slave state.
    c. Mexico and the United States agreed to a joint protectorate over Texas.
    d. Britain threatened the United States with war over Texas.
    e. the Texas government sought to expand westward to the Pacific.

13. The Panic of 1837 and the subsequent severe depression were caused primarily by

    a. the stock market collapse and a sharp decline in grain prices.
    b. a lack of new investment in industry and technology.
    c. the threat of war with Mexico over Texas.
    d. overspeculation and Jackson's hard-money financial policies.
    e. British investors' loss of confidence in American business.

14. Prominent leaders of the Whig party included

    a. Martin Van Buren and John C. Calhoun.
    b. David Crockett and Nicholas Biddle.
    c. Andrew Jackson and William Henry Harrison.
    d. Stephen Austin and Sam Houston.
    e. Henry Clay and Daniel Webster.

15. The real significance of William Henry Harrison's victory in the election of 1840 was that it

    a. constituted a sharp repudiation of Andrew Jackson and Jacksonianism.
    b. brought a fresh new face to American presidential politics.
    c. showed that the Whigs could win with a candidate other than Henry Clay.
    d. showed that the Whigs could practice the new mass democratic politics as successfully as the Democrats.
    e. showed that the public wanted serious debates as well as noisy "hoopla" in presidential politics.

C. Identification

Supply the correct identification for each numbered description.

1. _____ New, circus-like method of nominating presidential candidates that involved wider participation but usually left effective control in the hands of party bosses

2. _____ Small, short-lived third political party that originated a new method of nominating presidential candidates in the election campaign of 1831–1832

3. _____ Contemptuous Jacksonian term for the alleged political deal by which Clay threw his support to Adams in exchange for a high cabinet office

4. _____ Andrew Jackson's popular nickname, signaling his toughness and strength

5. _____ The arrangement under which public offices were handed out on the basis of political support rather than qualifications

6. _____ Scornful southern term for the high Tariff of 1828

7. _____ Theory promoted by John C. Calhoun and other South Carolinians that said states had the right to disregard federal laws to which they objected

8. _____ The "moneyed monster" that Clay tried to preserve and that Jackson killed with his veto in 1832

9. _____ Ritualistic secret societies that became the target of a momentarily powerful third party in 1832

10. _____ Religious believers, originally attracted to the Anti-Masonic party and then to the Whigs, who sought to use political power for moral and religious reform

11. _____ Any two of the southeastern Indian peoples who were removed to Oklahoma
_____

12. _____ The sorrowful path along which thousands of southeastern Indians were removed to Oklahoma

13. _____ Conflict of 1832 in which the Sauk and Fox Indians of Illinois and Wisconsin were defeated by federal troops and state militias.

14. _____ Economic crisis that precipitated an economic depression and doomed the presidency of Martin Van Buren

15. _____ Popular symbols of the flamboyant but effective campaign the Whigs used to elect "poor-boy" William Henry Harrison over Martin Van Buren in 1840

D. Matching People, Places, and Events

Match the person, place, or event in the left column with the proper description in the right column by inserting the correct letter on the blank line.

1. ___ John C. Calhoun

2. ___ Henry Clay

3. ___ Nicholas Biddle

4. ___ Sequoyah

5. ___ John Quincy Adams

6. ___ David Crocket

7. ___ Moses Austin

8. ___ Sam Houston

9. ___ Osceola

10. ___ Santa Anna

11. ___ Martin Van Buren

a. Cherokee leader who devised an alphabet for his people

b. Political party that generally stressed individual liberty, the rights of the common people, and hostility to privilege

c. Seminole leader whose warriors killed fifteen hundred American soldiers in years of guerrilla warfare

d. Former Tennessee governor whose victory at San Jacinto in 1836 won Texas its independence

e. Mexican general and dictator whose large army failed to defeat Texas rebels

12. ___   Black Hawk

13. ___   William Henry Harrison

14. ___   Whigs

15. ___   Democrats

f.   Former vice president, leader of South Carolina nullifiers, and bitter enemy of Andrew Jackson

g.   Political party that favored a more activist government, high tariffs, internal improvements, and moral reforms

h.   Original leader of American settlers in Texas who obtained a huge land grant from the Mexican government

i.   A frontier hero, Tennessee Congressman, and teller of tall tales who died in the Texas War for Independence

j.   "Old Tippecanoe," who was portrayed by Whig propagandists as a hard-drinking common man of the frontier

k.   Jackson's rival for the presidency in 1832, who failed to save the Bank of the United States

l.   The "wizard of Albany," whose economically troubled presidency was served in the shadow of Jackson

m.   Talented but high-handed bank president who fought a bitter losing battle with the president of the United States

n.   Aloof New England statesman whose elitism made him an unpopular leader in the new era of mass democracy

o.   Illinois-Wisconsin area Sauk leader who was defeated by American regulars and militia in 1832

E. Putting Things in Order

Put the following events in correct order by numbering them from 1 to 5.

1. ___   South Carolina threatens nullification of federal law and backs down in the face of Andrew Jackson's military threat.

2. ___   A strange four-way election puts an icy New Englander in office amid charges of a corrupt bargain.

3. ___   A campaign based on hoopla and "log cabins and hard cider slogans" demonstrates that both Whigs and Democrats can effectively play the new mass-party political game.

4. ____ A northern Mexican province successfully revolts and seeks admission to the United States.

5. ____ Despite attempting to follow white patterns of civilizing, thousands of American Indians are forcibly removed from their homes and driven across the Mississippi River.

F. Matching Cause and Effect

Match the historical cause in the left column with the proper effect in the right column by writing the correct letter on the blank line.

<table>
<tr><th>Cause</th><th>Effect</th></tr>
<tr><td>1. ____ The growth of American migration into northern Mexico</td><td>a. Brought many evangelical Christians into politics and showed that others besides Jackson could stir up popular feelings</td></tr>
<tr><td>2. ____ The demand of many whites to acquire Indian land in Georgia and other states</td><td>b. Provoked protests and threats of nullification from South Carolina</td></tr>
<tr><td>3. ____ The Anti-Masonic Party</td><td>c. Aroused popular anger and made Jackson's supporters determined to elect him in 1828</td></tr>
<tr><td>4. ____ The failure of any candidate to win an electoral majority in the four-way election of 1824</td><td>d. Laid the foundations for the spoils system that fueled the new mass political parties</td></tr>
<tr><td>5. ____ The alleged corrupt bargain between Adams and Clay for the presidency in 1824</td><td>e. Threw the bitterly contested election into the U.S. House of Representatives</td></tr>
<tr><td>6. ____ President Adams's strong nationalistic policies</td><td>f. Laid the basis for a political conflict that resulted in Texas independence</td></tr>
<tr><td>7. ____ The high New England–backed Tariff of 1828</td><td>g. Caused widespread human suffering and virtually guaranteed Martin Van Buren's defeat in 1840</td></tr>
<tr><td>8. ____ Andrew Jackson's war against Nicholas Biddle and his policies</td><td>h. Fueled the political pressures that led Andrew Jackson to forcibly remove the Cherokees and others</td></tr>
<tr><td>9. ____ Jackson's belief that any ordinary American could hold government office</td><td>i. Aroused the bitter opposition of westerners and southerners, who were increasingly sectionalist</td></tr>
<tr><td>10. ____ The Panic of 1837</td><td>j. Got the government out of banking but weakened the American financial system</td></tr>
</table>

G. Developing Historical Skills

Interpreting Political Cartoons and Satire

Political cartoons are an important historical source. Even when they are strongly biased one way or another, they can yield information about political conflicts and contemporary attitudes.

The anti-Jackson cartoon, *In Mother Bank's Sick Room*, reveals a number of things about how his opponents viewed Jackson. Answer the following questions.

1. What is the fundamental point of the cartoon's attack on the Bank of the United States and its supporters?

2. What visual means does the cartoonist use to develop its point?

3. In the pro-Jackson cartoon, *Symptom of a Locked Jaw*, how is Clay's frustration at Jackson's bank veto portrayed? How is Jackson's successful resistance represented?

4. In the satirical bank note mocking pro-Jackson pet banks, list at least three distinct visual symbols that identify the worthless note with Jackson and his policies.

5. List at least three verbal terms or phrases that underscore the supposed fraudulency of Jacksonian banking practices.

H. Map Mastery

Map Discrimination

Using the maps and charts in Chapter 13, answer the following questions.

1. *Election of 1824*: In the election of 1824, how many more electoral votes would Jackson have needed to win a majority and prevent the election from going to the House of Representatives?

2. *Presidential Election of 1828*: In the election of 1828, in which states outside New England did John Quincy Adams win electoral votes?

3. *Presidential Election of 1828*: In the election of 1828, which of the eastern middle states did Jackson carry completely?

4. *Presidential Election of 1828*: Which three states divided their electoral votes?

5. *The Removal of the Southern Tribes to the West*: Of the five southeastern Indian tribes, which two were located wholly within the boundaries of a single state? Which tribe was located in four states?

6. *The Texas Revolution, 1835–1836*: A) When Santa Anna's army entered Texas to attack the Alamo, what two major rivers did it cross? B) When Santa Anna's army moved from the site of its greatest victory to the site of its greatest defeat, what direction did it march?

PART III: APPLYING WHAT YOU HAVE LEARNED

1. Why was Andrew Jackson such a personally powerful embodiment of the new mass democracy in the 1820s and 1830s? Would mass democracy have developed without a popular hero like Jackson?

2. Why did Calhoun and the South see the Tariff of 1828 as such an abomination and raise threats of nullification over it?

3. What made Jackson's Indian Removal policy seem especially harsh and hypocritical? Was there any chance that the Cherokees and other civilized southeastern tribes could have maintained their own lands and identities if Jackson had not defied the Supreme Court?

4. How did Jackson's Bank War demonstrate the power of a modern mass democratic political machine and its propaganda? Was Biddle's Bank a real threat to the economic welfare of the less affluent citizens whom Jackson represented, or was it more important as a symbol of eastern wealth and elitism?

5. How did the Panic of 1837 and the subsequent depression reflect the weaknesses of Jackson's economic and financial policies? Why was Martin Van Buren unable to outmaneuver the Whig political opposition as Jackson had?

6. Does Andrew Jackson belong in the pantheon of great American presidents? Why or why not?

7. Argue for or against: the Texas Revolution against Mexico was more about the expansion of slavery into the West than about the rights of Anglo-American settlers in Texas.

8. Was the growing hoopla of American politics reflected in the "log cabin and hard cider" campaign of 1840 a violation of the republican virtue upheld by the Founders or an inevitable and even healthy reflection of the public's engagement with politics once it was opened up to the great mass of people?

9. What did the two new democratic parties, the Democrats and the Whigs, really stand for? Were they actual ideological opponents, or were their disagreements less important than their shared roots and commitment to America's new mass democracy?

10. Compare the two-party political system of the 1830s' New Democracy with the first two-party system of the early Republic (see Chapter 10). In what ways were the two systems similar, and in what ways were they different? Were both parties of the 1830s correct in seeing themselves as heirs of the Jeffersonian Republican tradition rather than the Hamiltonian Federalist tradition?

CHAPTER 14

Forging the National Economy, 1790–1860

PART I: REVIEWING THE CHAPTER

A. Checklist of Learning Objectives

After mastering this chapter, you should be able to:

1. Describe the growth and movement of America's population in the early nineteenth century.

2. Describe the largely German and Irish wave of immigration beginning in the 1830s and the reactions it provoked among native Americans.

3. Explain why America was relatively slow to embrace the industrial revolution and the factory.

4. Describe the early development of the factory system and Eli Whitney's system of interchangeable parts.

5. Outline early industrialism's effects on workers, including women and children.

6. Describe the impact of new technologies, including transportation and communication systems, on American business and agriculture.

7. Describe the development of a continental market economy and its revolutionary effects on both producers and consumers.

8. Explain why the emerging industrial economy could raise the general level of prosperity, while simultaneously creating greater disparities of wealth between rich and poor.

B. Glossary

To build your social science vocabulary, familiarize yourself with the following terms.

1. **caste** An exclusive or rigid social distinction based on birth, wealth, occupation, and so forth. "There was freedom from aristocratic caste and state church. . . ."

2. **nativist** One who advocates policies favoring native-born citizens and displays hostility or prejudice toward immigrants. "The invasion of this so-called immigrant 'rabble'. . . inflamed the prejudices of American 'nativists.' "

3. **factory** A large establishment for the manufacturing of goods, including buildings and substantial machinery. "The factory system gradually spread from England—'the world's workshop'—to other lands."

4. **trademark** A distinguishing symbol or word used by a manufacturer on its goods, usually registered by law to protect against imitators. ". . . unscrupulous Yankee manufacturers . . . learned to stamp their own products with faked English trademarks."

5. **patent** The legal certification of an original invention, product, or process, guaranteeing its holder sole rights to profits from its use or reproduction for a specified period of time. "For the decade ending in 1800, only 306 patents were registered in Washington. . . ."

6. **liability** Legal responsibility for loss or damage. "The principle of limited liability aided the concentration of capital. . . ."

7. **incorporation** The organization of individuals into an institutional entity with legally defined privileges and responsibilities. "Laws of 'free incorporation' were first passed in New York in 1848. . . ."

8. **labor union** An organization of workers—usually wage-earning workers—to promote the interests and welfare of its members, often by collective bargaining with employers. "They were forbidden by law to form labor unions. . . ."

9. **strike** An organized work stoppage by employees in order to obtain better wages, working conditions, and so on. "Not surprisingly, only twenty-four recorded strikes occurred before 1835."

10. **capitalist** An individual or group who uses its accumulated funds or private property to produce goods or services for profit in a market. "It made ambitious capitalists out of humble plowmen. . . ."

11. **turnpike** A toll road. "The turnpikes beckoned to the canvas-covered Conestoga wagons. . . ."

12. **posterity** Later descendants or subsequent generations. "He installed a powerful steam engine in a vessel that posterity came to know as the *Clermont*. . . ."

13. **productivity** In economics, the relative efficiency in the production of goods and services, measured in terms of the quantity of goods or services produced by workers in a certain length of time. "The principle of division of labor . . . spelled productivity and profits. . . ."

14. **barter** The direct exchange of goods or services for one another, without the use of cash or any other medium of exchange. "Most families . . . bartered with their neighbors for the few necessities they could not make themselves."

PART II: CHECKING YOUR PROGRESS

A. True-False

Where the statement is true, circle **T**; where it is false, circle **F**.

1. T   F   American frontier life was often plagued by poverty and illness.

2. T   F   Even as they often despoiled nature, Americans celebrated the spectacular American landscape and wilderness as a defining element of national culture and identity.

3. T   F   The growing cheapness and speed of transatlantic steamships made the United States the preferred destination for European immigrants.

4. T   F   The primary cause of nativist hostility to Irish immigrants was their frequent involvement in fights and street gangs.

5. T   F   The early industrial revolution was greatly advanced by Eli Whitney's introduction of the system of interchangeable parts.

6. T   F   Early labor unions made very slow progress, partly because the strike weapon was illegal and ineffective.

7. T   F   Most married women in the early nineteenth century worked only part-time and contributed their income to the support of their families.

8. T   F   The child-centered family developed in the early nineteenth century partly because Americans deliberately limited the number of their children.

9. T F   The Erie Canal greatly lowered the cost of Midwestern agricultural products in the markets of eastern big cities and even Europe.

10. T F   The railroad gained quick acceptance as a safer and more efficient alternative to waterbound transportation.

11. T F   In the sectional division of labor that developed before the Civil War, the South provided corn and meat to feed the nation, the Midwest produced industrial goods and textiles, and the Northeast supplied financial and communications services.

12. T F   The growth of the market economy increasingly undermined the family's role as a self-sufficient producing unit and made the home a place of refuge from work.

13. T F   By 1850, permanent telegraph lines had been stretched across both the Atlantic Ocean and the North American continent.

14. T F   The advances in manufacturing and transportation decreased the gap between rich and poor in America.

15. T F   In the 1830s, new legal and governmental policies prohibiting chartered business monopolies encouraged competition and aided the market economy.

B. Multiple Choice

Select the best answer and circle the corresponding letter.

1. In 1850, over one-half of the American population was

    a. foreign-born.
    b. living west of the Mississippi River.
    c. under the age of thirty.
    d. living in cities of over 100,000 people.
    e. Irish or German.

2. Writers like James Fenimore Cooper and Herman Melville explored characters who exemplified the American frontier's cultural emphasis on

    a. masculinity.
    b. rugged individualism.
    c. group conformity.
    d. environmental awareness.
    e. white racial superiority.

3. Americans came to look on their spectacular western wilderness areas especially as

    a. opportunities for imperialistic expansionism.
    b. a potential location for industrial development.
    c. a potential attraction for tourists from abroad.
    d. the sacred home of American Indian tribes.
    e. a distinctive and inspirational feature of American national identity.

4. Compared to European immigration to other countries like Australia and Argentina, immigrants to the United States were

    a. from a greater diversity of European countries.
    b. more affluent.
    c. primarily from European urban centers rather than rural areas.
    d. English-speaking.
    e. politically liberal or radical.

5. The two leading sources of European immigration to America in the 1840s and 1850s were
   a. France and Italy.
   b. Germany and France.
   c. Germany and Ireland.
   d. Ireland and Norway.
   e. Britain and the Netherlands.

6. Many nineteenth-century Americans feared and distrusted Roman Catholicism because
   a. American Catholics had been Loyalists during the American Revolution.
   b. French-Canadian Catholics were largely poor and uneducated.
   c. it was seen as a strange foreign religion under total control of an authoritarian pope.
   d. they disliked the Catholic belief in the Virgin Mary as the mother of Jesus.
   e. they saw Catholic monasteries and convents buying up choice western lands.

7. Industrialization was, at first, slow to arrive in America because
   a. there was a shortage of labor, capital, and consumers.
   b. low tariff rates invited foreign imports.
   c. the country lacked the educational system necessary to develop technology.
   d. the country lacked a patent system to guarantee investors the profits from new machines.
   e. most American consumers preferred hand-crafted goods.

8. The first industry to be substantially dominated by the new factory system of mass manufacturing was the
   a. shipbuilding industry.
   b. telegraph and communications industry.
   c. agricultural implement industry.
   d. iron-making industry.
   e. textile industry.

9. Wages for most American workers rose in the early nineteenth century, *except* for the most exploited workers like
   a. immigrants and westerners.
   b. textile and transportation workers.
   c. single men and women.
   d. women and children.
   e. American Indians.

10. A major change affecting the American family in the early nineteenth century was
    a. the rise of an organized feminist movement.
    b. the movement of most women into the work force.
    c. increased conflict between parents and children over moral questions.
    d. a decline in the average number of children per household.
    e. the growing opposition to families' use of children as economic assets.

11. In early nineteenth-century America, almost all the women who worked for wages in the new factories were
    a. young and single.
    b. middle aged.
    c. Irish or German immigrants.
    d. skilled workers.
    e. exploited by their husbands as well as factory owners.

12.   The greatest economic and political impact of New York's Erie Canal was to

   a.   make upstate New York the new center of American agriculture.
   b.   delay the development of railroads by several decades.
   c.   tie the agricultural Midwest by trade to the Northeast rather than to the South.
   d.   enable southern cotton to reach New England without ocean transport.
   e.   make the Ohio and Mississippi Rivers the primary paths of inland transportation.

13.   The new regional division of labor created by improved transportation meant that the South specialized in

   a.   cotton, the West in grain and livestock, and the East in manufacturing.
   b.   manufacturing, the West in transportation, and the East in grain and livestock.
   c.   cotton, the West in manufacturing, and the East in finance.
   d.   grain and livestock, the West in cotton, and the East in transportation.
   e.   manufacturing, the West in cotton, and the East in communications.

14.   Free incorporation laws, limited liability laws, and the Supreme Court's decision prohibiting state governments from granting irrevocable charters to corporations all greatly aided

   a.   private American colleges' ability to compete with state universities.
   b.   established businesses with large capital investments.
   c.   Americans' ability to compete with cheap British imports.
   d.   more entrepreneurial enterprises and greater market competition.
   e.   European investors in American business enterprises.

15.   One major effect of industrialization was a/an

   a.   increasing economic equality among all citizens.
   b.   strengthening of the family as an economic unit.
   c.   increasingly stable labor force.
   d.   rise in ethnic tensions.
   e.   rise in the gap between rich and poor.

C. Identification

Supply the correct identification for each numbered description.

1.   _____   New York Democratic machine organization that exemplified the growing power of Irish immigrants in American politics

2.   _____   Semisecret Irish organization that became a benevolent society aiding Irish immigrants in America

3.   _____   Liberal German refugees who fled failed democratic revolutions and came to America

4.   _____   Popular nickname of the secretive, nativist American Party that gained considerable, temporary success in the 1850s by attacking immigrants and Catholics

5.   _____   The transformation of manufacturing that began in Britain about 1750

6.   _____   Whitney's invention that enhanced cotton production and gave new life to black slavery

7.   _____   Principle that permitted individual investors to risk no more capital in a business venture than their own share of a corporation's stock

8. _____ Major European exposition in 1851 that provided a dazzling showcase for the American inventions of Samuel Morse, Cyrus McCormick, and Charles Goodyear

9. _____ Massachusetts Supreme Court decision of 1842 that overturned the widespread doctrine that labor unions were illegal conspiracies in restraint of trade

10. _____ Term for the widespread nineteenth-century cultural creed that glorified women's roles as wives and mothers in the home

11. _____ Cyrus McCormick's invention that vastly increased the productivity of the American grain farmer

12. _____ The only major highway constructed by the federal government before the Civil War (either of the two names for the highway are acceptable)

13. _____ The name of Robert Fulton's first steamship that sailed up the Hudson River in 1807

14. _____ Clinton's Big Ditch that transformed transportation and economic life across the Great Lakes region from Buffalo to Chicago

15. _____ Short-lived but spectacular service that carried mail from Missouri to California in only ten days

D. Matching People, Places, and Events

Match the person, place, or event in the left column with the proper description in the right column by inserting the correct letter on the blank line.

1. ____ Samuel Slater

2. ____ Maria Monk

3. ____ Samuel Colt

4. ____ Eli Whitney

5. ____ Elias Howe

6. ____ Samuel F.B. Morse

7. ____ Catharine Beecher

8. ____ Know-Nothings

9. ____ *Commonwealth* v. *Hunt*

10. ____ Cyrus McCormick

11. ____ Robert Fulton

12. ____ Cyrus Field

13. ____ Roger Taney

14. ____ Molly Maguires

15. ____ DeWitt Clinton

a. Inventor of the mechanical reaper that transformed grain growing into a business

b. Weapons manufacturer whose popular revolver used Whitney's system of interchangeable parts

c. New York governor who built the Erie Canal

d. Inventor of a machine that revolutionized the ready-made clothing industry

e. Supreme Court justice whose ruling in the Charles River Bridge case opened chartered monopolies to competition

f. Agitators against immigrants and Roman Catholics

g. Wealthy New York manufacturer who laid the first temporary transatlantic cable in 1858

h. Escaped nun whose lurid book *Awful Disclosures* became an anti-Catholic best seller in the 1830s

i. Immigrant mechanic who initiated American industrialization by setting up his cotton-spinning factory in 1791

j. Painter turned inventor who developed the first reliable system for instant communication across distance

k. Developer of a folly that made rivers two-way streams of transportation

l. Prominent figure who helped turn teaching into a largely female profession

m. Radical, secret Irish labor union of the 1860s and 1870s

n. Yankee mechanical genius who revolutionized cotton production and created the system of interchangeable parts

o. Pioneering Massachusetts Supreme Court decision that declared labor unions legal

E. Putting Things in Order

Put the following events in correct order by numbering them from 1 to 5.

1. ___ First telegraph message—"What hath God wrought?"—is sent from Baltimore to Washington.

2. ___ Industrial revolution begins in Britain.

3. ___ Telegraph lines are stretched across Atlantic Ocean and North American continent.

4. ___ Major water transportation route connects New York City to Lake Erie and points west.

5. ___ Invention of cotton gin and system of interchangeable parts revolutionized southern agriculture and northern industry.

F. Matching Cause and Effect

Match the historical cause in the left column with the proper effect in the right column by writing the correct letter on the blank line.

Cause

1. ____ The open, rough-and-tumble society of the American West

2. ____ Natural population growth and increasing immigration from Ireland and Germany

3. ____ The poverty and Roman Catholic faith of most Irish immigrants

4. ____ Eli Whitney's invention of the cotton gin

5. ____ The passage of general incorporation and limited-liability laws

6. ____ The early efforts of labor unions to organize and strike

7. ____ Improved western transportation and the new McCormick reaper

8. ____ The completion of the Erie Canal in 1825

9. ____ The development of a strong east-west rail network

10. ____ The replacement of household production by factory-made, store-bought goods

Effect

a. Made the fast-growing United States the fourth most populous nation in the Western world

b. Opened the Great Lakes states to rapid economic growth and spurred the development of major cities

c. Encouraged western farmers to specialize in cash-crop agricultural production for eastern and European markets

d. Made Americans strongly individualistic and self-reliant

e. Aroused nativist hostility and occasional riots

f. Bound the two northern sections together across the mountains and tended to isolate the South

g. Aroused fierce opposition from businesspeople and guardians of law

h. Enabled businesspeople to create more powerful and effective joint-stock capital ventures

i. Transformed southern agriculture and gave new life to slavery

j. Weakened many women's economic status and pushed them into a separate sphere of home and family

G. Developing Historical Skills

Reading a Chart and Bar Graph

Examine the bar graph *Population Increase, Including Slaves and Indians* to learn more about the character of the American population from 1790 to 1860.

Answer the following questions.

1. Which decade showed the largest absolute increase in total population?

2. During which decade did the nonwhite population begin to *decrease* as a percentage of the total population?

3. In which census year did the nonwhite population surpass the white population of 1790?

4. Using the bar graph, indicate about how many times larger the total population was in 1860 than it had been in 1820.

H. Map Mastery

Map Discrimination

Using the maps and charts in Chapter 14, answer the following questions.

1. *Cumberland (National) Road and Main Connections*: How many states did the Cumberland Road pass through? (Do not count Missouri.)

2. *Industry and Agriculture, 1860*: Which industry developed near Philadelphia?

3. *Industry and Agriculture, 1860*: If you were a tobacco farmer, in which state would you most likely live?

4. *Principal Canals in 1840*: If you had traveled from Albany, New York, to Evansville, Indiana, which two canals and one lake would you have traversed?

5. *Principal Canals in 1840*: If you had traveled from Columbia, Pennsylvania, to Cleveland, Ohio, which two canals and one river would you have traversed?

6. *The Railroad Revolution*: In 1860, how many direct rail lines linked the North and the South west of the Appalachians?

7. *The Railroad Revolution*: Which three Midwestern states had the greatest number of rail lines in 1860?

8. *Main Routes West Before the Civil War*: If you had traveled from Independence, Missouri, to Los Angeles, California, before the Civil War, which major trails would you have traversed?

Map Challenge

Using the maps of *Erie Canal and Main Branches*, *Principal Canals in 1840*, and *The Railroad Revolution*, write a brief essay explaining the economic importance of the Erie Canal and other canals and railroads for trade between the Northeast and the Northwest.

PART III: APPLYING WHAT YOU HAVE LEARNED

1. How did the migration into a vast western frontier shape Americans' values and society in the period 1790–1860?

2. Since all white Americans were descended from European immigrants, what made the Irish and German immigration of the 1830s and 1840s so controversial. Was the crucial factor in fueling nativist hostility really religion (that is, Catholicism) and poverty rather than immigration itself?

3. What were the effects of the new factory and corporate systems of production on early industrial workers. Why were Americans relatively slow to move from their traditional agricultural and craft forms of production to industrial factory manufacturing?

4. Argue for or against: Americans' love of technology and success in inventing labor-saving devices occurred in part because skilled labor was such a scarce commodity in the United States.

5. What was the impact of the new economic developments on the role of women in society? Which women were most affected by early industrialization and which least?

6. How did the American family change in the early nineteenth century? How did these changes especially affect the place of children within the family?

7.   In America, early industrialization, westward expansion, and growing sectional tension all occurred during the first half of the nineteenth century. How were these three developments connected? Which section of the nation gained the most from the transportation and communications revolutions of the period, and which gained least?

8.   Should the rise of early American industry and the market revolution be seen as an expression of American popular democracy and the rise of mass politics (see Chapter 13), or was the Jacksonian movement toward democracy and equality in part a response to the threat that expanding capitalism posed to those core American values?

CHAPTER 15

The Ferment of Reform and Culture, 1790–1860

PART I: REVIEWING THE CHAPTER

A. Checklist of Learning Objectives

After mastering this chapter, you should be able to:

1. Describe the widespread revival of religion in the early nineteenth century and its effects on American culture and social reform.

2. Describe the cause of the most important American reform movements of the period, identifying which were most successful and why.

3. Explain the origins of American feminism, describe its essential principles, and summarize its early successes and failures.

4. Describe the utopian and communitarian experiments of the period, and indicate how they reflected the essential spirit of early American culture despite their small size.

5. Identify the most notable early American achievements in science, medicine, the visual arts, and music, and explain why advanced science and culture had difficulty taking hold on American soil.

6. Analyze the American literary flowering of the early nineteenth century, especially the transcendentalist movement, and identify the most important writers who dissented from the optimistic spirit of the time.

B. Glossary

To build your social science vocabulary, familiarize yourself with the following terms.

1. **polygamy** The practice of having two or more spouses at one time. (More specifically, **polygyny** is marriage two or more wives; **polyandry** is marriage to two or more husbands.) "Accusations of polygamy likewise arose and increased in intensity."

2. **theocracy** Literally, rule by God; the term is often applied to a state where religious leaders exercise direct or indirect political authority. ". . . the community became a prosperous frontier theocracy and a cooperative commonwealth."

3. **zealot** One who is carried away by a cause to an extreme or excessive degree. "But less patient zealots came to believe that temptation should be removed by legislation."

4. **utopian** Referring to any theoretical plan that aims to establish an ideal social order, or a place founded on such principles. "Bolstered by the utopian spirit of the age, various reformers . . . set up more than forty [cooperative] communities. . . ."

5. **communistic** Referring to the economic theory or practice in which the means of production are owned by the community as a whole. ". . . various reformers . . . set up more than forty communities of a . . . communistic nature."

6. **communitarian** Referring to the belief in or practice of the superiority of community life or values over individual life, but not necessarily the common ownership of material goods. ". . . various reformers . . . set up more than forty communities of a . . . 'communitarian' nature."

7. **free love** The principle or practice of open sexual relations unrestricted by law, marriage, or religious constraints. "It practiced free love ('complex marriage'). . . ."

8. **eugenic** Concerning the improvement of the human species through selective breeding or genetic control. "It practiced . . . the eugenic selection of parents to produce superior offspring."

9. **coitus reservatus** The practice of sexual intercourse without the male's release of semen. "It practiced . . . birth control through 'male continence' or *coitus reservatus*."

10. **classical** Specifically, in Western civilization, the culture of ancient Greece and Rome, and the artistic or cultural values presumed to be based on those ancient principles; more generally, any cultural form whose value has been established and recognized over time. "He brought a classical design to his Virginia hilltop home, Monticello. . . ."

11. **mystical** Referring to the belief in the direct apprehension of God or divine mystery, without reliance on reason or human comprehension. "These mystical doctrines of transcendentalism defied precise definition. . . ."

12. **nonconformist** One who refuses to follow established or conventional ideas or habits. "Henry David Thoreau . . . was . . . a poet, a mystic, a transcendentalist, and a nonconformist."

13. **nonviolence** The principle of resolving hostilities or managing conflict without resort to physical force. "His writings . . . inspired the development of American civil rights leader Martin Luther King, Jr.'s thinking about nonviolence."

14. **urbane** Sophisticated, elegant, cosmopolitan. "Handsome and urbane, he lived a generally serene life. . . ."

15. **providential** Under the care and direction of God or other benevolent natural or supernatural forces. ". . . he lived among cannibals, from whom he providentially escaped uneaten."

PART II: CHECKING YOUR PROGRESS

A. True-False

Where the statement is true, circle **T**; where it is false, circle **F**.

1. T F The Second Great Awakening reversed the trends toward religious indifference and rationalism of the late eighteenth century.

2. T F The religious revivals of the Second Great Awakening occurred almost entirely in rural frontier communities.

3. T F The Mormon church migrated to the Utah frontier to escape persecution and to establish its tightly organized cooperative social order without persecution.

4. T F The primary purpose for establishing taxpayer-supported free public schools was to educate all citizens for participation in democracy, without regard to wealth.

5. T F Most practical, hard-working Americans disliked highly educated intellectuals and writers like Ralph Waldo Emerson.

6. T F Many early American reformers were middle-class idealists inspired by evangelical Protestantism.

7. T F   The key role of women in American reform movements was undergirded by a growing feminization of the churches that spawned many efforts at social improvement.

8. T F   The Seneca Falls Convention of 1848 was considered most radical for issuing the demand for women's right to vote.

9. T F   Many of the prominent utopian communities of early nineteenth century involved communal ownership of property and sexual practices different from the conventional norm.

10. T F   Advances in medicine and science raised the average life expectancy of Americans to nearly 60 years by 1850.

11. T F   The Knickerbocker group of American writers sharply criticized the militant nationalism and western expansionism that followed the War of 1812.

12. T F   Although it rejected most Americans' materialism and focus on practical concerns, transcendentalism strongly reflected American individualism, love of liberty, and hostility to formal institutions and authority.

13. T F   Ralph Waldo Emerson taught the doctrines of simple living and nonviolence, while his friend Henry David Thoreau emphasized self-improvement and the development of a uniquely American scholarship.

14. T F   The works of Walt Whitman, such as *Leaves of Grass*, revealed his love of democracy, the frontier, and the common people.

15. T F   The fiction of Edgar Allan Poe and Herman Melville reflected most Americans' optimism and belief in social progress and reform.

B. Multiple Choice

Select the best answer and circle the corresponding letter.

1. The tendency toward rationalism and indifference in religion was reversed beginning about 1800 by
    a. the rise of Deism and Unitarianism.
    b. the rise of new groups like the Mormons and Christian Scientists.
    c. the revivalist movement called the Second Great Awakening.
    d. a large influx of religiously traditional immigrants.
    e. the emergence of Roman Catholicism.

2. Two denominations that became the dominant faiths among the common people of the West and South were
    a. Episcopalians and Unitarians.
    b. Congregationalists and Presbyterians.
    c. Quakers and Seventh Day Adventists
    d. Lutherans and Catholics.
    e. Methodists and Baptists.

3. Which of the following was *not* characteristic of the Second Great Awakening?
    a. Enormous revival gatherings, over several days, featuring famous evangelical preachers
    b. A movement to overcome denominational divisions through a united Christian church
    c. The spilling over of religious fervor into missionary activity and social reform
    d. The prominent role of women in sustaining the mission of the evangelical churches
    e. An intense focus on emotional, personal conversion and a democratic spiritual equality

4. Evangelical preachers like Charles Grandison Finney linked personal religious conversion to

   a. the construction of large church buildings throughout the Midwest.

   b. the expansion of American political power across the North American continent.

   c. the Christian reform of social problems in order to build the Kingdom of God on earth.

   d. the organization of effective economic development and industrialization.

   e. a call for Christians to withdraw from worldly materialism and politics.

5. The term *Burned-Over District* refers to

   a. an area where fires were used to clear land for frontier revivals.

   b. areas where Baptist and Methodist revivalists fiercely battled one another for converts.

   c. the region of western New York State that experienced especially frequent and intense revivals.

   d. the areas of Missouri and Illinois where the Mormon settlements were attacked and destroyed.

   e. the church conventions where Baptists, Methodists, and Presbyterians split over slavery.

6. The major effect of the growing slavery controversy on the churches was

   a. a major missionary effort directed at converting African American slaves.

   b. the organization of the churches to lobby for the abolition of slavery.

   c. an agreement to keep political issues like slavery out of the religious area.

   d. a prohibition on slaveowning by clergy.

   e. a split of Baptists, Methodists, and Presbyterians into separate northern and southern churches.

7. Besides their practice of polygamy, the Mormons aroused hostility from many Americans because of

   a. their cooperative economic practices that ran contrary to American economic individualism.

   b. their efforts to convert members of other denominations to Mormonism.

   c. their populous settlement in Utah , which posed the threat of a breakaway republic in the West.

   d. their practice of baptizing the dead without the permission of living relatives.

   e. the political ambitions of their leaders Joseph Smith and Brigham Young.

8. The major promoter of an effective tax-supported system of free public education for all American children was

   a. Mary Lyons.

   b. Horace Mann.

   c. Noah Webster.

   d. Susan B. Anthony.

   e. Abraham Lincoln.

9. Reformer Dorothea Dix worked for the cause of

   a. women's right to higher education and voting.

   b. international peace.

   c. better treatment of the mentally ill.

   d. temperance.

   e. antislavery.

10. One primary cause of women's subordination in nineteenth-century America was

   a. the cult of domesticity that sharply separated women's sphere of the home from that of men in the workplace.

   b. women's primary involvement in a host of causes other than that of their own rights.

   c. the higher ratio of females to males in many communities.

   d. the prohibition against women's participation in religious activities.

   e. the widespread belief that women were morally inferior to men.

11. Besides the hostility and ridicule it suffered from most men, the pre–Civil War women's movement failed to make large gains because

   a.   it was overshadowed by the larger and seemingly more urgent antislavery movement.
   b.   women were unable to establish any effective organization to advance their cause.
   c.   several prominent feminist leaders were caught up in personal and sexual scandals.
   d.   it became bogged down in pursuing trivial issues like changing women's fashions.
   e.   most ordinary women could not see any advantage to gaining equal rights.

12. Many of the American utopian experiments of the early nineteenth century focused on all of the following except for

   a.   communal economics and alternative sexual arrangements.
   b.   temperance and diet reforms.
   c.   advanced scientific and technological ways of producing and consuming.
   d.   developing small-business enterprises and advanced marketing techniques.
   e.   doctrines of reincarnation and transcendental meditation.

13. Two leading female imaginative writers who added luster to New England's literary reputation were

   a.   Sarah Orne Jewett and Kate Chopin.
   b.   Toni Morrison and Mary McCarthy.
   c.   Sarah Grimké and Susan B. Anthony.
   d.   Harriet Beecher Stowe and Abigail Adams.
   e.   Louisa May Alcott and Emily Dickinson.

14. The Knickerbocker Group of American writers included

   a.   Henry David Thoreau, Thomas Jefferson, and Susan B. Anthony.
   b.   George Bancroft, Ralph Waldo Emerson, and Herman Melville.
   c.   Washington Irving, James Fenimore Cooper, and William Cullen Bryant.
   d.   Walt Whitman, Henry Wadsworth Longfellow, and Edgar Allan Poe.
   e.   Nathaniel Hawthorne, Edith Wharton, and Henry James

15. The transcendentalist writers such as Emerson, Thoreau, and Fuller stressed the ideas of

   a.   inner truth and individual self-reliance.
   b.   political democracy and economic progress.
   c.   personal guilt and fear of death.
   d.   love of chivalry and return to the medieval past.
   e.   religious tradition and social reform.

C. Identification

Supply the correct identification for each numbered description.

1. _____   Liberal religious belief, held by many of the Founders such as Paine, Jefferson, and Franklin, that stressed rationalism and moral behavior rather than Christian revelation while retaining belief in a Supreme Being

2. _____   Religious revival that began on the frontier and swept eastward, stirring an evangelical spirit in many areas of American life

3. _____
    _____   The two religious denominations that benefited most from the evangelical revivals of the early nineteenth century

4. _____   Religious group founded by Joseph Smith that eventually established a cooperative commonwealth in Utah

5. _____   Area of western New York state where frequent, fervent religious revivals produced intense religious controversies and numerous new sects

6. _____   Memorable 1848 meeting in New York where women made an appeal based on the Declaration of Independence

7. _____   Evangelical college in Ohio that was the first institution of higher education to admit blacks and women

8. _____   Short-lived intellectual commune in Massachusetts based on "plain living and high thinking"

9. _____   Thomas Jefferson's stately self-designed home in Virginia that became a model of American architecture

10. _____   Long-lived communal religious group, founded by Mother Ann Lee, that emphasized simple living and prohibited all marriage and sexual relationships

11. _____   Philosophical and literary movement, centered in New England, that greatly influenced many American writers of the early nineteenth century

12. _____   The doctrine, promoted by American writer Henry David Thoreau in an essay of the same name, that later influenced Gandhi and Martin Luther King, Jr.

13. _____   Walt Whitman's originally shocking poetic masterpiece that embraced sexual liberation and celebrated America as a great democratic experiment

14. _____   Herman Melville's great but commercially unsuccessful novel about Captain Ahab's obsessive pursuit of a white whale

15. _____   Popular nineteenth-century musical entertainments that featured white actors and singers with painted black faces

D. Matching People, Places, and Events

Match the person, place, or event in the left column with the proper description in the right column by inserting the correct letter on the blank line.

1. ___ Dorothea Dix

2. ___ Brigham Young

3. ___ Elizabeth Cady Stanton

4. ___ Lucretia Mott

5. ___ Emily Dickinson

6. ___ Charles Grandison. Finney

7. ___ Amelia Bloomer

8. ___ John Humphrey Noyes

9. ___ Mary Lyon

10. ___ Louisa May Alcott

11. ___ James Fenimore Cooper

12. ___ Ralph Waldo Emerson

13. ___ Walt Whitman

14. ___ Edgar Allan Poe

15. ___ Herman Melville

a. Leader of a radical New York commune that practiced complex marriage and eugenic birth control

b. Bold, unconventional poet who celebrated American democracy

c. The "Mormon Moses" who led persecuted Latter-Day Saints to their promised land in Utah

d. Influential evangelical revivalist of the Second Great Awakening

e. New York writer whose romantic sea tales were more popular than his dark literary masterpiece

f. Pioneering women's educator, founder of Mount Holyoke Seminary in Massachusetts

g.   Female reformer who promoted short skirts and trousers as a replacement for highly restrictive women's clothing

h.   Second-rate poet and philosopher, but first-rate promoter of transcendentalist ideals and American culture

i.   Eccentric genius whose tales of mystery, suffering, and the supernatural departed from general American literary trends

j.   Quietly determined reformer who substantially improved conditions for the mentally ill

k.   Reclusive New England poet who wrote about love, death, and immortality

l.   Leading feminist who wrote the "Declaration of Sentiments" in 1848 and pushed for women's suffrage

m.   A leading female transcendentalist who wrote *Little Women* and other novels to help support her family

n.   Path-breaking American novelist who contrasted the natural person of the forest with the values of modern civilization

o.   Quaker women's rights advocate who also strongly supported abolition of slavery

E. Putting Things in Order

Put the following events in correct order by numbering them from 1 to 5.

1. ___   A leading New England transcendentalist appeals to American writers and thinkers to turn away from Europe and develop their own literature and culture.

2. ___   A determined reformer appeals to a New England legislature to end the cruel treatment of the insane.

3. ___   A gathering of female reformers in New York declares that the ideas of the Declaration of Independence apply to both sexes.

4. ___   Great evangelical religious revival begins in western camp meetings.

5. ___   A visionary from New York state creates a controversial new religion.

F. Matching Cause and Effect

Match the historical cause in the left column with the proper effect in the right column by writing the correct letter on the blank line.

Cause

1. ___ The Second Great Awakening
2. ___ The Mormon practice of polygamy
3. ___ Women abolitionists' anger at being ignored by male reformers
4. ___ The women's rights movement
5. ___ Unrealistic expectations and conflict within perfectionist communes
6. ___ The Knickerbocker and transcendentalist use of new American themes in their writing
7. ___ Henry David Thoreau's theory of civil disobedience
8. ___ Walt Whitman's *Leaves of Grass*
9. ___ Herman Melville's and Edgar Allan Poe's concern with evil and suffering
10. ___ The Transcendentalist movement

Effect

a. Created the first literature genuinely native to America

b. Captured, in one long poem, the exuberant and optimistic spirit of popular American democracy

c. Caused most utopian experiments to decline or collapse in a few years

d. Inspired writers like Ralph Waldo Emerson, Henry David Thoreau, and Margaret Fuller

e. Aroused hostility and scorn in most of the male press and pulpit

f. Made their works little understood in their lifetimes by generally optimistic Americans

g. Aroused persecution from morally traditionalist Americans and delayed statehood for Utah

h. Inspired a widespread spirit of evangelical reform in many areas of American life

i. Led to expanding the crusade for equal rights to include women

j. Inspired later practitioners of nonviolence like Gandhi and King

G. Developing Historical Skills

Using Primary-Source Documents

Statements from historical contemporaries often reveal fundamental conflicts over values and demonstrate the shock that occurs when new ideas emerge. The quotations, in your textbook, from the London *Saturday Review* and from Walt Whitman illustrate such opposing views. Answer the following questions.

1. What is the London *Saturday Review*'s primary objection to Whitman's poetry?

2. How does Whitman answer such criticisms?

3. How does Whitman's statement reveal the values of individualism and democracy cherished by the emerging American culture?

4. What does the quotation from *Leaves of Grass* in the text indicate about Whitman's typically American view of Europe?

PART III: APPLYING WHAT YOU HAVE LEARNED

1. What was the relationship between the evangelical revivals of the Second Great Awakening and the spread of American social reform movements and utopian ideas?

2. Why did the Second Great Awakening inspire so many new American religions and sects like Mormonism, Adventism, the Shakers, and others? In what ways were these religions an expression of general American ideals of democracy, individualism, and opportunity? In what ways were they dissenting from the general norms of nineteenth-century American religion and American life?

3. What were the greatest successes and failures of the many American reform movements of the early nineteenth century? Why did most of the reformers, and their reforms, address the ideals and goals of religious, middle-class Americans, while largely overlooking the growing problems of factory workers and cities?

4. What inspired the many utopian communities of the early nineteenth century? What issues or problems did various utopias attempt to address? Should the utopias be viewed as failures because most did not last long or attain the perfection they sought? Or should they be seen as natural, intense outgrowths of America's own utopian ideals of liberty, equality, and democracy?

5. What were the motivations and goals of the first American feminists? Why did their movement spark such fierce opposition, including from some women themselves? Why was feminism generally less successful than abolitionism before the Civil War?

6. Compare the early American achievements in the sciences with those in the arts. Which were the most successful, and why?

7. What were the major concerns of America's greatest imaginative writers in the early nineteenth century? How did most of those writers fundamentally reflect the deepest values of American culture? Would you agree that the transcendentalism of Ralph Waldo Emerson and others was an especially American philosophy?

8. Why were almost all the religious, social, and intellectual movements of the early nineteenth century so positive and optimistic about human nature and society? Was their goal of uplifting or even perfecting human character inspiring or naïve? Why did a few more critical writers like Hawthorne, Poe, and Melville dissent from this optimistic vision?

9. Which American writer or thinker would you select as the most important and insightful figure of the early nineteenth century: Ralph Waldo Emerson, Henry David Thoreau, Elizabeth Cady Stanton, or Herman Melville? Defend your choice by explaining that person's impact on American culture and society.

CHAPTER 16

The South and the Slavery Controversy, 1793–1860

PART I: REVIEWING THE CHAPTER

A. Checklist of Learning Objectives

After mastering this chapter, you should be able to:

1. Describe the economic strengths and weaknesses of the Cotton Kingdom and its central role in the prosperity of Britain as well as the United States.

2. Outline the hierarchical social structure of the South, from the planter aristocracy to African American slaves.

3. Describe the nonslaveholding white majority of the South, and explain why most poorer whites supported slavery even though they owned no slaves.

4. Describe the workings of the peculiar institution of slavery, including the role of the domestic slave trade after the outlawing of international slave trading.

5. Describe African American life under slavery, including the role of the family and religion.

6. Describe the rise of abolitionism in both the United States and Britain, and explain why it was initially so unpopular in the North.

7. Describe the fierce southern resistance to abolitionism, and explain why southerners increasingly portrayed slavery as a positive good.

B. Glossary

To build your social science vocabulary, familiarize yourself with the following terms.

1. **oligarchy** Rule by a small elite. "Before the Civil War, the South was in some respects not so much a democracy as an oligarchy. . . ."

2. **medievalism** Devotion to the social values, customs, or beliefs of the European Middle Ages, especially a fixed social hierarchy and code of honor. "Southern aristocrats . . . strove to perpetuate a type of medievalism that had died out in Europe. . . ."

3. **commission** Fee paid to an agent in a transaction, usually as a percentage of the sale. "They were pained by the heavy outward flow of commissions. . . ."

4. **middlemen** In commerce, those who stand between the producer and the retailer or consumer. "[Southern planters] were pained by the heavy outward flow . . . to northern middlemen, bankers, agents, and shippers."

5. **racism** Belief in the superiority of one race over another or behavior reflecting such a belief. "Thus did the logic of economics join with the illogic of racism in buttressing the slave system."

6. **squadron** A medium-sized military unit, especially naval or air, assigned to a specific task or purpose. "... the Royal Navy's West African Squadron seized hundreds of slave ships. ..."

7. **bankruptcy** In law, the condition of being declared unable to meet legitimate financial obligations or debts, therefore requiring special supervision by the courts. "... families were separated with distressing frequency, usually for economic reasons such as bankruptcy. ..."

8. **overseer** Someone who governs or directs the work of another. "... under the watchful eyes and ready whip-hand of a white overseer or black 'driver.' "

9. **sabotage** Intentional destruction or damage of goods, machines, or productive processes. "They sabotaged expensive equipment. ..."

10. **fratricidal** Literally, concerning the killing of brothers; the term is often applied more broadly to the killing of relatives or countrymen in feuds or civil wars. (The killing of sisters is **sororicide**; of fathers **patricide**; and of mothers **matricide**.) "... supported a frightfully costly fratricidal war as the price of emancipation."

11. **barbarism (barbarian)** The condition of being crude, uneducated, or uncivilized. "It was good for the Africans, who were lifted from the barbarism of the jungle. ..."

12. **table (tabling)** In parliamentary rules of order, the act of setting aside a resolution or law without voting or taking action, positive or negative, on the proposal itself. "It required all such antislavery appeals to be tabled without debate."

PART II: CHECKING YOUR PROGRESS

A. True-False

Where the statement is true, circle **T**; where it is false, circle **F**.

1. T F   After 1800, the prosperity of both North and South became heavily dependent on growing, manufacturing, and exporting cotton.

2. T F   The southern planter aristocracy was strongly attracted to medieval cultural ideals.

3. T F   The growing of cotton on large plantations was economically efficient and agriculturally sound.

4. T F   Most white southern women were critical of slavery because it threatened their marriage and family.

5. T F   In 1860, three-fourths of all white southerners owned no slaves at all.

6. T F   Poor whites supported slavery because it made them feel racially superior and because they hoped someday to be able to buy slaves.

7. T F   Free blacks enjoyed considerable status and wealth in both the North and the South before the Civil War.

8. T F   Despite the outlawing of the international slave trade in 1807–1808, African slaves continued to be smuggled into the United States as well as Brazil and the West Indies.

9. T F   Most slaveowners treated their black slaves as a valuable economic investment.

10. T F   Slavery almost completely destroyed the black family.

11. T F   The *Amistad* uprising of 1839 was the most successful rebellion by American slaves in the South before the Civil War.

12. T   F   The greatest opposition to abolitionism in the North and Britain came from evangelical Christians.

13. T   F   The most prominent black abolitionist, Frederick Douglass, supported William Lloyd Garrison's absolutist principles and refusal to seek a political solution to the sin of slavery.

14. T   F   After about 1830, all criticism of slavery was suppressed in the South, including a prohibition of delivery of abolitionist materials through the U.S. mail.

15. T   F   By 1860, most northerners had come to agree with the abolitionists that slavery was an evil to be immediately abolished.

B. Multiple Choice

Select the best answer and circle the corresponding letter.

1. By 1840, cotton had become central to the whole American economy because
    a. the United States was still largely an agricultural nation.
    b. cotton exports provided much of the capital that fueled American economic growth.
    c. the North became the largest market for southern cotton production.
    d. western expansion depended on continually increasing the acreage devoted to cotton.
    e. northern agricultural products like wheat and corn could not be grown for a profit.

2. A large portion of the profits from the South's cotton growing went to
    a. northern traders and European cloth manufacturers.
    b. southern and northern slave traders.
    c. southern textile industrialists.
    d. Midwestern farmers and cattlemen.
    e. small cotton growers.

3. Which of the following was *not* characteristic of the few thousand wealthiest southern plantation owners holding a hundred or more slaves?
    a. They promoted the ideals of feudal, hierarchical medieval Europe.
    b. They provided their children with elite private educations in Europe or the North.
    c. They controlled a large proportion of the wealth and power of the entire South.
    d. They felt a large sense of public obligation to pursue education and statecraft.
    e. They did not permit their wives to have any role in managing their slaves and plantations.

4. Most southern slaveowners held
    a. over a hundred slaves.
    b. over fifty slaves.
    c. about twenty slaves.
    d. fewer than ten slaves.
    e. only one slave.

5. Even though they owned no slaves, most southern whites strongly supported the slave system because they
    a. were bribed by the planter class.
    b. enjoyed the economic benefits of slavery.
    c. felt racially superior to blacks and hoped to be able to buy slaves.
    d. disliked the northern abolitionists.
    e. accepted the idea that slavery was approved in the Bible.

6.   The only group of white southerners who hated both slaveowners and blacks were

   a.   poor southern whites in the frontier areas of Texas and Arkansas.
   b.   urban merchants and manufacturers.
   c.   religious leaders.
   d.   Appalachian mountain whites.
   e.   women.

7.   The condition of the 500,000 or so free blacks was

   a.   considerably better in the North than in the South.
   b.   notably improving in the decades before the Civil War.
   c.   causing a majority of them to favor emigration to Africa or the West Indies.
   d.   politically threatened but economically secure.
   e.   as bad or worse in the North than in the South.

8.   One major consequence of the outlawing of the international slave trade by Britain and the United States was

   a.   a boom in slave trading inside the United States.
   b.   a complete end to the importation of any slaves from African into the United States.
   c.   a decline in the growth of the American slave population.
   d.   slaveowners' growing support for black family life so that natural reproduction would increase.
   e.   a movement to end the domestic U.S. slave trade as well.

9.   Most slaveowners treated their slaves as

   a.   objects to be beaten and brutalized as often as possible.
   b.   economically profitable investments.
   c.   members of their extended family.
   d.   potential converts to evangelical Christianity.
   e.   sexual objects.

10. The African American family under slavery was

   a.   generally stable and mutually supportive.
   b.   almost nonexistent.
   c.   largely female-dominated.
   d.   seldom able to raise children to adulthood.
   e.   more stable on the small farms of the upper South than on large plantations.

11. Most of the early abolitionists were motivated by

   a.   a desire to send African Americans back to Africa.
   b.   anger at the negative economic impact of slavery on poorer whites.
   c.   a belief that slavery violated the Declaration of Independence and the Constitution.
   d.   a philosophical commitment to racial equality.
   e.   religious feeling against the sin of slavery.

12. Frederick Douglass and some other black and white abolitionists sought to end slavery by

   a.   encouraging slave rebellions in the South.
   b.   calling on the North to secede from the Union and invade the South.
   c.   getting northern churches to condemn the sin of slavery.
   d.   promoting antislavery political movements like the Free Soil and Republican parties.
   e.   promoting education and economic opportunity for free blacks.

13. The last open debate inside the South regarding proposals to gradually abolish slavery occurred in

   a. southern colleges in the 1830s.
   b. the Southern Baptist Convention in 1850.
   c. the Tennessee Appalachian Mountain areas in 1840–1841.
   d. the Virginia state legislature in 1830–1831.
   e. the Texas state legislature in 1848–1850.

14. The northern political leader who successfully defended the *Amistad* slave rebels and overturned the Gag Resolution in Congress was

   a. congressman and former president John Quincy Adams.
   b. black abolitionist leader Frederick Douglass.
   c. Senator Daniel Webster.
   d. religious revivalist Theodore Dwight Weld.
   e. Illinois state legislator and congressman Abraham Lincoln.

15. By the 1850s, most northerners could be described as

   a. opposed to slavery but also hostile to immediate abolitionists.
   b. fervently in favor of immediate abolition.
   c. sympathetic to white southern arguments in defense of slavery.
   d. eager to let the slaveholding South break apart the Union.
   e. hostile to the slave trade but tolerant of slavery.

C. Identification

Supply the correct identification for each numbered description.

1. _____ Term for the ante-bellum South that emphasized its economic dependence on a single staple product

2. _____ British naval unit that seized hundreds of slave ships in the process of suppressing the illegal slave trade in the early 1800s

3. _____ Harriet Beecher Stowe's powerful 1852 novel that focused on slavery's cruel effects in separating black family members from one another

4. _____ The fertile region of the Deep South, stretching across Alabama, Mississippi, and Louisiana, where the largest concentration of black slaves worked on rich cotton plantations

5. _____ Spanish slave ship, seized by revolting African slaves, that led to a dramatic U.S. Supreme Court case that freed the slaves.

6. _____ Theodore Dwight Weld's powerful antislavery book

7. _____ Organization founded in 1817 to transport American blacks back to Africa

8. _____ African republic founded by freed American slaves in 1822

9. _____ The group of theology students, led by Theodore Dwight Weld, who were expelled from their seminary for abolitionist activity and later became leading preachers of the anti-slavery gospel

10. _____ William Lloyd Garrison's fervent abolitionist newspaper that preached an immediate end to slavery

11. _____ Garrisonian abolitionist organization, founded in 1833, that included the eloquent Wendell Phillips among its leaders

12. _____ Classic autobiography written by the leading African American abolitionist,

13. _____ The line across the southern boundary of Pennsylvania that formed the boundary between free states and slave states in the East

14. _____ Strict rule passed by pro-southern Congressmen in 1836 to prohibit all discussion of slavery in the House of Representatives

15. _____ Northern antislavery politicians, like Abraham Lincoln, who rejected radical immediate abolitionism, but fought to prohibit the expansion of slavery in the western territories

D. Matching People, Places, and Events

Match the person, place, or event in the left column with the proper description in the right column by inserting the correct letter on the blank line.

1. ___ Eli Whitney

2. ___ Harriet Beecher Stowe

3. ___ Nat Turner

4. ___ William Wilberforce

5. ___ Theodore Dwight Weld

6. ___ Wendell Phillips

7. ___ Denmark Vesey

8. ___ William Lloyd Garrison

9. ___ David Walker

10. ___ Sojourner Truth

11. ___ Martin Delany

12. ___ Frederick Douglass

13. ___ Lewis Tappan

14. ___ John Quincy Adams

15. ___ Elijah Lovejoy

a. New England patrician and Garrison follower whose eloquent attacks on slavery earned him the title "abolition's golden trumpet"

b. Visionary black preacher whose bloody slave rebellion in 1831 tightened the reins of slavery in the South

c. Free black whose failed attempt to lead a slave revolt in Charleston, South Carolina, led to the execution of more than thirty of his followers

d. New York free black woman who fought for emancipation and women's rights

e. Leading radical abolitionist who burned the Constitution as "a covenant with death and an agreement with hell"

f. Author of an abolitionist novel that portrayed the separation of slave families by auction

g. Wealthy New York abolitionist merchant whose home was ransacked by a proslavery mob in 1834

h. Inventor of a machine for extracting seeds from cotton that revolutionized the southern economy

i. Black abolitionist who visited West Africa in 1859 to examine sites where African Americans might relocate

j. Former president who won the *Amistad* rebellious slaves' freedom and fought for the right to discuss slavery in Congress

k. Illinois editor whose death at the hands of a mob made him an abolitionist martyr

l. British evangelical Christian reformer who in 1833 achieved the emancipation of slaves in the British West Indies

m. Escaped slave and great black abolitionist who fought to end slavery through political action

n. Black abolitionist writer who called for a bloody end to slavery in an appeal of 1829

o. Leader of the Lane Rebels who wrote the powerful antislavery work *American Slavery As It Is*

E. Putting Things in Order

Put the following events in correct order by numbering them from 1 to 5.

1. ___   The last slaves to be legally imported from Africa enter the United States.

2. ___   A radical abolitionist editor is murdered, and so becomes a martyr to the antislavery cause.

3. ___   A radical abolitionist newspaper and a slave rebellion spread fear through the South.

4. ___   A new invention increases the efficiency of cotton production, laying the basis for the vast Cotton Kingdom.

5. ___   A group of seminary students expelled for their abolitionist views spread the antislavery gospel far and wide.

F. Matching Cause and Effect

Match the historical cause in the left column with the proper effect in the right column by writing the correct letter on the blank line.

Cause		**Effect**	
1. ___	Whitney's cotton gin and southern frontier expansionism	a.	Often resulted in the cruel separation of black families
2. ___	Excessive soil cultivation and financial speculation	b.	Kept poor, nonslaveholding whites committed to a system that actually harmed them
3. ___	Belief in white superiority and the hope of owning slaves	c.	Aroused deep fears of rebellion and ended rational discussion of slavery in the South
4. ___	The selling of slaves at auctions	d.	Made abolitionists personally unpopular but convinced many Northerners that slavery was a threat to American

freedom

5. ___ The slaves' love of freedom and hatred of their condition

6. ___ The religious fervor of the Second Great Awakening

7. ___ Politically minded abolitionists like Frederick Douglass

8. ___ Garrison's *Liberator* and Nat Turner's bloody slave rebellion

9. ___ White southern defenses of slavery as a positive good

10. ___ The constant abolitionist agitation in the North

e. Caused slaves to work slowly, steal from their masters, and frequently run away

f. Stirred a fervent abolitionist commitment to fight the sin of slavery

g. Turned the South into a booming one-crop economy where "cotton was king"

h. Opposed Garrison and organized the Liberty party and the Free Soil party

i. Created dangerous weaknesses beneath the surface prosperity of the southern cotton economy

j. Widened the moral and political gap between the white South and the rest of the Western world

G. Developing Historical Skills

Visual Images and Slavery

The bitter controversy over slavery is reflected in the visual images (drawings, prints, photographs) of the peculiar institution. Some images present slavery from an abolitionist viewpoint, as a moral horror. Others depict it in benign or even favorable terms. Examine the following photos or illustrations in this chapter: 1) A Market in People; 2) A Slave Auction; 3) The Cruelty of Slavery; 4) Slave Nurse and Young White Master; 5) Slaves Being Marched from Staunton, Virginia, to Tennessee; 6) Am I Not a Man and a Brother. Am I Not a Woman and a Sister?; and 7) In Defense of Slavery. Then answer the following questions.

1. Which five images plainly depict negative features of the slave system? Which visual details point to the mistreatment of the slaves?

2. How does the image, In Defense of Slavery, present the peculiar institution in a positive light. What are the visual points of contrast with the condition of British workers?

3. The photograph of Slave Nurse and Young White Master seems neither directly "proslavery" nor "antislavery." How might supporters or opponents of slavery each interpret this image of a slave nanny with a white child?

H. Map Mastery

Map Discrimination

Using the maps and charts in Chapter 16, answer the following questions.

1. *Southern Cotton Production, 1860*: Which six states contained nearly all the major cotton-production areas of the South in 1860?

2. *Slaveowning Families, 1850*: Approximately how many slaveowning families owned fifty or more slaves?

3. *Distribution of Slaves, 1820*: Which five states contained a substantial number of slave-majority counties in 1820?

4. *Distribution of Slaves, 1860*: List the six slaveholding states, not counting Texas and Florida, that contained the most counties with less than 10 percent slaves in 1860.

Map Challenge

Using the maps of *Southern Cotton Production, 1820, Southern Cotton Production, 1860, Distribution of Slaves, 1820*, and *Distribution of Slaves, 1860*, write a brief essay explaining the relation between the areas of cotton production and the areas with the heaviest concentration of slaves in 1820 and 1860. Include some discussion of why Virginia and the Carolinas had substantial areas with more than 50 percent slaves but almost no major cotton-production areas.

PART III: APPLYING WHAT YOU HAVE LEARNED

1. Describe the complex structure of southern society. How was the wealth and status of plantation owners, small slaveholders, independent white farmers, poor whites, free blacks, and black slaves each fundamentally shaped by the peculiar institution of slavery?

2. Compare the attitudes and practices regarding slavery and race relations in the North and the South. Were northerners, at bottom, any more or less racist in their attitudes toward blacks than southern whites.

3. How did the reliance on cotton production and slavery affect the South economically, socially, and morally, and how did this reliance affect its relations with the North?

4. How did slavery affect the lives of African Americans in both the South and the North?

5. A large majority of Americans, both North and South, strongly rejected radical abolitionism. How, then, was radical abolitionism able to transform the public atmosphere regarding slavery, creating fierce sectional polarization around the issue by the 1850s?

6. In what ways did slavery make the South a fundamentally different kind of society from the North? In suppressing debate and free speech and declaring slavery to be a positive good and a great achievement, was the South really turning against the American Revolutionary heritage of freedom and equality in favor of a medieval ideal of hierarchy and inequality?

7. If you had been an ordinary northern citizen in the 1830s or 1840s, what would you have proposed to do about the Central American problem of slavery, and why? Would either William Lloyd Garrison's radical abolitionism or Frederick Douglass's political abolitionism or Abraham Lincoln's free soil doctrine have appealed to you. Why or why not?

CHAPTER 17

Manifest Destiny and Its Legacy, 1841–1848

PART I: REVIEWING THE CHAPTER

A. Checklist of Learning Objectives

After mastering this chapter, you should be able to:

1. Explain the spirit and meaning of the Manifest Destiny that inspired American expansionism in the 1840s.

2. Outline the major conflicts between Britain and the United States over debts, Maine, Canada, Texas, Oregon, and growing British hostility to slavery.

3. Explain why the U.S. government increasingly saw the independent Texas Republic as a threat and sought to pursue annexation.

4. Indicate how the issues of Oregon and Texas became central in the election of 1844 and why Polk's victory was seen as a mandate for Manifest Destiny.

5. Explain how President Polk's goals for his administration, especially the acquisition of California, led to the Texas boundary crisis and war with Mexico.

6. Describe how the dramatic American victory in the Mexican War led to the breathtaking territorial acquisition of the whole Southwest.

7. Describe the consequences of the Mexican War, and especially how the Mexican territorial acquisitions explosively opened the slavery question.

B. Glossary

To build your social science vocabulary, familiarize yourself with the following terms.

1. **caucus** An unofficial organization or consultation of like-minded people to plan a political course or advance their cause, often within some larger body. " . . . the stiff-necked Virginian was formally expelled from his party by a caucus of Whig congressmen. . . ."

2. **royalty** The payments to an inventor, author, composer, and so on, usually as a percentage of the sales or profits from their work. ". . . they were being denied rich royalties by the absence of an American copyright law."

3. **default** To fail to pay a loan or interest due. ". . . several states defaulted on their bonds. . . ."

4. **repudiate** To refuse to accept responsibility for paying a bill or debt. "When . . . several states . . . repudiated [their bonds] openly, honest English citizens assailed Yankee trickery."

5. **protectorate** The relation of a strong nation to a weaker political entity, which comes under its control and protection but still retains elements of autonomy; a **colony** is a territory under direct ownership or control of the imperial power. ". . . Texas was driven to open negotiations . . . in the hope of securing the defensive shield of a protectorate."

6. **colossus** In politics, an entity of extraordinary size and power. "Such a republic would check the southward surge of the American colossus. . . ."

7. **resolution** In government, a formal statement of policy or judgment by a legislature, but requiring no legal statute. "He therefore arranged for annexation by a joint resolution."

8. **intrigue** A plot or scheme formed by secret, underhanded means. ". . . the Lone Star Republic had become a danger spot, inviting foreign intrigue that menaced the American people."

9. **parallel** In geography, the imaginary east-west lines, parallel to the earth's equator, marking latitude. **Meridians** are the imaginary north-south lines, marking longitude on the globe. " . . . the United States had sought to divide the vast domain at the forty-ninth parallel."

10. **deadlock** To completely block or stop action as a consequence of the mutual pressure of equal and opposed forces. "The Democrats, meeting later in the same city, seemed hopelessly deadlocked."

11. **dark horse** In politics, a candidate with little apparent support who unexpectedly wins a nomination or election. "Polk may have been a dark horse, but he was hardly an unknown or decrepit nag."

12. **mandate** In politics, the belief that an official has been issued a clear charge by the electorate to pursue some particular policy goal. "Land-hungry Democrats . . . proclaimed that they had received a mandate from the voters to take Texas."

13. **platform** The campaign document stating a party's or candidate's position on the issues, and upon which they "stand" for election. "Polk . . . had no intention of insisting on the . . . pledge of his own platform."

14. **no-man's-land** A territory to which neither of two disputing parties has clear claim and where they may meet as combatants. ". . . Polk was careful to keep American troops out of virtually all of the explosive no-man's-land between the Nueces and the Rio Grande. . . ."

15. **indemnity** A repayment for loss or damage inflicted. "Victors rarely pay an indemnity. . . ."

PART II: CHECKING YOUR PROGRESS

A. True-False

Where the statement is true, circle **T**; where it is false, circle **F**.

1. T F   After President Harrison's death, Vice President John Tyler carried on the strong Whig policies of party leaders like Clay and Webster.

2. T F   By the 1840s, American relations with British Canada were largely peaceful.

3. T F   The Aroostook War, over the Maine boundary, was settled by a territorial compromise in the Webster-Ashburton Treaty.

4. T F   A primary motive driving Americans to annex Texas was fear that the Lone Star Republic would become an ally or protectorate of Britain.

5. T F   Texas was annexed by a simple majority resolution of both houses of Congress because the two-thirds vote necessary for a treaty of annexation could not be obtained in the Senate.

6. T F   The British claim to the disputed Oregon country was considerably strengthened by the thousands of British settlers in the region supported by the Hudson's Bay Company.

7. T F In the election of 1844, Clay lost to Polk partly because he tried to straddle the Texas annexation issue and thus lost antislavery support.

8. T F Polk's victory in the election of 1844 was interpreted as a mandate for Manifest Destiny and led directly to the annexation of Texas and a favorable settlement of the Oregon dispute.

9. T F President Polk proved unable to implement his four-point program for his presidency because of strong opposition from anti-imperialist Whigs.

10. T F The immediate cause of the Mexican War was an attempt by Mexico to reconquer Texas.

11. T F Polk's primary objective in fighting the Mexican War was to obtain California for the United States.

12. T F The overwhelming American military victory over Mexico led some expansionist Americans to call for the United States to take over all of Mexico.

13. T F The Treaty of Guadalupe Hidalgo added Texas to the territory of the United States.

14. T F The outcome of the Mexican War became a source of continuing bad feeling between the United States and much of Latin America.

15. T F The Wilmot Proviso prohibiting slavery in territory acquired from Mexico enabled the slavery issue to be temporarily removed from national politics.

B. Multiple Choice

Select the best answer and circle the corresponding letter.

1. The conflict between President Tyler and Whig leaders like Henry Clay took place over issues of

   a. slavery and expansion.
   b. banking and tariff policy.
   c. foreign policy.
   d. agriculture and transportation policy.
   e. Whig party leadership and patronage.

2. Among the major sources of the tension between Britain and the United States in the 1840s was

   a. American involvement in Canadian rebellions and border disputes.
   b. British support for American abolitionists.
   c. American anger at British default on canal and railroad loans.
   d. American intervention in the British West Indies.
   e. American involvement in the prohibited international slave trade.

3. The Aroostook War involved a

   a. battle between American and French fishermen over Newfoundland fishing rights.
   b. conflict over fugitive slaves escaping across the Canadian border.
   c. battle between British and American sailors over impressment.
   d. battle between Americans and Mexicans over the western boundary of Louisiana.
   e. battle between American and Canadian lumberjacks over the northern Maine boundary.

4. During the early 1840s, Texas maintained its independence by

   a. waging constant small-scale wars with Mexico.
   b. refusing to sign treaties with any outside powers.
   c. relying on the military power of the United States.
   d. establishing friendly relations with Britain and other European powers.
   e. declaring absolute neutrality in the conflicts between the United States, Britain, and Mexico.

5. Which of the following was *not* among the reasons why Britain strongly supported an independent Texas?

    a. Britain was interested in eventually incorporating Texas into the British Empire.
    b. British abolitionists hoped to make Texas an antislavery bastion.
    c. British manufacturers looked to Texas as a way to reduce their dependence on American cotton.
    d. A puppet Texas nation could be used to check the power of the United States.
    e. An independent Texas would provide a shield for European powers to re-enter the Americas and overturn the Monroe Doctrine.

6. Texas was finally admitted to the Union in 1844 as a result of

    a. the Mexican War.
    b. the Texans' willingness to abandon slavery.
    c. an agreement that Texas would eventually be divided into five smaller states.
    d. a compromise agreement with Britain.
    e. President Tyler's interpretation of the election of 1844 as a mandate to acquire Texas.

7. Manifest Destiny represented the widespread nineteenth-century American belief that

    a. Americans were destined to uphold democracy and freedom.
    b. the irrepressible conflict over slavery was destined to result in a Civil War.
    c. Mexico was destined to be acquired by the United States.
    d. the American Indians were doomed to disappear as white settlement advanced.
    e. God had destined the United States to expand across the whole North American continent.

8. The British finally agreed to concede to the United States the disputed Oregon territory between the Columbia River and the forty-ninth parallel because

    a. they did not really want to fight a war over territory that American settlers might overrun.
    b. they recognized that the Lewis and Clark expedition has established America's prior claim to the territory.
    c. they determined that their own harbors at Vancouver and Victoria, British Columbia, were superior to those on Puget Sound.
    d. the Americans had concentrated superior military and naval forces in the region.
    e. the Hudson's Bay Company no longer considered the area economically valuable.

9. Henry Clay lost the election of 1844 to James Polk primarily because

    a. his attempt to straddle the Texas annexation issue lost him votes to the antislavery Liberty party in New York.
    b. his strong stand for expansion in Texas and Oregon raised fears of war with Britain.
    c. he supported lower tariffs and an independent Treasury system.
    d. he lacked experience in presidential politics.
    e. Polk persuaded voters that Clay would not aggressively seek to acquire California for the United States.

10. The direct cause of the Mexican War was

    a. American refusal to pay Mexican claims for damages caused by the Texas war for independence.
    b. Mexico's refusal to sell California to the United States.
    c. Mexican support for the antislavery movement in Texas.
    d. American determination to conquer and annex northern Mexico.
    e. Mexican anger at American discrimination against Latinos in Texas.

11.   President Polk was especially determined that the United States must acquire San Francisco from Mexico because

    a.   it was the most strategic fort on the entire Pacific Coast.

    b.   it was the home of most of the American settlers in Mexican California.

    c.   the discovery of gold in California meant that San Francisco would be the gateway to the gold fields.

    d.   the harbor of San Francisco Bay was considered the crucial gateway to the entire Pacific Ocean.

    e.   the Franciscan Catholic missionaries there were using it as a base to counteract American Protestant missions in Oregon.

12.   The phrase "spot resolutions" refers to

    a.   President Polk's message asking Congress to declare war on Mexico on the spot.

    b.   the amendment introduced after the Mexican War declaring that not one new spot of land could be opened to slavery.

    c.   Congressman Abraham Lincoln's resolution demanding that President Polk specify the exact spot, on American soil, where American blood had supposedly been shed.

    d.   the congressional act determining which spots of Mexican land should be ceded to the United States.

    e.   Congress's resolution declaring that the key spot America should seize from Mexico was San Francisco Bay.

13.   The brilliant American military campaign that finally captured Mexico City was commanded by General

    a.   Stephen W. Kearny.

    b.   John C. Frémont.

    c.   Zachary Taylor.

    d.   Robert E. Lee.

    e.   Winfield Scott.

14.   The Treaty of Guadalupe Hidalgo ending the Mexican War provided for

    a.   a return to the status quo that had existed before the war.

    b.   the eventual American acquisition of all of Mexico.

    c.   American acquisition of about half of Mexico and payment of several million dollars in compensation.

    d.   the acquisition of California and joint U.S.-Mexican control of Arizona and New Mexico.

    e.   American guarantees of fair treatment for the Mexican citizens annexed by the United States.

15.   The major domestic consequence of the Mexican War was

    a.   the decline of the Democratic party.

    b.   a sharp revival of the issue of slavery.

    c.   a large influx of Mexican immigrants into the southwestern United States.

    d.   a significant increase in taxes to pay the costs of the war.

    e.   a public revulsion against the doctrines of Manifest Destiny and expansionism.

C. Identification

Supply the correct identification for each numbered description.

1.   _____   American ship involved in supplying Canadian rebels that was sunk by British forces, sparking an international crisis between Britain and the United States

2.   _____   Outbreak of fighting between American and Canadian lumberjacks over disputed Maine boundary

3. _____ Antislavery Whigs who strongly opposed the annexation of Texas as a conspiracy by the slave power

4. _____ Northern boundary of Oregon territory jointly occupied with Britain, advocated by Democratic party and others as the desired line of American expansion

5. _____ Two-thousand-mile-long path along which thousands of Americans journeyed to the Willamette Valley in the 1840s

6. _____ The widespread American belief that God had ordained the United States to occupy all the territory of North America

7. _____ Small antislavery party that took enough votes from Henry Clay to cost him the election of 1844

8. _____ Reduced tariff law sponsored by President Polk's secretary of the Treasury that produced substantial revenue and bolstered the U.S. economy

9. _____ Rich Mexican province that Polk was determined to buy and Mexico refused to sell

10. _____ River that Mexico claimed as the Texas-Mexico boundary, crossed by Taylor's troops in 1846

11. _____ Resolution offered by Congressman Abraham Lincoln demanding to know the precise location where Mexicans had allegedly shed American blood on American soil

12. _____ Short-lived West Coast republic proclaimed by American rebels against Mexican rule just before the arrival of U.S. troops in the province

13. _____ Site of major victory by American troops under Zachary Taylor over Mexican troops under Santa Anna.

14. _____ Treaty ending Mexican War and granting vast territories to the United States

15. _____ Controversial amendment, which passed the House but not the Senate, stipulating that slavery should be forbidden in all territory acquired from Mexico

D. Matching People, Places, and Events

Match the person, place, or event in the left column with the proper description in the right column by inserting the correct letter on the blank line.

1. ___ John Tyler

2. ___ Henry Clay

3. ___ Aroostook War

4. ___ Daniel Webster

5. ___ Texas

6. ___ Oregon

7. ___ James K. Polk

8. ___ John C. Fremont

9. ___ Abraham Lincoln

a. Congressional author of the spot resolutions criticizing the Mexican War

b. "Old Fuss and Feathers," whose conquest of Mexico City brought U.S. victory in the Mexican War

c. Leader of Senate Whigs and unsuccessful presidential candidate against Polk in 1844

d. Long-winded American diplomat who negotiated the Treaty of Guadalupe Hidalgo

10. ___ Rio Grande

11. ___ Zachary Taylor

12. ___ Winfield Scott

13. ___ Santa Anna

14. ___ Nicholas Trist

15. ___ David Wilmot

e. Whig leader and secretary of state who negotiated an end to Maine boundary dispute in 1842

f. Claimed by United States as southern boundary of Texas

g. Dashing explorer/adventurer who led the overthrow of Mexican rule in California after war broke out

h. Clash between Canadians and Americans over disputed timber country

i. Mexican military leader who failed to stop humiliating American invasion of his country

j. Independent nation that was the object of British, Mexican, and French scheming in the early 1840s

k. American military hero who invaded northern Mexico from Texas in 1846–1847

l. Congressional author of resolution forbidding slavery in territory acquired from Mexico

m. Dark-horse presidential winner in 1844 who effectively carried out ambitious expansionist campaign plans

n. Northwestern territory in dispute between Britain and United States, subject of Manifest Destiny rhetoric in 1844

o. Leader elected vice president on the Whig ticket who spent most of his presidency in bitter feuds with his fellow Whigs

E. Putting Things in Order

Put the following events in correct order by numbering them from 1 to 5.

1. ___ United States ends a long courtship by incorporating an independent republic that had once been part of Mexico.

2. ___ The first American president to die in office is succeeded by his controversial vice president.

3. ___ A treaty adding vast territory to the United States is hastily pushed through the Senate.

4. ___ American and Mexican troops clash in disputed border territory, leading to a controversial declaration of war.

5. ___ An ambitious "dark horse" wins an election against an opponent trapped by the Texas annexation issue.

F. Matching Cause and Effect

Match the historical cause in the left column with the proper effect in the right column by writing the correct letter on the blank line.

Cause	**Effect**
1. ___ Tyler's refusal to carry out his own Whig party's policies	a. Thwarted a growing movement calling for the United States to annex all of Mexico
2. ___ Strong American hostility to Britain	b. Enabled the United States to take vast territories in the Treaty of Guadalupe Hidalgo
3. ___ British support for the Texas Republic	c. Helped lead to a controversial confrontation with Mexico along the Texas border
4. ___ Rapidly growing American settlement in Oregon	d. Increased American determination to annex Texas
5. ___ The upsurge of Manifest Destiny in the 1840s	e. Split the Whigs and caused the entire cabinet except Webster to resign
6. ___ Clay's unsuccessful attempts to straddle the Texas issue	f. Heated up the slavery controversy between North and South
7. ___ Polk's frustration at Mexico's refusal to sell California	g. Sparked bitter feuds over Canadian rebels, the boundaries of Maine and Oregon, and other issues
8. ___ The overwhelming American military victory over Mexico	h. Turned antislavery voters to the Liberty party and helped elect the expansionist Polk
9. ___ The rapid Senate ratification of the Treaty of Guadalupe Hidalgo	i. Created widespread popular support for Polk's expansionist policies on Texas, Oregon, and California
10. ___ The Wilmot Proviso	j. Strengthened American claims to the Columbia River country and made Britain more willing to compromise

G. Developing Historical Skills

Reading Maps for Routes

Historical maps often include the routes taken in connection with particular events. The map of the *Major Campaigns of the Mexican War* includes a number of such routes. Answer the following questions.

1. Near what Mexican port city did both General Taylor and General Scott pass?

2.   From which city (and battle site) did American forces move both west to California and south toward Buena Vista?

3.   According to the map, where did American naval forces come from? Where did they go during the course of the war? Where were they involved in battles?

4.   Across what territories did Kearny and Frémont pass during the war? In which significant battles did each of them take part?

H. Map Mastery

Map Discrimination

Using the maps and charts in Chapter 17, answer the following questions.

1.   *Maine Boundary Settlement, 1842*: The Webster-Ashburton Treaty line settled the boundary between the American state of Maine and which two Canadian provinces?

2.   *The Oregon Controversy, 1846*: The part of the Oregon Country that was in dispute between the United States and Britain lay between what two boundaries?

3.   *The Oregon Controversy, 1846*: How many degrees and minutes (°, ′) of latitude were there between the northern and southern boundaries of the *whole* Oregon Country?

4.   *Major Campaigns of the Mexican War*: Which major western river did Stephen Kearney have to cross on his route from Santa Fe to the Battle of San Pasquial in December 1846?

5.   *Major Campaigns of the Mexican War*: Name any three of the cities within present-day Mexico that were occupied by the armies of generals Taylor or Scott.

Map Challenge

Using the map of *Major Campaigns of the Mexican War*, write a brief essay explaining the relation between the movement of American military forces during the war and the political issues of the Mexican War.

PART III: APPLYING WHAT YOU HAVE LEARNED

1.   What led to the rise of the spirit of Manifest Destiny in the 1840s, and how did that spirit show itself in the American expansionism of the decade?

2.   How did rivalry with Britain affect the American decision to annex Texas, the Oregon dispute, and other controversies of the 1840s?

3.   Most Americans believed that expansion across North America was their destiny. Was expansion actually inevitable? What forces might have stopped it? How would American history have changed if, say, the Mexican War had not occurred?

4.   Could the United States have accepted a permanently independent Texas? Why or why not?

5.   Did James Polk really receive a mandate for expansion in the election of 1844?

6.   Did Polk deliberately provoke the Mexican War, as Congressman Abraham Lincoln charged? Or was the war largely inevitable given U.S.-Mexican tensions following the annexation of Texas?

7.   How was the Manifest Destiny of the 1840s—particularly the expansion into Texas and Mexico—related to the sectional conflict over slavery?

8.   Many conscience Whigs and others believed that the annexation of Texas and the Mexican War itself were part of a conspiracy by the slave power to expand slavery and guarantee its future in the United States. Is there any evidence to suggest such goals on the part of Polk or others?

9.   Why was the Wilmot Proviso proposal, prohibiting slavery in the whole territory acquired from Mexico, so divisive and explosive? Was it intended to reignite sectional controversy or actually to defuse it?

CHAPTER 18

Renewing the Sectional Struggle, 1848–1854

PART I: REVIEWING THE CHAPTER

A. Checklist of Learning Objectives

After mastering this chapter, you should be able to:

1.   Explain how the issue of slavery in the territories acquired from Mexico disrupted American politics from 1848 to1850.

2.   Point out the major terms of the Compromise of 1850 and indicate how this agreement attempted to defuse the sectional crisis over slavery.

3.   Explain why the Fugitive Slave Law included in the Compromise of 1850 stirred moral outrage and fueled antislavery agitation in the North.

4.   Indicate how the Whig party's disintegration over slavery signaled the end of nonsectional political parties.

5.   Describe how the Pierce administration, as well as private American adventurers, pursued numerous overseas and expansionist ventures primarily designed to expand slavery.

6.   Describe Americans' first ventures into China and Japan in the 1850s and their diplomatic, economic, cultural, and religious consequences.

7.   Describe the nature and purpose of Douglas's Kansas-Nebraska Act, and explain why it fiercely rekindled the slavery controversy that the Compromise of 1850 had been designed to settle.

B. Glossary

To build your social science vocabulary, familiarize yourself with the following terms.

1.   **self-determination** In politics, the right of a people to assert its own national identity and determine its own form of government without outside influence. "The public liked it because it accorded with the democratic tradition of self-determination."

2.   **homestead** A family home or farm with buildings and land sufficient for survival. ". . . they broadened their appeal . . . by urging free government homesteads for settlers."

3.   **vigilante** Concerning self-appointed groups that claim to punish crime and maintain order without legal authority to do so. ". . . violence was only partly discouraged by rough vigilante justice."

4.   **sanctuary** A place of refuge or protection, where people are made safe from punishment by the law. ". . . scores of . . . runaway slaves . . . were spirited . . . to the free-soil sanctuary of Canada."

5.   **fugitive** A person who flees from danger or prosecution. ". . . southerners were demanding a new and more stringent fugitive-slave law."

6. **topography** The precise surface features and details of a place—for example, rivers, coastlines, hills—in relation to one another. "The good Lord had decreed—through climate, topography, and geography—that a plantation economy . . . could not profitably exist in the Mexican Cession territory. . . ."

7. **mundane** Belonging to this world, as opposed to a higher or spiritual world. "Seward argued earnestly that Christian legislators must obey God's moral law as well as mundane human law."

8. **statecraft** The art of government leadership. "The Whigs . . . missed a splendid opportunity to capitalize on their record in statecraft."

9. **isthmian (isthmus)** Concerning a narrow strip of land connecting two larger bodies of land. ". . . neither America nor Britain would fortify or secure exclusive control over any future isthmian water-way."

10. **filibustering (filibuster)** Adventurers who conduct a private war against a foreign country. "During 1850–1851 two 'filibustering' expeditions descended upon Cuba." (In a different definition, **filibuster** also refers to deliberately prolonging speechmaking in order to block legislation.)

11. **dynasty** A succession of monarchs or emperors all descended from the same family; hence, the entire period of time (usually lengthy) in which such a family rules. "The long- ruling warrior dynasty known as the Tokugawa Shogunate. . . . "

12. **cloak-and-dagger** Concerning the activities of spies or undercover agents, especially involving elaborate deceptions. "An incredible cloak-and-dagger episode followed."

13. **manifesto** A proclamation or document aggressively asserting a controversial position or advocating a daring course of action. " . . . rose in an outburst of wrath against this 'manifesto of brigands.'"

14. **booster** One who promotes a person or enterprise, especially in a highly enthusiastic way. "An ardent booster for the West, he longed to . . . stretch a line of settlements across the continent."

15. **truce** A temporary suspension of warfare by agreement of the hostile parties. "This bold step Douglas was prepared to take, even at the risk of shattering the uneasy truce patched up by the Great Compromise of 1850."

PART II: CHECKING YOUR PROGRESS

A. True-False

Where the statement is true, circle **T**; where it is false, circle **F**.

1. T F   Democratic party politicians and others attempted to avoid the issue of slavery in the territories by saying it should be left to popular sovereignty.

2. T F   The Free Soil party consisted of a small, unified band of radical abolitionists.

3. T F   After the gold rush of 1849, California sought direct admission to the Union as a slave state.

4. T F   Southerners demanded a more effective fugitive-slave law to stop the Underground Railroad from running escaped slaves to Canada.

5. T F   In the Senate debate of 1850, Calhoun and Webster each spoke for their respective sections in opposition to a compromise over slavery.

6.   T   F   In the key provisions of the Compromise of 1850, New Mexico and Utah were admitted as slave states, while California was left open to popular sovereignty.

7.   T   F   The provision of the Compromise of 1850 that aroused the fiercest northern opposition was the Fugitive Slave Law.

8.   T   F   The Whig Party disappeared because its northern and southern wings were too deeply split over the Fugitive Slave Law and other sectional issues.

9.   T   F   The Pierce administration's expansionist efforts in Central America, Cuba, and the Gadsden Purchase were basically designed to serve southern proslavery interests.

10.   T   F   The Ostend Manifesto was designed to secure a peaceful solution to the crisis between the United States and Spain over Cuba.

11.   T   F   In negotiating the first American treaty with China in 1844, diplomat Caleb Cushing made sure that the United States followed a more culturally respectful policy than that of the imperialistic European great powers in China.

12.   T   F   Douglas's Kansas-Nebraska Act was intended to organize western territories so that a transcontinental railroad could be built along a northern route.

13.   T   F   Both southerners and northerners were outraged by Douglas's plan to repeal the Missouri Compromise.

14.   T   F   The Kansas-Nebraska Act wrecked the Compromise of 1850 and created deep divisions within the Democratic Party.

15.   T   F   The Republican Party was initially organized as a northern protest movement against Douglas's Kansas-Nebraska Act.

B. Multiple Choice

Select the best answer and circle the corresponding letter.

1.   Popular sovereignty was the idea that
   a.   the government of each new territory should be elected by the people.
   b.   the American public should have a popular vote on whether to admit states with or without slavery.
   c.   presidential candidates should be nominated by popular primaries rather than party conventions.
   d.   the United States should assume popular control of the territory acquired from Mexico.
   e.   the people of a territory should determine for themselves whether or not to permit slavery.

2.   In the election of 1848, the response of the Whig and Democratic parties to the rising controversy over slavery was
   a.   a strong proslavery stance by the Democrats and a strong antislavery stance by the Whigs.
   b.   to attack the sectional divisiveness of the antislavery Free Soil party.
   c.   an attempt to ignore the issue by shoving it out of sight.
   d.   to permit each individual candidate to take his own stand on the issue.
   e.   to promise to seek a sectional compromise no matter which party won the presidency.

3.   Rapid formation of an effective state government in California seemed especially urgent because

a.   proslavery Californians were gaining effective control of the territory.

b.   of the threat that Mexico would reconquer the territory.

c.   of the need to provide state subsidies for a transcontinental railroad.

d.   there was no legal authority to suppress the violence and lawlessness that accompanied the California gold rush.

e.   the influx of gold-seekers from around the world was causing ethnic conflict.

4.   The proposed direct admission of California into the Union, without passing through territorial status, was dangerously controversial because

a.   the territory was in a condition of complete lawlessness and anarchy.

b.   the Mexicans were threatening renewed warfare if California joined the Union.

c.   California's admission as a free state would destroy the equal balance of slave and free states in the U.S. Senate.

d.   there was a growing movement to declare California an independent nation.

e.   southern California and northern California did not want to be part of the same state.

5.   Southerners hated the Underground Railroad and demanded a stronger federal Fugitive Slave Law especially because

a.   the numbers of runaway slaves had grown dramatically.

b.   they feared that railroad conductors might foment a slave rebellion.

c.   northern toleration of slave runaways reflected a moral judgment against slavery.

d.   southern states were forced to spend large sums on slave patrols and slave catchers.

e.   the risk of uncaptured runaways was beginning to depress the price of slaves.

6.   Senator Daniel Webster's fundamental view regarding the issue of slavery expansion into the West was that

a.   Congress had no authority to prohibit slavery in the territories.

b.   new slave and free states should always be admitted in pairs so as to preserve the sectional balance.

c.   there was no need to legislate because climate and geography guaranteed that plantation slavery could not exist in the West.

d.   slavery should be prohibited in the West but that the South could expand slavery into Central America and the Caribbean.

e.   the South should be permitted to expand slavery if it abandoned its demand for a Fugitive Slave Law.

7.   It appeared that the Compromise of 1850 would fail to be enacted into law when

a.   Senator John C. Calhoun agreed that the Compromise was the best solution available.

b.   President Zachary Taylor suddenly died and the new president Fillmore backed the Compromise.

c.   Senator William Seward stated that a higher law demanded preservation of the Union.

d.   violence between radical abolitionists and southern fire-eaters made Congress realize compromise was essential.

e.   Henry Clay persuaded President Taylor to reverse his opposition to the Compromise.

8.   Under the terms of the Compromise of 1850

a.   California was admitted to the Union as a free state, and the issue of slavery in Utah and New Mexico territories would be left up to popular sovereignty.

b.   California was admitted as a free state, and Utah and New Mexico as slave states.

c.   California, Utah, and New Mexico were kept as territories but with slavery prohibited.

d.   New Mexico and Texas were admitted as slave states and Utah and California as free states.

e.   the South and North agreed that the number of slave and free states should remain equal.

9. The greatest winner in the Compromise of 1850 was

    a. the North.
    b. the South.
    c. the Whig party.
    d. the border states.
    e. President Millard Fillmore.

10. The most significant effect of the Fugitive Slave Law, passed as part of the Compromise of 1850, was

    a. an end to slave escapes and the Underground Railroad.
    b. the extension of the Underground Railroad into Canada.
    c. a sharp rise in northern antislavery feeling.
    d. a growing determination by radical abolitionists to foment violent slave rebellions.
    e. growing northern hostility to radical abolitionists.

11. The conflict over slavery following the election of 1852 led shortly to the

    a. death of the Whig party.
    b. death of the Democratic party.
    c. death of the Republican party.
    d. rise of the Free Soil party.
    e. takeover of the Whig party by proslavery elements.

12. Southerners seeking to expand the territory of slavery undertook filibustering military expeditions to acquire

    a. Canada and Alaska.
    b. Venezuela and Colombia.
    c. Nicaragua and Cuba.
    d. Hawaii and Samoa.
    e. northern Mexico.

13. The primary goal of the Treaty of Kanagawa , which Commodore Matthew Perry signed with Japan in 1854, was

    a. establishing a balance of power in East Asia.
    b. opening Japan to American missionaries.
    c. guaranteeing the territorial integrity of China.
    d. establishing American naval bases in Hawaii and Okinawa.
    e. opening Japan to American trade.

14. The Gadsden Purchase was fundamentally designed to

    a. enable the United States to guarantee control of California.
    b. permit the construction of a transcontinental railroad along a southern route.
    c. block Mexican raids into Arizona and New Mexico.
    d. serve the political interests of Senator Stephen Douglas.
    e. divert attention from the Pierce administration's secret plan to seize Cuba.

15. Northerners especially resented Douglas's Kansas-Nebraska Act because it

    a. would encourage the building of a transcontinental railroad along the southern route.
    b. would make Douglas the leading Democratic candidate for the presidency.
    c. repealed the Missouri Compromise prohibiting slavery in northern territories.
    d. would bring Kansas into the Union as a slave state.
    e. would end the equal balance of free and slave states in the Union.

C. Identification

Supply the correct identification for each numbered description.

1. _____ Hotheaded southern agitators who pushed for southern interests and favored secession from the Union

2. _____ The doctrine that the issue of slavery should be decided by the residents of a territory themselves, not by the federal government

3. _____ Antislavery political party in the election of 1848 that included moral opponents of slavery as well as white workers who disliked black competition.

4. _____ The informal network of people who helped runaway slaves travel from the South to the safe haven of Canada

5. _____ Senator William Seward's doctrine that slavery should be excluded from the territories because it was contrary to a divine morality standing above even the Constitution

6. _____ The provision of the Compromise of 1850 that comforted southern slave-catchers and aroused the wrath of northern abolitionists

7. _____
   _____ The two territories that were organized under the Compromise of 1850 with the choice of slavery left open to popular sovereignty

8. _____ A series of agreements between North and South that temporarily dampened the slavery controversy and led to a short-lived era of national good feelings

9. _____ Political party that fell apart and disappeared after losing the election of 1852

10. _____ An 1850 treaty between Britain and America stating that neither country would exclusively control or fortify any Central American canal.

11. _____ A top-secret dispatch, drawn up by American diplomats in Europe, that detailed a plan for seizing Cuba from Spain

12. _____ British military victory over China that gained Britain's right to sell drugs in China and colonial control of the island of Hong Kong

13. _____ Treaty of 1844, between the United States and China that opened China to American trade and missionary activity

14. _____ Southwestern territory acquired by the Pierce administration to facilitate a southern transcontinental railroad

15. _____ A new political party organized as a protest against the Kansas-Nebraska Act

D. Matching People, Places, and Events

Match the person, place, or event in the left column with the proper description in the right column by inserting the correct letter on the blank line.

1. ___ Lewis Cass

2. ___ Zachary Taylor

3. ___ Martin Van Buren

4. ___ Caleb Cushing

a. American naval commander who opened Japan to the West in 1854

b. Democratic presidential candidate in 1848, original proponent of the idea of popular sovereignty

5. ____ Harriet Tubman

6. ____ Daniel Webster

7. ____ William Seward

8. ____ Millard Fillmore

9. ____ Franklin Pierce

10. ____ Winfield Scott

11. ____ John C. Calhoun

12. ____ Matthew Perry

13. ____ William Walker

14. ____ James Gadsden

15. ____ Stephen A. Douglas

c. Weak Democratic president whose pro-southern cabinet pushed aggressive expansionist schemes

d. Famous conductor on the Underground Railroad who rescued more than three hundred slaves from bondage

e. Illinois politician who helped smooth over sectional conflict in 1850, but then reignited it in 1854

f. South Carolina senator who fiercely defended southern rights and opposed compromise with the North in the debates of 1850

g. Military hero of the Mexican War who became the Whigs' last presidential candidate in 1852

h. Whig president who nearly destroyed the Compromise of 1850 before he died in office

i. American proslavery filibusterer who seized control of Nicaragua and made himself president in the 1850s

j. American diplomat who negotiated the Treaty of Wanghia with China in 1844

k. American minister to Mexico in the 1850s who acquired land for the United States that would enable the building of a southern transcontinental railroad

l. New York senator who argued that the expansion of slavery was forbidden by a higher law

m. New Yorker who supported and signed the Compromise of 1850 after he suddenly became president that same year

n. Northern spokesman whose support for the Compromise of 1850 earned him the hatred of abolitionists

o. Former president who became the candidate of the antislavery Free Soil party in the election of 1848

E. Putting Things in Order

Put the following events in correct order by numbering them from 1 to 5.

1. ___ A series of delicate agreements between the North and South temporarily smoothes over the slavery conflict.

2. ___ A Mexican War hero is elected president, as the issue of how a deal with slavery in the territory acquired from Mexico arouses national controversy.

3. ___ A spectacular growth of settlement in the far West creates demand for admission of a new free state and agitates the slavery controversy.

4. ___ Stephen A. Douglas's scheme to build a transcontinental railroad leads to repeal of the Missouri Compromise, which reopens the slavery controversy and spurs the formation of a new party.

5. ___ The Pierce administration acquires a small Mexican territory to encourage a southern route for the transcontinental railroad.

F. Matching Cause and Effect

Match the historical cause in the left column with the proper effect in the right column by writing the correct letter on the blank line.

Cause

1. ___ The evasion of the slavery issue by Whigs and Democrats in 1848

2. ___ The California gold rush

3. ___ The Underground Railroad

4. ___ The Free Soil Party

5. ___ The Compromise of 1850

6. ___ The Fugitive Slave Law

7. ___ The Pierce administration's schemes to acquire Cuba

8. ___ The Gadsden Purchase

9. ___ Stephen Douglas's indifference to slavery and desire for a northern railroad route

10. ___ The Kansas-Nebraska Act

Effect

a. Was the predecessor of the antislavery Republican Party

b. Fell apart after the leaking of the Ostend Manifesto

c. Caused a tremendous northern protest and the birth of the Republican party

d. Made the issue of slavery in the Mexican Cession areas more urgent

e. Created a short-lived national mood of optimism and reconciliation

f. Heightened competition between southern and northern railroad promoters over the choice of a transcontinental route

g. Led to the formation of the new Free Soil antislavery party

h. Aroused active northern resistance to legal enforcement and prompted attempts at nullification in Massachusetts

i. Led to the passage of the Kansas-Nebraska Act, without regard for the consequences

j. Aroused southern demands for an effective fugitive-slave law

G. Developing Historical Skills

Understanding Cause and Effect

It is often crucial to understand how certain historical forces or events cause other historical events or developments. In the pairs of historical events listed below, designated (A) and (B), indicate which was the cause and which was the effect. Then indicate in a brief sentence how the cause led to the effect.

1.   (A) The acquisition of California   (B) The Mexican War

2.   (A) The entry of California into the Union (B) The California gold rush

3.   (A) The death of President Zachary Taylor   (B) The passage of the Compromise of 1850

4.   (A) Northern aid to fugitive slaves (B) The passage of the Fugitive Slave Law

5.   (A) The disappearance of the Whig party   (B) The election of 1852

6.   (A) The Compromise of 1850   (B) Southern filibuster ventures

7.   (A) The Gadsden Purchase   (B) The southern plan for a transcontinental railroad

8.   (A) Douglas's plan for a transcontinental railroad   (B) The Kansas-Nebraska Act

9.   (A) The Ostend Manifesto (B) The end of Pierce administration schemes to acquire Cuba

10.   (A) The rise of the Republican party   (B) The Kansas-Nebraska Act

H. Map Mastery

Map Discrimination

Using the maps and charts in Chapter 18, answer the following questions.

1. *Texas and the Disputed Area Before the Compromise of 1850*: A large territory claimed by Texas was taken from it in the Compromise of 1850, and parts of it were later incorporated into five other states. Which were they?

2. *Slavery After the Compromise of 1850*: Under the Compromise of 1850, which free state was partially located south of the line 36°30' (the southern border of Missouri), which had been established by the Missouri Compromise as the border between slave and free territories?

3. *Slavery After the Compromise of 1850*: Under the Compromise of 1850, which territory located *north* of 36°30' *could* have adopted slavery if it had chosen to do so?

4. *Slavery After the Compromise of 1850*: After 1850, how many organized territories prohibited slavery? Identify them.

5. *Central America c. 1850*: In Central America, British influence extended along the Atlantic coasts of which two nations?

6. *Central America c. 1850*: In the 1850s, the territory of the future Panama Canal was part of which South American country?

7. *The Gadsden Purchase, 1853*: The proposed southern transcontinental railroad was supposed to run through which two Texas cities?

8. *Kansas and Nebraska, 1854*: The proposed northern transcontinental railroad was supposed to run through which territory organized by Stephen Douglas's act of 1854?

9. *The Legal Status of Slavery, from the Revolution to the Civil War*: In 1854, what was the status of slavery in the only state that bordered on the Kansas Territory?

10. *The Legal Status of Slavery, from the Revolution to the Civil War*: Under the Kansas-Nebraska Act, how far north could slavery have extended had it been implemented in Nebraska territory?

Map Challenge

Using the map of *The Legal Status of Slavery, from the Revolution to the Civil War*, write a brief essay in which you describe how the Missouri Compromise, the Compromise of 1850, and the Kansas-Nebraska Act each affected the legal status of slavery in various territories.

PART III: APPLYING WHAT YOU HAVE LEARNED

1. What were the most fundamental issues causing the sectional crisis and threatening to split the Union in 1850?

2. Why did the two major political parties, the Whigs and the Democrats, both strive mightily to keep the most important problem facing America, slavery, out of national political discussion?

3. How did the Compromise of 1850 attempt to deal with the most difficult issues concerning slavery? Was the Compromise a success? By what standard?

4. Most northerners strongly supported the Compromise of 1850, except for the Fugitive Slave Act. Why did the South insist on the Act when only about a thousand slaves a year escaped? Why was the Fugitive Slave Act such a point of horror for many northerners? Could the Compromise of 1850 have succeeded longer if the fugitive law had not been included?

5. Why were proslavery southerners and the Pierce administration they controlled so eager to push for further American expansion into Nicaragua, Cuba, and elsewhere in the 1850s?

6. What fundamentally motivated the new American engagement with China and Japan in the 1840s and 1850s? Were the treaties negotiated by Caleb Cushing and Matthew Perry expressions of the expansionist spirit of manifest destiny and general Western imperialism, or were Americans genuinely interested in economic and cultural exchange with East Asia?

7. What were the causes and consequences of the Kansas-Nebraska Act? Did Senator Stephen A. Douglas genuinely believe that he could repeal the Missouri Compromise without arousing a new sectional crisis?

8. How similar was the Compromise of 1850 to the Missouri Compromise of 1820 (see Chapter 13)? How did each sectional compromise affect the balance of power between North and South? Why could sectional issues be compromised in 1820 and 1850, but not after 1854?

9. Because Senator Stephen A. Douglas's Kansas-Nebraska Act reignited the slavery issue after the Compromise of 1850 appeared to have calmed it down, should he bear responsibility as an instigator of the Civil War?

10. How could a single issue—the Kansas-Nebraska Act—cause the formation of a powerful new political party out of nothing?

CHAPTER 19

Drifting Toward Disunion, 1854–1861

PART I: REVIEWING THE CHAPTER

A. Checklist of Learning Objectives

After mastering this chapter, you should be able to:

1. Enumerate the sequence of major crises, beginning with the Kansas-Nebraska Act, that led up to secession, and explain the significance of each event.

2. Explain how and why the territory of bleeding Kansas became the scene of a dress rehearsal for the Civil War.

3. Trace the growing power of the Republican party in the 1850s and the increasing domination of the Democratic party by its militantly proslavery wing.

4. Explain how the *Dred Scott* decision and John Brown's Harpers Ferry raid deepened sectional antagonism.

5. Trace the rise of Lincoln as a Republican spokesman, and explain why his senatorial campaign debates with Stephen Douglas made him a major national figure despite losing the election.

6. Analyze the election of 1860, including the split in the Democratic party, the four-way campaign, the sharp sectional divisions, and Lincoln's northern-based minority victory.

7. Describe the secession of seven southern states following Lincoln's victory, the formation of the Confederacy, and the failure of the last compromise effort.

B. Glossary

To build your social science vocabulary, familiarize yourself with the following terms.

1. **puppet government** A weak government created or controlled by more powerful outside forces. "The slavery supporters triumphed and then set up their own puppet government at Shawnee Mission."

2. **bigoted** Blindly or narrowly intolerant. ". . . the allegation . . . alienated many bigoted Know-Nothings. . . ."

3. **public domain** Land or other property belonging to the whole nation, controlled by the federal government. "Financial distress . . . gave a new vigor to the demand for free farms of 160 acres from the public domain."

4. **bandwagon** In politics, a movement or candidacy that gains rapid momentum because of people's purported desire to join a successful cause. "After mounting the Republican bandwagon, he emerged as one of the foremost politicians and orators of the Northwest."

5. **apportionment** The allotment or distribution of legislative representatives in districts according to population. (**Reapportionment** occurs after each census according to growth or loss of population.) "Yet thanks to inequitable apportionment, the districts carried by Douglas supporters represented a smaller population. . . ."

6. **splintering** Concerning the small political groups that result when a larger organization has divided or broken apart. "But Douglas . . . hurt his own chances . . . while further splitting his splintering party."

7. **affidavit** A sworn, written testimony, usually attested to by a notary public or legal officer, that may be admitted as evidence in court. "His presumed insanity was supported by affidavits from seventeen friends and relatives. . . ."

8. **martyr** One who is tortured or killed for adherence to a belief. ". . . Ralph Waldo Emerson compared the new martyr-hero with Jesus."

9. **border state** The northernmost slave states contested by North and South; during the Civil War the four border states (Maryland, Delaware, Kentucky, and Missouri) remained within the Union, though they contained many Confederate sympathizers and volunteers. " . . . a man of moderate views from the border state of Kentucky."

10. **vassalage** The service and homage given by a feudal subordinate to an overlord; by extension, any similar arrangement between political figures or entities. ". . . secession [w]as a golden opportunity to cast aside their generations of 'vassalage' to the North."

PART II: CHECKING YOUR PROGRESS

A. True-False

Where the statement is true, circle **T**; where it is false, circle **F**.

1. T   F   Harriet Beecher Stowe's *Uncle Tom's Cabin* proved to be the most influential publication in arousing the northern and European publics against the evils of slavery.

2. T   F   Hinton Helper's *The Impending Crisis of the South* stirred slaveholders' wrath by predicting that the slaves would eventually rise up in violent revolt.

3. T   F   Prosouthern Kansas pioneers brought numerous slaves with them in order to guarantee that Kansas would not become a free state.

4. T   F   The violence in Kansas was provoked by both radical abolitionists and militant proslavery forces who sought to control the territory.

5. T   F   Senator Stephen Douglas's support for the proslavery Lecompton Constitution demonstrated that the Democratic party was completely beholden to its southern wing.

6. T   F   After Congressman Preston Brooks nearly beat Senator Charles Sumner to death on the Senate floor, South Carolina reelected Brooks and Massachusetts reelected Sumner.

7. T   F   Although Republican John C. Frémont lost the presidency to Democrat James Buchanan, the election of 1856 demonstrated the growing power of the new antislavery party.

8. T   F   The *Dred Scott* decision upheld the doctrine of popular sovereignty that the people of each territory should determine whether or not to permit slavery.

9. T   F   In the Lincoln-Douglas debates, Lincoln's criticisms forced Douglas to back away from his support for popular sovereignty as the solution to the slavery question in the West.

10. T   F   The South was enraged by many northerners' celebration of John Brown as a martyr.

11. T   F   Northern Democrats walked out of the Democratic party convention in 1860 when southerners nominated Vice President John Breckenridge for president.

12. T   F   The election of 1860 was really two campaigns, Lincoln versus Douglas in the North and Bell versus Breckinridge in the South.

13. T   F   The overwhelming support for Lincoln in the North gave him a majority of the total popular vote despite winning almost no votes in the South.

14. T   F   Seven states seceded and formed the Confederate States of America during the "lame-duck" period between Lincoln's election and his inauguration.

15. T   F   Lincoln made a strong effort to get the South to accept the Crittenden Compromise in order to avoid a civil war.

B. Multiple Choice

Select the best answer and circle the corresponding letter.

1. Harriet Beecher Stowe's *Uncle Tom's Cabin*

    a.   was strongly rooted in religiously based antislavery sentiments.
    b.   argued that nonslaveholding whites suffered the most from slavery.
    c.   helped northerners understand that southerners disliked the cruelty of slavery.
    d.   was based on Stowe's extensive personal experience with slavery in the Deep South.
    e.   portrayed black slaves as seething with anger and potential violence.

2. Hinton R. Helper's *The Impending Crisis of the South* contended that

    a.   the Founders had intended that slavery should eventually be eliminated.
    b.   slavery was contrary to the religious values held by most Americans.
    c.   slavery did great harm to the poor whites of the South.
    d.   slavery violated the human rights of African Americans.
    e.   wealthy plantation owners would eventually seek to enslave poor whites as well.

3. Southerners were especially enraged by abolitionists' funding of antislavery settlers in Kansas because

    a.   proslavery settlers from Missouri could not receive the same kind of funding.
    b.   such sponsored settlement would make a mockery of Douglas's popular sovereignty doctrine.
    c.   the settlers included fanatical and violent abolitionists like John Brown.
    d.   most ordinary westward-moving pioneers would be sympathetic to slavery.
    e.   Douglas's Kansas-Nebraska had seemed to imply that Kansas would become a slave state.

4. As submitted to Congress, the Lecompton Constitution was designed to

    a.   bring Kansas into the Union as a free state.
    b.   bring Kansas into the Union as a slave state and Nebraska as a free state.
    c.   prohibit both antislavery New Englanders or proslavery Missourians from interference in Kansas politics.
    d.   insure that the future of slavery would be determined according to Douglas's principle of popular sovereignty.
    e.   bring Kansas into the Union, while making it impossible to prohibit slavery there.

5. The fanatical abolitionist John Brown made his first entry into violent antislavery politics by

    a.   killing five proslavery settlers at Pottawatomie Creek, Kansas.
    b.   organizing a slave rebellion in Missouri.
    c.   leading an armed raid on the federal arsenal at Harpers Ferry, Virginia.
    d.   organizing an armed militia of blacks and whites to conduct escaped slaves to Canada.
    e.   soliciting funds from abolitionists intellectuals in Massachusetts to finance a slave revolt.

6. Congressman Preston Brooks beat Senator Charles Sumner nearly to death on the Senate floor because

    a. Sumner had helped to fund John Brown's violent activities in Kansas.
    b. Sumner had used abusive language to describe the South and a South Carolina senator.
    c. Sumner had personally blocked the admission of Kansas to the Union as a slave state.
    d. Sumner had threatened to kill Brooks if he had the opportunity.
    e. Democrats believed that Sumner would be a dangerous Republican candidate for president.

7. The election of 1856 was most noteworthy for

    a. Democrat James Buchanan's surprisingly easy victory over John Frémont.
    b. the support immigrants and Catholics gave to the American party.
    c. the dramatic rise of the Republican party.
    d. the absence of the slavery issue from the campaign.
    e. the strong showing of former president Millard Fillmore as the American party candidate.

8. In the *Dred Scott* decision, the Supreme Court

    a. avoided controversy by ruling that the slave Dred Scott had no right to sue in federal court.
    b. ruled that the Kansas-Nebraska Act was unconstitutional.
    c. ruled that Congress could not prohibit slavery in any of the territories because slaves were private property of which owners could not be deprived.
    d. ruled that Dred Scott was still a slave because he had not filed suit until he had been returned to the slave state of Missouri.
    e. ruled that Dred Scott had to be freed because his owner had taken him into the free state of Illinois.

9. The financial and economic collapse of 1857 increased northern anger at the South's refusal to support

    a. banking regulation and development of a sound paper currency.
    b. a transcontinental railroad and transatlantic telegraph.
    c. publicly supported state universities.
    d. the admission of any more free states into the Union.
    e. higher tariffs and free western homesteads for farmers.

10. The crucial Freeport Question that Lincoln demanded that Douglas answer during their debates was whether

    a. secession from the Union was legal.
    b. the people of a territory could prohibit slavery in light of the *Dred Scott* decision.
    c. Illinois should continue to prohibit slavery.
    d. Kansas should be admitted to the Union as a slave or a free state.
    e. Douglas still supported the brutal Fugitive Slave Law as part of the Compromise of 1850.

11. Southerners were particularly enraged by the John Brown affair because

    a. so many slaves had joined the insurrection.
    b. northerners' celebration of Brown as a martyr seemed to indicate their support for slave insurrection.
    c. Brown had used vicious language to describe southerners and their way of life.
    d. Brown escaped punishment by pleading insanity.
    e. prominent Republican leaders like William Seward and Abraham Lincoln expressed admiration for Brown.

12. In the campaign of 1860, the Democratic party

    a. tried to unite around the compromise popular sovereignty views of Stephen A. Douglas.
    b. campaigned on a platform of restoring the compromises of 1820 and 1850.
    c. split in two, with each faction nominating its own presidential candidate.
    d. threatened to support secession if the sectionally-based Republicans won the election.
    e. attempted to keep its militant fire-eating southern wing out of sight.

13. During the campaign of 1860, Abraham Lincoln and the Republican party

    a. opposed the expansion of slavery but did not threaten to attack slavery in the South.
    b. waged a national campaign to win votes in the South as well as the Midwest and the Northeast.
    c. promised, if elected, to seek peaceful, compensated abolition of slavery in the South.
    d. were forced to be cautious about limiting the expansion of slavery because of Stephen A. Douglas's threats to support secession.
    e. focused entirely on the slavery question.

14. Within two months after the election of Lincoln

    a. Northerners were mobilizing for a civil war.
    b. seven southern states had seceded and formed the Confederate States of America.
    c. all the slaveholding states had held conventions and passed secessionist resolutions.
    d. President Buchanan appealed for troops to put down the secessionist rebellion.
    e. the southern states had demanded a new constitutional convention to guarantee the future of slavery.

15. Lincoln rejected the proposed Crittenden Compromise primarily because

    a. it left open the possibility that slavery could expand south into Mexico, Central America, or the Caribbean.
    b. it permitted the further extension of slavery north of the line of 36° 30′.
    c. it represented essentially the continuation of Douglas's popular sovereignty doctrine.
    d. the Supreme Court would probably have ruled it unconstitutional.
    e. it would have restored a permanent equal balance of slave and free states within the Union.

C. Identification

Supply the correct identification for each numbered description.

1. _____ A powerful, evangelical antislavery novel that altered the course of American politics

2. _____ A book by a southern writer that argued that slavery was most oppressive for poor whites

3. _____ Nickname for rifles paid for by New England abolitionists and brought to Kansas by antislavery pioneers

4. _____ Term that described the prairie territory where a small-scale civil war between abolitionists and proslavery border ruffians erupted in 1856

5. _____ Tricky proslavery document designed to bring Kansas into the Union; blocked by Stephen A. Douglas

6. _____ Anti-immigrant party headed by former president Millard Fillmore that competed with Republicans and Democrats in the election of 1856 (either official name or informal nickname)

7. _____ Controversial Supreme Court ruling that blacks had no civil or human rights and that Congress could not prohibit slavery in the territories

8. _____ Sharp economic decline that increased northern demands for a high tariff and convinced southerners that the North was economically vulnerable

9. _____ Stephen Douglas's assertion in the Lincoln-Douglas debates that, despite the *Dred Scott* decision, the people of a territory could block slavery by refusing to pass legislation enforcing it

10. _____ Newly formed, middle-of-the-road party of elderly politicians that sought compromise in 1860, but carried only three border states

11. _____ Western Virginia town where a violent abolitionist seized a federal arsenal in hopes of sparking a widespread slave rebellion

12. _____ A new nation that proclaimed its independence in Montgomery, Alabama, in February 1861

13. _____ A last-ditch plan to save the Union by guaranteeing that slavery would be protected in territories lying south of the line of 36° 30′

14. _____ Four-way race for the presidency that resulted in the election of a sectional minority president

15. _____ Period between Lincoln's election and his inauguration, during which the ineffectual President Buchanan passively stood by as seven states seceded

D. Matching People, Places, and Events

Match the person, place, or event in the left column with the proper description in the right column by inserting the correct letter on the blank line.

1. ____ Harriet Beecher Stowe

2. ____ Hinton R. Helper

3. ____ Henry Ward Beecher

4. ____ John Brown

5. ____ James Buchanan

6. ____ Charles Sumner

7. ____ Preston Brooks

8. ____ John C. Frémont

9. ____ Dred Scott

10. ____ Harpers Ferry, Virginia

11. ____ Stephen A. Douglas

12. ____ Pottawatomie Creek, Kansas

13. ____ John C. Breckenridge

14. ____ Montgomery, Alabama

15. ____ Jefferson Davis

a. Southern congressman whose bloody attack on a northern senator fueled sectional hatred

b. Leading northern Democrat whose presidential hopes fell victim to the conflict over slavery

c. Black slave whose unsuccessful attempt to win his freedom deepened the sectional controversy

d. Former United States senator who, in 1861, became the president of what called itself a new nation

e. "The little woman who wrote the book that made this great war" (the Civil War)

f. Fanatical and bloody-minded abolitionist martyr admired in the North and hated in the South

g. Southern-born author whose book attacking slavery's effects on whites aroused northern opinion

h.   Scene of militant abolitionist John Brown's massacre of proslavery men in 1856

i.   Site where seven seceding states united to declare their independence from the United States

j.   Romantic western hero and the first Republican candidate for president

k.   Abolitionist senator whose verbal attack on the South provoked a physical assault that severely injured him

l.   Site of a federal arsenal where a militant abolitionist attempted to start a slave rebellion

m.   Buchanan's vice president, nominated for president by breakaway southern Democrats in 1860

n.   Weak Democratic president whose manipulation by proslavery forces divided his own party

o.   Preacher-abolitionist who funded weapons for antislavery pioneers in Kansas

E. Putting Things in Order

Put the following events in correct order by numbering them from 1 to 6.

1.   ___   A black slave's attempt to win freedom produces a controversial Supreme Court decision.

2.   ___   A newly organized territory becomes a bloody battleground between proslavery and antislavery forces.

3.   ___   The hanging of a fanatically violent abolitionist makes him a martyr in the North and a hated symbol in the South.

4.   ___   A black Republican whose minority sectional victory in a presidential election provokes southern secession.

5.   ___   The fictional tale of a black slave's vicious treatment by the cruel Simon Legree touches millions of northern hearts and creates stronger opposition to slavery.

6.   ___   A group of states calling itself a new southern nation declares its independence and chooses its first president.

F. Matching Cause and Effect

Match the historical cause in the left column with the proper effect in the right column by writing the correct letter on the blank line.

Cause	**Effect**
1. ___ H. B. Stowe's *Uncle Tom's Cabin*	a. Moved South Carolina to declare immediate secession from the Union
2. ___ The exercise of popular sovereignty in Kansas	b. Shattered one of the last links between the sections and almost guaranteed Lincoln's victory in 1860
3. ___ Buchanan's support for the proslavery Lecompton Constitution	c. Convinced southerners that the North generally supported murder and slave rebellion
4. ___ The *Dred Scott* case	d. Made Lincoln a leading national Republican figure and hurt Douglas's presidential chances
5. ___ The 1858 Illinois senate race	e. Ended the last hopes of a peaceable sectional settlement and an end to secession
6. ___ John Brown's raid on Harpers Ferry	f. Paralyzed the North while the southern secessionist movement gained momentum
7. ___ The splitting of the Democratic party in 1860	g. Infuriated Republicans and made them determined to defy the Supreme Court
8. ___ The election of Lincoln as president	h. Offended Senator Douglas and divided the Democratic party
9. ___ The "lame-duck" period and Buchanan's indecisiveness	i. Persuaded millions of northerners and Europeans that slavery was evil and should be eliminated
10. ___ Lincoln's rejection of the Crittenden Compromise	j. Led to a mini prairie civil war between proslavery and antislavery factions

G. Developing Historical Skills

Interpreting Primary-Source Documents

In order properly to interpret primary-source documents in history, two skills are essential: first, the ability to read closely and carefully for the intended meaning; and second, the ability to understand the historical context and possible implications of a text or statement.

The small, boxed samples of primary documents in this chapter demonstrate these principles. The questions below will help you practice the skills of textual interpretation by asking you to read the documents very carefully for meaning and to consider some of their implications.

1. Lincoln's statement from the Lincoln-Douglas debate (p. 450)

    a. In what ways does Lincoln claim that blacks are equal to whites, and in what ways does he claim that whites are superior?

    b. What do the first two sentences tell you about the reason Lincoln is making a distinction between equality of natural rights and complete equality of the races?

2. John Brown's letter before his hanging (p. 451)

    a. What does Brown mean when he writes that "I am worth inconceivably more to hang than for any other purpose. . . ."?

    b. What does Brown's statement imply about how abolitionists might make use of Brown's impending death?

3. Greeley's New York *Tribune* editorial (p. 456)

    a. What two arguments does Greeley use for letting the seceding states "go in peace"?

    b. The editorial was written three days after Lincoln's election. What fear is motivating Greeley?

4.   Letter of South Carolina Senator Hammond (p. 457)

    a.   What does the letter suggest will be the federal government's response to secession?

    b.   Why did the attitude reflected in the letter make efforts like the Crittenden Compromise fail?

5.   London *Times* editorial (p. 458)

    a.   What is the editorial's view of the relation between the southern states and the United States government?

    b.   What position does it appear the London *Times* would advocate the British government take regarding the American Civil War?

6.   Harriet Beecher Stowe's *Uncle Tom's Cabin* (pp. 438–439).

    a.   What details in Stowe's account of Tom's last morning in the cabin before the sale of his family might especially appeal to female readers?

    b.   How does Stowe characterize the black slave Tom and his wife Chloe?

    c.   What details in the excerpts in *Examining the Evidence* (p. 439) and on p. 438 show Stowe's explicit appeal to the religious sentiments of her readers?

H. Map Mastery

Map Discrimination

Using the maps and charts in Chapter 19, answer the following questions.

1.   *Presidential Election of 1856*: In the presidential election of 1856, how many electoral votes did Buchanan get from the free states? (See map of *The Legal Status of Slavery*, Chapter 17, for free and slave states.)

2. *Presidential Election of 1856; Presidential Election of 1860 (electoral vote by state)*: Which four states carried by Democrat Buchanan in 1856 were also carried completely by Republican Lincoln in 1860?

3. *Presidential Election of 1860 (showing popular vote by county)* Using this map of the presidential voting by counties in 1860, indicate which five states gave Douglas his strongest support.

4. *Presidential Election of 1860 (showing popular vote by county)*: In which five states did Bell receive his strongest support?

5. *Presidential Election of 1860 (showing popular vote by county)*: Which Border State was the most closely divided among Douglas, Bell, and Breckenridge?

6. *Presidential Election of 1860 (showing popular vote by county)*: Which state was the only one divided among Lincoln, Douglas, and Breckenridge?

7. *Presidential Election of 1860 (showing vote by county)*: In which six northern states did Lincoln carry every single country?

8. *Southern Opposition to Secession, 1860–1861*: In which four future Confederate states was the *opposition* to secession strongest?

9. *Southern Opposition to Secession, 1860–1861*: In which three states did every single county for which returns are available support secession?

10. *Southern Opposition to Secession, 1860–1861*: In which two states were many county conventions divided about secession?

Map Challenge

Using the electoral maps of *The Presidential Election of 1856* and *The Presidential Election of 1860*, write a brief essay in which you describe what political changes enabled the Republicans to turn defeat in 1856 into victory in 1860.

PART III: APPLYING WHAT YOU HAVE LEARNED

1. How did the development of a violent mini civil war in the territory of Kansas demonstrate a fatal flaw in Stephen Douglas's popular sovereignty doctrine that the people of each territory should settle the slavery question for themselves?

2. Argue for or against: John Brown was actually a terrorist who successfully used violence to polarize North and South and help bring on the Civil War.

3. Why was the Democratic party, as the only remaining national party, unable to avoid the growing sectional polarization of the 1850s.

4. Explain the crucial role of Stephen A. Douglas in the political events of the 1850s. Why did Douglas's attempts to keep the conflict over slavery out of national politics fail? Might he have succeeded if proslavery extremists had not tried to bring Kansas in as a slave state under the Lecompton Constitution?

5. Some historians argue that American political parties have been strictly practical coalitions, not ideological movements. Yet the Republican Party came into existence primarily to oppose the extension of slavery. What explains the rise of such an ideological single-issue party in the 1850s? Why did the other single-issue party of the time—the anti-immigrant Know-Nothings—eventually fail, while the Republicans not only survived but took power in 1860?

6. If Congress had passed and the states ratified the Crittenden Compromise, could it have prevented or at least postponed the Civil War? Was Lincoln wrong to kill the Crittenden Compromise without trying it? Why was compromise successful in 1820 and 1850 but not 1860?

7. Why did so many northerners, including prominent intellectuals like Ralph Waldo Emerson, celebrate a violent fanatic like John Brown as a noble martyr comparable to Jesus. Why did southerners refuse to believe it when mainstream Republicans like Abraham Lincoln condemned Brown?

8. Abraham Lincoln and the Republicans frequently declared that they sought only to prevent the expansion of slavery and not to overturn slavery where it existed. Yet immediately after Lincoln's election seven southern states marched out of the Union, without waiting to see what Lincoln's policies would be. Why? Were southern fears of Lincoln rational or irrational?

CHAPTER 20

Girding for War: The North and the South, 1861–1865

PART I: REVIEWING THE CHAPTER

A. Checklist of Learning Objectives

After mastering this chapter, you should be able to:

1. Explain how the South's firing on Fort Sumter galvanized the North and how Lincoln's call for troops prompted four more states to join the Confederacy.

2. Explain why the slaveholding Border States were so critical to both sides and how Lincoln maneuvered to keep them in the Union.

3. Indicate the strengths and weaknesses of both sides at the onset of the war, what strategies each pursued, and why the North's strengths could be brought to bear as the war dragged on.

4. Describe the contest for European political support and intervention, and explain why Britain and France finally refused to recognize the Confederacy.

5. Compare Lincoln's and Davis's political leadership during the war.

6. Describe Lincoln's policies on civil liberties and how both sides mobilized the military manpower to fight the war.

7. Analyze the economic and social consequences of the war for both sides.

B. Glossary

To build your social science vocabulary, familiarize yourself with the following terms.

1. **balance of power** The theory and practice of distributing political and military strength evenly among several nations so that no one of them becomes too strong or dangerous. "They could gleefully transplant to America their ancient concept of the balance of power."

2. **moral suasion** The effort to move others to a particular course of action through appeals to moral values and beliefs, without the use of economic incentives or military force. "In dealing with the Border States, President Lincoln did not rely solely on moral suasion. . . ."

3. **martial law** The imposition of military rule above or in place of civil authority and law during times of war and emergency. "In Maryland he declared martial law where needed. . . ."

4. **ultimatum** A final proposal or demand, as by one nation to another, that if rejected, will likely lead to war. "The London Foreign Office prepared an ultimatum. . . ."

5. **loophole(d)** Characterized by small exceptions or conditions that enable escape from the general rule or principle. "These vessels were not warships within the meaning of the loopholed British law. . . ."

6. **merchant marine**   The ships and manpower of a nation devoted to waterborne commerce and trade, as distinct from naval vessels and personnel devoted to military purposes. "Confederate commerce-destroyers . . . captured more than 250 Yankee ships, severely crippling the American merchant marine. . . ."

7. **arbitration**   The settlement of a dispute by putting the mandatory decision in the hands of a third, neutral party. (**Mediation** is using the services of a third party to promote negotiations and suggest solutions, but without the power of mandatory decision making.) "It agreed in 1871 to submit the *Alabama* dispute to arbitration. . . ."

8. **appropriation**   A sum of money or property legally authorized to be spent for a specific purpose. "He directed the secretary of the treasury to advance $2 million without appropriation. . . ."

9. **habeas corpus**   In law, a judicial order requiring that a prisoner be brought before a court at a specified time and place in order to determine the legality of the imprisonment (literally, "produce the body.") "He suspended the precious privilege of the writ of habeas corpus. . . ."

10. **arbitrary**   Governed by indeterminate preference or whim rather than by settled principle or law. "Jefferson Davis was less able than Lincoln to exercise arbitrary power. . . ."

11. **quota**   The proportion or share of a larger number of things that a smaller group is assigned to contribute. ". . . with each state assigned a quota based on population."

12. **greenback**   In the United States, popular term for paper currency, especially that printed before the establishment of the Federal Reserve System in 1913; named for the original color of the printed money. "Greenbacks thus fluctuated with the fortunes of Union arms. . . ."

13. **bond**   In finance, an interest-bearing certificate issued by a government or business that guarantees repayment to the purchaser on a specified date at a predetermined rate of interest. ". . . the Treasury was forced to market its bonds through the private banking house of Jay Cooke and Company. . . ."

14. **graft**   The corrupt acquisition of funds, through overt theft or embezzling or through questionably legal methods such as kickbacks or insider trading. "But graft was more flagrant in the North than in the South. . . ."

15. **profiteer**   One who takes advantage of a shortage of supply to charge excessively high prices and thus reap large profits. "One profiteer reluctantly admitted that his profits were 'painfully large.' "

PART II: CHECKING YOUR PROGRESS

A. True-False

Where the statement is true, circle **T**; where it is false, circle **F**.

1. T   F   Lincoln deliberately decided to provoke a war by sending strong military reinforcements to Fort Sumter.

2. T   F   In order to appease the Border States, Lincoln first insisted that the North was fighting only to preserve the Union and not to abolish slavery.

3. T   F   The South's advantage in the Civil War was that it only had to fight to a stalemate on its own territory, while the North had to fight a war of conquest against a hostile population.

4. T   F   The North generally had superior military leadership, while the South struggled to find successful commanders for its armies.

5.   T   F   In the long run, Northern economic and population advantages effectively wore down Southern resistance.

6.   T   F   The antislavery feelings of many in the British working class restrained the pro-Confederate sympathies of the British aristocracy and government.

7.   T   F   Northern pressure eventually forced the British Navy to stop the *Alabama* from raiding Union shipping.

8.   T   F   The French Emperor Napoleon III took advantage of America's Civil War to invade Mexico and install his puppet Emperor Maximilian as the ruler there.

9.   T   F   Abraham Lincoln's lack of political experience in high administrative office made him less effective in leading public opinion than the highly experienced Confederate president Jefferson Davis.

10.   T   F   The Civil War draft reflected the North's commitment to fighting a war based on the ideal of equal treatment of citizens from all economic conditions.

11.   T   F   Lincoln's temporary violations of civil liberties were strongly opposed by Congress.

12.   T   F   The North effectively financed its Civil War effort through an income tax, higher tariffs, and the sale of federal government bonds.

13.   T   F   The South in effect used severe inflation as a means of financing its war effort.

14.   T   F   Northern women effectively supported the Union cause through hospital and relief work in ways that southern women were prevented from doing.

15.   T   F   Despite losing the Civil War, the South emerged with its basic agricultural and transportation infrastructure fairly intact.

B. Multiple Choice

Select the best answer and circle the corresponding letter.

1.   Lincoln's plan for the besieged federal forces in Fort Sumter was to
   a.   order the soldiers there to open fire on the surrounding Confederate army.
   b.   send about 3,000 soldiers and marines to reinforce the fort.
   c.   make a symbolic show of support and then withdraw the forces.
   d.   send U.S. naval forces to gain control of Charleston Harbor.
   e.   send supplies for the existing soldiers but not to add new reinforcements.

2.   The firing on Fort Sumter had the effect of
   a.   pushing ten other states to join South Carolina in seceding from the Union.
   b.   causing Lincoln to declare a war to free the slaves.
   c.   strengthening many Northerners' view that the South should be allowed to secede.
   d.   arousing enthusiastic Northern support for a war to put down the South's rebellion.
   e.   making the North aware that the Civil War would be long and costly.

3.   The four states that joined the Confederacy only after Lincoln's call for troops to suppress the rebellion in April 1861 were
   a.   Florida, Louisiana, Texas, and Oklahoma.
   b.   Virginia, Arkansas, Tennessee, and North Carolina.
   c.   Missouri, Maryland, Kentucky, and Delaware.
   d.   South Carolina, North Carolina, Virginia, and Mississippi.
   e.   Tennessee, Kentucky, West Virginia, and North Carolina.

4. Lincoln at first declared that the war was being fought

    a. only to save the Union and not to free the slaves.
    b. in order to end slavery everywhere except the Border States.
    c. in order to restore the Missouri Compromise.
    d. only to punish South Carolina for firing on Fort Sumter.
    e. only to restore federal control over the forts and arsenals in the South.

5. Which of the following was *not* among the Border States?

    a. Missouri
    b. Kentucky
    c. Oklahoma
    d. Maryland
    e. Delaware

6. The term *Butternut region* refers to the

    a. mountain areas of the South that remained loyal to the Union.
    b. Border States, especially Kentucky and Missouri, that contained large numbers of Confederate supporters.
    c. areas of the upper Midwest that supplied a large portion of the committed Union volunteers.
    d. areas of southern Pennsylvania and New York that supported the war but hated the draft.
    e. areas of southern Ohio, Indiana, and Illinois that opposed an antislavery war.

7. In the Indian Territory (Oklahoma), most of the Five Civilized Tribes

    a. supported the Confederacy and sent warriors to fight for it.
    b. supported a war for the Union but not a war against slavery.
    c. sent many young warriors to fight for the Union cause.
    d. tried to stay neutral in the "white man's war."
    e. used the Civil War to reassert their independence.

8. Among the significant advantages the Confederacy possessed at the beginning of the Civil War was

    a. a stronger and more balanced economy.
    b. a stronger navy.
    c. better-trained officers and soldiers.
    d. a larger reserve of manpower.
    e. better political leadership.

9. Among the advantages the Union possessed at the beginning of the Civil War was

    a. better preparation of its ordinary soldiers for military life.
    b. a continuing influx of immigrant manpower from Europe.
    c. more highly educated and experienced generals.
    d. the ability to fight a primarily defensive war.
    e. strong support from the British and French aristocracy.

10. The response to the Civil War in Europe was

    a. almost unanimous support for the North.
    b. support for the South among the upper classes and for the North among the working classes.
    c. almost unanimous support for the South.
    d. support for the South in France and Spain and for the North in Britain and Germany.
    e. support for the North in the large cities and for the South in rural areas.

11. The South's weapon of King Cotton failed to draw Britain into the war on the side of the Confederacy because
    a. the British discovered that they could substitute flax and wool for cotton.
    b. the British proved able to grow sufficient cotton in their own land.
    c. the British found sufficient cotton from previous stockpiles and from new sources like Egypt and India.
    d. the threat of war with France distracted British attention for several years.
    e. Confederate smugglers evaded the Union blockade and delivered sufficient cotton supplies to Britain.
12. The U.S. minister in London warned that the United States would declare war against Britain if
    a. the British navy did not help to sink the Confederate raider *Alabama*.
    b. Confederate agents continued to use Canada as a safe base for raids into the North.
    c. the British did not withdraw their support for French intervention in Mexico.
    d. the British aristocracy continued to express public support for the Confederacy.
    e. the British government delivered the Laird ram warships it had built to the Confederacy.
13. Lincoln argued that his assertion of sweeping executive powers and suspension of certain civil liberties was justified because
    a. he was confident that Congress and the Supreme Court would approve his actions.
    b. the South had committed even larger violations of the Constitution.
    c. during wartime, a president has unlimited power over the civilian population.
    d. he had plainly stated that he would take such steps during his campaign for the presidency.
    e. it was necessary to set aside small provisions of the Constitution in order to save the Union.
14. Many of the new millionaires who emerged in the North during the Civil War
    a. committed their personal fortunes to the Union cause.
    b. made their fortunes by providing poorly made, shoddy goods to the Union armies.
    c. made their highest profits by selling captured cotton to British textile manufacturers.
    d. earned public distrust by secretly advocating a negotiated settlement with the Confederacy.
    e. paid the largest portion of the taxes that financed the Union war effort.
15. Northern women made particular advances during the Civil War by
    a. advocating the right to vote for both African Americans and women.
    b. entering industrial employment and providing medical aid for soldiers on both sides.
    c. pushing for women to take up noncombatant roles in the military.
    d. upholding the feminine ideals of peace and reconciliation.
    e. operating farms and shops while their men were away fighting the war.

C. Identification

Supply the correct identification for each numbered description.

1. _____   The four original Border States where secession failed but slavery still survived
   _____
   _____
   _____

2. _____   The federal military installation in Charleston Harbor against which the first shots of the Civil War were fired

3. _____   A British ship from which two Confederate diplomats were forcibly removed by the U.S. Navy, creating a major crisis between London and Washington

4. _____   Confederate navy warship built in Britain that wreaked havoc on Northern shipping until it was finally sunk in 1864

5. _____   Ironclad warships that were kept out of Confederate hands by Minister Adams's stern protests to the British government

6. _____   Constitutional protection against arbitrary arrest and imprisonment that was suspended by President Lincoln on the grounds that the Union was at risk of destruction

7. _____   Violent protests by largely Irish working class citizens against being forced to serve in a war against slavery that they opposed

8. _____   Popular term for the paper currency that was issued by the wartime Union government to help finance the war

9. _____   Financial institution set up by the wartime federal government to sell war bonds and issue a stable paper currency

10. _____   Federal law of 1862 that offered free land in the West to pioneers willing to settle on it, even during the Civil War

11. _____   Union agency organized by Dr. Elizabeth Blackwell and others to provide field hospitals, supplies, and nurses to U.S. soldiers.

12. _____   New profession that Clara Barton and others first opened to many women during the Civil War

D. Matching People, Places, and Events

Match the person, place, or event in the left column with the proper description in the right column by inserting the correct letter on the blank line.

1. ___ Napoleon III

2. ___ Charles Francis Adams

3. ___ Thomas J. Jackson

4. ___ Maximilian

5. ___ Sally Tompkins

6. ___ Jay Cooke

7. ___ Abraham Lincoln

8. ___ Jefferson Davis

9. ___ Elizabeth Blackwell

10. ___ Clara Barton

a.   American envoy whose shrewd diplomacy helped keep Britain neutral during the Civil War

b.   An Old World aristocrat, manipulated as a puppet in Mexico, who was shot when his puppet-master deserted him

c.   An inexperienced leader in war but a genius at inspiring and directing his nation's cause

d.   Leader whose conflict with states' rights advocates and rigid personality harmed his ability to mobilize and direct his nation's war effort

e.   Head of a major New York bank that marketed war bonds for the Union government at a profit

f.   Slippery French dictator who ignored the Monroe Doctrine by intervening in Mexican politics

g.   Robert E. Lee's brilliant military assistant for much of the Civil War whose nickname symbolized his strength and determination

h. Helped transform nursing into a respected profession during the Civil War

i. Leading organizer of medical services for the South, who was made a captain in the Confederate army for her efforts

j. First woman physician, organizer of the United States Sanitary Commission

E. Putting Things in Order

Put the following events in correct order by numbering them from 1 to 5.

1. ___   Secretary of State Seward threatens to send an American army against the French-installed government of Mexico.

2. ___   Napoleon III's puppet emperor is removed from power in Mexico under threat of American intervention.

3. ___   The firing on Fort Sumter unifies the North and leads to Lincoln's call for troops.

4. ___   The *Alabama* escapes from a British port and begins wreaking havoc on Northern shipping.

5. ___   Charles Francis Adams's successful diplomacy prevents the Confederacy from obtaining two Laird ram warships.

F. Matching Cause and Effect

Match the historical cause in the left column with the proper effect in the right column by writing the correct letter on the blank line.

Cause	Effect
1. ___ South Carolina's assault on Fort Sumter	a. Enabled textile mills to keep functioning despite the Civil War and expanded Britain's share of global markets
2. ___ Lincoln's first call for troops to suppress the rebellion	b. Enabled Northern generals to wear down Southern armies, even at the cost of many lives
3. ___ Lincoln's careful use of moral suasion, politics, and military force	c. Unified the North and made it determined to preserve the Union by military force
4. ___ The large Northern advantage in human resources	d. Eventually gave the Union a crucial economic advantage over the mostly agricultural South
5. ___ The North's naval blockade and industrial superiority	e. Deterred the British from recognizing and aiding the Confederacy
6. ___ The British aristocracy's sympathy with the South	
7. ___ American minister C. F. Adams's diplomacy	
8. ___ British expansion of cotton growing in colonial Egypt and India	

9. ___ The class-biased unfairness of the Civil War draft

10. ___ Lincoln's belief that the Civil War emergency required drastic action

f. Caused four more Upper South states to secede and join the Confederacy

g. Kept the Border States in the Union

h. Led the British government toward actions that aided the Confederacy and angered the Union

i. Led to riots by underprivileged Northern whites, especially Irish Americans

j. Led to temporary infringements on civil liberties and Congress's constitutional powers

G. Developing Historical Skills

Interpreting Tables

Tables convey a great deal of data, often numerical, in concise form. Properly interpreted, they can effectively aid historical understanding.

The following questions will help you interpret some of the tables in this chapter.

1. *Manufacturing by Sections, 1860*

   a. Compare the number of manufacturing establishments in the South and New England. Now compare the amount of invested capital, the number of laborers, and the product value of these same two sections. What do you conclude about the character of the manufacturing establishments in the South and New England?

   b. Approximately how many laborers were employed in the average Southern manufacturing establishment? About how many in the average New England establishment? How many in the average establishment in the middle states?

2. *Immigration to United States, 1860–1866*

   a. From which country did immigration decline rather sharply at the end as well as at the beginning of the Civil War?

   b. From which country did immigration rise most sharply after the end of the Civil War?

   c. From which country did the coming of the Civil War evidently cause the sharpest decline in immigration?

   d. How was immigration affected by the first year of the Civil War? How was it affected by the second year of war? By the third? How long did it take for immigration from each country to return to its prewar level?

3. *Number of Men in Uniform at Date Given*

   a. In what period did the absolute difference in military manpower between the two sides increase most dramatically?

   b. What was the approximate manpower ratio of Union to Confederate forces on each of the following dates: July 1861, March 1862, January 1863, and January 1865?

   c. What happened to the military manpower ratio in the last two years of the war?

PART III: APPLYING WHAT YOU HAVE LEARNED

1. Why did Lincoln decide only to send supplies to Fort Sumter, rather than abandoning it or militarily reinforcing it? How did this decision prove to work to his political advantage? What would have been the consequences had he pursued one of the other two strategies?

2. Why did Lincoln's call for federal troops after the firing on Fort Sumter cause such a furious reaction in the South and lead four more states to secede? Would those states have stayed in the Union had Lincoln not called out troops to suppress the original seven-state Confederacy?

3. Why were the Border States absolutely critical to the Union cause in 1861–1862? How did Lincoln use both political strategy and force to keep the Border States from joining the Confederacy? Was the use of martial law and other harsh means necessary?

4. Which of the advantages that the Confederacy enjoyed at the beginning of the Civil War was the greatest and provided the largest opportunity for the South to successfully win its independence? Did the South fail to exploit its initial advantages to the extent it could have, or were the North's advantages, finally, just greater?

5. How close did the United States and Britain really come to going to war over British sympathy and aid for the Confederacy? Do you agree with most historians that British intervention would probably have secured Confederate independence?

6. Compare Abraham Lincoln and Jefferson Davis as political and military leaders of their two countries during the Civil War. How did their personal strengths and weaknesses to some extent reflect the character of the North and of the South, respectively?

7. How did the North and the South each address their economic and human resources needs? Given the South's economic and manpower disadvantages from the beginning, did it make the most effective use of the resources it did possess?

8. What changes did the Civil War bring about in civilian society, North and South? How did the war particularly affect women?

9. Some historians have called the Civil War "the Second American Revolution." What was revolutionary about the political, social, and economic conduct of the war?

10. Some historians have argued that the North's inherent superiority in manpower and industrial strength made its victory in the Civil War inevitable from the beginning. Do you agree or disagree? Why?

CHAPTER 21

The Furnace of Civil War, 1861–1865

PART I: REVIEWING THE CHAPTER

A. Checklist of Learning Objectives

After mastering this chapter, you should be able to:

1. Describe the consequences for both sides of the North's defeat at the First Battle of Bull Run.

2. Outline Union's original military strategy and how Lincoln was forced to adjust it during the course of the War.

3. Explain the critical importance of the failed Peninsula Campaign and the Battle of Antietam in changing the Civil War from a limited war for the Union into a total war against slavery.

4. Describe the role that African Americans played during the war.

5. Explain why the battles of Gettysburg in the East and Vicksburg in the West decisively turned the tide toward Union victory and Confederate defeat.

6. Describe the politics of the War in both North and South, and the end of the South's hope for winning independence through a defeat of Lincoln in the election of 1864.

7. Describe the end of the war and list its final consequences.

B. Glossary

To build your social science vocabulary, familiarize yourself with the following terms.

1. **intelligence** In military affairs or diplomacy, specific information and analysis regarding an adversary's forces, deployments, production, and so on. "He consistently but erroneously believed that the enemy outnumbered him, partly because . . . his intelligence reports were unreliable."

2. **reconnaissance** Operations designed specifically to observe and ferret out pertinent information about an adversary. ". . . 'Jeb' Stuart's cavalry rode completely around his army on reconnaissance."

3. **proclamation** An official announcement or publicly declared order. "Thus, the Emancipation Proclamation was stronger on proclamation than emancipation."

4. **flank** The side of an army, where it is vulnerable to attack. "Lee . . . sent 'Stonewall' Jackson to attack the Union flank."

5. **court-martial** A military court, or a trial held in such a court under military law. "Resigning from the army to avoid a court-martial for drunkenness, he failed at various business ventures. . . ."

6. **garrison** A military fortress, or the troops stationed at such a fortress, usually designed for defense or occupation of a territory. "Vicksburg at length surrendered . . . , with the garrison reduced to eating mules and rats."

7. **morale** The condition of courage, confidence, and willingness to endure hardship. "One of his major purposes was . . . to weaken the morale of the men at the front by waging war on their homes."

8. **pillaging** Plundering, looting, destroying property by violence. ". . . his army . . . engaged in an orgy of pillaging."

9. **tribunal** An agency or institution (sometimes but not necessarily a court) constituted to render judgments and assign punishment, especially in the military. "But he was convicted by a military tribunal in 1863 for treasonable utterances. . . ."

10. **running mate** In American politics, the candidate for the lesser of two offices when they are decided together—for example, the U.S. vice presidency. "Lincoln's running mate was ex-tailor Andrew Johnson. . . ."

PART II: CHECKING YOUR PROGRESS

A. True-False

Where the statement is true, circle **T**; where it is false, circle **F**.

1. T F The South's victory in the First Battle of Bull Run gave it a great advantage in morale during the first year of the Civil War.

2. T F General George McClellan's Peninsula Campaign failed through a combination of his own excessive caution and Robert E. Lee's vigorous attacks.

3. T F The failed Peninsula Campaign forced the Union to turn toward a total war designed to crush the entire South.

4. T F The Battle of Antietam was a turning point of the war because it prevented British and French recognition of the Confederacy and enabled Lincoln to issue the preliminary Emancipation Proclamation.

5. T F Lincoln's decision to turn the Civil War into a war to abolish slavery greatly enhanced his political standing in the North.

6. T F Black soldiers often faced execution as escaped slaves if they were captured during battle.

7. T F Lee's invasion of Pennsylvania in 1863 was intended to win the war by encouraging the Northern peace movement and bringing foreign intervention on behalf of the Confederacy.

8. T F The Northern victories at Vicksburg and Gettysburg effectively spelled doom for the Confederacy's efforts to win its independence on the battlefield.

9. T F In the final year of the conflict, Grant and Sherman waged a total war that aimed to destroy the South's economy and morale as well as defeat its armies.

10. T F The Northern Democrats were deeply divided between War Democrats who supported the war effort and Peace Democrats who sought a negotiated settlement with the South.

11. T F At the Democratic party convention of 1864, the openly antiwar Copperheads enjoyed little influence.

12. T F A series of Union military victories just before the election of 1864 guaranteed Lincoln's victory over McClellan and ended the South's last hope.

13. T F   Lee's turn to defensive tactics in the last year of the war forced Grant into an offensive strategy that caused enormous casualties in direct frontal assaults on Confederate lines.

14. T F   Lincoln's assassination added to northern bitterness and determination to punish the South.

15. T F   In terms of percentage of soldiers killed, the Civil War was the second deadliest war in American history after World War II.

B. Multiple Choice

Select the best answer and circle the corresponding letter.

1. A major effect of the First Battle of Bull Run was to
   a. convince the North that it would not be that difficult to conquer Richmond.
   b. increase the South's already dangerous overconfidence.
   c. demonstrate the superiority of Southern volunteer soldiers over Northern draftees.
   d. cause a wave of new Southern enlistments in the army.
   e. lead Lincoln to consider abandoning Washington and moving the government elsewhere.

2. The primary weakness of General George McClellan as a military commander was his
   a. inability to gain the support of his troops.
   b. tendency to rush into battle with inadequate plans and preparation.
   c. lack of confidence in his own abilities.
   d. excessive caution and reluctance to use his troops in battle.
   e. tendency to rely on artillery and cavalry rather infantry troops.

3. After the failed Peninsula Campaign, Lincoln and the Union turned to a
   a. new strategy based on total war against the Confederacy.
   b. new strategy based on an invasion through the mountains of western Virginia and Tennessee.
   c. strategy of defensive warfare designed to protect Washington, D.C.
   d. reliance on the navy rather than the army to win the war.
   e. strategy based on encouraging political divisions within the South.

4. The Union blockade of Confederate ports was
   a. initially leaky but eventually effective.
   b. challenged by the powerful navies of Britain and France.
   c. immediately effective in capturing Confederate blockade-running ships.
   d. largely ineffective in shutting off the sale of Confederate cotton in Europe.
   e. more effective on the Atlantic coast than along the Gulf coast.

5. Antietam was one of the crucial battles of the Civil War because
   a. it ended any further possibility of Confederate invasion of the North.
   b. it was the last chance for the Confederates to win a major battle.
   c. it fundamentally undermined Confederate morale.
   d. the death of Lee's greatest general, Stonewall Jackson, crippled his military effectiveness.
   e. it prevented British and French recognition of the Confederacy.

6. Officially, the Emancipation Proclamation freed only slaves
   a. who had fled their masters and joined the Union Army.
   b. under control of the rebellious Confederate states.
   c. in the Border States and in areas under Union Army control.
   d. in Washington, D.C.
   e. whose masters were loyal to the Confederacy.

7. The political effects of the Emancipation Proclamation were to

    a. bolster public support for the war and the Republican party.
    b. increase conflict between Lincoln and the radical wing of the Republican party.
    c. turn the Democratic party from support of the war toward favoring recognition of the Confederacy.
    d. weaken support for the Union among British and French public opinion.
    e. strengthen the North's moral cause but weaken the Lincoln administration in the Border States and parts of the North.

8. The thousands of black soldiers in the Union Army

    a. added a powerful new weapon to the antislavery dimension of the Union cause.
    b. were largely prevented from participating in combat.
    c. **were enlisted primarily to compensate for the military advantage that the South enjoyed because of slavery.**
    d. saw relatively little direct military action during the war.
    e. were enthusiastic but relatively ineffective in combat.

9. Lee's primary goal in invading the North in the summer of 1863 was to

    a. capture major Northern cities like Philadelphia and Pittsburgh.
    b. deflect attention from "Stonewall" Jackson's movements against Washington.
    c. strengthen the Northern peace movement and encourage foreign intervention in the war.
    d. cut off Northern supply lines and damage the Union's economic foundations.
    e. drive through to Canada and thus split the North in two.

10. Grant's capture of Vicksburg was especially important because it

    a. quelled Northern peace agitation and cut off the Confederate trade route across the Mississippi.
    b. ended the threat of a Confederate invasion of southern Illinois and Indiana.
    c. blocked the French army in Mexico from moving to aid the Confederacy.
    d. destroyed Southern naval power.
    e. enabled the North to completely suppress the South's cotton trade with Europe.

11. Lincoln dealt with the leading Copperhead, Clement Vallandigham, by

    a. banishing him to Canada.
    b. persuading the Democratic party to repudiate him.
    c. drafting him into the Union army.
    d. using Union troops to harass him into silence.
    e. convicting him of treason in a military tribunal and then shipping him to the South.

12. Andrew Johnson, Lincoln's vice-presidential running mate in 1864, was a

    a. Copperhead.
    b. War Democrat.
    c. conservative Republican.
    d. radical Republican.
    e. Peace Democrat.

13. Lincoln's election victory in 1864 was sealed by Union military successes at

    a. Gettysburg, Antietam, and Vicksburg.
    b. the Wilderness, Lookout Mountain, and Appomattox.
    c. Bull Run, the Peninsula, and Fredericksburg.
    d. Mobile, Atlanta, and the Shenandoah Valley.
    e. Chancellorsville, the Wilderness, and Cold Harbor.

14. Sherman's march "from Atlanta to the sea" was especially notable for its
    a. tactical brilliance against Confederate cavalry forces.
    b. effective use of public relations to turn Southern sympathies against the Confederacy.
    c. brutal use of total war tactics of destruction and pillaging against Southern civilian populations.
    d. impact in inspiring Northern public opinion to turn against slavery.
    e. commitment to emancipate slaves and bring them into the Union army.
15. As the Democratic Party nominee in 1864, General George McClellan
    a. denounced Lincoln as a traitor and called for an immediate end to the war.
    b. repudiated the Copperhead platform that called for a negotiated settlement with the Confederacy.
    c. indicated that, if elected president, he would take personal command of all Union armies.
    d. called for waging a total war against the civilian population in the South.
    e. effectively attacked Lincoln's constant turnover of top Union generals.

C. Identification

Supply the correct identification for each numbered description.

1. _____ First major battle of the Civil War, in which untrained Northern troops and civilian picnickers fled back to Washington (either battle name acceptable)

2. _____ McClellan's disastrously unsuccessful attempt to end the war quickly by a back-door conquest of Richmond

3. _____ Key battle of 1862 that forestalled European intervention to aid the Confederacy and led to the Emancipation Proclamation

4. _____ Document that proclaimed slaves in territories in rebellion to be free and guaranteed a fight to the finish

5. _____ Constitutional amendment, passed eight months after the Civil War, that permanently ended slavery throughout the United States.

6. _____ Crucial Confederate fortress on the Mississippi whose fall to Grant in 1863 cut the South in two

7. _____ Pennsylvania battle that ended Lee's last hopes of achieving victory through an invasion of the North

8. _____ Campaign through Georgia that stirred southern hatred by waging total war against the southern civilian economy and morale

9. _____ Northern Democrats who openly opposed the Civil War and sympathized with the South

10. _____ Edward Everett Hale's fictional story of treason and banishment, inspired by the actual wartime banishing of Copperhead Clement Vallandigham

11. _____ Georgia city captured and burned by Sherman just before the election of 1864

12. _____ The temporary 1864 coalition of Republicans and War Democrats that backed Lincoln's re-election

13. _____ Washington site where Lincoln was assassinated by John Wilkes Booth on April 14, 1865

14. _____ Virginia site where Lee surrendered to Grant in April 1865

15. _____ English law under which Britain became a modern democracy, influenced by the Union victory in the Civil War

D. Matching People, Places, and Events

Match the person, place, or event in the left column with the proper description in the right column by inserting the correct letter on the blank line.

1. ___ Bull Run

2. ___ George McClellan

3. ___ Robert E. Lee

4. ___ Antietam

5. ___ Thomas J. "Stonewall" Jackson

6. ___ George Pickett

7. ___ Ulysses S. Grant

8. ___ Gettysburg

9. ___ Vicksburg

10. ___ William T. Sherman

11. ___ Clement Vallandigham

12. ___ Salmon P. Chase

13. ___ The Wilderness

14. ___ Andrew Johnson

15. ___ John Wilkes Booth

a. Daring Southern commander killed at the Battle of Chancellorsville

b. Southern officer whose failed charge at Gettysburg marked "the high water mark of the Confederacy"

c. Ruthless Northern general who waged a march through Georgia

d. Fortress whose capture split the Confederacy in two

e. Site where Lee's last major invasion of the North was turned back

f. Gentlemanly top commander of the Confederate army

g. Site of one of Grant's bloody battles with the Confederates near Richmond in 1864

h. Crucial battle in Maryland that staved off European recognition of the Confederacy

i. Ambitious secretary of the treasury who wanted to replace Lincoln as president in 1864

j. Fanatical actor whose act of violence actually harmed the South

k. Union commander who first made his mark with victories in the West

l. Southern War Democrat who ran as Lincoln's Union party vice-presidential candidate in 1864

m. Notorious Copperhead, convicted of treason, who ran for governor of Ohio while exiled to Canada

n. Union general who repudiated his party's Copperhead platform and polled 45 percent of the popular vote in 1864

o. Site of two important Civil War battles, the first a Union defeat in very early days of the war

E. Putting Things in Order

Put the following events in correct order by numbering them from 1 to 5.

1. _____   Within one week, two decisive battles in Mississippi and Pennsylvania almost ensured the Confederacy's eventual defeat.

2. _____   Defeat in a battle near Washington, D.C., ends Union military complacency.

3. _____   A militarily indecisive battle in Maryland enables Lincoln to declare that the Civil War has become a war on slavery.

4. _____   The Civil War ends with the defeated army granted generous terms of surrender.

5. _____   In both Georgia and Virginia, determined Northern generals wage bloody and destructive total war against a weakened but still-resisting South.

F. Matching Cause and Effect

Match the historical cause in the left column with the proper effect in the right column by writing the correct letter on the blank line.

Cause	**Effect**
1. ___ Political dissent by Copperheads and jealous Republicans	a. Enabled Lincoln to issue the Emancipation Proclamation and blocked British and French intervention
2. ___ A series of Union military victories in late 1864	b. Split the South in two and opened the way for Sherman's invasion of Georgia
3. ___ The assassination of Lincoln	c. Deprived the nation of experienced leadership during Reconstruction
4. ___ Grant's Tennessee and Mississippi River campaigns	d. Made it difficult for Lincoln to prosecute the war effectively
5. ___ The Battle of Bull Run	e. Helped lead to the enlistment of black fighting men in the Union Army
6. ___ The Battle of Antietam	f. Ended the South's effort to win the war by aggressive invasion
7. ___ The Battle of Gettysburg	g. Guaranteed that the South would fight to the end to try to save slavery
8. ___ Grant's final brutal campaign in Virginia	h. Forced Lee to surrender at Appomattox
9. ___ The Emancipation Proclamation	i. Led some southerners to believe they would win an easy victory
10. ___ The growing Union manpower shortage in 1863	j. Ensured Lincoln's reelection and ended the South's last hope of achieving independence by political means

G. Developing Historical Skills

Interpreting Painting

Paintings may depict historical subjects and, in the process, convey information about an artist's interpretation of an event, a problem, or a whole society. Answer these questions about the Winslow Homer painting *Prisoners from the Front.* (p. 508)

1. Study the clothing carefully. Who is in what kind of uniform, and who is not? What is the artist suggesting about the economic and military condition of the two sides? What is suggested about the condition of civilians in the two sections?

2. Describe the posture and facial expressions of the five main figures. What kind of attitude does each suggest?

3. Look at the weapons in the painting and at the distance between the Northern officer and the Confederates. What does Homer seem to be suggesting about the relations between the sections after the war?

H. Map Mastery

Map Discrimination

Using the maps and charts in Chapter 21, answer the following questions.

1. *Main Thrusts, 1861–1865*: Which two states of the Southeast saw little of the major fighting of the Civil War?

2. *Emancipation in the South*: In which four states were the slaves all freed by state action—without any federal involvement?

3. *Emancipation in the South*: Which two states kept slavery until it was finally abolished by the Thirteenth Amendment to the Constitution?

4. *The Mississippi River and Tennessee, 1862–1863*: On what three rivers were the major Confederate strategic points that Grant successfully assaulted in 1862–1863?

5. *Sherman's March, 1864–1865*: What major secessionist South Carolina city was *not* in the direct path of Sherman's army in 1864–1865?

6. *Grant's Virginia Campaign, 1864–1865*: What major battle of Grant's final campaign was fought very close to the Confederate capital city?

Map Challenge

Using the maps in this chapter, write a brief essay explaining Union military strategy in the Civil War.

PART III: APPLYING WHAT YOU HAVE LEARNED

1. Why did both sides initially expect the Civil War to be relatively short? How did this expectation shape their strategy and actions? How did the strategies and meaning of the war change as it became increasingly long and bloody?

2. Why was George McClellan such a popular and politically influential general, despite his military weaknesses and failures? Why did Lincoln support him for so long despite McClellan's contempt for him? Should Lincoln have fired McClellan much earlier than he did?

3. Why was Lincoln so slow to declare the Civil War as a fight against slavery? Was he wise to move slowly, or could an early Emancipation Proclamation have undermined the Union cause?

4. Which should be viewed is the single most critical turning point in the War: a) the Battle of Antietam in September 1862, b) Gettysburg and Vicksburg in July 1863, or c) Atlanta, Mobile, and the Shenandoah Valley in fall 1864. Defend your answer.

5. Why was the enlistment and successful use of black soldiers such a radical and important development in affecting Americans' view of the Civil War and race. Why did the use of black soldiers stir such fury in the South—including establishing the policy of executing captured black soldiers?

6. What qualities made Ulysses S. Grant so successful, when all the numerous generals Lincoln had earlier tried had largely failed?

7. Compare Grant and Lee as commanders of their respective armies. Is the traditional view of Lee as the "greatest general of the Civil War," despite his defeat, a justified one? Why or why?

8. What were the causes and consequences of Sherman's and Grant's turn toward total war in the conquest of the South? Was Sherman's aim of destroying southern civilian morale a fundamentally immoral one? In what ways is it fair to call the Civil War "the first modern war"?

9. Why did peace sentiment remain fairly strong in the North right up until Lincoln's victory in the election of 1864? Was Lincoln too harsh in dealing with the Copperheads or not harsh enough?

10. Were the costs of the Civil War worth the results to the nation as a whole? What issues were settled by the war, and what new problems were created?

CHAPTER 22

The Ordeal of Reconstruction, 1865–1877

PART I: REVIEWING THE CHAPTER

A. Checklist of Learning Objectives

After mastering this chapter, you should be able to:

1. Define the major problems facing the nation and the South after the Civil War.

2. Describe the responses of both whites and African Americans to the end of slavery.

3. Analyze the differences between the presidential and congressional approaches to Reconstruction.

4. Explain how the blunders of President Johnson and the resistance of the white South opened the door to the Republicans' radical Reconstruction.

5. Describe the intentions and the actual effects of radical Reconstruction in the South.

6. Indicate how militant southern white opposition and growing northern weariness with military Reconstruction gradually undermined Republican attempt to empower Southern blacks.

7. Explain why the radical Republicans impeached Johnson but failed to convict him.

8. Explain the legacy of Reconstruction, and assess its successes and failures.

B. Glossary

To build your social science vocabulary, familiarize yourself with the following terms.

1. **treason** The crime of betrayal of one's country, involving some overt act violating an oath of allegiance or providing illegal aid to a foreign state. In the United States, treason is the only crime specified in the Constitution. "What should be done with the captured Confederate ringleaders, all of whom were liable to charges of treason?"

2. **civil disabilities** Legally imposed restrictions of a person's civil rights or liberties. "But Congress did not remove all remaining civil disabilities until thirty years later. . . ."

3. **legalistically** In accord with the exact letter of the law, sometimes with the intention of thwarting its broad intent. "Some planters resisted emancipation more legalistically. . . ." (p. 481)

4. **mutual aid societies** Nonprofit organizations designed to provide their members with financial and social benefits, often including medical aid, life insurance, funeral costs, and disaster relief. "These churches . . . gave rise to other benevolent, fraternal, and mutual aid societies."

5. **confiscation (confiscated)** Legal government seizure of private property *without* compensation, often as a penalty; under **eminent domain**, the government may take private property for public purposes, but *with* fair compensation. ". . . the bureau was authorized to settle former slaves on forty-acre tracts confiscated from the Confederates. . . ."

6. **pocket veto** The presidential act of blocking a Congressionally passed law not by direct veto but by simply refusing to sign it at the end of a session. (A president can pocket-veto ten days of a session's end.) "Lincoln 'pocket-vetoed' this bill by refusing to sign it after Congress had adjourned."

7. **lease** To enter into a contract by which one party gives another use of land, buildings, or other property for a fixed time and fee. ". . . some [codes] even barred blacks from renting or leasing land."

8. **chain gang** A group of prisoners chained together while engaged in forced labor. "A black could be punished for 'idleness' by being sentenced to work on a chain gang."

9. **sharecrop** An agricultural system in which a tenant receives land, tools, and seed on credit and pledges in return a predetermined share of the crop to the creditor. ". . . former slaves slipped into the status of sharecropper farmers. . . ."

10. **peonage** A system, once common in Latin America, in which debtors are bound, in permanent or semi-permanent servitude, to labor for their creditors. "Luckless sharecroppers gradually sank into a morass of virtual peonage. . . ."

11. **scalawag** Disparaging term for a white Southerner who supported Republican Reconstruction after the Civil War. "The so-called scalawags were Southerners, often former Unionists and Whigs."

12. **carpetbagger** Disparaging term for a Northern politician who came south to exploit the unsettled conditions after the Civil War; hence, any politician who relocates for political advantage. "The carpet-baggers, on the other hand, were supposedly sleazy Northerners. . . ." (p. 495)

13. **felony** A major crime for which severe penalties are exacted under the law. "The crimes of the Reconstruction governments were no more outrageous than the scams and felonies being perpetrated in the North at the same time. . . ."

14. **terror (terrorist)** Using violence or the threat of violence in order to create intense fear in the attempt to promote some political policy or objectives. "Such tomfoolery and terror proved partially effective."

15. **president pro tempore** In the United States Senate, the officer who presides in the absence of the vice president. "Under existing law, the president pro tempore of the Senate . . . would then become president."

PART II: CHECKING YOUR PROGRESS

A. True-False

Where the statement is true, circle **T**; where it is false, circle **F**.

1. T   F   Most of the aristocratic southern plantation owners lost their wealth during the Civil War.

2. T   F   Most white southerners recognized that secession had been a mistake and welcomed returning to the United States as American citizens.

3. T   F   Many newly emancipated slaves undertook travel to demonstrate their freedom or to seek separated loved ones.

4. T   F   The focus of black community life after emancipation became the black church.

5.   T   F   The newly established Freedmen's Bureau proved effective as a social agency providing economic opportunity as well as food, clothing, and medical care to emancipated blacks.

6.   T   F   Lincoln's 10 percent Reconstruction plan was designed to return the Southern states to the Union quickly and with few restrictions.

7.   T   F   Andrew Johnson's first Reconstruction actions pleased radical Republicans by harshly punishing Southern leaders and refusing to grant them pardons.

8.   T   F   The sharecropping system, developed during Reconstruction, trapped most blacks and many poor whites in a condition of perpetual debt to their creditors.

9.   T   F   The Black Codes, enacted by the Johnson-established southern state governments, provided freed slaves with basic political rights but not social integration.

10.   T   F   Congressional Republicans demanded that the Southern states ratify the Fourteenth Amendment in order to be readmitted to the Union.

11.   T   F   Radical Republicans succeeded in their goal of redistributing land to the former slaves.

12.   T   F   During Reconstruction, blacks controlled most of the Southern state legislatures.

13.   T   F   Many women felt betrayed when the Fifteenth Amendment gave voting rights to black males but not to women.

14.   T   F   The federal government made no effort to attempt to suppress the violent white supremacists in the Ku Klux Klan.

15.   T   F   The Republicans impeached Andrew Johnson essentially because of his opposition to their Reconstruction policies and not on the basis of "high crimes and misdemeanors."

B. Multiple Choice

Select the best answer and circle the corresponding letter.

1. Which of the following was *not* among the critical questions that faced the United States during Reconstruction?
   a. Would the president, Congress, or the states direct Reconstruction?
   b. How would liberated blacks manage as free men and women?
   c. Would the South be granted some kind of regional autonomy short of independence?
   d. How would the economically and socially devastated South be rebuilt?
   e. How would the southern states be reintegrated into the Union?

2. The Freedmen's Bureau was originally established to provide
   a. land, supplies, and seed for black farmers.
   b. job registration.
   c. food, clothing, and education for emancipated slaves.
   d. political training in citizenship for black voters.
   e. transportation and assistance in reuniting separated family members.

3. Lincoln's original plan for Reconstruction in 1863 was that a state could be reintegrated into the Union when

    a. it repealed its original secession act and withdrew its soldiers from the Confederate Army.
    b. 10 percent of its voters took an oath of allegiance to the Union and pledged to abide by emancipation.
    c. it formally adopted a plan guaranteeing black political and economic rights.
    d. it ratified the Fourteenth and Fifteenth Amendments to the Constitution.
    e. it barred from office and punished those who had voted for secession or served in the Confederate government.

4. The Black Codes, passed by many of the Johnson-approved Southern state governments in late 1865, aimed to

    a. provide economic assistance to get former slaves started as sharecroppers.
    b. prohibit interracial sexual relations.
    c. permit blacks to vote if they met certain educational or economic standards.
    d. force blacks to leave the South.
    e. ensure a stable and subservient labor force under white control.

5. The congressional elections of 1866 resulted in a

    a. victory for Johnson and his pro-Southern Reconstruction plan.
    b. further political stalemate between the Republicans in Congress and Johnson.
    c. decisive defeat for Johnson and a veto-proof Republican Congress.
    d. gain for Northern Democrats and their moderate compromise plan for Reconstruction.
    e. split between moderate Republicans in the Senate and radical Republicans in the House.

6. In contrast to radical Republicans, moderate Republicans generally

    a. favored states' rights and opposed direct federal involvement in individuals' lives.
    b. favored the use of federal power to alter the Southern economic system.
    c. favored emancipation but opposed the Fourteenth Amendment.
    d. favored returning the Southern states to the Union without significant Reconstruction.
    e. supported policies favorable to poor southern whites as well as blacks.

7. Besides putting the South under the rule of federal soldiers, the Military Reconstruction Act of 1867 required that all the reconstructed southern states must

    a. give blacks the vote as a condition of readmission to the Union.
    b. give blacks and carpetbaggers majority control of Southern legislatures.
    c. provide former slaves with land and education at state expense.
    d. try former Confederate officials and military officers for treason.
    e. effectively suppress the Ku Klux Klan and other white supremacist groups.

8. Which of the following was *not* among the provisions of the Fourteenth Amendment?

    a. Disqualification from federal and state office for former Confederate officials who had violated their oaths
    b. Reduction in Congressional representation and Electoral College vote for states that did not let blacks vote
    c. Repudiation of any Confederate debts
    d. Citizenship and full civil rights (except voting) for former slaves
    e. Elimination of one senator from each southern state until Reconstruction was complete

9. The Fifteenth Amendment provided for

    a. readmitting Southern states to the Union.
    b. full citizenship and civil rights for former slaves.
    c. voting rights for former slaves.
    d. voting rights for women.
    e. racial integration of public schools and public facilities.

10. Women's-rights leaders opposed the Fourteenth and Fifteenth Amendments because
    a. they objected to racial integration in the women's movement.
    b. the amendments granted citizenship and voting rights to black and white men but not to women.
    c. they favored passage of the Equal Rights Amendment first.
    d. most of them were Democrats who would be hurt by the amendments.
    e. they feared interracial sex and marriage.
11. Achieving the right to vote encouraged southern black men to
    a. form a third political party as an alternative to the Democrats and Republicans.
    b. seek a formal apology and reparations for slavery.
    c. organize the Union League as a vehicle for political empowerment and self-defense.
    d. organize large-scale migrations out of the South to the West.
    e. demand that each southern state grant blacks "forty acres and a mule."
12. The radical Reconstruction regimes in the Southern states
    a. took away white Southerners' civil rights and voting rights.
    b. consisted almost entirely of blacks.
    c. established public education and adopted many needed reforms.
    d. were largely the pawns of white northern carpetbaggers.
    e. were almost one hundred percent honest and free from corruption.
13. The major long-term effect of white terrorist organizations like the Ku Klux Klan was to
    a. disempower blacks politically and restore white supremacy.
    b. drive the U.S. Army out of the South.
    c. create a permanent secret government of former Confederates in the southern states.
    d. make most southerners forget their nostalgia for the lost cause of the Confederacy.
    e. encourage many blacks to arm themselves for self-defense.
14. The radical Republicans' impeachment of President Andrew Johnson resulted in
    a. Johnson's acceptance of the radicals' Reconstruction plan.
    b. a revision in the impeachment clause of the Constitution to make such an action more difficult.
    c. Johnson's conviction on the charge of violating the Tenure of Office Act.
    d. Johnson's resignation and appointment of Ulysses Grant as his successor.
    e. a failure to convict and remove Johnson from the presidency by a margin of only one vote.
15. The skeptical public finally accepted Secretary of State William Seward's purchase of Alaska partly because it
    a. learned that there were extensive oil deposits in the territory.
    b. was found to be strategically vital to American defense in the northern Pacific.
    c. realized that Alaska would be the last frontier after the settling of the West.
    d. was grateful to Russia as the only great power friendly to the Union during the Civil War.
    e. became entranced by the natural beauty and wildlife of the territory.

C. Identification

Supply the correct identification for each numbered description.

1. _____ Federal agency that greatly assisted blacks educationally but failed in other aid efforts

2. _____ The two largest African American denominations (church bodies) by the end of Reconstruction

3. _____ Lincoln's 1863 program for a rapid Reconstruction of the South

4. _____ The congressional bill of 1864 requiring 50 percent of a state's voters to take an oath of allegiance before rejoining Union; vetoed by Lincoln

5. _____ The harsh Southern state laws of 1865 that limited black rights and imposed harsh restrictions to ensure a stable black labor supply

6. _____ The constitutional amendment granting civil rights to freed slaves and barring former Confederates from office

7. _____ Law of March 1867 that imposed military rule on the South and disenfranchised former thousands of former Confederates

8. _____ Laudatory term for white southerners who worked to overthrow Reconstruction and establish Home Rule regimes in the southern states

9. _____ The black political organization that promoted self-help and defense of political rights during Reconstruction

10. _____ Supreme Court ruling that military tribunals could not try civilians when the civil courts were open

11. _____ Derogatory term for white Southerners who cooperated with the Republican Reconstruction governments

12. _____ Derogatory term for Northerners who came to the South during Reconstruction and sometimes took part in Republican state governments

13. _____ Constitutional amendment guaranteeing blacks the right to vote

14. _____ White supremacist organization that created a reign of terror against blacks until it was largely suppressed by federal troops

D. Matching People, Places, and Events

Match the person, place, or event in the left column with the proper description in the right column by inserting the correct letter on the blank line.

1. ___ Exodusters

2. ___ Oliver O. Howard

3. ___ Andrew Johnson

4. ___ Abraham Lincoln

5. ___ Andrew Stephens

6. ___ Charles Sumner

7. ___ Thaddeus Stevens

8. ___ Military Reconstruction Act of 1867

9. ___ Hiram Revels

10. ___ Ku Klux Klan

11. ___ Force Acts of 1870 and 1871

12. ___ "swing around the circle"

13. ___ Union League

a. President Andrew Johnson's angry, disastrous political trip attacking Congress in the campaign of 1866

b. Former Confederate vice president whose election to Congress in 1865 infuriated northerners

c. Born a poor white southerner, he became the white South's champion against radical Reconstruction

d. Secretary of state who arranged an initially unpopular but valuable land deal in 1867

e. Laws designed to stamp out Ku Klux Klan terrorism in the South

f. Black Republican senator from Mississippi during Reconstruction

14. ___ Benjamin Wade

15. ___ William Seward

g. Secret organization that intimidated blacks and worked to restore white supremacy

h. Blacks who left the South for Kansas and elsewhere during Reconstruction

i. Congressional law that imposed military rule on the South and demanded harsh conditions for readmission of the seceded states

j. Beaten in the Senate chamber before the Civil War, he became the leader of Senate Republican radicals during Reconstruction

k. Pro-black general who led an agency that tried to assist the freedmen

l. Leading black political organization during Reconstruction

m. Author of the moderate 10 percent Reconstruction plan that ran into congressional opposition

n. The president pro tempore of the Senate who hoped to become president of the United States after Johnson's impeachment conviction

o. Leader of radical Republicans in the House of Representatives

E. Putting Things in Order

Put the following events in correct order by numbering them from 1 to 5.

1. _____ Constitution is amended to guarantee former slaves the right to vote

2. _____ Lincoln announces a plan to rapidly restore southern states to the Union.

3. _____ Northern troops are finally withdrawn from the South, and Southern state governments are reconstituted without federal constraint.

4. _____ An unpopular antiradical president escapes conviction and removal from office by one vote.

5. _____ Johnson's attempt to restore the South to the Union is overturned because of congressional hostility to ex-Confederates and southern passage of the Black Codes.

F. Matching Cause and Effect

Match the historical cause in the left column with the proper effect in the right column by writing the correct letter on the blank line.

Cause

1. ___ The South's military defeat in the Civil War

2. ___ The Freedmen's Bureau

3. ___ The Black Codes of 1865

4. ___ The election of ex-Confederates to Congress in 1865

5. ___ Johnson's "swing around the circle" in the election of 1866

6. ___ Military Reconstruction and the Fourteenth and Fifteenth Amendments

7. ___ The radical Southern state Reconstruction governments

8. ___ The Ku Klux Klan

9. ___ The radical Republicans' hatred of Johnson

10. ___ The whole Reconstruction era

Effect

a. Provoked a politically motivated trial to remove the president from office

b. Intimidated black voters and tried to keep blacks "in their place"

c. Prompted Republicans to refuse to seat Southern delegations in Congress

d. Destroyed the Southern economy but strengthened Southern hatred of yankees

e. Successfully educated former slaves but failed to provide much other assistance to them

f. Forced all the Southern states to establish governments that upheld black voting and other civil rights

g. Embittered white Southerners while doing little to really help blacks

h. Engaged in some corruption but also enacted many valuable social reforms

i. Weakened support for mild Reconstruction policies and helped elect overwhelming Republican majorities to Congress

j. Imposed slavery-like restrictions on blacks and angered the North

G. Developing Historical Skills

Interpreting Photographs and Drawings

Answer the following questions about the photographs and drawings in this chapter.

1. *Educating Young Freedmen and Women, 1870s*

   What appears to be the average age of the students in the photograph? What does the dress of the students suggest about the freedmen's attitudes toward education? From their positioning in the photograph, how might you describe the teachers' relationships with the children?

2. *Sharecroppers Picking Cotton*

    What tasks are the sharecroppers engaged in? Is there possibly a gender division of labor among the field workers? How does the white man in the background—likely the landowner—display his social and economic superiority to the black sharecroppers?

3. *Freedmen Voting, Richmond, Virginia, 1871*

    What appears to be the economic status of the new black voters portrayed here? How does their condition differ from that of the voting officials, black and white? What does the drawing suggest about the power of the newly enfranchised freedmen?

PART III: APPLYING WHAT YOU HAVE LEARNED

1. What were the major problems facing the South and the nation after the Civil War? How did Reconstruction address them or fail to do so?

2. How did freed blacks react to the end of slavery? How did both Southern and Northern whites react?

3. Why did the white South's treatment of the freed slaves so enrage many northerners in 1865. Was the Republican anger at Johnson motivated primarily by concern that the fruits of emancipation would be lost or by fear that a restored white South would be more powerful than ever?

4. What was the purpose of congressional Reconstruction, and what were its actual effects in the South?

5. What did the attempt at black political empowerment achieve? Why did it finally fail? Could it have succeeded with a stronger Northern political will behind it?

6. How did African Americans take advantage of the political, economic, religious, and social opportunities of Reconstruction, despite their limitations? In what areas were blacks most successful, and in which least?

7. The legend of the Reconstruction state governments is that they were vicious and corrupt failures run by unprepared blacks and greedy northern carpetbaggers. How did the reality of Reconstruction compare with this portrayal?

8. The radical Republicans believed that only a complete economic and social revolution, including redistribution of land and property, could permanently guarantee black rights in the South. Were they right? Why were most northerners of the time, including the moderate Republicans, unwilling to support such a drastic government-sponsored transformation?

9. Why did Reconstruction apparently fail so badly? Was the failure primarily one of immediate political circumstances, or was it more deeply rooted in the history of American sectional and race relations?

10. What was the greatest success of Reconstruction? Would you agree with historians who argue that even though Reconstruction failed at the time, it laid the foundations for the later successes of the civil rights movement?

CHAPTER 23

Political Paralysis in the Gilded Age, 1869–1896

PART I: REVIEWING THE CHAPTER

A. Checklist of Learning Objectives

After mastering this chapter, you should be able to:

1. Describe the political corruption of the Grant administration and the mostly unsuccessful efforts to reform politics in the Gilded Age.

2. Describe the economic crisis of the 1870s, and explain the growing conflict between hard-money and soft-money advocates.

3. Explain the intense political partisanship of the Gilded Age, despite the parties' lack of ideological difference and poor quality of political leadership.

4. Indicate how the disputed Hayes-Tilden election of 1876 led to the Compromise of 1877 and the end of Reconstruction.

5. Describe how the end of Reconstruction led to the loss of black rights and the imposition of the Jim Crow system of segregation in the South.

6. Explain the rise of class conflict between business and labor in the 1870s and the growing hostility to immigrants, especially the Chinese.

7. Explain the economic crisis and depression of the 1890s, and indicate how the Cleveland administration failed to address it.

8. Show how the farm crisis of the depression of the 1890s stirred growing social protests and class conflict, and fueled the rise of the radical Populist Party.

B. Glossary

To build your social science vocabulary, familiarize yourself with the following terms.

1. **coalition** A temporary alliance of political factions or parties for some specific purpose. "The Republicans, now freed from the Union party coalition of war days, enthusiastically nominated Grant. . . ."

2. **corner** To gain exclusive control of a commodity in order to fix its price. "The crafty pair concocted a plot in 1869 to corner the gold market."

3. **censure** An official statement of condemnation passed by a legislative body against one of its members or some other official of government. While severe, a censure itself stops short of penalties or **expulsion**, which is removal from office. "A newspaper exposé and congressional investigation led to formal censure of two congressmen. . . ."

4. **amnesty** A general pardon for offenses or crimes against a government. "The Republican Congress in 1872 passed a general amnesty act. . . ."

5. **civil service** Referring to regular employment by government according to a standardized system of job descriptions, merit qualifications, pay, and promotion, as distinct from **political appointees** who receive positions based on affiliation and party loyalty. "Congress also moved to reduce high Civil War tariffs and to fumigate the Grant administration with mild civil service reform."

6. **unsecured loans** Money loaned without identification of collateral (existing assets) to be forfeited in case the borrower defaults on the loan. "The Freedman's Savings and Trust Company had made unsecured loans to several companies that went under."

7. **contraction** In finance, reducing the available supply of money, thus tending to raise interest rates and lower prices. "Coupled with the reduction of greenbacks, this policy was called 'contraction.' "

8. **deflation (ary)** An increase in the value of money in relation to available goods, causing prices to fall. **Inflation**, a decrease in the value of money in relation to goods, causes prices to rise. "It had a noticeable deflationary effect—the amount of money per capita in circulation actually *decreased*. . . ."

9. **fraternal organization** A society of men drawn together for social purposes and sometimes to pursue other common goals. ". . . the Grand Army of the Republic [was] a politically potent fraternal organization of several hundred thousand Union veterans of the Civil War."

10. **consensus** Common or unanimous opinion. "How can this apparent paradox of political consensus and partisan fervor be explained?"

11. **kickback** The return of a portion of the money received in a sale or contract, often secretly or illegally, in exchange for favors. "The lifeblood of both parties was patronage—disbursing jobs by the bucketful in return for votes, kickbacks, and party service."

12. **lien** A legal claim by a lender or another party on a borrower's property as a guarantee against repayment, and prohibiting any sale of the property. " . . . storekeepers extended credit to small farmers for food and supplies and in return took a lien on their harvest."

13. **assassination** Politically motivated murder of a public figure. " . . . he asked all those who had benefited politically by the assassination to contribute to his defense fund."

14. **laissez-faire** The doctrine of noninterference, especially by the government, in matters of economics or business (literally, "leave alone"). "[The new president was] a staunch apostle of the hands-off creed of laissez-faire. . . ."

15. **pork barrel** In American politics, government appropriations for political purposes, especially projects designed to please a legislator's local constituency. "One [way to reduce the surplus] was to squander it on pensions and 'pork-barrel' bills. . . ."

PART II: CHECKING YOUR PROGRESS

A. True-False

Where the statement is true, circle **T**; where it is false, circle **F**.

1. T   F   Ulysses Grant's status as a military hero enabled him to become a successful president who stood above partisan politics.

2. T   F   The scandals of the Grant administration included bribes and corrupt dealings reaching to the cabinet and the vice president of the United States.

3. T   F   The Liberal Republican movement's political skill enabled it to clean up the corruption of the Grant administration.

4. T F   The severe economic downturn of the 1870s caused business failures, labor conflict, and battles over currency.

5. T F   The close, fiercely contested elections of the Gilded Age reflected the deep divisions between Republicans and Democrats over national issues.

6. T F   The battles between the Stalwart and Half-Breed Republican factions were mainly over who would get patronage and spoils.

7. T F   The disputed Hayes-Tilden election was settled by a political deal in which Democrats got the presidency and Republicans got economic and political concessions.

8. T F   The Compromise of 1877 purchased political peace between North and South by sacrificing southern blacks and removing federal troops in the South.

9. T F   The sharecropping and tenant farming systems forced many Southern blacks into permanent economic debt and dependency.

10. T F   Western hostility to Chinese immigrants arose in part because the Chinese provided a source of cheap labor that competed with white workers.

11. T F   By reducing politicians' use of patronage, the new civil-service system inadvertently made them more dependent on big campaign contributors.

12. T F   The Cleveland-Blaine campaign of 1884 was conducted primarily as a debate about the issues of taxes and the tariff.

13. T F   The Republican party, in the post–Civil War era, relied heavily on the political support of veterans' groups, to which it gave substantial pension benefits in return.

14. T F   The Populist party's attempt to form a coalition of farmers and workers failed partly because of the racial division between poor whites and blacks in the South.

15. T F   President Cleveland's deal to save the gold standard by borrowing $65 million from J.P. Morgan enhanced his popularity among both Democrats and Populists.

B. Multiple Choice

Select the best answer and circle the corresponding letter.

1. Financiers Jim Fisk and Jay Gould involved the Grant administration in a corrupt scheme to
    a. skim funds from the Bureau of Indian Affairs.
    b. sell watered railroad stock at artificially high prices.
    c. corner the gold market.
    d. bribe congressmen in exchange for federal land grants.
    e. provide federal subsidies for bankrupt Wall Street stockbrokers.
2. Boss Tweed's widespread corruption was finally brought to a halt by
    a. federal prosecutors who uncovered the theft.
    b. outraged citizens who rebelled against the waste of public money.
    c. the journalistic exposés of the *New York Times* and cartoonist Thomas Nast.
    d. Tweed's political opponents in New York City.
    e. bank officials who disclosed Tweed's illegal financial maneuvers.

3.   The Credit Mobilier scandal involved

    a.   the abuse of federal loans intended for urban development.

    b.   railroad corporation fraud and the subsequent bribery of congressmen to cover it up.

    c.   Secretary of War Belknap's fraudulent sale of contracts to supply Indian reservations.

    d.   the attempt of insiders to gain control of New York's gold and stock markets.

    e.   illegal gifts and loans to members of President Grant's White House staff.

4.   Grant's greatest failing in the scandals that plagued his administration was his

    a.   refusal to turn over evidence to congressional investigators.

    b.   toleration of corruption and his loyalty to crooked friends.

    c.   acceptance of behind-the-scenes payments for performing his duties as president.

    d.   use of large amounts of dirty money in his political campaigns.

    e.   inability to distinguish innocent members of his staff from the guilty.

5.   The depression of the 1870s led to increasing demands for

    a.   a new federally controlled Bank of the United States.

    b.   federal programs to create jobs for the unemployed.

    c.   restoration of sound money by backing all paper currency with gold.

    d.   stronger regulation of the banking system.

    e.   inflation of the money supply by issuing more paper or silver currency.

6.   The political system of the Gilded Age was generally characterized by

    a.   split-ticket voting, low voter turnout, and single-issue special-interest groups.

    b.   strong party loyalties, low voter turnout, and deep ideological differences.

    c.   third-party movements, high voter turnout and strong disagreement on foreign-policy issues.

    d.   strong party loyalties, high voter turnout, and few disagreements on national issues.

    e.   weak party loyalties, high voter turnout, and focus on personalities rather than parties.

7.   The primary goal for which all factions in both political parties contended during the Gilded Age was

    a.   racial justice.

    b.   a sound financial and banking system.

    c.   patronage.

    d.   a more assertive American foreign policy.

    e.   rapid expansion of the national railway system.

8.   The key tradeoff featured in the Compromise of 1877 was that

    a.   Republicans got the presidency in exchange for the final removal of federal troops from the South.

    b.   Democrats got the presidency in exchange for federal guarantees of black civil rights.

    c.   Republicans got the presidency in exchange for Democratic control of the cabinet.

    d.   Democrats got the presidency in exchange for increased immigration quotas from Ireland.

    e.   Republicans got the presidency in exchange for permitting former Confederate officers to vote.

9.   Which of the following was *not* among the changes that affected African Americans in the South after federal troops were withdrawn in the Compromise of 1877?

    a.   The forced relocation of black farmers to the Kansas and Oklahoma dust bowl

    b.   The imposition of literacy requirements and poll taxes to prevent black voting

    c.   The development of the tenant farming and share-cropping systems

    d.   The introduction of legal systems of racial segregation

    e.   The rise of mob lynching as a means of suppressing blacks who challenged the racial system

10. The Supreme Court's ruling in *Plessy* v. *Ferguson* upholding "separate but equal" public facilities in effect legalized
    a.   southern blacks' loss of voting rights.
    b.   the right of blacks to establish separate colleges admitting blacks only.
    c.   the program of separate black and white economic development endorsed by Booker T. Washington.
    d.   the rights to "equal protection of the law" guaranteed by the Fourteenth Amendment.
    e.   the system of unequal segregation between the races.

11. The great railroad strike of 1877 revealed the
    a.   growing strength of American labor unions.
    b.   refusal of the U.S. federal government to intervene in private labor disputes.
    c.   ability of American workers to cooperate across ethnic and racial lines.
    d.   growing threat of class warfare in response to the economic depression of the mid-1870s.
    e.   American economy's capacity to find alternatives to railroad transportation.

12. The final result of the widespread anti-Chinese agitation in the West was
    a.   a program to encourage Chinese students to enroll in American colleges and universities.
    b.   a congressional law to prohibit any further Chinese immigration.
    c.   the stripping of citizenship even from native-born Chinese Americans.
    d.   legal segregation of all Chinese into Chinatown districts in San Francisco and elsewhere.
    e.   the forced emigration of all but a handful of Chinese back to China.

13. President James Garfield was assassinated by a(n)
    a.   fanatically anti-Republican Confederate veteran.
    b.   mentally unstable disappointed office seeker.
    c.   anticapitalist immigrant anarchist.
    d.   corrupt gangster under federal criminal indictment.
    e.   bitter supporter of his defeated Democratic opponent, Winfield Scott Hancock.

14. In its first years, the Populist Party advocated, among other things
    a.   free silver, a graduated income tax, and government ownership of the railroads, telegraph, and telephone.
    b.   higher tariffs and federally sponsored unemployment insurance and pensions.
    c.   tighter restriction on black economic, social, and political rights.
    d.   a Homestead Act to permit farmers and unemployed workers to obtain free federal land in the West.
    e.   greater support for land grant colleges to enhance scientific agriculture.

15. Grover Cleveland stirred a furious storm of protest when, in response to the extreme financial crisis of the 1890s, he
    a.   lowered tariffs to permit an influx of cheaper foreign goods into the country.
    b.   signed a bill introducing a federal income tax that cut into workers' wages.
    c.   pushed the Federal Reserve Board into sharply raising interest rates.
    d.   borrowed $65 million dollars from J.P. Morgan and other bankers in order to save the monetary gold standard.
    e.   seized federal control of the railroad industry.

C. Identification

Supply the correct identification for each numbered description.

1. _____ The symbol of the Republican political tactic of attacking Democrats with reminders of the Civil War

2. _____ Corrupt construction company whose bribes and payoffs to congressmen and others created a major Grant administration scandal

3. _____ Short-lived third party of 1872 that attempted to curb Grant administration corruption

4. _____ Precious metal that soft-money advocates demanded be coined again to compensate for the Crime of '73

5. _____ Soft-money third party that polled over a million votes and elected fourteen congressmen in 1878 by advocating inflation

6. _____ Mark Twain's sarcastic name for the post–Civil War era, which emphasized its atmosphere of greed and corruption

7. _____ Civil War Union veterans' organization that became a potent political bulwark of the Republican party in the late nineteenth century

8. _____ Republican party faction led by Senator Roscoe Conkling that opposed all attempts at civil-service reform

9. _____ Republican party faction led by Senator James G. Blaine that paid lip service to government reform while still battling for patronage and spoils

10. _____ The complex political agreement between Republicans and Democrats that resolved the bitterly disputed election of 1876

11. _____ Asian immigrant group that experienced discrimination on the West Coast

12. _____ System of choosing federal employees on the basis of merit rather than patronage introduced by the Pendleton Act of 1883

13. _____ Sky-high Republican tariff of 1890 that caused widespread anger among farmers in the Midwest and the South

14. _____ Insurgent political party that gained widespread support among farmers in the 1890s

15. _____ Notorious clause in southern voting laws that exempted from literacy tests and poll taxes anyone whose ancestors had voted in 1860, thereby excluding blacks

D. Matching People, Places, and Events

Match the person, place, or event in the left column with the proper description in the right column by inserting the correct letter on the blank line.

1. ___ Ulysses S. Grant

2. ___ Jim Fisk

3. ___ Boss Tweed

4. ___ Horace Greeley

a. Heavyweight New York political boss whose widespread fraud landed him in jail in 1871

b. Bold and unprincipled financier whose plot to corner the U.S. gold market nearly succeeded in 1869

5. ___ Samuel Tilden

6. ___ Denis Kearney

7. ___ Tom Watson

8. ___ Roscoe Conkling

9. ___ James G. Blaine

10. ___ Rutherford B. Hayes

11. ___ James Garfield

12. ___ Jim Crow

13. ___ Grover Cleveland

14. ___ William Jennings Bryan

15. ___ J. P. Morgan

c. Winner of the contested 1876 election who presided over the end of Reconstruction and a sharp economic downturn

d. Great military leader whose presidency foundered in corruption and political ineptitude

e. Term for the racial segregation laws imposed in the 1890s

f. Eloquent young Congressman from Nebraska who became the most prominent advocate of free silver in the early 1890s

g. President whose assassination after only a few months in office spurred the passage of a civil-service law

h. Irish-born leader of the anti-Chinese movement in California

i. Radical Populist leader whose early success turned sour and who then became a vicious racist

j. New York prosecutor of Boss Tweed who later lost in the disputed presidential election of 1876

k. Imperious New York senator and leader of the Stalwart faction of Republicans

l. First Democratic president since the Civil War; defender of laissez-faire economics and low tariffs

m. Enormously wealthy banker whose secret bailout of the federal government in 1895 aroused fierce public anger

n. Colorful, eccentric newspaper editor who carried the Liberal Republican and Democratic banners against Grant in 1872

o. Charming but corrupt Half-Breed Republican senator and presidential nominee in 1884

E. Putting Things in Order

Put the following events in correct order by numbering them from 1 to 5.

1. _____ A bitterly disputed presidential election is resolved by a complex political deal that ends Reconstruction in the South.

2. _____ Two unscrupulous financiers use corrupt means to manipulate New York gold markets and the U.S. Treasury.

3. _____ A major economic depression causes widespread social unrest and the rise of the Populist party as a vehicle of protest.

4. _____ Grant administration scandals split the Republican party, but Grant overcomes the inept opposition to win reelection.

5. _____ Monetary deflation and the high McKinley Tariff lead to growing agitation for free silver by Congressman William Jennings Bryan and others.

F. Matching Cause and Effect

Match the historical cause in the left column with the proper effect in the right column by writing the correct letter on the blank line.

Cause	**Effect**
1. ___ Favor-seeking businesspeople and corrupt politicians	a. Created fierce partisan competition and high voter turnouts, even though the parties agreed on most national issues
2. ___ The *New York Times* and cartoonist Thomas Nast	b. Caused anti-Chinese violence and restrictions against Chinese immigration
3. ___ Upright Republicans' disgust with Grant administration scandals	c. Led to the formation of the Liberal Republican party in 1872
4. ___ The economic crash of the mid-1870s	d. Induced Grover Cleveland to negotiate a secret loan from J. P. Morgan's banking syndicate
5. ___ Local cultural, moral, and religious differences	e. Forced Boss Tweed out of power and into jail
6. ___ The Compromise of 1877 that settled the disputed Hayes-Tilden election	f. Helped ensure passage of the Pendleton Act
7. ___ White workers' resentment of Chinese labor competition	g. Caused numerous scandals during President Grant's administration
8. ___ Public shock at Garfield's assassination by Guiteau	h. Led to failure of the third-party revolt in the South and a growing racial backlash
9. ___ The 1890s depression and the drain of gold from the federal treasury	i. Caused unemployment, railroad strikes, and a demand for cheap money
10. ___ The inability of Populist leaders to overcome divisions between white and black farmers	j. Led to the withdrawal of troops from the South and the virtual end of federal efforts to protect black rights there

G. Developing Historical Skills

Historical Fact and Historical Explanation

Historians uncover a great deal of information about the past, but often that information takes on significance only when it is analyzed and interpreted. In this chapter, many facts about the presidents and elections of the Gilded Age are presented: for example, the very close elections in 1876, 1884, 1888, and 1892; the large voter turnouts; and the lack of significant issues in most elections.

These facts take on larger meaning, however, when we examine the reasons for them. Reread the section "Pallid Politics in the Gilded Age" (pp.543–544) and answer each of the following questions in a sentence or two.

1. What fundamental difference between the two parties made partisan politics so fiercely contested in the Gilded Age?

2. Why did this underlying difference *not* lead to differences over issues at the national level?

3. Why were so many of the elections extremely close, no matter who the candidates were?

4. Why was winning each election so very important to both parties, even though there was little disagreement on issues?

H. Map Mastery

Map Discrimination

Using the maps and charts in Chapter 23, answer the following questions.

1. *Hayes-Tilden Disputed Election of 1876*: In the controversial Hayes-Tilden election of 1876, how many undisputed electoral votes did Republican Hayes win in the former Confederate states?

2. *Hayes-Tilden Disputed Election of 1876*: Democrat Tilden carried four states in the North—states that did not have slavery before 1865. Which were they?

3. *Growth of Classified Civil Service*: The percentage of offices classified under civil service was approximately how many times greater under President McKinley than under President Arthur: two, three, four, five, or ten?

4. *Presidential Election of 1884*: Which of the following states gained the most electoral votes between 1876 and 1884: New York, Indiana, Missouri, or Texas?

5. *Presidential Election of 1884*: How many states that were carried by Republican Hayes in 1876 were carried by Democrat Cleveland in 1884?

Map Challenge

Using the election map on p. 545 and the account of the Compromise of 1877 in the text (pp. 545–546), discuss the election of 1876 in relation to both Reconstruction and the political balance of the Gilded Age. Include some analysis of the reasons why this was the last time for nearly a century that the states in the Deep South voted Republican.

PART III: APPLYING WHAT YOU HAVE LEARNED

1. What made politics in the Gilded Age so extremely popular—with over 80 percent voter participation—yet so often corrupt and unconcerned with important national issues?

2. What caused the end of the Reconstruction? In particular, why did the majority of Republicans abandon their earlier policy of support for black civil rights and voting in the South?

3. What were the results of the Compromise of 1877 for race relations? How did the suppression of blacks through the sharecropping and crop-lien systems depress the economic condition of the South for whites and blacks alike?

4. What caused the rise of the money issue in American politics? What were the backers of greenback and silver money each trying to achieve?

5. What were the causes and political results of the rise of agrarian protest in the 1880s and 1890s? Why were the Populists' attempts to form a coalition of white and black farmers and industrial workers ultimately unsuccessful?

6. White laborers in the West fiercely resisted Chinese immigration, and white farmers in the South turned toward race-baiting rather than forming a populist alliance with black farmers. How and why did racial animosity trump the apparent economic self-interests of these lower-class whites?

7. In what ways did the political conflicts of the Gilded Age still reflect the aftermath of the Civil War and Reconstruction (see Chapter 22)? To what extent did the political leaders of the time address issues of race and sectional conflict, and to what extent did they merely shove them under the rug?

8. Was the apparent failure of the American political system to address the industrial conflicts and racial tensions of the Gilded Age a result of the two parties' poor leadership and narrow self-interest, or was it simply the natural inability of a previously agrarian, local, democratic nation to face up to a modern, national industrial economy?

CHAPTER 24

Industry Comes of Age, 1865–1900

PART I: REVIEWING THE CHAPTER

A. Checklist of Learning Objectives

After mastering this chapter, you should be able to:

1. Explain how the transcontinental railroad network provided the basis for an integrated national market and the great post–Civil War industrial transformation.

2. Identify the abuses in the railroad industry and discuss how these led to the first efforts at industrial regulation by the federal government.

3. Describe how the economy came to be dominated by giant trusts, such as those headed by Carnegie and Rockefeller in the steel and oil industries, and the growing class conflict it precipitated.

4. Describe how new technological inventions fueled new industries and why American manufacturers increasingly turned toward the mass production of standardized goods.

5. Indicate how industrialists and their intellectual and religious supporters attempted to explain and justify great wealth, and increasing class division through natural law and the Gospel of Wealth.

6. Explain why the South was generally excluded from American industrial development and remained in a Third World economic subservience to the North.

7. Analyze the social changes brought by industrialization, particularly the altered position of working men and women.

8. Explain the failures of the Knights of Labor and the modest success of the American Federation of Labor.

B. Glossary

To build your social science vocabulary, familiarize yourself with the following terms.

1. **pool** In business, an agreement to divide a given market in order to avoid competition. "The earliest form of combination was the 'pool'. . . ."

2. **rebate** A return of a portion of the amount paid for goods or services. "Other rail barons granted secret rebates. . . ."

3. **free enterprise** An economic system that permits unrestricted entrepreneurial business activity; capitalism. "Dedicated to free enterprise . . . , they cherished a traditionally keen pride in progress."

4. **regulatory commission** In American government, any of the agencies established to control a special sphere of business or other activity; members are usually appointed by the president and confirmed by Congress. "It heralded the arrival of a series of independent regulatory commissions in the next century. . . ."

5. **trust** A combination of corporations, usually in the same industry, in which stockholders trade their stock to a central board in exchange for trust certificates. (By extension, the term came to be applied to any large, semi-monopolistic business.) "He perfected a device for controlling bothersome rivals—the 'trust.'"

6. **syndicate** An association of financiers organized to carry out projects requiring very large amounts of capital. "His prescribed remedy was to . . . ensure future harmony by placing officers of his own banking syndicate on their various boards of directors."

7. **patrician** Characterized by noble or high social standing. "An arrogant class of 'new rich' was now elbowing aside the patrician families. . . ."

8. **plutocracy** Government by the wealthy. "Plutocracy . . . took its stand firmly on the Constitution."

9. **Third World** Term developed during the Cold War between the United States and the Soviet Union (1946–1991) for the non-Western (first world) and noncommunist (second world) nations of the world, most of them formerly under colonial rule and still economically poor and dependent. "The net effect was to keep the South in a kind of 'Third World' servitude to the Northeast. . . ."

10. **socialist (socialism)** Political belief in promoting social and economic equality through the ownership and control of the major means of production by the whole community (usually but not necessarily in the form of the state) rather than by individuals or corporations. "Some of it was envious, but much of it rose from the small and increasingly vocal group of socialists. . . ."

11. **radical** One who believes in fundamental change in the political, economic, or social system. ". . .much of [this criticism] rose from . . . socialists and other radicals, many of whom were recent European immigrants."

12. **lockout** The refusal by an employer to allow employees to work unless they agree to his or her terms. "Employers could lock their doors against rebellious workers—a process called the 'lockout'. . . ."

13. **yellow dog contract** A labor contract in which an employee must sign a document pledging not to join a union as a condition of holding the job. "[Employers] could compel them to sign 'ironclad oaths' or 'yellow dog contracts'. . . ."

14. **cooperative** An organization for producing, marketing, or consuming goods in which the members share the benefits. ". . . they campaigned for . . . producers' cooperatives. . . ."

15. **anarchist (anarchism)** Political belief that all organized, coercive government is wrong in principle, and that society should be organized solely on the basis of free cooperation. (Some anarchists practiced violence against the state, while others were nonviolent pacifists.) "Eight anarchists were rounded up, although nobody proved that they had anything to do directly with the bomb."

PART II: CHECKING YOUR PROGRESS

A. True-False

Where the statement is true, circle **T**; where it is false, circle **F**.

1. T F Private railroad companies built the transcontinental rail lines by raising their own capital funds without the assistance of the federal government.

2. T F The rapid expansion of the railroad industry was often accompanied by rapid mergers, bankruptcies, and reorganizations.

3.   T   F   The railroads created an integrated national market, stimulated the growth in cities, and encouraged European immigration.

4.   T   F   The practice of artificially inflating railroads' stock prices (stock watering) often left the companies deeply in debt after promoters absconded with the profits.

5.   T   F   The new Interstate Commerce Commission did end some of the worst railroad abuses, but served more to stabilize the railroad industry than to seriously reform it.

6.   T   F   The Rockefeller oil company technique of horizontal integration involved combining into one organization all the phases of manufacturing from the raw material to the customer.

7.   T   F   Rockefeller, Morgan, and others organized monopolistic trusts and interlocking directorates in order to consolidate business and eliminate cutthroat competition.

8.   T   F   Defenders of unrestrained capitalism like Herbert Spencer and William Graham Sumner primarily used natural law and laissez-faire economics rather than Charles Darwin's theories to justify the "survival of the fittest."

9.   T   F   The pro-industry ideology of the New South enabled that region to make rapid economic gains by 1900.

10.   T   F   Two new inventions that brought large numbers of women into the workplace were the typewriter and the telephone.

11.   T   F   The most successful American manufacturers concentrated on producing high-quality, specialized goods for luxury markets in the United States and Europe.

12.   T   F   The impact of new machines and mass immigration held down wages and gave employers advantages in their dealings with labor.

13.   T   F   The Knights of Labor achieved spectacular growth by enlisting all workers, including skilled and unskilled, male and female, black and white.

14.   T   F   The Haymarket Square bombing severely damaged the Knights of Labor by linking it with anarchist violence, even though the organization had nothing to do with the bombs.

15.   T   F   The American Federation of Labor tried hard but failed to organize unskilled workers, women, and blacks.

B. Multiple Choice

Select the best answer and circle the corresponding letter.

1.   The federal government contributed to the building of the national rail network by
   a.   importing substantial numbers of Chinese immigrants to build the railroads.
   b.   providing free grants of federal land to the railroad companies.
   c.   building and operating the first transcontinental rail lines.
   d.   transporting the mail and other federal shipments over the rail lines.
   e.   establishing clear national standards for railroad routes, track gauge, safety, and fair pricing.

2.   A large share of the capital that financed the growth of American industry came from
   a.   workers' pension funds and other pooled resources.
   b.   the federal government.
   c.   European investment in private American corporations.
   d.   a system of revolving industrial development loans run by individual states.
   e.   immigrants and investors fleeing political instability in Latin America.

3. The railroad most significantly stimulated American industrialization by

    a. opening up the West to settlement.
    b. creating a single national market for raw materials and consumer goods.
    c. eliminating the inefficient canal system.
    d. inspiring greater federal investment in technical research and development.
    e. ending the agricultural domination of the American economy.

4. The railroad barons aroused considerable public opposition by practices such as

    a. forcing Indians off their traditional hunting grounds.
    b. refusing to pay their employees decent wages.
    c. refusing to build railroad lines in less settled areas.
    d. stock watering, rate discrimination, and bribery of public officials.
    e. using federal land grants and other subsidies to finance their construction and operations.

5. The railroads affected even the organization of time in the United States by

    a. introducing regularly scheduled departures and arrivals on railroad timetables.
    b. introducing daylight savings time during the summer.
    c. introducing four standard time zones across the country.
    d. turning travel that had once taken days into a matter of hours.
    e. establishing the practice of a fixed 10-hour work day for all employees.

6. Congress finally stepped in to pass the Interstate Commerce Act to regulate the railroad industry because

    a. labor unions and social reformers demanded a public voice in the railroad industry.
    b. railroad corporations themselves were demanding an end to corruption and cutthroat competition.
    c. President Grover Cleveland gave strong backing for the law.
    d. the Supreme Court had ruled in the *Wabash* case that the states had no power to regulate interstate commerce.
    e. the spectacular failure of several railroads threatened the survival of the industry.

7. Financier J. P. Morgan exercised his tremendous economic power most effectively by

    a. promoting horizontal integration of the oil industry.
    b. lending money to the federal government.
    c. consolidating and controlling rival industries through interlocking directorates.
    d. serving as the middleman between American industrialists and foreign governments.
    e. steering bank loans and investments to the most promising new industries.

8. Two late-nineteenth-century technological inventions that especially drew women out of the home and into the workforce were the

    a. railroad and the telegraph.
    b. electric light and the phonograph.
    c. cash register and the stock ticker.
    d. typewriter and the telephone.
    e. mimeograph and the moving picture.

9. Andrew Carnegie's industrial system of vertical integration involved the

    a. construction of large, vertical steel factories in Pittsburgh and elsewhere.
    b. cooperation between manufacturers like Andrew Carnegie and financiers like J. P. Morgan.
    c. integration of diverse immigrant ethnic groups into the steel industry labor force.
    d. combination of all phases of the steel industry from mining to manufacturing into a single organization.
    e. allying of competitors to monopolize a given market.

10. The large trusts like Standard Oil and Swift and Armour justified their economic domination of their industries by claiming that
    a. they were fundamentally concerned with serving the public interest over private profit.
    b. only large-scale methods of production and distribution could provide superior products at low prices.
    c. competition among many small firms was contrary to the law of economics.
    d. only large American corporations could compete with huge British and German international companies.
    e. price wars were necessary to make a profit.

11. So-called Social Darwinists like Herbert Spencer and William Graham Sumner justified harsh competition and vast disparities in wealth by arguing that
    a. industrialists like Rockefeller and Carnegie foreshadowed the evolution of the human race.
    b. such developments were a natural consequence of the New World environment.
    c. large fortunes could be used to invest in research that would improve the human gene pool.
    d. Charles Darwin had uncovered the scientific basis of economics as well as biology.
    e. the wealthy who came out on top were simply displaying their natural superiority to others.

12. Andrew Carnegie's "Gospel of Wealth" proclaimed his belief that
    a. wealth was God's reward for hard work, while poverty resulted from laziness and immorality.
    b. churches needed to take a stronger stand on the economic issues of the day.
    c. faith in capitalism and progress should take the place once reserved for religion.
    d. those who acquired great wealth were morally responsible to use it for the public good.
    e. Jesus' teachings had revealed the fundamental principles of successful business.

13. The attempt to create an industrialized New South in the late nineteenth century generally failed because
    a. most southerners cherished the aristocratic ideals of leisure and education and looked down on hard work and economic pursuits.
    b. Southerners were too still too bitter at the Union to engage in productive economic pursuits that might benefit the nation.
    c. continued political violence made the South an unattractive place for investment.
    d. there was little demand for southern products like textiles and cigarettes.
    e. the South was discriminated against and kept in constant debt as a supplier of raw materials to northern industry.

14. For American workers, industrialization generally meant
    a. a steady, long-term decline in wages and the standard of living.
    b. an opportunity to create small businesses that would enable them eventually to achieve economic independence.
    c. a long-term rise in the standard of living but a loss of independence and control of work.
    d. a stronger sense of identification with their jobs and employers.
    e. the ability to join unions and achieve solidarity with their fellow workers.

15. In contrast to the Knights of Labor, the American Federation of Labor advocated
    a. uniting both skilled and unskilled workers into a single large union.
    b. concentrating on improving wages and hours and avoiding general social reform.
    c. working for black and female labor interests as well as those of white men.
    d. using secrecy and violence against employers.
    e. using politics and government rather than strikes to achieve labor's goals.

C. Identification

Supply the correct identification for each numbered description.

1. _____ Federally owned acreage granted to the railroad companies in order to encourage the building of rail lines

2. _____ The original transcontinental railroad, commissioned by Congress, which built its rail line west from Omaha

3. _____ The California-based railroad company, headed by Leland Stanford, that employed Chinese laborers in building lines across the mountains

4. _____ The luxurious railroad cars that enabled passengers to travel long distances in comfort and elegance

5. _____ Dishonest device by which railroad promoters artificially inflated the price of their stocks and bonds

6. _____ Supreme Court case of 1886 that prevented states from regulating railroads or other businesses engaging in interstate commerce

7. _____ The region of northern Minnesota that supplied most of the iron ore for tremendously profitable American steel industry

8. _____ Late-nineteenth-century invention that revolutionized communications and created a large new industry that relied heavily on female workers

9. _____ First of the great industrial trusts, organized through the principle of horizontal integration, that ruthlessly incorporated or destroyed competitors in an energy industry.

10. _____ The first billion-dollar American corporation, organized when J. P. Morgan bought out Andrew Carnegie

11. _____ Term that southern promoters used to proclaim their belief in a technologically advanced, industrial South

12. _____ Somewhat misleading term to describe the ideas of theorists like Herbert Spencer and William Graham Sumner, who claimed that vast wealth was the result of the natural superiority of those who achieved it.

13. _____ Secret, ritualistic labor organization that enrolled many skilled and unskilled workers but collapsed suddenly after the Haymarket Square bombing

14. _____ Shorthand term for the image of the independent and athletic new woman created by a popular magazine illustrator of the late nineteenth century.

15. _____ The conservative labor group that successfully organized a minority of American workers but left others out

D. Matching People, Places, and Events

Match the person, place, or event in the left column with the proper description in the right column by inserting the correct letter on the blank line.

1. ____ Leland Stanford

2. ____ Russell Conwell

3. ____ James J. Hill

a. Inventive genius of industrialization who worked on devices such as the electric light, the phonograph, and the motion picture

4. ____ Cornelius Vanderbilt

5. ____ James Buchanan Duke

6. ____ Alexander Graham Bell

7. ____ Thomas Edison

8. ____ Andrew Carnegie

9. ____ John D. Rockefeller

10. ____ J. Pierpont Morgan

11. ____ Henry Grady

12. ____ Terence V. Powderly

13. ____ William Graham Sumner

14. ____ John P. Altgeld

15. ____ Samuel Gompers

b. The only businessperson in America wealthy enough to buy out Andrew Carnegie and organize the United States Steel Corporation

c. Illinois governor who pardoned the Haymarket anarchists

d. Southern newspaper editor who tirelessly promoted industrialization as the salvation of the economically backward South

e. Aggressive energy-industry monopolist who used tough means to build a trust based on horizontal integration

f. Wealthy southern industrialist whose development of mass-produced cigarettes led him to endow a university that later bore his name

g. Aggressive eastern railroad builder and consolidator who scorned the law as an obstacle to his enterprise

h. Pro-business clergyman whose "Acres of Diamonds" speeches criticized the poor

i. Scottish immigrant who organized a vast new industry on the principle of vertical integration

j. Former California governor and organizer of the Central Pacific Railroad

k. Organizer of a conservative craft-union group and advocate of more wages for skilled workers

l. Eloquent leader of a secretive labor organization that made substantial gains in the 1880s before it suddenly collapsed

m. Public-spirited railroad builder who assisted farmers in the northern areas served by his rail lines

n. Intellectual defender of laissez-faire capitalism who argued that the wealthy owed nothing to the poor

o. Former teacher of the deaf whose invention created an entire new industry

E. Putting Things in Order

Put the following events in correct order by numbering them from 1 to 5.

1. _____   J. P. Morgan buys out Andrew Carnegie to form the first billion-dollar U.S. corporation.

2. _____   The first federal law regulating railroads is passed.

3. _____   The killing of policemen during a labor demonstration results in the execution of radical anarchists and the decline of the Knights of Labor.

4. _____   A teacher of the deaf invents a machine that greatly eases communication across distance.

5. _____   A golden spike is driven, fulfilling the dream of linking the nation by rail.

F. Matching Cause and Effect

Match the historical cause in the left column with the proper effect in the right column by writing the correct letter on the blank line.

Cause	**Effect**
1. ___ The vast American national market and the high cost of skilled labor in the United States	a. Eliminated competition and created monopolistic trusts in many industries
2. ___ The building of a transcontinental rail network	b. Provided a large share of the capital for the growth of American industry
3. ___ Corrupt financial dealings and political manipulations by the railroads	c. Created a strong but narrowly based union organization
4. ___ New developments in steel making, oil refining, and communication	d. Stimulated the growth of a huge unified national market for American manufactured goods
5. ___ The ruthless competitive techniques of Rockefeller and other industrialists	e. Created a public demand for railroad regulation, such as the Interstate Commerce Act
6. ___ The economic investments of European financiers	f. Often made laborers feel powerless and vulnerable to their well-off corporate employers
7. ___ The North's use of discriminatory price practices against the South	g. Helped destroy the Knights of Labor and increased public fear of labor agitation
8. ___ The growing mechanization and depersonalization of factory work	h. Laid the technological basis for huge new industries and spectacular economic growth
9. ___ The Haymarket Square bombing	i. Encouraged industrialists to develop technological innovations that would enable them to produce goods with limited, unskilled labor
10. ___ The American Federation of Labor's concentration on skilled craft workers	j. Kept the South in economic dependency as a poverty-stricken supplier of farm products and raw materials to the Northeast

G. Developing Historical Skills

Interpreting Historical Paintings and Photographs

Historical paintings, lithographs, and photographs not only convey substantive information; they can also tell us how an artist or photographer viewed and understood the society and events of his or her day. Examine the photographs and painting indicated below and answer the following questions about them.

1. Examine the working people in the images on pp. 568, 570, 580, 581, 584, 585, and 587. What is the relationship of the workers in each image to their workplace? What is their relation to one another? What does each of the photos reveal about the nature of industrial labor?

2. Examine the painting of "The Strike" by Robert Koehler on p. 588. Where is the scene taking place? What is the relationship between the place of work and the scene in the painting? What has likely happened to bring the workers to this scene?

3. Analyze the clothing of all the figures in the Koehler painting. What does it tell you about the economic and social condition of the various people?

4. Two main conversations seem to be taking place in the foreground of the painting. What might each be about? What is the artist suggesting by presenting both conversations?

PART III: APPLYING WHAT YOU HAVE LEARNED

1. What was the impact of the transcontinental rail system on the American economy and society in the late nineteenth century?

2. How did the huge industrial trusts develop in industries such as steel and oil, and what was their effect on the economy? Was the growth of enormous, monopolistic corporations simply the natural end result of economic competition, or did it partly result from corrupt practices designed to eliminate competition?

3. What early efforts were made to control the new corporate industrial giants, and how effective were these efforts?

4. What was the effect of the new industrial revolution on American laborers, and how did various labor organizations attempt to respond to the new conditions?

5. Compare the impact of the new industrialization on the North and the South. Why was the New South more a propagandistic slogan than a reality?

6. William Graham Sumner and other so-called Social Darwinists argued that the wealth and luxury enjoyed by millionaires was justifiable as a "good bargain for society" and that natural law should prevent the wealthy classes from aiding the working classes and poor. Why were such views so popular during the Gilded Age? What criticisms of such views might be offered?

7. The text states that "no single group was more profoundly affected by the new industrial age than women." Why was women's role in society so greatly affected by these economic changes?

8. In what ways did industrialization bring a revolution in cultural views of labor, opportunity, and even time?

9. How did the vast scale of the continent-wide American market affect the development of American production, technology, and labor practices?

10. What strains did the new industrialization bring to the American ideals of democracy and equality? Was the growth of huge corporations and great fortunes a successful realization of American principles or a threat to them?

CHAPTER 25

America Moves to the City, 1865–1900

PART I: REVIEWING THE CHAPTER

A. Checklist of Learning Objectives

After mastering this chapter, you should be able to:

1. Describe the rise of the American industrial city, and place it in the context of worldwide trends of urbanization and mass migration (the European diaspora).

2. Describe the New Immigration, and explain how it differed from the Old Immigration and why it aroused opposition from many native-born Americans.

3. Discuss the efforts of social reformers and churches to aid the New Immigrants and alleviate urban problems, and the immigrants' own efforts to sustain their traditions while assimilating to mainstream America.

4. Analyze the changes in American religious life in the late nineteenth century, including the expansion of Catholicism, Orthodoxy, and Judaism, and the growing Protestant division between liberals and fundamentalists over Darwinism and biblical criticism.

5. Explain the changes in American education and intellectual life, including the debate between DuBois and Washington over the goals of African American education.

6. Describe the literary and cultural life of the period, including the widespread trend towards realism in art and literature, and the city beautiful movement led by urban planners.

7. Explain the growing national debates about morality in the late nineteenth century, particularly in relation to the changing roles of women and the family.

B. Glossary

To build your social science vocabulary, familiarize yourself with the following terms.

1. **megalopolis** An extensive, heavily populated area, containing several dense urban centers. " . . . gave way to the immense and impersonal megalopolis. . . ."

2. **tenement** A multidwelling building, often poor or overcrowded. "The cities . . . harbored . . . towering skyscrapers and stinking tenements."

3. **affluence** An abundance of wealth. "These leafy 'bedroom communities' eventually ringed the brick-and-concrete cities with a greenbelt of affluence."

4. **despotism** Government by an absolute or tyrannical ruler. ". . . people had grown accustomed to cringing before despotism."

5. **parochial** Concerning a religious parish or small district. (By extension, the term is used, often negatively, to refer to narrow or local perspectives as distinct from broad or cosmopolitan outlooks.) "Catholics expanded their parochial-school system. . . ."

6. **sweatshop** A factory where employees are forced to work long hours under difficult conditions for meager wages. "The women of Hull House successfully lobbied in 1893 for an Illinois antisweatshop law that protected women workers. . . ."

7. **pauper** A poor person, often one who lives on tax-supported charity. "The first restrictive law . . . banged the gate in the faces of paupers. . . ."

8. **convert** A person who turns from one religion or set of beliefs to another. "A fertile field for converts was found in America's harried, nerve-racked, and urbanized civilization. . . ."

9. **Fundamentalism** A conservative Protestant movement that rejects religious modernism in religion and culture, including biblical higher criticism, and adheres to a strict and literal interpretation of Christian doctrine and Scriptures. "Their rejection of scientific consensus spawned a muscular view of biblical authority that eventually gave rise to fundamentalism...."

10. **philanthropist** A person or organization that works to benefit society through uncompensated gifts, services, or benefits; literally, a "lover of humanity." "Some help came from northern philanthropists. . . . "

11. **behavioral psychology** The branch of psychology that examines human action, often considering it more important than mental or inward states. "His [work] helped to establish the modern discipline of behavioral psychology."

12. **syndicated (syndication)** In journalism, featured writing or drawing that is sold by an organization for publication in several newspapers. "Bare-knuckle editorials were, to an increasing degree, being supplanted by feature articles and non-controversial syndicated material."

13. **tycoon** A wealthy businessperson, especially one who openly displays power and position. "Two new journalistic tycoons emerged."

14. **feminist (feminism)** One who promotes complete political, social, and economic equality of opportunity for women. " . . . in 1898 they heard the voice of a major feminist prophet."

15. **prohibition** Forbidding by law the manufacture, sale, or consumption of liquor. (**Temperance** is the voluntary abstention from liquor consumption.) "Statewide prohibition . . . was sweeping new states into the 'dry' column."

PART II: CHECKING YOUR PROGRESS

A. True-False

Where the statement is true, circle **T**; where it is false, circle **F**.

1. T F   Rapid and uncontrolled growth made American cities places of both exciting opportunity and severe social problems.

2. T F   The United States was unique in the rapidity and scale of growth in its large cities.

3. T F   The largest root cause of the New Immigration was the inability of the European economy to support millions of peasants who were driven off the land.

4. T F   Female social workers established settlement houses to aid struggling immigrants and promote social reform, while also advancing women's opportunities.

5. T F   American Protestantism was dominated by liberal denominations that adapted religious ideas to modern culture and promoted a social gospel rather than biblical literalism.

6. T F Catholic, Jewish, and Orthodox immigrants often initially clustered in their own neighborhoods, places of worship, and schools.

7. T F Almost all American Protestants eventually accepted Charles Darwin's evolutionary theories as well as nonliteral interpretations of the Bible.

8. T F In the late nineteenth century, secondary (high school) education was increasingly carried on by private schools.

9. T F Booker T. Washington believed that the most talented blacks should be educated for political leadership in academically rigorous black colleges.

10. T F American higher education depended on both public land-grant funding and private donations for its financial support.

11. T F Urban newspapers often promoted a sensational yellow journalism that emphasized sex and scandal rather that politics or social reform.

12. T F Post–Civil War writers like Mark Twain and William Dean Howells turned from social realism toward fantasy and science fiction in their novels.

13. T F There was growing tension in the late nineteenth century between women's traditionally defined sphere of family and home, and the social and cultural changes of the era.

14. T F The new urban environment generally weakened the family but offered new opportunities for women to achieve social and economic independence.

15. T F American urban planners focused on preserving greenbelt suburbs rather than the grand schemes for urban beautification developed in Paris and other European cities.

B. Multiple Choice

Select the best answer and circle the corresponding letter.

1. The new cities' glittering consumer economy was symbolized especially by the rise of
    a. separate districts for retail merchants.
    b. fine restaurants and grocery stories.
    c. large, elegant department stores.
    d. large, carefully constructed urban parks.
    e. large arenas for sports and other forms of urban entertainment.
2. One of the most difficult new problems generated by the rise of cities and the urban American life-style was
    a. dealing with horses and other animals in crowded urban settings.
    b. developing means of communication in densely populated city centers.
    c. disposing of large quantities of consumer-generated waste material.
    d. finding effective methods of high-rise construction for limited urban space.
    e. developing methods for accurately recording urban population growth and movement.
3. Two new technological developments of the late nineteenth century that especially contributed to the spectacular growth of cities in America and elsewhere around the world were the
    a. telegraph and the railroad.
    b. steam drill and the internal combustion engine.
    c. phonograph and the motion picture.
    d. oil furnace and the air conditioner.
    e. electric trolley and the skyscraper.

4. Among the primary countries from which many of the New Immigrants came were

    a. Sweden and Great Britain.
    b. Germany and Ireland.
    c. Poland and Italy.
    d. China and Japan.
    e. Mexico and Cuba.

5. Among the factors driving tens of millions of European peasants from their homeland to America and elsewhere in the late nineteenth century were the

    a. rapid rise of population and cheap American food imports.
    b. rise of European nation-states and the decline of the Catholic Church.
    c. rise of tyrannical communist and fascist regimes.
    d. major international wars among the European great powers.
    e. attempt to impose compulsory state education on tradition-minded parents.

6. Besides providing direct services to immigrants, the reformers of Hull House worked to implement social reforms such as

    a. the secret ballot and direct election of senators.
    b. antisweatshop and child labor laws to protect women and child laborers.
    c. social security and unemployment compensation.
    d. conservation and federal aid to municipal governments.
    e. public ownership of municipal transportation systems.

7. The one immigrant group that was totally banned from America after 1882, as a result of fierce nativist agitation, was the

    a. Irish.
    b. Greeks.
    c. Africans.
    d. Chinese.
    e. Jews.

8. The religious groups that grew most dramatically because of the New Immigration were

    a. Methodists, Baptists, and Disciples of Christ.
    b. Christian Scientists, the Salvation Army, and Buddhists.
    c. Episcopalians, Unitarians, and Congregationalists.
    d. Jews, Roman Catholics, and Orthodox.
    e. Lutherans, Christian Reformed, and Assemblies of God.

9. The phrase "social Gospel" refers to the

    a. evangelical movement that urged people to turn to God as the solution to social problems and class conflict.
    b. theories that Protestant liberals developed to reconcile Darwinian theories with the biblical views of human origins and the special creation of species.
    c. new theories of Biblical interpretation that emphasized the social contexts of ancient religious texts.
    d. conflict between socialists and traditional religious believers.
    e. efforts of Christian reformers like Walter Rauschenbusch to apply their religious beliefs to new social problems.

10. Traditional American Protestant religion received a substantial blow from the

    a. psychological ideas of William James.
    b. theological ideas of the Fundamentalists.
    c. chemical theories of Charles Eliot.
    d. biological ideas of Charles Darwin.
    e. the sermons of Dwight Moody.

11. Unlike Booker T. Washington, W. E. B. Du Bois advocated

    a. economic opportunity for blacks.
    b. turning to wealthy white philanthropist for funds to support black causes.
    c. practical as well as theoretical education for blacks.
    d. that blacks remain in the South rather than move north.
    e. advanced education and complete political and social equality for blacks.

12. In the late nineteenth century, American colleges and universities benefited especially from

    a. federal and state land-grant assistance and the private philanthropy of wealthy donors.
    b. the growing involvement of the churches in higher education.
    c. the fact that a college degree was becoming a prerequisite for employment in industry.
    d. the growth of federal grants and loans to college students.
    e. the growing belief that classical learning and the liberal arts were essential to a well-rounded life.

13. The widely popular American social reformers Henry George and Edward Bellamy advocated

    a. utopian reforms to end poverty and eliminate class conflict.
    b. an end to racial prejudice and segregation.
    c. the resettlement of the urban poor on free western homesteads.
    d. a transformation of the traditional family through communal living arrangements.
    e. detailed urban planning and low-cost housing as keys to ending inequality.

14. Authors like Mark Twain, Stephen Crane, and Jack London turned American literature toward a greater concern with

    a. close observation and contemplation of nature.
    b. postmodernism and deconstruction of traditional narratives.
    c. fantasy and romance.
    d. social realism and contemporary problems.
    e. history and religion.

15. Drawing on European models, American urban planners like Daniel Burnham believed that

    a. public buildings like libraries and museums should be subordinated to planned commercial development.
    b. suburban sprawl should be controlled through strict land use and zoning regulations.
    c. grand urban buildings and public spaces would stimulate progress and inspire civic virtue and loyalty in the city's residents.
    d. a dense concentration of urban skyscrapers and apartments was the best way to inspire civic pride and eliminate slums.
    e. the key to urban planning was a cheap, efficient mass transportation system.

C. Identification

Supply the correct identification for each numbered description.

1. _____   High-rise urban buildings that provided barracks-like housing for urban slum dwellers

2. _____   Term for the post-1880 newcomers who came to America primarily from southern and eastern Europe

3. _____   Term for the passion for migration to the New World that swept across Europe in the late nineteenth century

4. _____   The religious doctrines preached by those who believed that churches should directly address and work to reform economic and social problems

5. _____ Settlement house in the Chicago slums that became a model for women's involvement in urban social reform

6. _____ Profession established by Jane Addams and others that opened new opportunities for women while engaging urban problems

7. _____ Nativist organization that attacked New Immigrants and Roman Catholicism in the 1880s and 1890s

8. _____ Protestant believers who strongly resisted liberal Protestantism's attempts to adapt doctrines to Darwinian evolution and biblical criticism

9. _____ Black educational institution founded by Booker T. Washington to provide training in agriculture and crafts

10. _____ Organization founded by W. E. B. Du Bois and others to advance black social and economic equality

11. _____ Henry George's best-selling book that advocated social reform through the imposition of a single tax on land

12. _____ Federal law promoted by a self-appointed morality crusader and used to prosecute moral and sexual dissidents

13. _____ The American philosophical theory, especially advanced by William James, that the test of the truth of an idea was its practical consequences

14. _____ Urban planning movement, begun in Paris and carried on in Chicago and other American cities, that emphasized harmony, order, and monumental public buildings

15. _____ Women's organization founded by reformer Frances Willard and others to oppose alcohol consumption

D. Matching People, Places, and Events

Match the person, place, or event in the left column with the proper description in the right column by inserting the correct letter on the blank line.

1. ___ Louis Sullivan

2. ___ Walter Rauschenbusch

3. ___ Jane Addams

4. ___ Charles Darwin

5. ___ Horatio Alger

6. ___ Booker T. Washington

7. ___ W. E. B. Du Bois

8. ___ William James

9. ___ Henry George

10. ___ Emily Dickinson

11. ___ Mark Twain

12. ___ Victoria Woodhull

a. Controversial reformer whose book, *Progress and Poverty*, advocated solving problems of economic inequality by a tax on land

b. Midwestern-born writer and lecturer who created a new style of American literature based on social realism and humor

c. Well-connected and socially prominent historian who feared modern trends and sought relief in the beauty and culture of the past

d. Popular novelist whose tales of young people rising from poverty to wealth through hard work and good fortune enhanced Americans' belief in individual opportunity

e. Leading Protestant advocate of the social gospel who tried to make Christianity relevant to urban and industrial problems

13. ___ Daniel Burnham

14. ___ Charlotte Perkins Gilman

15. ___ Henry Adams

f. Former slave who promoted industrial education and economic opportunity but not social equality for blacks

g. Harvard scholar who made original contributions to modern psychology and philosophy

h. Radical feminist propagandist whose eloquent attacks on conventional social morality shocked many Americans in the 1870s

i. Brilliant feminist writer who advocated cooperative cooking and child-care arrangements to promote women's economic independence and equality

j. Leading social reformer who lived with the poor in the slums and pioneered new forms of activism for women

k. American architect and planner who helped bring French Baron Haussman's City Beautiful movement to the United States.

l. Harvard-educated scholar and advocate of full black social and economic equality through the leadership of a talented tenth

m. Chicago-based architect whose high-rise innovation allowed more people to crowd into limited urban space

n. British biologist whose theories of human and animal evolution by means of natural selection created religious and intellectual controversy

o. Gifted but isolated New England poet, the bulk of whose works were not published until after her death

E. Putting Things in Order

Put the following events in correct order by numbering them from 1 to 5.

1. _____ Well-educated young midwesterner moves to Chicago slums and creates a vital center of social reform and activism.

2. _____ Introduction of a new form of high-rise slum housing drastically increases the overcrowding of the urban poor.

3. _____ Nativist organization is formed to limit the New Immigration and attack Roman Catholicism.

4. _____ The formation of a new national organization signals growing strength for the women's suffrage movement.

5. _____ A western territory becomes the first U.S. government to grant full voting rights to women.

F. Matching Cause and Effect

Match the historical cause in the left column with the proper effect in the right column by writing the correct letter on the blank line.

Cause	**Effect**
1. ____ New industrial jobs and urban excitement	a. Encouraged the mass urban public's taste for scandal and sensation
2. ____ Uncontrolled rapid growth and the New Immigration from Europe	b. Created intense poverty and other problems in the crowded urban slums
3. ____ Cheap American grain exports to Europe	c. Weakened the religious influence in American society and created divisions within the churches
4. ____ The cultural strangeness and poverty of southern and eastern European immigrants	d. Led women and men to delay marriage and have fewer children
5. ____ Social gospel ministers and settlement-house workers	e. Helped uproot European peasants from their ancestral lands and sent them seeking new opportunities in America and elsewhere
6. ____ Darwinian science and growing urban materialism	f. Supported the substantial improvements in American undergraduate and graduate education in the late nineteenth century
7. ____ Government land grants and private philanthropy	g. Lured millions of rural Americans off the farms and into the cities
8. ____ Popular newspapers and yellow journalism	h. Assisted immigrants and other slum dwellers and pricked middle-class consciences about urban problems
9. ____ Changes in moral and sexual attitudes	i. Provoked sharp hostility from some native-born Americans and organized labor groups
10. ____ The difficulties of family life in the industrial city	j. Created sharp divisions about the new morality and issues such as divorce

G. Developing Historical Skills

Interpreting a Line Graph

A line graph is another visual way to convey information. It is often used to present notable historical changes occurring over substantial periods of time. Study the line graph on p.600 and answer the following questions.

1. There are five major peaks of immigration and four major valleys. What factors helped cause each of the periods of heavy immigration? What helped cause each of the sharp declines?

2. About how long did each of the first four periods of major immigration last? About how long did each of the four valleys last? How long has the current (to 2006) phase of rising or steady immigration lasted?

3. During what five-year period was there the sharpest rise in immigration? What five-year period saw the sharpest fall?

4. In about what three years did approximately 800,000 immigrants enter the United States? In about what seven years did approximately 200,000 immigrants enter the United States?

5. Approximately how many fewer immigrants came in 1920 than in 1914? About how many more immigrants came in 1990 than in 1950?

PART III: APPLYING WHAT YOU HAVE LEARNED

1. What new opportunities and social problems did the cities create for Americans?

2. In what ways was American urbanization simply part of a worldwide trend, and in what ways did it reflect particular American circumstances? How did the influx of millions of mostly European immigrants create a special dimension to America's urban problems?

3. How did the New Immigration differ from the Old Immigration, and how did Americans respond to it?

4. How was American religion affected by the urban transformation, the New Immigration, and cultural and intellectual changes?

5. Why was Darwinian evolution such a controversial challenge for American religious thinkers? Why were religious liberals able to dominate Americans' cultural response to evolution? How did a minority resistance to evolution lay the basis for the later rise of fundamentalism?

6. How did American social criticism, fiction writing, and art all reflect and address the urban industrial changes of the late nineteenth century? Which social critics and novelists were most influential, and why?

7. How and why did women assume a larger place in American society at this time? (Compare their status in this period with that of the pre–Civil War period described in Chapter 16.) How were changes in their condition related to changes in both the family and the larger social order?

8. What was the greatest single cultural transformation of the Gilded Age?

9. In what ways did Americans positively and enthusiastically embrace the new possibilities of urban life, and in what ways did their outlooks and actions reflect worries about the threats that cities presented to traditional American democracy and social ideals?

CHAPTER 26

The Great West and the Agricultural Revolution, 1865–1896

PART I: REVIEWING THE CHAPTER

A. Checklist of Learning Objectives

After mastering this chapter, you should be able to:

1. Describe the nature of the cultural conflicts and battles that accompanied the white American migration into the Great Plains and the Far West.

2. Explain the development of federal policy towards Native Americans in the late nineteenth century.

3. Analyze the brief flowering and decline of the cattle and mining frontiers, and the settling of the arid West by small farmers increasingly engaged with a worldwide economy.

4. Summarize Frederick Jackson Turner's thesis regarding the significance of the frontier in American history, describe its strengths and weaknesses, and indicate the ways in which the American West became and remains a distinctive region of the United States.

5. Describe the economic forces that drove farmers into debt, and describe how the Populist Party organized to protest their oppression, attempted to forge an alliance with urban workers, and vigorously attacked the two major parties after the onset of the depression of the 1890s.

6. Describe the Democratic party's revolt against President Cleveland and the rise of the insurgent William Jennings Bryan's free silver campaign.

7. Explain why William McKinley proved able to defeat Bryan's populist campaign and how the Republicans' triumph signaled the rise of urban power and the end of the third party system in American politics.

B. Glossary

To build your social science vocabulary, familiarize yourself with the following terms.

1. **nomadic (nomad)** A way of life characterized by frequent movement from place to place for economic sustenance. ". . . the Sioux transformed themselves from foot-traveling, crop-growing villagers to wide-ranging nomadic traders. . . ."

2. **immunity** Freedom or exemption from some imposition. ". . . [the] militia massacred . . . four hundred Indians who apparently thought they had been promised immunity."

3. **reservation** Public lands designated for use by Indians. "The vanquished Indians were finally ghettoized on reservations. . . ."

4. **ward** Someone considered incompetent to manage his or her own affairs and therefore placed under the legal guardianship of another person or group. ". . . there [they had] to eke out a sullen existence as wards of the government."

5.   **probationary** Concerning a period of testing or trial, after which a decision is made based on performance. "The probationary period was later extended. . . ."

6.   **folklore** The common traditions and stories of a people. "These bowlegged Knights of the Saddle . . . became part of American folklore."

7.   **irrigation** Watering land artificially, through canals, pipes, or other means. ". . . irrigation projects . . . caused the 'Great American Desert' to bloom. . . ."

8.   **meridian** In geography, any of the imaginary lines of longitude running north and south on the globe. ". . . settlers . . . rashly pushed . . . beyond the 100th meridian. . . ."

9.   **contiguous** Joined together by common borders. "Only Oklahoma, New Mexico, and Arizona remained to be lifted into statehood from contiguous territory on the mainland of North America."

10.   **safety valve** Anything, such as the American frontier, that allegedly serves as a necessary outlet for built-up pressure, energy, and so on. "But the 'safety-valve' theory does have some validity."

11.   **loan shark** A person who lends money at an exorbitant or illegal rate of interest. "The [farmers] . . . cried out in despair against the loan sharks. . . ."

12.   **serfdom** The feudal condition of being permanently bound to land owned by someone else. ". . . the farmers were about to sink into a status suggesting Old World serfdom."

13.   **mumbo jumbo** Mysterious and unintelligible words or behavior. "Kelley, a Mason, even found farmers receptive to his mumbo jumbo of passwords and secret rituals. . . ."

14.   **prophet** A person believed to speak with divine power or special gifts, sometimes including predicting the future (hence any specially talented or eloquent advocate of a cause). "Numerous fiery prophets leapt forward to trumpet the Populist cause."

15.   **citadel** A fortress occupying a commanding height. " . . . join hands with urban workers, and mount a successful attack on the northeastern citadels of power."

PART II: CHECKING YOUR PROGRESS

A. True-False

Where the statement is true, circle **T**; where it is false, circle **F**.

1.   T   F   The acquisition of Spanish horses transformed the Sioux and Cheyenne from crop-growing villagers into nomadic buffalo hunters.

2.   T   F   The Plains Indians were rather quickly and easily defeated by the U.S. Army.

3.   T   F   A crucial factor in defeating the Indians was the destruction of the buffalo, a vital source of food and other supplies.

4.   T   F   Humanitarian reformers respected the Indians' traditional culture and tried to preserve their tribal way of life.

5.   T   F   Individual gold and silver miners proved unable to compete with large mining corporations and trained engineers.

6.   T   F   During the peak years of the Long Drive, the cattlemen's prosperity depended on driving large beef herds great distances to railroad terminal points.

7.   T   F   The fair administration of the Homestead Act enabled many poorer farmers to achieve economic success on the plains of the arid, frontier West.

8. T F   Although very few city dwellers ever migrated west to take up farming, the frontier "safety valve" did have some positive effects by luring some immigrants to the West and helping to keep urban wages higher than they otherwise might have been.

9. T F   The farmers who settled the Great Plains were usually single-crop producers who became increasingly dependent on competitive and unstable world markets to sell their agricultural products.

10. T F   Western and southern farmers were able to organize quickly and effectively to break their cycle of debt, falling prices, and exploitation by the railroads and other "middlemen."

11. T F   A fundamental problem of the Farmers' Alliance in the South was their inability to overcome the racial division between poor white and black farmers.

12. T F   The economic crisis of the 1890s strengthened the Populists' belief that farmers and industrial workers should form an alliance against economic and political oppression.

13. T F   Republican political manager Mark Hanna struggled to raise enough funds to combat William Jennings Bryan's pro-silver campaign.

14. T F   Bryan's populist campaign failed partly because he was unable to persuade enough urban workers to join his essentially rural-based cause.

15. T F   McKinley's victory in 1896 ushered in an era marked by Republican domination, weakened party organization, and the fading of the money issue in American politics.

B. Multiple Choice

Select the best answer and circle the corresponding letter.

1. The Indians of the western plains offered strong resistance to white expansion through their effective use of
    a. artillery and infantry tactics.
    b. Canada and Mexico as safe havens from which to conduct warfare.
    c. nighttime and winter campaigning.
    d. eastern journalists and artists to publicize their cause.
    e. superb horsemanship and mobility.

2. The federal government's attempt to confine Indians to certain areas through formal treaties was largely ineffective because
    a. the nomadic Plains Indians largely rejected the idea of formal authority and defined territory.
    b. Congress refused to ratify treaties signed with the Indians.
    c. the treaties made no effective provisions for enforcement.
    d. the largest tribe, the Sioux, refused to sign any treaties with the whites.
    e. the Indians repeatedly broke out of the proposed reservations and resumed open warfare.

3. The warfare that led up to the Battle of the Little Big Horn was set off by
    a. white intrusion into the previously reserved Indian territory of Oklahoma.
    b. Indian attacks on the transcontinental railroad construction crews.
    c. the Indians' defeat and killing of Captain William Fetterman's entire military unit in Montana.
    d. a conflict over the interpretation of the second Treaty of Fort Laramie.
    e. white intrusions into the Indians' sacred Black Hills after the discovery of gold there.

4. Which of the following was *not* among the factors that finally led to the defeat of the Plains Indians and their confinement to reservations?
    a. The federal government's willingness to deploy unrelenting military force
    b. The constant political infighting among the Sioux, Cheyenne, Arapaho, and Apache tribes
    c. The destruction of the buffalo upon which the Indian way of life depended
    d. The railroads' intrusive penetration of Indian lands
    e. The Indians' vulnerability to white people's diseases and liquor

5. Many religious reformers, federal boarding schools, and the Dawes Act were all focused on the goal of
    a. enabling Indians to achieve economic opportunity on the reservations.
    b. assisting Indians who chose to migrate from the remote reservations to towns and cities.
    c. helping Indians form an effective pan-Indian alliance beyond their tribal identity.
    d. undermining Indians' traditional culture and assimilating them into white American culture and society.
    e. weakening the Bureau of Indian Affairs' monopoly on Indian policy.

6. Both the mining and cattle frontiers of the late nineteenth-century West saw a/an
    a. increase of ethnic and class conflict.
    b. loss of economic viability after an initial boom.
    c. turn from large-scale investment to the individual entrepreneur.
    d. brief flourishing of individual enterprise eventually followed by large corporate takeovers.
    e. influx of immigrant miners and cowboys from Europe.

7. The problem of sustaining agriculture in the arid West was solved most successfully through
    a. concentrating agriculture in the more fertile mountain valleys.
    b. the use of small-scale family farms rather than large bonanza farms.
    c. the use of irrigation from dammed western rivers.
    d. the turn to desert crops like olives and dates.
    e. revising the Homestead Act to give away free farms of 640 acres instead of the inadequate 160 acres.

8. The safety valve theory of the frontier claims that
    a. Americans were able to divert the most violent elements of the population to the West.
    b. the conflict between farmers and ranchers was relieved by the Homestead Act.
    c. class and labor conflict in America was alleviated because eastern workers could always migrate to the West and become independent farmers.
    d. political movements such as the Populists provided relief for the most serious grievances of western farmers.
    e. the wide-open spaces of the West provided an arena where Americans' attachment to guns and violence could be pursued without threatening the social fabric.

9. Which one of these factors did *not* make the trans-Mississippi West a unique part of the American frontier experience?
    a. The large-scale engagement and struggle between white Anglo and Hispanic cultures.
    b. The problem of applying new technologies in a hostile wilderness
    c. The scale and severity of environmental challenges in an arid environment
    d. The large role of the federal government in economic and social development
    e. The final military defeat of American Indians and their continuing substantial presence in the region.

10. By the 1880s, most western farmers faced hard times because

    a. free land was no longer available under the Homestead Act.

    b. they were unable to increase grain production to keep up with demand.

    c. they were being strangled by excessive federal regulation of agriculture.

    d. they resisted the adoption of technologically improved farming techniques.

    e. they were forced to sell their grain at declining prices in volatile and depressed world markets.

11. Which of the following was *not* among the political goals advocated by the Populist party in the 1890s?

    a. Nationalizing the railroad, telegraph, and telephone

    b. Creation of a national system of unemployment insurance and old-age pensions

    c. A graduated income tax

    d. Free and unlimited coinage of silver money

    e. Federally-owned warehouses where farmers could store their grain until prices rose.

12. The federal government's use of the U.S. Army to crush the Pullman strike in Chicago aroused great anger from both organized labor and the Populists because

    a. it seemed to reflect an alliance of big business and government to destroy the organizing efforts of workers and farmers.

    b. it broke apart the growing alliance between urban workers and farmers.

    c. it undermined efforts to organize federal workers like those in the postal service.

    d. it turned their most effective leader, Eugene V. Debs, into a cautious conservative.

    e. many of the soldiers used to defeat the union were themselves from rural or working class backgrounds.

13. William Jennings Bryan gained the Democratic nomination in 1896 because he strongly advocated

    a. unlimited coinage of silver in order to inflate the currency.

    b. higher tariffs in order to protect the American farmer.

    c. government ownership of the railroads and the telegraph system.

    d. a coalition between white and black farmers in the South and Midwest.

    e. enlisting President Cleveland and other conservative Democrats in the reform cause.

14. McKinley defeated Bryan primarily because he was able to win the support of

    a. white southern farmers.

    b. eastern wage earners and city dwellers.

    c. urban and rural blacks.

    d. former Populists and Greenback Laborites.

    e. western ranchers and miners.

15. Which of the following was *not* a feature of the end of the third party system and its replacement by a fourth party system after the pivotal election of 1896?

    a. The weakening of strong, patronage-driven political party organizations

    b. The end of razor-thin elections and the beginning of an era of Republican domination

    c. The rise of third parties that threatened to replace either the Democrats or Republicans as a major party

    d. The decline of the money issue that had dominated American politics since the Civil War

    e. Gradual decline in voter participation in politics and elections

C. Identification

Supply the correct identification for each numbered description.

1. _____   Major northern Plains Indian nation that fought and eventually lost a bitter war against the U.S. Army, 1876–1877

2. _____   Southwestern Indian tribe led by Geronimo that carried out some of the last fighting against white conquest

3. _____   Generally poor areas where vanquished Indians were eventually confined under federal control

4. _____   Indian religious movement, originating out of the sacred Sun Dance that the federal government attempted to stamp out in 1890

5. _____   Federal law that attempted to dissolve tribal landholding and establish Indians as individual farmers

6. _____   Huge silver and gold deposit that brought wealth and statehood to Nevada

7. _____   General term for the herding of cattle from the grassy plains to the railroad terminals of Kansas, Nebraska, and Wyoming

8. _____   Federal law that offered generous land opportunities to poorer farmers but also provided the unscrupulous with opportunities for hoaxes and fraud

9. _____   Historian Frederick Jackson Turner's argument that the continual westward migration into unsettled territory has been the primary force shaping American character and American society

10. _____   Former Indian Territory where illegal sooners tried to get the jump on boomers when it was opened for settlement in 1889

11. _____   Third political party that emerged in the 1890s to express rural grievances and mount major attacks on the Democrats and Republicans

12. _____   Popular pamphlet written by William Hope Harvey that portrayed pro-silver arguments triumphing over the traditional views of bankers and economics professors

13. _____   Bitter labor conflict in Chicago that brought federal intervention and the jailing of union leader Eugene V. Debs

14. _____   Spectacular convention speech by a young pro-silver advocate that brought him the Democratic presidential nomination in 1896

15. _____   Popular term for those who favored the status quo in metal money and opposed the pro-silver Bryanites in 1896

D. Matching People, Places, and Events

Match the person, place, or event in the left column with the proper description in the right column by inserting the correct letter on the blank line.

1. ___ Sand Creek, Colorado

2. ___ Little Big Horn

a. Ohio industrialist and organizer of McKinley's victory over Bryan in the election of 1896

3. ___ Sitting Bull

4. ___ Chief Joseph

5. ___ Geronimo

6. ___ Helen Hunt Jackson

7. ___ John Wesley Powell

8. ___ Frederick Jackson Turner

9. ___ Jacob S. Coxey

10. ___ William Hope Harvey

11. ___ Eugene V. Debs

12. ___ Oliver H. Kelley

13. ___ James B. Weaver

14. ___ Mary E. Lease

15. ___ Marcus Alonzo Hanna

b. Leader of the Nez Percé tribe who conducted a brilliant but unsuccessful military campaign in 1877

c. Author of the popular pro-silver pamphlet Coin's Financial School

d. Minnesota farm leader whose Grange organization first mobilized American farmers and laid the groundwork for the Populists

e. Former Civil War general and Granger who ran as the Greenback Labor party candidate for president in 1880

f. Leader of the Sioux during wars of 1876–1877

g. Explorer and geologist who warned that traditional agriculture could not succeed west of the 100th meridian

h. Ohio businessman who led his Commonweal Army to Washington, seeking relief and jobs for the unemployed

i. Leader of the Apaches of Arizona in their warfare with the whites

j. Site of Indian massacre by militia forces in 1864

k. Massachusetts writer whose books aroused sympathy for the plight of the Native Americans

l. Site of major U.S. Army defeat in the Sioux War of 1876–1877

m. American historian who argued that the encounter with the ever-receding West had fundamentally shaped America

n. Railway union leader who converted to socialism while serving jail time during the Pullman strike

o. Eloquent Kansas Populist who urged farmers to "raise less corn and more hell"

E. Putting Things in Order

Put the following events in correct order by numbering them from 1 to 5.

1. _____ A sharp economic depression leads to a major railroad strike and the intervention of federal troops in Chicago.

2. _____ The violation of agreements with the Dakota Sioux leads to a major Indian war and a military disaster for the U.S. cavalry.

3. _____ A federal law grants 160 acres of land to farmers at token prices, thus encouraging the rapid settlement of the Great West.

4. _____ The U.S. Census Bureau declares that there is no longer a clear line of frontier settlement, ending a formative chapter of American history.

5. _____ Despite a fervent campaign by their charismatic young champion, pro-silver Democrats lose a pivotal election to Gold Bug Republicans.

F. Matching Cause and Effect

Match the historical cause in the left column with the proper effect in the right column by writing the correct letter on the blank line.

Cause		**Effect**	
1. ___	The encroachment of white settlement and the violation of treaties with Indians	a.	Caused widespread protests and strikes like the one against the Pullman Company in Chicago
2. ___	Railroad building, disease, and the destruction of the buffalo	b.	Threatened the two-party domination of American politics by the Republicans and Democrats
3. ___	Reformers' attempts to make Native Americans conform to white ways	c.	Created new psychological and economic problems for a nation accustomed to a boundlessly open West
4. ___	The coming of big-business mining and stock-raising to the West		
5. ___	Dry farming, barbed wire, and irrigation	d.	Ended the romantic, colorful era of the miners' and the cattlemen's frontier
6. ___	The passing of the frontier in 1890	e.	Decimated Indian populations and hastened their defeat at the hands of advancing whites
7. ___	The growing economic specialization of western farmers		
8. ___	The rise of the Populist party in the early 1890s	f.	Effectively ended the free-silver agitation and the domination of the money question in American politics
9. ___	The economic depression that began in 1893	g.	Made settlers vulnerable to vast industrial and market forces beyond their control
10. ___	The return of prosperity after 1897 and new gold discoveries in Alaska, South Africa, and elsewhere	h.	Made it possible to farm the dry, treeless areas of the Great Plains and the West

          i.   Further undermined Native Americans'
                traditional tribal culture and morale

          j.   Led to nearly constant warfare with
                Plains Indians from 1868 to about 1890

G. Developing Historical Skills

Reading Meteorological/Agricultural Maps

The map on p. 647 is designed to demonstrate the relationship between a key variation in climate and weather, average annual precipitation, and the patterns of agriculture. Study the map to discern these patterns, and then answer the following questions.

1.   In 1900, which was the only grain crop regularly grown in areas receiving less than 20 inches of annual rainfall?

2.   In 1900, which two grain crops were produced in areas receiving over sixty inches a year of annual precipitation?

3.   Which type of livestock evidently thrived *only* in areas receiving moderate rainfall (20–40 inches per year)?

4.   Which type of livestock could be raised in low-rainfall country (under 20 inches per year) as well as in moderate rainfall areas?

H. Map Mastery

Map Discrimination

Using the map on p. 663, answer the following questions.

1.   In the election of 1896, how many states west of the Mississippi River did William McKinley carry (counting Minnesota as west of the Mississippi)?

2.   How many electoral votes did William Jennings Bryan win in the five Border States of Delaware, Maryland, West Virginia, Kentucky, and Missouri?

3. Given the regional division and pattern of the election, which candidate would Oklahoma, New Mexico, and Arizona likely have favored had they been admitted to the Union?

4. How many electoral votes did McKinley win in the eleven southern states of the old Confederacy?

Map Challenge

Using the maps of *American Agriculture in 1900* (p. 647) and *Presidential Election of 1896* (p. 663), discuss the relationship between the Populist and pro-silver movements and the patterns of American agriculture. Include in your analysis some analysis of those Midwestern agricultural states that may have been influenced by Populism but did not vote for Bryan in 1896.

PART III: APPLYING WHAT YOU HAVE LEARNED

1. How did whites finally overcome resistance of the Plains Indians, and what happened to the Indians after their resistance ceased?

2. What social, ethnic, environmental, and economic factors made the trans-Mississippi West a unique region among the successive American frontiers? What makes the West continue to be a region quite distinctive from other regions such as the Northeast, the Midwest, and the South? How does the myth of the frontier West differ from the actual reality, in the late nineteenth century, and after?

3. What were the actual effects of the frontier on American society at different stages of its development? What was valuable in Frederick Jackson Turner's frontier thesis, despite its being discredited by subsequent historians.

4. Why did landowning small American farmers—traditionally considered by Jefferson, Jackson, and others the backbone of American society—suddenly find themselves trapped in a cycle of debt, deflation, and exploitation in the late nineteenth century? Was their plight due primarily to deliberate economic oppression corporate business, as they saw it, or was it simply an inevitable consequence of agriculture's involvement in world markets and economy?

5. Were the Populist and pro-silver movements of the 1880s and 1890s essentially backward-looking protests by a passing rural America, or were they, despite their immediate political failure, genuine prophetic voices raising central critical questions about democracy and economic justice in the new corporate industrial America?

6. What were the major issues in the crucial campaign of 1896? Why did McKinley win, and what were the long-term effects of his victory?

7. Some historians have seen Bryan as the political heir of Jefferson and Jackson, and McKinley as the political heir of Hamilton and the Whigs. Are such connections valid? Why or why not (see Chapters 10, 12, and 13)?

8. The settlement of the Great West and the farmers' revolt occurred at the same time as the rise of industrialism and the growth of American cities. To what extent were the defeat of the Indians, the destruction and exploitation of western resources, and the populist revolt of the farmers in the 1890s caused by the Gilded Age forces of industrialization and urbanization?

CHAPTER 27

Empire and Expansion, 1890–1909

PART I: REVIEWING THE CHAPTER

A. Checklist of Learning Objectives

After mastering this chapter, you should be able to:

1. Explain why the United States suddenly abandoned its isolationism and turned outward at the end of the nineteenth century.

2. Describe the forces pushing for American overseas expansion and the causes of the Spanish-American War.

3. Describe and explain the unintended results of the Spanish-American War, especially the conquest of Puerto Rico and the Philippines.

4. Explain McKinley's decision to keep the Philippines, and list the opposing arguments in the debate about imperialism.

5. Analyze the consequences of the Spanish-American War, including the Filipino rebellion against U.S. rule and the war to suppress it.

6. Explain the growing U.S. involvement in East Asia, and summarize America's Open Door policy toward China.

7. Discuss the significance of the pro-imperialist Republican victory in 1900 and the rise of Theodore Roosevelt as a strong advocate of American power in international affairs.

8. Describe Roosevelt's assertive policies in Panama and elsewhere in Latin America, and explain why his corollary to the Monroe Doctrine aroused such controversy.

9. Discuss Roosevelt's foreign policies and diplomatic achievements, especially regarding Japan.

B. Glossary

To build your social science vocabulary, familiarize yourself with the following terms.

1. **arbitration** An arrangement in which a neutral third party conclusively determines the mandatory outcome of a dispute between two parties. (In **mediation** the third party only serves as a go-between and proposes solutions that the disputing parties may or may not accept.) "A simmering argument between the United States and Canada . . . was resolved by arbitration in 1893."

2. **scorched-earth policy** The policy of burning and destroying all the property in a given area so as to deny it to an enemy. "The desperate insurgents now sought to drive out their Spanish overlords by adopting a scorched-earth policy."

3. **reconcentration** The policy of forcibly removing a population to confined areas in order to deny support to enemy forces. " He undertook to crush the rebellion by herding many civilians into barbed-wire reconcentration camps."

4. **atrocity** A specific act of extreme cruelty. "Where atrocity stories did not exist, they were invented."

5. **proviso** An article or clause in a statute, treaty, or contract establishing a particular stipulation or condition that qualifies or modifies the whole document. "This proviso proclaimed . . . that when the United States had overthrown Spanish misrule, it would give the Cubans their freedom. . . ."

6. **hostage** A person or thing forcibly held in order to obtain certain goals or agreements. "Hereafter these distant islands were to be . . . a kind of indefensible hostage given to Japan."

7. **Americanization** The process of originally non-American people assimilating to American character, manner, institutions, culture, and so on. "The Filipinos, who hated compulsory Americanization, preferred liberty."

8. **sphere of influence** In international affairs, the territory where a powerful state exercises the dominant control over weaker states or territories. ". . . they began to tear away valuable leaseholds and economic spheres of influence from the Manchu government."

9. **partition** In politics, the act of dividing a weaker territory or government among several more powerful states. "Those principles helped to spare China from possible partition in those troubled years. . . .

10. **blue blood** A person of supposedly" pure blood," presumed to be descended directly from nobility or aristocracy. "Born into a wealthy and distinguished New York family, Roosevelt, a red-blooded blue blood. . . ."

11. **bellicose** Disposed to fight or go to war. "Incurably boyish and bellicose, Roosevelt ceaselessly preached the virile virtues. . . ."

12. **preparedness** The accumulation of sufficient armed forces and matériel to go to war. "An ardent champion of military and naval preparedness. . . ."

13. **corollary** A secondary inference or deduction from a main proposition that is assumed to be established or proven. "[Roosevelt] therefore devised a devious policy of 'preventive intervention,' better known as the Roosevelt Corollary of the Monroe Doctrine."

14. **indemnity** A payment assessed to compensate for an injury or illegal action. "Japan was forced to drop its demands for a cash indemnity. . . ."

PART II: CHECKING YOUR PROGRESS

A. True-False

Where the statement is true, circle **T**; where it is false, circle **F**.

1. T F The American people and their government were deeply involved in the key international developments of the 1860s and 1870s.

2. T F The South American boundary dispute over Guyana in 1895–1896 nearly resulted in a U.S. war with Venezuela.

3. T F President Cleveland refused to annex Hawaii because he believed that the white American planters there had unjustly deposed Hawaii's Queen Liliuokalani.

4. T F Americans first became involved in Cuba because they sympathized with the Cubans' revolt against imperialist Spain.

5. T F   When war broke out between the United States and Spain, Admiral George Dewey's squadron attacked Spanish forces in the Philippines because of secret orders given by Assistant Navy Secretary Theodore Roosevelt.

6. T F   When the United States refused to hand over the Philippines to Filipino rebels, a vicious guerrilla war with racial overtones broke out between the former allies.

7. T F   The American military conquest of Cuba was efficient but very costly in battlefield casualties.

8. T F   President McKinley declared that religion played a crucial role in his decision to keep the Philippines as an American colony.

9. T F   The peace treaty with Spain that made the Philippines an American colony was almost universally popular with the U.S. Senate and the American public.

10. T F   The Supreme Court decided in the insular cases that American constitutional law and the Bill of Rights applied to the people under American rule in Puerto Rico and the Philippines.

11. T F   American male and female Protestant missionaries helped to foster a strong, sentimental American attachment to China in the early 1900s.

12. T F   John Hay's Open Door notes were designed in consultation with the Chinese and welcomed by the European imperialist powers.

13. T F   Theodore Roosevelt believed that the United States should exercise caution and restraint in its exercise of power in international affairs.

14. T F   President Roosevelt's anger at Colombia's refusal to authorize a canal across Panama led him to unofficially encourage and assist a movement for Panamanian independence.

15. T F   The Roosevelt Corollary to the Monroe Doctrine stated that only the United States but no other nation had the right to intervene in Latin American nations' internal affairs.

16. T F   In the San Francisco school crisis of 1906, President Roosevelt forced the integration of Japanese children into schools while persuading Japan to stop further immigration to the United States.

B. Multiple Choice

Select the best answer and circle the corresponding letter.

1.   The military theorist Captain Alfred Thayer Mahan promoted American overseas expansion by
   a.   developing a lurid yellow press that stimulated popular excitement.
   b.   arguing that control of the seas through naval power was the key to world domination.
   c.   provoking naval incidents with Germany and Britain in the Pacific.
   d.   arguing that the Monroe Doctrine required American control of Latin American waters.
   e.   pressing the United States to establish naval bases throughout the Pacific Ocean.

2. Which of the following was *not* among the factors propelling America toward overseas expansion in the 1890s?
    a. The desire to expand overseas agricultural and manufacturing exports
    b. The yellow press of Joseph Pulitzer and William Randolph Hearst
    c. Some Protestant leaders' belief that America should spread its religion and culture to backward people
    d. The ideologies of Anglo-Saxon superiority and social Darwinism
    e. The intervention of the German Kaiser in Latin America

3. President Grover Cleveland refused to annex Hawaii in 1893 because
    a. white planters had illegally overthrown Queen Liliuokalani against the wishes of most native Hawaiians.
    b. there was no precedent for the United States to acquire territory except by purchase.
    c. the Germans and the British threatened possible war.
    d. he knew the public disapproved and the Senate would not ratify a treaty of annexation.
    e. he knew that many Americans would object to the incorporation of a non-white territory into the United States.

4. Americans first became actively involved with the situation in Cuba because
    a. it was clear that Spanish control of Cuba violated the Monroe Doctrine.
    b. imperialists and business leaders were looking to acquire colonial territory for the United States.
    c. leading Cuban rebels began advocating that Cuban be incorporated into the United States.
    d. the Battleship *Maine* exploded in Havana harbor.
    e. Americans sympathized with Cuban rebels in their fight for democratic freedom from Spanish imperial rule.

5. Even before the sinking of the *Maine*, the American public's indignation at Spain had been whipped into a frenzy by
    a. Spanish Catholics' persecution of the Protestant minority in Cuba.
    b. Spain's aggressive battleship-building program.
    c. William Randolph Hearst's sensational newspaper accounts of Spanish atrocities in Cuba.
    d. the Spanish government's brutal treatment of American sailors on leave in Havana.
    e. the mistreatment of white American women by Spanish businessmen.

6. Assistant Secretary of the Navy Roosevelt took full advantage of the outbreak of war between the United States and Spain over Cuba by
    a. pushing for the annexation of Hawaii to the United States.
    b. establishing American naval bases at Pearl Harbor, Guam, and Samoa in the Pacific.
    c. secretly ordering Admiral George Dewey to attack the Spanish in the distant Philippines.
    d. organizing an American naval squadron to trap the Spanish fleet in Havana harbor.
    e. ordering the American navy to blockade all shipments in and out of Cuba.

7. Emilio Aguinaldo was the
    a. leader of Cuban insurgents against Spanish rule.
    b. leader of Filipino insurgents against Spanish rule.
    c. commander of the Spanish navy in the Battle of Manila Bay.
    d. first native Hawaiian to become governor of the islands after the American takeover.
    e. scheming Panamanian engineer who helped Panama to declare independence from Colombia.

8. Besides the Philippines, which two other colonial territories did the United States acquire in the Spanish-American War?

    a. Trinidad and Tobago
    b. Puerto Rico and Guam
    c. Cuba and the Dominican Republic
    d. Hawaii and American Samoa
    e. The Virgin Islands and the Panama Canal Zone

9. Which of the following was *not* among the reasons that President McKinley and other pro-imperialists gave for acquiring the Philippines as an American territory?

    a. Other imperial nations like Germany or Japan would seize the Philippines if the United States left.
    b. McKinley believed that handing them back to Spain's cruel misrule would betray American ideals.
    c. Many believed that Manila could open rich trading opportunities in China.
    d. McKinley believed that God had told him to Christianize and civilize the Filipinos.
    e. The Filipinos had been mostly Catholic Christians for centuries and so would welcome American rule.

10. Which of the following was *not* among the arguments that anti-imperialists used to oppose American acquisition of the Philippines?

    a. The Philippines had a large population of a different culture, language, and racial composition.
    b. The Filipinos would never voluntarily convert to Protestantism if they were forced under American rule.
    c. Acquiring colonial territory would violate Americans' historic commitment to self-determination and anti-colonialism.
    d. Ruling over people without their consent was despotism and would undermine American democracy at home.
    e. Ruling the Philippines would be expensive, and the United States could never adequately defend them.

11. The most immediate consequence of American acquisition of the Philippines was

    a. the establishment of Manila as a crucial American defense post in East Asia.
    b. an agreement between Americans and Filipinos to move toward Philippine independence.
    c. an outbreak of vicious guerrilla warfare between the United States and Filipino rebels.
    d. threats by Japan to seize the Philippines from American control.
    e. a successful program to Americanize the Filipinos by bringing them U.S. culture and education.

12. In the Open Door notes, Secretary of State John Hay called on all the imperial powers to

    a. acknowledge American control of the Philippines as the gateway to China.
    b. limit their military forces and control the arms race in China and the Pacific.
    c. respect Chinese rights and uphold China's territorial integrity rather than breaking it up into colonies.
    d. grant the United States an equal share in any possible colonization of China.
    e. treat China fairly despite the attacks on foreigners during the Boxer Rebellion.

13. As president, Theodore Roosevelt gained political strength especially through

    a. his careful use of traditional diplomacy.
    b. his constant threats of military intervention around the world.
    c. his vigorous use of his personal popularity and presidential power to lead Congress and the public.
    d. his ability to quietly mobilize his cabinet to promote his policy objectives.
    e. creating a personal political organization separate from the Republican party.

14. Roosevelt overcame Colombia's refusal to approve a canal treaty by
    a. increasing the amount of money the United States was willing to pay for a canal zone.
    b. encouraging Panamanian rebels to revolt and declare independence from Colombia.
    c. threatening to build the canal on a route through Nicaragua.
    d. seeking mediation of the dispute by other Latin American nations.
    e. sending in U.S. marines to seize control of the canal route.
15. Theodore Roosevelt's slogan that stated his essential foreign policy principle was
    a. "Open covenants openly arrived at."
    b. "Millions for defense but not one cent for tribute."
    c. "Speak softly and carry a big stick."
    d. "Democracy and liberty in a New World Order."
    e. "American does not go abroad in search of monsters to destroy."

C. Identification

Supply the correct identification for each numbered description.

1. _____ Remote Pacific site of a naval clash between the United States and Germany in 1889

2. _____ South American nation that nearly came to blows with the United States in 1892 over an incident involving the deaths of American sailors

3. _____ The principle of American foreign policy invoked by Secretary of State Olney to justify American intervention in the Venezuelan boundary dispute

4. _____ Term for the sensationalistic and jingoistic pro-war journalism practiced by W. R. Hearst and Joseph Pulitzer

5. _____ American battleship sent on a friendly visit to Cuba that ended in disaster and war

6. _____ Site of the dramatic American naval victory that led to U.S. acquisition of rich, Spanish-owned Pacific islands

7. _____ Colorful volunteer regiment of the Spanish-American War led by a militarily inexperienced but politically influential colonel

8. _____ The Caribbean island conquered from Spain in 1898 that became an important American colony

9. _____ Supreme Court cases of 1901 that determined that the U.S. Constitution and Bill of Rights did not apply in colonial territories under the American flag

10. _____ John Hay's clever diplomatic efforts to preserve Chinese territorial integrity and maintain American access to China

11. _____ Antiforeign Chinese revolt of 1900 that brought military intervention by Western troops, including Americans

12. _____ Diplomatic agreement of 1901 that permitted the United States to build and fortify a Central American canal alone, without British involvement

13. _____ Nation whose senate, in 1902, refused to ratify a treaty permitting the United States to build a canal across its territory

14. _____ Questionable extension of a traditional American policy; declared an American right to intervene in Latin American nations under certain circumstances

15. _____ Diplomatic understanding of 1907–1908 that ended a Japanese-American crisis over treatment of Japanese immigrants to the U.S.

D. Matching People, Places, and Events

Match the person, place, or event in the left column with the proper description in the right column by inserting the correct letter on the blank line.

1. ___ Josiah Strong
2. ___ Alfred Thayer Mahan
3. ___ Emilio Aguinaldo
4. ___ Queen Liliuokalani
5. ___ Richard Olney
6. ___ "Butcher" Weyler
7. ___ William Randolph Hearst
8. ___ William McKinley
9. ___ George E. Dewey
10. ___ Theodore Roosevelt
11. ___ John Hay
12. ___ Philippe Bunau-Varilla
13. ___ William James
14. ___ William Jennings Bryan
15. ___ George Washington Goethals

a. Imperialist advocate, aggressive assistant navy secretary, Rough Rider, vice president, and president

b. Harvard philosopher and one of the leading anti-imperialists opposing U.S. acquisition of the Philippines

c. Spanish general whose brutal tactics against Cuban rebels outraged American public opinion

d. Native Hawaiian ruler overthrown in a revolution led by white planters and aided by U.S. troops

e. Scheming engineer who helped stage a revolution in Panama and then became the new country's instant foreign minister

f. American naval officer who wrote influential books emphasizing sea power and advocating a big navy

g. Naval commander whose spectacular May Day victory in 1898 opened the doors to American imperialism in Asia

h. Vigorous promoter of sensationalistic anti-Spanish propaganda and eager advocate of imperialistic war

i. American military engineer who built the Panama Canal

j. American clergyman who preached Anglo-Saxon superiority and called for stronger U.S. missionary effort overseas

k. Filipino leader of a guerrilla war against American rule from 1899 to 1901

l. President who initially opposed war with Spain but eventually supported U.S. acquisition of the Philippines

m. Democratic party nominee who campaigned and lost on a platform opposing imperialism in the presidential election of 1900

n. U.S. secretary of state whose belligerent notes to Britain during the Guiana boundary crisis nearly caused a war

o. American secretary of state who attempted to preserve Chinese independence and protect American interests in China

E. Putting Things in Order

Put the following events in correct order by numbering them from 1 to 5.

1. _____ American rebels in Hawaii seek annexation by the United States, but the American president turns them down.

2. _____ A battleship explosion arouses fury in America and leads the nation into a splendid little war with Spain.

3. _____ A South American boundary dispute leads to aggressive American assertion of the Monroe Doctrine against Britain.

4. _____ Questionable Roosevelt actions in Central America help create a new republic and pave the way for a U.S.-built canal.

5. _____ A San Francisco School Board dispute leads to intervention by President Roosevelt and a Gentleman's Agreement to prohibit further Japanese immigration to the United States.

F. Matching Cause and Effect

Match the historical cause in the left column with the proper effect in the right column by writing the correct letter on the blank line.

Cause	**Effect**
1. ___ Economic expansion, the yellow press, and competition with other powers	a. Brought American armed forces onto the Asian mainland for the first time
2. ___ The Venezuelan boundary dispute	b. Created an emotional and irresistible public demand for war with Spain
3. ___ The white planter revolt against Queen Liliuokalani	c. Strengthened the Monroe Doctrine and made Britain more willing to accommodate U.S. interests
4. ___ The Cuban revolt against Spain	
5. ___ The *Maine* explosion	d. Led to the surprising U.S. victory over Spain at Manila Bay

6. ___ Theodore Roosevelt's secret orders to Commodore Dewey

7. ___ The Boxer Rebellion that attempted to drive all foreigners out of China

8. ___ McKinley's decision to keep the Philippines

9. ___ Colombia's refusal to permit the United States to build a canal across its province of Panama

10. ___ The Spanish-American War

e. Set off the first debate about the wisdom and rightness of American overseas imperialism

f. Turned America away from isolationism and toward international involvements in the 1890s

g. Aroused strong sympathy from most Americans

h. Enhanced American national pride and made the United States an international power in East Asia

i. Set off a bitter debate about imperialism in the Senate and the country

j. Led President Theodore Roosevelt to encourage a revolt for Panamanian independence

G. Map Mastery

Map Discrimination

Using the maps and charts in Chapter 27, answer the following questions.

1. *United States Expansion, 1857–1917*: Of the new American territories acquired in 1898–1899, which three were directly acquired from Spain as a result of conquest in the Spanish-American War (see also text, p. 679)?

2. *United States Expansion, 1857–1917*: Which new American acquisition was located the farthest south in the Pacific Ocean?

3. *Dewey's Route in the Philippines, 1898*: Manila Bay lies off the coast of which island of the Philippine archipelago?

4. *The Cuban Campaign, 1898*: Which of the two battles fought by Rough Riders—San Juan Hill and El Caney—occurred nearer Santiago Harbor?

5. *The Cuban Campaign, 1898*: Which of the two Spanish-owned Caribbean islands conquered by the United States in 1898 was farthest from Florida?

Map Challenge

Using the map of *United States Expansion* on p. 673, discuss the exact geographical relation of each of America's new Pacific colonies—Samoa, Hawaii, the Philippines—to (a) the United States mainland and (b) China and Japan. Which of the colonies was most strategically important to America's position in the Pacific, which least, and which was most vulnerable? Why?

PART III: APPLYING WHAT YOU HAVE LEARNED

1. What were the causes and signs of America's sudden turn toward international involvement at the end of the nineteenth century?

2. How did the United States get into the Spanish-American War over the initial objections of President McKinley?

3. What role did the press and public opinion play in the origin, conduct, and results of the Spanish-American War?

4. What were the key arguments for and against U.S. imperialism?

5. What were some of the short-term and long-term results of American acquisition of the Philippines and Puerto Rico?

6. How was U.S. overseas imperialism in 1898 similar to and different from earlier American expansion across North America or Manifest Destiny (see especially Chapter 13)? Was this new imperialism a fundamental departure from America's traditions or simply a further extension of westward migration?

7. Theodore Roosevelt was an accidental president due to the McKinley's assassination, yet he quickly became one of the most powerful presidents ever. What elements in Roosevelt's personality and political outlook enabled him to dominate American politics as few others have? How did his view of presidential power differ radically from that of most late nineteenth-century American presidents (see Chapter 23)?

8. What were the essential principles of Theodore Roosevelt's foreign policy, and how did he apply them to specific situations?

9. How did Roosevelt's policies in Latin America demonstrate American power in the region, and why did they arouse opposition from many Latin Americans?

10. What were the central issues in America's relations with China and Japan? How did Roosevelt handle tense relations with Japan?

11. What were the strengths and weaknesses of Theodore Roosevelt's aggressive foreign policy? What were the benefits of TR's activism, and what were its drawbacks?

12. The text states that the Roosevelt corollary to the Monroe Doctrine distorted the original policy statement of 1823. How did it do so (see Chapter 10)? Compare the circumstances and purposes of the two policies.

CHAPTER 28

Progressivism and the Republican Roosevelt, 1901–1912

PART I: REVIEWING THE CHAPTER

A. Checklist of Learning Objectives

After mastering this chapter, you should be able to:

1. Discuss the origin, leadership, and goals of progressivism.

2. Describe how the early progressive movement developed at the local and state level and spread to become a national movement.

3. Describe the major role that women played in progressive social reform, and explain why progressivism meshed with many goals of the women's movement.

4. Tell how President Roosevelt began applying progressive principles to the national economy, including his attention to conservation and consumer protection.

5. Explain why Taft's policies offended progressives, including Roosevelt.

6. Describe how Roosevelt led a progressive revolt against Taft that openly divided the Republican party.

B. Glossary

To build your social science vocabulary, familiarize yourself with the following terms.

1. **progressive** In politics, one who believes in continuing social advancement, improvement, or reform. "The new crusaders, who called themselves 'progressives,' waged war on many evils. . ."

2. **conspicuous consumption** The theory, developed by economist Thorstein Veblen, that much spending by the affluent occurs primarily to display wealth and status to others rather than from enjoyment of the goods or services. " . . . a savage attack on 'predatory wealth' and 'conspicuous consumption.' "

3. **direct primary** In politics, the nomination of a party's candidates for office through a special election of that party's voters. "These ardent reformers pushed for direct primary elections. . . ."

4. **initiative** In politics, the procedure whereby voters can, through petition, present proposed legislation directly to the electorate. "They favored the 'initiative' so that voters could directly propose legislation. . . ."

5. **referendum** The submission of a law, proposed or already in effect, to a direct vote of the electorate. "Progressives also agitated for the 'referendum.' "

6. **recall** In politics, a procedure for removing an official from office through popular election or other means. "The 'recall' would enable the voters to remove faithless elected officials. . . ."

7. **city manager** An administrator appointed by the city council or other elected body to manage affairs, supposedly in a nonpartisan or professional way. "Other communities adopted the city-manager system. . . ."

8. **red-light district** A section of a city where prostitution is officially or unofficially tolerated. ". . . wide-open prostitution (vice-at-a-price) . . . flourished in red-light districts. . . ."

9. **franchise** In government, a special privilege or license granted to a company or group to perform a specific function. "Public-spirited city-dwellers also moved to halt the corrupt sale of franchises for streetcars. . . ."

10. **bureaucracy (bureaucrat)** The management of government or business through departments and subdivisions manned by a system of officials (bureaucrats) following defined rules and processes. (The term is often, though not necessarily, disparaging.) "These wedges into the federal bureaucracy, however small, gave female reformers a national stage. . . ."

11. **workers' (workmen's) compensation** Insurance, provided either by government or employers or both, providing benefits to employees suffering work-related injury or disability. " . . . by 1917 thirty states had put workers' compensation laws on the books. . . ."

12. **reclamation** The process of bringing or restoring wasteland to productive use. "Settlers repaid the cost of reclamation. . . ."

13. **collectivism** A political or social system in which individuals are subordinated to mass organization and direction. "He strenuously sought the middle road between unbridled individualism and paternalistic collectivism."

14. **insubordination** Deliberate disobedience or challenge to proper authority. ". . . Taft dismissed Pinchot on the narrow grounds of insubordination. . . ."

PART II: CHECKING YOUR PROGRESS

A. True-False

Where the statement is true, circle **T**; where it is false, circle **F**.

1. T F The progressive movement believed that social and economic problems should be solved at the community level without involvement by the federal government.

2. T F Muckraking journalists, social-gospel ministers, and women reformers all aroused Americans' concern about economic and social problems.

3. T F Early twentieth-century progressivism found its home almost entirely in the Republican party.

4. T F Many female progressives saw the task of improving life in factories and slums as an extension of their traditional roles as wives and mothers.

5. T F President Theodore Roosevelt ended the anthracite coal strike by threatening to use federal troops to break the miners' union.

6. T F Some progressive reforms such as the municipal ownership of utilities were modeled on the admired practices of contemporary German cities.

7. T F Roosevelt believed that all the monopolistic corporate trusts should be broken up so that competition could be restored among smaller businesses.

8. T F Upton Sinclair's novel, *The Jungle*, was intended to arouse consumers' concern about unsanitary practices in the meat industry.

9. T F   Conservation of forests, water, and other natural resources was probably Theodore Roosevelt's most popular and enduring presidential achievement.

10. T F   Defenders of nature became divided between fervent preservationists who wanted to stop all human intrusions into wilderness areas and more moderate conservationists who thought nature should be available for multiple use.

11. T F   Roosevelt effectively used the power of the presidency and the federal government to tame and regulate unbridled capitalism while preserving the basic foundations of the market system and American business.

12. T F   William Howard Taft demonstrated his skill as a political campaigner and leader throughout his presidency.

13. T F   Progressive Republicans became angry with President Taft because he began to form alliances with Democrats and Socialists.

14. T F   The Ballinger-Pinchot conservation controversy pushed Taft further into an alliance with the reactionary Republican Old Guard and against the pro-Roosevelt progressives.

15. T F   President Taft used his firm control of the Republican party machinery to deny Theodore Roosevelt the nomination in 1912.

B. Multiple Choice

Select the best answer and circle the corresponding letter.

1. The two primary goals of the progressive movement, as a whole, were to
    a. restore business competition and stimulate entrepreneurship in new areas of the economy.
    b. protect farmers and create a more flexible monetary system.
    c. improve the quality of urban life and help immigrants adjust to American life.
    d. organize workers into class-conscious unions and develop consumer cooperatives.
    e. use the state to curb monopoly power and improve the lives of ordinary people.
2. Prominent among those who aroused the progressive movement by stirring the public's sense of concern were
    a. socialists, social gospelers, women, and muckraking journalists.
    b. union leaders, machine politicians, immigrants, and engineers.
    c. bankers, salesmen, congressmen, and scientists.
    d. athletes, entertainers, filmmakers, and musicians.
    e. farmers, miners, Latinos, and African Americans.
3. Which of the following was *not* among the targets of muckraking journalistic exposés?
    a. Urban politics and government
    b. The oil, insurance, and railroad industries
    c. The U.S. Army and Navy
    d. Child labor and the white slave traffic in women
    e. Makers of patent medicines and other adulterated or dangerous drugs
4. Most progressives were
    a. poor farmers.
    b. urban workers.
    c. immigrants.
    d. wealthy people.
    e. urban middle-class people.

5. Among the political reforms sought by the progressives were

   a. an end to political parties, political conventions, and the Supreme Court's right to judicial review of legislation.
   b. an Equal Rights Amendment, federal financing of election campaigns, and restrictions on negative campaigning.
   c. civil-service reform, racial integration, and free silver.
   d. initiative and referendum, direct election of senators, and women's suffrage.
   e. expanded immigration, literacy tests for voting, and federal loans for higher education.

6. The states where progressivism first gained great influence were

   a. Massachusetts, Maine, and New Hampshire.
   b. Wisconsin, Oregon, and California.
   c. Michigan, Kansas, and Nevada.
   d. New York, Florida, and Texas.
   e. Alabama, Maryland, and Utah.

7. The Supreme Court case of *Muller* v. *Oregon* was seen as a victory for both progressivism and women's rights because it

   a. upheld the right of women to vote in state and local elections.
   b. upheld a law requiring that women receive "equal pay for equal work."
   c. upheld workplace safety regulations to prevent disasters like the Triangle Shirtwaist fire.
   d. opened almost all categories of the new industrial employment to women.
   e. upheld the constitutionality of state laws granting special protections to women in the workplace.

8. President Theodore Roosevelt ended the major Pennsylvania coal strike by

   a. asking Congress to pass a law improving miners' wages and working conditions.
   b. passing federal legislation legalizing unions.
   c. forcing the mine owners and workers to negotiate by threatening to seize the coal mines and operate them with federal troops.
   d. declaring a national state of emergency and ordering the miners back to work.
   e. mobilizing the public to write letters urging the two parties to settle their dispute.

9. The Roosevelt-backed Elkins Act and Hepburn Act were aimed at

   a. better protection for industrial workers.
   b. more effective regulation of the railroad industry.
   c. protection for consumers of beef and fresh produce.
   d. breaking up the Standard Oil and United States Steel monopolies.
   e. prohibiting nonfarm child labor for anyone under age fourteen.

10. The controversy over the Hetch Hetchy Valley in Yosemite National Park revealed

   a. a philosophical disagreement between wilderness preservationists and more moderate multiple-use conservationists.
   b. President Roosevelt's hostility toward creating any more national parks.
   c. a political conflict between the lumber industry and conservationists.
   d. a split between urban California's need for water and environmentalists' concerns to preserve free-flowing streams.
   e. a disagreement over whether or not the National Park system should permit commercial vendors inside the parks.

11. Two issues that President Roosevelt especially promoted as part of his progressive policies were
     a.   agricultural exports and housing reform.
     b.   stock market regulation and restrictions on false advertising.
     c.   freer immigration and racial integration.
     d.   consumer protection and conservation of nature.
     e.   the advancement of science and federal support for the arts.
12. Roosevelt was blamed by big business for the Panic of 1907 because
     a.   his progressive boat-rocking tactics had allegedly unsettled industry and undermined business confidence.
     b.   his policies of regulating and protecting industrial workers had caused a depression.
     c.   his inability to establish a stable monetary policy led to a Wall Street crash.
     d.   the public wanted him to run again for president in 1908.
     e.   his administration had run up enormous federal deficits.
13. As a result of his successful presidential campaign in 1908, William Howard Taft was widely expected to
     a.   advance the issues of women's suffrage and prohibition of alcohol.
     b.   forge a coalition with William Jennings Bryan and the Democrats.
     c.   emphasize foreign policy instead of Roosevelt's domestic reforms.
     d.   turn away from Theodore Roosevelt and toward the conservative wing of the Republican party.
     e.   continue and extend Theodore Roosevelt's progressive policies.
14. Progressive Republicans grew deeply disillusioned with Taft, especially over the issues of
     a.   dollar diplomacy and military intervention in the Caribbean and Central America.
     b.   labor union protections and women's rights.
     c.   trust-busting, tariffs, and conservation.
     d.   regulation of the banking and railroad industries.
     e.   tax policy and international trade.
15. Roosevelt finally decided to break with the Republicans and form a third party because
     a.   he had always regarded the Republican party as too conservative.
     b.   he could no longer stand to be in the same party with Taft.
     c.   Taft had used his control of the Republican party machine to deny Roosevelt the nomination.
     d.   Roosevelt believed that he would have a better chance of winning the presidency as a third-party candidate.
     e.   he believed he could win the support of Woodrow Wilson and other mainstream Democrats.

C. Identification

Supply the correct identification for each numbered description.

1. _____   A largely middle-class movement that aimed to use the power of government to correct the economic and social problems of industrialism

2. _____   Popular journalists who used publicity to expose corruption and attack abuses of power in business and government

3. _____   Progressive proposal to allow voters to bypass state legislatures and propose legislation themselves

4. _____   Progressive device that would enable voters to remove corrupt or ineffective officials from office

5. _____ Roosevelt's policy of having the federal government promote the public interest by dealing evenhandedly with both labor and business

6. _____ Effective railroad-regulation law of 1906 that greatly strengthened the Interstate Commerce Commission

7. _____ Disastrous industrial fire of 1911 that spurred workmen's compensation laws and some state regulation of wages and hours in New York

8. _____ Upton Sinclair's novel that inspired pro-consumer federal laws regulating meat, food, and drugs

9. _____ Powerful women's reform organization led by Frances Willard

10. _____ Brief but sharp economic downturn of 1907, blamed by conservatives on the supposedly dangerous president

11. _____ Generally unsuccessful Taft foreign policy in which government attempted to encourage overseas business ventures

12. _____ Powerful corporation broken up by a Taft-initiated antitrust suit in 1911

D. Matching People, Places, and Events

Match the person, place, or event in the left column with the proper description in the right column by inserting the correct letter on the blank line.

1. ___ Thorstein Veblen

2. ___ Lincoln Steffens

3. ___ Ida Tarbell

4. ___ Seventeenth Amendment

5. ___ Robert M. La Follette

6. ___ Hiram Johnson

7. ___ Triangle Shirtwaist Company fire

8. ___ Women's Christian Temperance Union

9. ___ Anthracite coal strike

10. ___ Jane Addams

11. ___ Upton Sinclair

12. ___ *Muller* v. *Oregon*

13. ___ William Howard Taft

14. ___ *Lochner* v. *New York*

15. ___ Gifford Pinchot

a. Politically inept inheritor of the Roosevelt legacy who ended up allied with the reactionary Republican Old Guard

b. Powerful progressive women's organization that sought to "make the world homelike" by outlawing the saloon and the product it sold

c. Case that upheld protective legislation on the grounds of women's supposed physical weakness

d. New York City disaster that underscored urban workers' need for government protection

e. The most influential of the state-level progressive governors and a presidential aspirant in 1912

f. Leading female progressive reformer whose advocacy of pacifism as well as social welfare set her at odds with more muscular and militant progressives

g. Eccentric economist who criticized the wealthy for conspicuous consumption and failure to serve real human needs

h. Leading muckraking journalist whose articles documented the Standard Oil Company's abuse of power

i. Progressive governor of California who broke the stranglehold of the Southern Pacific Railroad on the state's politics

j. Pro-conservation federal official whose dismissal by Taft angered Roosevelt progressives

k. Dangerous labor conflict resolved by Rooseveltian negotiation and threats against business people

l. Early muckraker who exposed the political corruption in many American cities

m. Progressive novelist who sought to aid industrial workers, but found his book, *The Jungle*, instead inspiring middle-class consumer protection.

n. Progressive measure that required U.S. senators to be elected directly by the people rather than by state legislatures

o. Supreme court ruling that overturned a progressive law mandating a ten-hour workday

E. Putting Things in Order

Put the following events in correct order by numbering them from 1 to 5.

1. _____ A former president opposes his handpicked successor for the Republican presidential nomination.

2. _____ Sensational journalistic accounts of corruption and abuse of power in politics and business spur the progressive movement.

3. _____ A progressive forestry official feuds with Taft's secretary of the interior, deepening the division within the Republican party.

4. _____ A novelistic account of Chicago's meat-packing industry sparks new federal laws to protect consumers.

5. _____ A brief but sharp financial crisis leads to conservative criticism of Roosevelt's progressive policies.

F. Matching Cause and Effect

Match the historical cause in the left column with the proper effect in the right column by writing the correct letter on the blank line.

Cause

1. ___ Old-time Populists, muckraking journalists, social-gospel ministers, and European socialist immigrants

2. ___ Progressive concern about political corruption

3. ___ Governors like Robert La Follette

4. ___ Roosevelt's threat to seize the anthracite coal mines

5. ___ Settlement houses and women's clubs

6. ___ Upton Sinclair's *The Jungle*

7. ___ Roosevelt's personal interest in conservation

8. ___ Taft's political mishandling of tariff and conservation policies

9. ___ Russia's and Japan's hostility to an American role in China

10. ___ Roosevelt's feeling that he was cheated out of the Republican nomination by the Taft machine

Effect

a. Ended the era of uncontrolled exploitation of nature and involved the federal government in preserving natural resources

b. Led to reforms like the initiative, referendum, and direct election of senators

c. Forced a compromise settlement of a strike that threatened the national well-being

d. Outraged consumers and led to the Meat Inspection Act and the Pure Food and Drug Act

e. Laid the basis for a third-party crusade in the election of 1912

f. Incensed pro-Roosevelt progressives and increased their attacks on the Republican Old Guard

g. Led the way in using universities and regulatory agencies to pursue progressive goals

h. Made Taft's dollar-diplomacy policy a failure

i. Provided the pioneering forces who laid the foundations for the Progressive movement.

j. Served as the launching pads for widespread female involvement in progressive reforms

G. Developing Historical Skills

Classifying Historical Information

Often a broad historical movement, such as progressivism, can best be understood by breaking it down into various component parts. Among the varieties of progressive reform discussed in this chapter are (A) political progressivism, (B) economic or industrial progressivism, (C) consumer progressivism, and (D) environmental progressivism.

Put each of the following progressive acts, policies, or court cases into one of those categories by writing in the correct letter.

1. _____ The Newlands Act of 1902

2. _____ The ten-hour law for bakers

3. _____ The movement for women's suffrage

4. _____ The anthracite coal strike of 1902

5. _____ Direct election of senators

6. _____ The Meat Inspection Act of 1906

7. _____ The Pure Food and Drug Act

8. _____ Initiative, referendum, and recall

9. _____ *Muller* v. *Oregon*

10. _____ The Hepburn Act of 1906

11. _____ Yosemite and Grand Canyon National Parks

12. _____ Workmen's compensation laws

PART III: APPLYING WHAT YOU HAVE LEARNED

1. The text says that progressivism was less a minority movement than a dominant majority mood. What were the basic social and political conditions that created that reforming mood, and what diverse people and ideas were all sheltered under the broad progressive umbrella?

2. What did the progressive movement accomplish at the local, state, and national levels?

3. What made women such central forces in the progressive crusade? What specific backgrounds and ideologies did they bring to the public arena? What were the strengths and limitations of the progressive emphasis on providing special protection to children and women?

4. The text says that Theodore Roosevelt sought to tame unbridled capitalism, including the largest corporations, without fundamentally altering the American economic system. How do his policies regarding the trusts, labor, and consumer protection reflect this middle way? Why was Roosevelt regarded with hostility by many industrialists and Wall Street financiers, even though he sought to reform rather than attack them?

5. Why were consumer protection and conservation among Theodore Roosevelt's most successful progressive achievements? What does the high visibility of these causes reveal about the character and strength of progressivism, as well as its limits?

6. What caused the Taft-Roosevelt split, and how did it reflect the growing division between Old Guard and progressive Republicans?

7. How was progressivism a response to the development of the new urban and industrial order in America (see Chapters 24 and 25)?

8. It is sometimes argued that progressivism was a uniquely American phenomenon because it addressed the most profound social and economic problems without engaging in the rhetoric of class conflict or economic warfare. Is this true? How did progressives address the problems of the working classes and poor without adopting the ideologies of socialism or communism. How did progressives borrow some ideas from European models, while adapting them to uniquely American conditions?

9.   The two key goals of progressivism, according to the text, were to use the government to curb monopolistic corporations and to enhance the ordinary citizen's welfare. How successful was it in attaining these two goals?

CHAPTER 29

Wilsonian Progressivism at Home and Abroad, 1912–1916

PART I: REVIEWING THE CHAPTER

A. Checklist of Learning Objectives

After mastering this chapter, you should be able to:

1. Discuss the key issues of the pivotal 1912 election and the basic principles of Wilsonian progressivism.

2. Describe how Wilson successfully reformed the "triple wall of privilege."

3. State the basic features of Wilson's moralistic foreign policy, and explain how, despite his intentions, it drew him into intervention in Mexico and elsewhere in Latin America.

4. Describe America's initial neutral response to World War I, Wilson's increasingly tough policies on Germany's submarine warfare, and the sharp political divisions over the prospect of American entry into the war.

5. Explain how Wilson's progressive domestic agenda and provisionally successful maintenance of American neutrality enabled him to win a narrow victory in 1916 over still-divided Republicans.

B. Glossary

To build your social science vocabulary, familiarize yourself with the following terms.

1. **entrepreneurship** The process whereby an individual initiates a business at some risk in order to expand it and thereby earn a profit. "Wilson's New Freedom, by contrast, favored small enterprise, entrepreneurship, and the free functioning of . . . markets."

2. **self-determination** In politics, the right of a people to shape its own national identity and form of government, without outside coercion or influence. ". . . [the Confederacy] . . . partly inspired his ideal of self-determination for people of other countries."

3. **piety** Devotion to religious duty and practices. ". . . Wilson was reared in an atmosphere of fervent piety."

4. **graduated income tax** A tax on income in which the taxation rates grow progressively higher for those with higher income. "Congress enacted a graduated income tax. . . ."

5. **levy** A forcible tax or other imposition. ". . . [the] income tax [began] with a modest levy on income over $3,000. . . ."

6. **inelasticity** The inability to expand or contract rapidly. "[The] most serious shortcoming [of the country's financial structure] was the inelasticity of the currency."

7. **commercial paper** Any business document having monetary or exchangeable value. "The . . . paper money [was] backed by commercial paper. . . ."

8. **promissory note** A written pledge to pay a certain person a specified sum of money at a certain time. "The . . . paper money [was] backed by commercial paper, such as promissory notes of business people."

9. **Magna Carta** The "Great Charter" of England, which feudal nobles of England forced King John I to sign in 1215. As the first written guarantee of certain traditional rights, such as trial by a jury of peers, against arbitrary royal power, it served as a model for later assertions of Anglo-Saxon liberties. "Union leader Samuel Gompers hailed the [Clayton] act as the Magna Carta of labor...."

10. **agricultural extension** The system of providing services and advice to farmers through dispersed local agents. "Other laws benefited rural America by providing for . . . the establishment of agricultural extension work in the state colleges."

11. **enclave** A small territory surrounded by foreign or hostile territory. "Though often segregated in Spanish-speaking enclaves, they helped to create a unique borderland culture. . . ."

12. **gringo** Contemptuous Latin American term for North Americans. "Challenging Carranza's authority while also punishing the gringos. . . ."

13. **censor** An official who examines publications, mail, literature, and so forth in order to remove or prohibit the distribution of material deemed dangerous or offensive. "Their censors sheared away war stories harmful to the Allies. . . ."

14. **torpedo** To launch from a submarine or airplane a self-propelled underwater explosive designed to detonate on impact. ". . . the British passenger liner *Lusitania* was torpedoed and sank. . . ."

15. **draft** In politics, to choose an individual to run for office without that person's prior solicitation of the nomination. (A *military* draft, or conscription, legally compels individuals into the armed services.) "Instead, they drafted Supreme Court Justice Charles Evans Hughes, a cold intellectual who had achieved a solid record as governor of New York."

PART II: CHECKING YOUR PROGRESS

A. True-False

Where the statement is true, circle **T**; where it is false, circle **F**.

1. T F Wilson won the election of 1912 largely because the Republican party split in two.

2. T F In the 1912 campaign, Wilson's New Freedom favored a socially activist government and regulating trusts, while Roosevelt's New Nationalist favored strict antitrust laws that would favor small business.

3. T F Wilson was an intellectually gifted leader who tended to look down on ordinary politics and politicians.

4. T F Wilson successfully used his eloquence and popular appeal to push through progressive reforms of the tariff, monetary systems, and trusts.

5. T F Wilson's progressive outlook showed itself clearly in his attempt to improve the conditions and treatment of blacks.

6. T F Wilson initially attempted to overturn the imperialistic big-stick and dollar-diplomacy foreign policies of Roosevelt and Taft in Asia and Latin America.

7. T F Wilson consistently refused to send American troops to intervene in the Caribbean.

8.   T   F   Wilson's initial policy toward the revolutionary Mexican government of General Huerta was to display moral disapproval while trying to avoid American military intervention.

9.   T   F   The mediation of three Latin American nations after the Tampico incident saved Wilson from a full-scale war with Mexico.

10.   T   F   General Pershing's expedition into Mexico was an attempt to bring the pro-American faction of Mexican revolutionaries to power.

11.   T   F   In the early days of World War I, more Americans sympathized with Germany than with Britain.

12.   T   F   The American economy benefited greatly from supplying goods to the Allies.

13.   T   F   After the *Lusitania*'s sinking, the Midwest and West favored war with Germany, while the more isolationist East generally favored attempts at negotiation.

14.   T   F   After the sinking of the *Sussex*, Wilson successfully pressured Germany into stopping submarine attacks against neutral shipping.

15.   T   F   In the 1916 campaign, Wilson ran on the slogan "He Kept Us Out of War," while his opponent Hughes tried to straddle the issue of a possible war with Germany.

B. Multiple Choice

Select the best answer and circle the corresponding letter in the space provided.

1.   The basic contrast between the two progressive candidates, Roosevelt and Wilson, was that
   a.   Roosevelt wanted genuine political and social reforms, while Wilson wanted only to end obvious corruption.
   b.   Roosevelt wanted to promote free enterprise and competition, while Wilson wanted the federal government to regulate the economy and promote social welfare.
   c.   Wilson saw advancing women's interests as central to the progressive agenda, while Roosevelt believed women were best served by supporting progressivism outside politics.
   d.   Roosevelt wanted to focus on issues of jobs and economic growth, while Wilson pushed for social legislation to protect women, children, and city-dwellers.
   e.   Roosevelt wanted the federal government to regulate the corporate economy and expand social welfare, while Wilson wanted to restore economic competition and social equality by breaking up large corporate trusts.

2.   Wilson won the election of 1912 primarily because
   a.   his policies were more popular with the public.
   b.   Taft and Roosevelt split the former Republican vote.
   c.   the Socialists took nearly a million votes from Roosevelt.
   d.   he was able to win over many of the embittered Roosevelt Republicans to his cause.
   e.   his charismatic personal appeal exceeded that of Roosevelt and Taft.

3.   Wilson's primary weakness as a politician was his
   a.   lack of skill in public speaking.
   b.   inability to grasp the complexity of governmental issues.
   c.   tendency to be inflexible and refuse to compromise.
   d.   lack of overarching political ideals.
   e.   background as a professor and college president.

4. The "triple wall of privilege" that Wilson set out to reform consisted of

    a. farmers, shippers, and the military.
    b. the tariffs, the banks, and the trusts.
    c. Ivy League universities, private dining clubs, and segregated urban neighborhoods.
    d. congressional leaders, lobbyists, and lawyers.
    e. labor union officials, big city bosses, and wealthy southern landlords.

5. Under the Wilson administration, Congress exercised the authority granted by the newly enacted Sixteenth Amendment to pass

    a. prohibition of liquor.
    b. women's suffrage.
    c. voting rights for blacks.
    d. rules for the direct election of U.S. Senators.
    e. a progressive federal income tax.

6. The new regulatory agency, created by the Wilson administration in 1914, that attacked unfair business competition, false and misleading advertising, and consumer fraud was the

    a. Federal Trade Commission.
    b. Interstate Commerce Commission.
    c. Federal Reserve System.
    d. Consumer Products Safety Commission.
    e. Antitrust Division of the Justice Department.

7. While outlawing business monopolies, the Clayton Anti-Trust Act created exemptions from antitrust prosecution for

    a. industries essential to national defense.
    b. agricultural and labor organizations.
    c. the oil and steel industries.
    d. professional organizations of doctors and lawyers.
    e. colleges and universities.

8. Wilson effectively reformed the banking and financial system by

    a. requiring that all banks be federally chartered and carry effective deposit insurance.
    b. taking the United States off the gold standard.
    c. establishing a publicly controlled Federal Reserve Board to issue currency and control credit.
    d. transferring authority to regulate banking and currency from the federal government to the states and the private sector.
    e. creating a system of currency exchanges so that people without bank accounts could cash checks and obtain credit.

9. Wilson's general progressive support for the less fortunate in American society was weakened by his actively hostile policies toward

    a. labor unions.
    b. blacks.
    c. farmers.
    d. women.
    e. immigrants.

10. Wilson's initial attitude toward the Mexican revolutionary government was to

    a. refuse recognition of General Huerta's regime but avoid American intervention.
    b. intervene with troops on behalf of threatened American business interests.
    c. provide military and economic assistance to the Huerta regime.
    d. mobilize other Latin American governments to oust Huerta.
    e. follow the lead of publisher William Randolph Hearst.

11. The threatened war between the United States and Mexico in 1914 was avoided by the mediation of the ABC powers, which consisted of

    a. Australia, Britain, and Canada.
    b. Antigua, Brazil, and Cuba.
    c. Angola, Belgium, and China.
    d. the Association of British Commonwealth nations.
    e. Argentina, Brazil, and Chile.

12. General Pershing's expedition into Mexico was sent in direct response to the

    a. refusal of Huerta to abandon power.
    b. threat of German intervention in Mexico.
    c. arrest of American sailors in the Mexican port of Tampico.
    d. killing of American citizens in New Mexico by Pancho Villa.
    e. Mexican revolutionary persecution of the Catholic Church.

13. An early event of World War I that led many Americans to sympathize with the Allies against Germany was

    a. German bribes and payoffs to American journalists.
    b. the Germans' involvement in overseas imperialism.
    c. Germany's invasion of neutral Belgium.
    d. the British refusal to use poison gas in warfare.
    e. Germany's aerial bombing of civilians in France.

14. After the *Lusitania, Arabic,* and *Sussex* sinkings, Wilson successfully pressured the German government to

    a. end the use of the submarine against British warships.
    b. end its attempt to blockade the British Isles.
    c. publish warnings to all Americans considering traveling on unarmed ships.
    d. cease from sinking neutral merchant and passenger ships without warning.
    e. permit Red Cross officials to travel on German submarines to monitor civilian deaths.

15. Wilson's most effective slogan in the campaign of 1916 was

    a. "The full dinner pail."
    b. "Free and unlimited coinage of silver in the ratio of sixteen to one."
    c. "A war to make the world safe for democracy."
    d. "He kept us out of war."
    e. "I will not send your boys to fight in a foreign war."

C. Identification

Supply the correct identification for each numbered description.

1. _____   Four-footed symbol of Roosevelt's Progressive third party in 1912

2. _____   A fourth political party, led by a former railroad labor union leader, that garnered nearly a million votes in 1912

3. _____   Wilson's political philosophy of restoring democracy through trust-busting and economic competition

4. _____   A twelve-member agency appointed by the president to oversee the banking system under a new federal law of 1913

5. _____   New presidentially appointed regulatory commission designed to prohibit unfair business competition, unethical advertising, and labeling practices

6. _____   Wilsonian trust-busting law that prohibited interlocking directorates and other monopolistic business practices, while legalizing labor and agricultural organizations

7. _____   Wilson-backed law that promised the Philippines eventual independence from the United States, but only when a stable and secure government was attained

8. _____   Troubled Caribbean island nation where a president's murder led Wilson to send in the marines and assume American control of the police and finances

9. _____   Term for the three Latin American nations whose mediation prevented war between the United States and Mexico in 1914

10. _____   World War I alliance headed by Germany and Austria-Hungary

11. _____   The coalition of powers—led by Britain, France, and Russia—that opposed Germany and its partners in World War I

12. _____   New underwater weapon that threatened neutral shipping and seemed to violate all traditional norms of international law

13. _____   Large British passenger liner whose sinking in 1915 prompted some Americans to call for war against Germany

14. _____   Germany's carefully conditional agreement in 1916 not to sink passenger and merchant vessels without warning

15. _____   Key electoral state where a tiny majority for President Wilson tipped the balance against Republican Charles Evans Hughes in 1916

D. Matching People, Places, and Events

Match the person, place, or event in the left column with the proper description in the right column by inserting the correct letter on the blank line.

1. ___ Thomas Woodrow Wilson

2. ___ Theodore Roosevelt

3. ___ Eugene V. Debs

4. ___ Samuel Gompers

5. ___ Louis D. Brandeis

6. ___ Virgin Islands

7. ___ General Huerta

8. ___ Venustiano Carranza

9. ___ Vera Cruz

10. ___ Pancho Villa

11. ___ John J. Pershing

12. ___ Belgium

13. ___ Serbia

14. ___ Kaiser Wilhelm II

15. ___ Charles Evans Hughes

a. Small European nation in which an Austro-Hungarian heir was killed, leading to the outbreak of World War I

b. Mexican revolutionary whose assaults on American citizens and territory provoked a U.S. expedition into Mexico

c. Port where clashes between Mexicans and American military forces nearly led to war in 1914

d. Socialist party leader who garnered nearly a million votes for president in the election of 1912.

e. Caribbean territory purchased by the United States from Denmark in 1917

f. Narrowly unsuccessful presidential candidate who tried to straddle both sides of the fence regarding American policy toward Germany

g. Small European nation whose neutrality was violated by Germany in the early days of World War I

h. Commander of the American military expedition into Mexico in 1916–1917

i. Southern-born intellectual who pursued strong moral goals in politics and the presidency

j. Leading progressive reformer and the first Jew appointed to the Supreme Court

k. Energetic progressive and vigorous nationalist whose failed third-party effort contributed to Wilson's victory in the election of 1912

l. Labor leader who hailed the Clayton Anti-Trust Act as the "Magna Carta of labor"

m. Second revolutionary Mexican president, who took aid from the United States but strongly resisted American military intervention in his country

n. Autocratic ruler who symbolized ruthlessness and arrogance to many pro-Allied Americans

o. Mexican revolutionary whose bloody regime Wilson refused to recognize and nearly ended up fighting

E. Putting Things in Order

Put the following events in correct order by numbering them from 1 to 5.

1. _____ Wilson extracts a dangerously conditional German agreement to halt submarine warfare.

2. _____ Wilson's superb leadership pushes major reforms of the tariff and monetary system through Congress.

3. _____ The bull moose and the elephant are both electorally defeated by a donkey bearing the banner of "New Freedom."

4. _____ The heavy loss of American lives to German submarines nearly leads the United States into war with Germany.

5. _____ Despite efforts to avoid involvement in the Mexican revolution, Wilson's occupation of a Mexican port raises the threat of war.

F. Matching Cause and Effect

Match the historical cause in the left column with the proper effect in the right column by writing the correct letter on the blank line.

1. ___ The split between Taft and Roosevelt

2. ___ Wilson's presidential appeals to the public over the heads of Congress

3. ___ The Federal Reserve Act

4. ___ Conservative justices of the Supreme Court

5. ___ Political turmoil in Haiti and Santo Domingo (Dominican Republic)

6. ___ The Mexican revolution

7. ___ Pancho Villa's raid on Columbus, New Mexico

8. ___ America's close cultural and economic ties with Britain

9. ___ Germany's sinking of the *Lusitania, Arabic,* and *Sussex*

10. ___ Wilson's apparent success in keeping America at peace through diplomacy

a. Caused most Americans to sympathize with the Allies rather than the Central Powers

b. Helped push through sweeping reforms of the tariff and the banking system in 1913

c. Enabled the Democrats to win a narrow presidential victory in the election of 1916

d. Allowed Wilson to win a minority victory in the election of 1912

e. Declared unconstitutional progressive Wilsonian measures dealing with labor unions and child labor

f. Caused President Wilson and other outraged Americans to demand an end to unrestricted submarine warfare

g. Created constant political instability south of the border and undermined Wilson's hopes for better U.S. relations with Latin America

h. Was the immediate provocation for General Pershing's punitive expedition into Mexico

i. Finally established an effective national banking system and a flexible money supply

j. Caused Wilson to send in U.S. marines to restore order and supervise finances

G. Developing Historical Skills

Understanding Documents in Context

Historical documents cannot usually be understood in isolation. Awareness of the circumstances and conditions under which they were written is essential to comprehending their importance. The text reproduces on p. 741 the advertisement with notice from the German government that appeared in the New York *Herald* on May 1, 1915, six days before the *Lusitania* was sunk. Read the ad carefully, and reread text pp. 739–742 to understand and evaluate the context in which the warning appeared. Then answer the following questions.

1. What was the policy of the German government regarding submarine use at the time the ad was taken out?

2.   Why might the German government be particularly concerned about warning American passengers thinking of traveling on a British liner? How would the notice be useful even if some Americans did travel on the ship?

3.   What fact about the *Lusitania*'s cargo did the German government know that it did not put into the warning?

4.   Why were many Americans outraged about the *Lusitania* sinking despite the warning?

PART III: APPLYING WHAT YOU HAVE LEARNED

1.   What were the essential qualities of Wilson's presidential leadership, and how did he display them in 1913–1914?

2.   What were the results of Wilson's great reform assault on the "triple wall of privilege"—the tariff, the banks, and the trusts?

3.   In what ways was Wilson the most pro-labor president up to that point in American history? Which specific laws, policies, and appointments reflect his support for ordinary workers?

4.   How was Wilson's foreign policy an attempt to expand idealistic progressive principles from the domestic to the international arena? Why did Wilson's progressive democratic idealism lead to the very kind of U.S. interventions in other countries that he professed to dislike?

5.   What were the causes and consequences of U.S. entanglement with Mexico in the wake of the Mexican Revolution? Could the United States have avoided involvement in Mexican affairs?

6.   Why was it so difficult for Wilson to maintain America's neutrality from 1914 to 1916?

7.   How did Wilson's prejudicial attitudes toward non-whites, in the United States and elsewhere, affect his domestic and foreign policies? Should these policies be seen as a major blot on his overall progressive reputation or as simply a reflection of the general racial prejudice of the time?

8.   How did Wilson's foreign policy differ from that of the other great progressive president, Theodore Roosevelt (see Chapter 27)? Which president was more effective in foreign policy and why?

9.   Wilsonianism is defined as an approach to American foreign policy that seeks to spread democracy and freedom throughout the whole world. In what ways does Wilson's foreign policy from 1913 to 1916 fit this definition? In what ways was his administration's policy during this period *not* Wilsonian?

10.   Why was America so determined to stay out of World War I during the early years of the conflict? What were the factors that gradually turned the government and the majority of Americans against Germany?

CHAPTER 30

The War to End War, 1917–1918

PART I: REVIEWING THE CHAPTER

A. Checklist of Learning Objectives

After mastering this chapter, you should be able to:

1. Explain what caused America to enter World War I.

2. Describe how Wilsonian idealism turned the war into an ideological crusade for democracy that inspired public fervor and suppressed dissent.

3. Discuss America's mobilization for war and its reliance primarily on voluntary methods rather than government force.

4. Explain the consequences of World War I for labor, women, and African Americans.

5. Describe America's participation in the War, and explain why its economic and political importance exceeded its military contribution to the Allied victory and German defeat.

6. Analyze Wilson's attempt to forge a peace based on his idealistic Fourteen Points, the political mistakes that weakened his hand, and the compromises he was forced to make by the other Allied statesmen at Versailles.

7. Discuss how Lodge and others resisted Wilson's League of Nations, how Wilson's total refusal to compromise doomed the Treaty of Versailles, and why Harding's victory in the election of 1920 became the final death sentence for the League.

B. Glossary

To build your social science vocabulary, familiarize yourself with the following terms.

1. **isolationism** In American diplomacy, the traditional belief that the United States should refrain from involvement in overseas politics, alliances, or wars, and confine its national security interest to its own borders (sometimes along with the Caribbean and Central America). **Internationalism or Wilsonianism** is the contrasting belief that America's national security requires involvement and sometimes diplomatic or military alliances overseas. "But their obstruction was a powerful reminder of the continuing strength of American isolationism."

2. **collective security** In international affairs, reliance on a group of nations or an international organization as protection against aggressors, rather than on national self-defense alone. " . . . an international organization that Wilson dreamed would provide a system of collective security."

3. **mobilization** The organization of a nation and its armed forces for war. "Creel typified American war mobilization. . . ."

4. **pardon** The official release of a person from punishment for a crime. ". . . presidential pardons were rather freely granted. . . ."

5. **ration** A fixed allowance of food or other scarce commodity. "He deliberately rejected issuing ration cards. . . ."

6. **conscientious objector** A person who refuses to participate in war on grounds of conscience or belief. ". . . about 4,000 conscientious objectors were excused."

7. **Bolshevik** The radical majority faction of the Russian Socialist party that seized power in the October 1917 revolution; they later took the name *Communist*. (Bolshevik is the Russian word for "majority"; their rivals for power were **Mensheviks**, or minority.) "The Bolsheviks long resented these 'capitalistic' interventions. . . ."

8. **salient** A portion of a battle line that extends forward into enemy territory. ". . . nine American divisions . . . joined four French divisions to push the Germans from the St. Mihiel salient. . . ."

9. **parliamentary** Concerning political systems in which the government is constituted from the controlling party's members in the legislative assembly. "Unlike all the parliamentary statesmen at the table, [Wilson] did not command a legislative majority at home."

10. **protectorate** In international affairs, a weaker or smaller country held to be under the guidance or protection of a major power; the arrangement is a weaker form of imperialism or colonialism. (A **colony** is a territory owned outright by a more powerful nation.) ". . . preventing any vengeful parceling out of the former colonies and protectorates of the vanquished powers."

11. **trustee** A nation that holds the territory of a former colony as the conditional agent of an international body under defined terms. "The victors would . . . receive the conquered territory . . . only as trustees of the League of Nations."

12. **mandate** Under the League of Nations (1919–1939), a specific commission that authorized a trustee to administer a former colonial territory. "Japan was conceded the strategic Pacific islands under a League of Nations mandate. . . ."

13. **self-determination** The Wilsonian doctrine that each people should have the right to freely choose its own political affiliation and national future, e.g., independence or incorporation into another nation. "Faced with fierce Wilsonian opposition to this violation of self-determination...."

14. **reservation** A portion of a deed, contract, or treaty that places conditions or restrictions on the general obligations. ". . . he finally came up with fourteen formal reservations. . . ."

15. **demagogue** A politician who arouses fervor by appealing to the lowest emotions of a mass audience, such as fear, hatred, and greed. " . . . a debacle that played into the hands of the German demagogue Adolf Hitler."

PART II: CHECKING YOUR PROGRESS

A. True-False

Where the statement is true, circle **T**; where it is false, circle **F**.

1. T   F   Germany responded to Wilson's call for "peace without victory" with a proposal for a negotiated settlement of the war.

2. T   F   Wilson's proclamation of the war as a crusade to end all war and spread democracy around the world inspired intense ideological enthusiasm among Americans.

3. T   F   Among Wilson's Fourteen Points were freedom of the seas, national self-determination for oppressed smaller nations, and an international organization to secure peace.

4. T   F   The Committee on Public Information used varied forms of propaganda to stir fervent American patriotism and support for the war.

5. T F The primary targets of prosecution under the Espionage and Sedition Acts were German and Austrian agents in the United States.

6. T F Even during the war mobilization, Americans were extremely reluctant to grant the federal government extensive powers over the civilian economy.

7. T F Despite bitter and sometimes violent strikes, American labor made economic and organizational gains as a result of World War I.

8. T F War-inspired black migration into northern cities led to major racial riots in 1917–1919.

9. T F America's granting of women's right to vote under the Nineteenth Amendment represented the first breakthrough for women's suffrage in the world.

10. T F One of the few major instances of using coercive power during the war was the federal government's seizure and operation of the nation's railroads.

11. T F The arrival of the main force American troops in May 1918 came just in time to block the last German offensive and turn the tide toward Allied victory.

12. T F When Woodrow Wilson first arrived in Europe, the European public hailed him as a hero and a peacemaking savior.

13. T F Wilson successfully thwarted other Allied nations' attempts to make imperialistic gains from the war.

14. T F Wilson's unwillingness to compromise or accept any Republican reservations to the Treaty of Versailles guaranteed that the whole treaty would go down to defeat.

15. T F In the election of 1920, Republican Harding supported the League of Nations, while Democrat Cox tried to straddle both sides of the issue.

B. Multiple Choice

Select the best answer and circle the corresponding letter.

1. The immediate cause of American entry into World War I was
   a. German support for a possible Mexican invasion of the southwestern United States.
   b. Germany's resumption of unrestricted submarine warfare.
   c. the imminent danger of a French surrender to Germany.
   d. desire of the American munitions makers to gain larger profits.
   e. Wilson's recognition that German militarism threatened the ideals of American democracy.

2. Wilson and his administration aroused the still-divided American people to fervent support of the war by
   a. seizing control of the means of communication and demanding national unity.
   b. declaring the German people to be immoral Huns and barbarians.
   c. proclaiming the conflict an ideological war to end all war and make the world safe for democracy.
   d. proclaiming the war a religious crusade to save Western, Christian civilization
   e. asserting that a victorious Germany might well attack or invade the United States.

3.   The capstone Fourteenth Point of Wilson's declaration of war aims called for
    a.   the establishment of parliamentary democracies throughout Europe.
    b.   guarantees of basic human rights for all people in the world.
    c.   an international organization to guarantee collective security.
    d.   freedom of travel without restrictions.
    e.   a severe limitation on all nations' military forces and armaments as soon as the war ended.

4.   George Creel's Committee on Public Information typified the entire American war effort because it
    a.   maintained respect for American ideals of free speech and dissent even as it promoted the war.
    b.   effectively used statistics and scientific information to enable the government to mobilize for war.
    c.   relied more on whipped-up patriotism and voluntary compliance than on formal laws or government coercion.
    d.   brought all the resources of private business into support of the war effort.
    e.   used the constant threat of government takeover to force business and labor to support the war.

5.   The two key laws aimed at enforcing loyalty and suppressing antiwar dissent were the
    a.   War Mobilization Act and the National Defense Act.
    b.   Selective Service Act and the Public Information Act.
    c.   Eighteenth Amendment and the Anti-German Language Act.
    d.   Espionage Act and the Sedition Act.
    e.   War Industries Act and the Council of National Defense authorization law.

6.   Two groups that experienced the most direct attacks and suppression during the war were
    a.   German Americans and socialists.
    b.   communists and labor leaders.
    c.   Mexican Americans and immigrants.
    d.   African Americans and feminists.
    e.   conscientious objectors and draft dodgers.

7.   The immediate postwar passage of the Nineteenth Amendment, granting American women the right to vote
    a.   was the breakthrough that opened the door to worldwide women's suffrage.
    b.   enabled women to consolidate the permanent economic gains they had made during the war.
    c.   came in the face of continued opposition by President Wilson.
    d.   reflected the general American belief that the war should really lead to an expansion of democracy.
    e.   followed similar adoption of suffrage in many Western nations.

8.   Particularly violent strikes erupted during and after World War I in
    a.   the shipping and railroad industries.
    b.   the steel industry.
    c.   the textile and clothing manufacturing industries.
    d.   factories employing women war workers.
    e.   Chicago and East St. Louis.

9.   The major result of the substantial wartime migration of blacks to northern cities was
    a.   a growing acceptance of the idea of a strong black presence in the military.
    b.   federal government efforts to block further black migration from southern farms.
    c.   a growing agitation by blacks and northern liberals for racial integration.
    d.   the incorporation of blacks into the major industrial unions.
    e.   a series of vicious race riots in northern cities.

10. A major difference between the World War I Selective Service Act and the Civil War draft was that in World War I

    a. women as well as men were drafted.
    b. there was no provision for conscientious objection as there had been during the Civil War.
    c. draftees were sent immediately into front line combat.
    d. draftees received the same training as professional soldiers.
    e. it was not possible to purchase an exemption or to hire a substitute as during the Civil War.

11. American soldiers were especially needed in France in the spring of 1918 because

    a. the Allied invasion of Germany was stalling and in danger of failing.
    b. the Italian front was about to collapse and permit the Austro-Hungarians to join German forces in France.
    c. the British were in danger of starving due to German submarine warfare.
    d. the Russians had left the Allied war effort and were threatening to switch to the German side.
    e. a renewed German offensive was threatening to break through to Paris and force France to surrender.

12. The major American military contribution to Germany's decision to give up fighting was

    a. American armies' victories in a dozen critical battles during 1918.
    b. the U.S. Navy's successful destruction of most German submarines.
    c. the prospect of endless supplies of future, fresh American troops to fight the war.
    d. General Pershing's brilliant strategy that final broke the stalemate of trench warfare.
    e. the effective use of new American military weapons like the tank and the airplane.

13. Wilson blundered badly when leading the American peace delegation to Paris by

    a. failing to develop any set of clear diplomatic goals for the peace treaty.
    b. refusing to include any Republican senators in the American delegation.
    c. not consulting with his key allies, Britain and France, about their war aims.
    d. suggesting that he would abandon his idealistic Fourteen Points in order to appease the Allies.
    e. believing Senator Henry Cabot Lodge when he said he supported Wilson one hundred percent.

14. The European Allied powers and Japan were able to undermine Wilson's goal of a nonimperialistic peace treaty partly because

    a. they regarded his proposed League of Nations as largely a useless symbol.
    b. American ethnic groups were working for imperialistic goals of their own.
    c. they knew he could not promise continuing American aid and involvement in European affairs.
    d. Germany's constant threat to resume fighting made them insistent on harshly punishing the war's loser.
    e. Republicans were forcing Wilson to change the League of Nations covenant to guarantee the Monroe Doctrine and other American interests.

15. Wilson bore considerable responsibility for the failure of the United States to join the League of Nations because he

    a. linked the League too closely to European politics.
    b. ordered Democratic senators to defeat the pro-League treaty with the Lodge reservations.
    c. failed to take the case for the League to the American public.
    d. had agreed that America would pay most of the cost of the League.
    e. failed to effectively campaign for pro-League Governor James Cox in the 1920 election.

C. Identification

Supply the correct identification for each numbered description.

1. _____   Message sent to Mexico from the German foreign minister proposing a secret German-Mexican alliance and possible support for Mexico's recovery of Texas, New Mexico, and Arizona

2. _____   Wilson's idealistic statement of American war aims in January 1918 that inspired the Allies and demoralized the Germans

3. _____   American government propaganda agency that aroused zeal for Wilson's ideals and whipped up hatred for the Kaiser

4. _____   Radical antiwar labor union whose members were prosecuted under the Espionage and Sedition Act

5. _____   Originally weak wartime agency that gradually expanded the federal government's power over the economy by setting production quotas and allocating natural resources.

6. _____   Constitutional revision endorsed by Wilson as a war measure whose ratification finally achieved a goal long sought by American women

7. _____   Treasury Department bond-selling drives that raised about $21 billion to provide most of the funds to finance the American war effort

8. _____   Popular term for American soldiers during World War I

9. _____   Collective term for the major powers that dominated the Paris Peace Conference—Britain, France, Italy, and the United States

10. _____   Wilson's proposed international body that constituted the key provision of the Versailles treaty

11. _____   Controversial peace agreement that compromised many of Wilson's idealistic Fourteen Points but retained his cherished League of Nations among its provisions

12. _____   Senatorial committee whose chairman used delaying tactics and hostile testimony to develop opposition to Wilson's treaty and League of Nations

13. _____   A hard core of isolationist senators who bitterly opposed any sort of league; also called the "Battalion of Death"

14. _____   Amendments to the proposed Treaty of Versailles, sponsored by Wilson's hated senatorial opponent, that attempted to guarantee America's sovereign rights in relation to the League of Nations

15. _____   Wilson's belief that the presidential election of 1920 should constitute a direct popular vote on the League of Nations

D. Matching People, Places, and Events

Match the person, place, or event in the left column with the proper description in the right column by inserting the correct letter on the blank line.

1. ___   George Creel

2. ___   Eugene V. Debs

a.   Inspirational leader of the Western world in wartime who later stumbled as a peacemaker

3. ___ Bernard Baruch

4. ___ Herbert Hoover

5. ___ John J. Pershing

6. ___ Alice Paul

7. ___ Franklin D. Roosevelt

8. ___ Kaiser Wilhelm II

9. ___ Woodrow Wilson

10. ___ Henry Cabot Lodge

11. ___ Georges Clemenceau

12. ___ William Borah

13. ___ James Cox

14. ___ Calvin Coolidge

15. ___ Warren G. Harding

b. Senatorial leader of the isolationist irreconcilables who absolutely opposed all American involvement in Europe

c. Exciting vice-presidential candidate from New York in the losing Democratic campaign of 1920.

d. The "tiger" of France, whose drive for security forced Wilson to compromise at Versailles

e. Head of the American propaganda agency that mobilized public opinion for World War I

f. Folksy Ohio senator whose 1920 presidential victory ended the last hopes for U.S. participation in the League of Nations

g. Hated leader of America's enemy in World War I

h. Head of the Food Administration who pioneered successful voluntary mobilization methods

i. Leader of the pacifist National Women's Party who opposed U.S. involvement in World War I

j. Defeated Democratic presidential candidate in the election of 1920

k. Commander of the overseas American Expeditionary Force in World War I

l. Massachusetts governor and Warren G. Harding's vice presidential running mate in the election of 1920

m. Wilson's great senatorial antagonist who fought to keep America out of the League of Nations

n. Head of the War Industries Board, which attempted to impose some order on U.S. war production

o. Socialist leader who won nearly a million votes as a presidential candidate while in federal prison for antiwar activities

E. Putting Things in Order

Put the following events in correct order by numbering them from 1 to 5.

1. _____ Germany's resumption of submarine warfare forces the United States into a declaration of war.

2. _____ The Senate's final defeat of the Versailles treaty and a Republican election victory end Wilson's last hopes for American entry into the League of Nations.

3. _____ The United States takes the first hesitant steps toward preparedness in the event of war.

4. _____ The effectiveness of American combat troops in crucial battles helps bring about an Allied victory in World War I.

5. _____ Wilson struggles with other Allied leaders in Paris to hammer out a peace treaty and organize the postwar world.

F. Matching Cause and Effect

Match the historical cause in the left column with the proper effect in the right column by writing the correct letter on the blank line.

<table>
<tr><th colspan="2" align="center">Cause</th><th colspan="2" align="center">Effect</th></tr>
<tr><td>1. ___</td><td>Germany's resumption of unrestricted submarine warfare</td><td>a.</td><td>Led to major racial violence in Chicago and East St. Louis, Illinois</td></tr>
<tr><td>2. ___</td><td>Wilson's Fourteen Points</td><td>b.</td><td>Forced Democrats to vote against a modified treaty and killed American participation in the League of Nations</td></tr>
<tr><td>3. ___</td><td>The wartime atmosphere of emotional patriotism and fear</td><td></td><td></td></tr>
<tr><td>4. ___</td><td>Women's labor in wartime factories</td><td>c.</td><td>Stopped the final German offensive and turned the tide toward Allied victory</td></tr>
<tr><td>5. ___</td><td>The migration of African Americans to northern cities</td><td></td><td></td></tr>
<tr><td>6. ___</td><td>American troops' entry into combat in the spring and summer of 1918</td><td>d.</td><td>Allowed domestic disillusionment and opposition to the treaty and League to build strength</td></tr>
<tr><td>7. ___</td><td>Wilson's political blunders in the fall of 1918</td><td>e.</td><td>Finally pushed the United States into World War I</td></tr>
<tr><td>8. ___</td><td>The strong diplomatic demands of France, Italy, and Japan</td><td>f.</td><td>Weakened the president's position during the peacemaking process</td></tr>
<tr><td>9. ___</td><td>Senator Lodge's tactics of delaying and proposing reservations in the Versailles treaty</td><td>g.</td><td>Caused harsh attacks on German Americans and other Americans who opposed the war</td></tr>
<tr><td>10. ___</td><td>Wilson's refusal to accept any reservations supported by Lodge.</td><td>h.</td><td>Lifted Allied and American spirits and demoralized Germany and its allies</td></tr>
<tr><td></td><td></td><td>i.</td><td>Forced Wilson to compromise his Fourteen Points in order to keep the League as part of the peace treaty</td></tr>
<tr><td></td><td></td><td>j.</td><td>Helped pass the Nineteenth Amendment but did not really change society's emphasis on the maternal role</td></tr>
</table>

G. Developing Historical Skills

Analyzing Visual Propaganda

This exercise involves analyzing visual propaganda designed to make emotional appeals on behalf of a cause. In this case, the propaganda was designed to enlist the American public's support for the war effort against Germany. The kinds of propaganda used on behalf of a cause can tell the historian a great deal about what issues were perceived to be at stake and what public values were being appealed to.

Answer the following questions about the cartoons and drawings in this chapter.

1. *Anti-German Propaganda* (p.749): How do the words and image of this poster work together to persuade an American audience to buy liberty loans? Besides the specific message, what general portrait of Germany, the war, and America's reasons for fighting are conveyed?

2. *Patriotic Persuasion* (p. 749): How does this army recruitment poster convey the idea that both patriotism and social solidarity can be served by joining the military? At what social class of young man is the poster evidently aimed?

3. *Food for Thought* (p. 755): How does this poster visually make the connection between the patriotic war effort and gardens? What specific words or phrases create the link between women's food-growing effort and military service on fields of combat? What specific appeal is this image making to women?

PART III: APPLYING WHAT YOU HAVE LEARNED

1. What caused American entry into World War I, and how did Wilson turn the war into an ideological crusade?

2. What did American women gain from their participation in the war effort? What did they fail to obtain?

3. What was America's military and ideological contribution to the Allied victory?

4. How were the goals of the war presented to the American public? Did these lofty and idealistic goals eventually contribute to the deep American disillusionment at the conclusion of the war? Why or why not?

5. How was Wilson forced to compromise during the peace negotiations, and why did America, in the end, refuse to ratify the treaty and join the League of Nations?

6. Do you agree that despite Wilson's failure to obtain all his goals, he made the Versailles Peace Treaty much better than it would have been had he not been in Paris? Why or why not?

7. Apart from such immediate factors as the Lodge-Wilson antagonism, what general features of earlier American history worked against American involvement in European affairs and participation in the League of Nations?

8. Do you agree that the final responsibility for the failure of America to join the League of Nations lies with Woodrow Wilson rather than with his opponents like Henry Cabot Lodge? Why or why not?

9. What really caused the overwhelming Republican victory in the election of 1920?

10. Ever since World War I and its aftermath, many of the fundamental debates about American foreign policy have been defined by whether the United States should pursue Wilsonianism or not. Using the account of Wilson's policies in the text and "Varying Viewpoints," outline the essential principles of Wilsonianism and explain why they have been so powerful and yet so controversial in American history.

CHAPTER 31

American Life in the "Roaring Twenties," 1919–1929

PART I: REVIEWING THE CHAPTER

A. Checklist of Learning Objectives

After mastering this chapter, you should be able to:

1. Explain and analyze America's turn toward social conservatism and normalcy following World War I.

2. Describe the cultural conflicts of the 1920s over such issues as immigration, cultural pluralism, and prohibition; and describe the rise of organized crime during the decade.

3. Describe the rise of Protestant Fundamentalism and its apparent defeat in the landmark Scopes Trial.

4. Discuss the rise of the mass-consumption economy, led by the automobile industry.

5. Describe the cultural revolution brought about by radio, films, and changing sexual standards, and the resulting anxiety it produced.

6. Explain how new ideas and values were reflected and promoted in the innovative American literature and music of the 1920s, including the African American Harlem Renaissance.

7. Explain how the era's cultural changes affected women and African Americans.

B. Glossary

To build your social science vocabulary, familiarize yourself with the following terms.

1. **syndicalism** A theory or movement that advocates bringing all economic and political power into the hands of labor unions by means of strikes. ". . . a number of legislatures . . . passed criminal syndicalism laws."

2. **Bible Belt** The region of the American South, extending roughly from North Carolina west to Oklahoma and Texas, where Protestant Fundamentalism and belief in literal interpretation of the Bible have traditionally been strongest. ". . . the Klan spread with astonishing rapidity, especially in the Midwest and the 'Bible Belt' South."

3. **provincial** Narrow and limited; isolated from cosmopolitan influences. "Isolationist America of the 1920s, ingrown and provincial, had little use for the immigrants. . . ."

4. **racketeer** A person who obtains money illegally by fraud, bootlegging, gambling, or threats of violence. "Racketeers even invaded the ranks of local labor unions. . . ."

5. **underworld** Those who live outside society's laws, by vice or crime. ". . . the annual 'take' of the underworld was estimated to be from $12 billion to $18 billion. . . ."

6.   **credit** In business, the arrangement of purchasing goods or services immediately but making the payment at a later date. "Buying on credit was another innovative feature of the postwar economy."

7.   **installment plan** A credit system by which goods already acquired are paid for in a series of payments at specified intervals. ". . . encouraged by tempting installment-plan buying, countless Americans with shallow purses acquired the habit of riding as they paid."

8.   **magnate** An influential person in a large-scale enterprise. ". . . an outraged public forced the screen magnates to set up their own rigorous code of censorship."

9.   **repression** In psychology, the forcing of instincts or ideas painful to the conscious mind into the unconscious, where they continue to exercise influence. "The Viennese physician appeared to argue that sexual repression was responsible for a variety of nervous and emotional ills."

10.   **charismatic** Concerning the personal magnetism or appeal of a leader for his or her followers; literally, "gift of grace." "Harlem in the 1920s also spawned a charismatic political leader, Marcus Garvey."

11.   **functionalism** The theory that a plan or design should be derived from practical purpose. "Architecture also married itself to the new materialism and functionalism."

12.   **surtax** A special tax, usually involving a raised percentage increase on an already existing tax. ". . . Congress . . . abolish[ed] the surtax, the income tax, and estate taxes."

PART II: CHECKING YOUR PROGRESS

A. True-False

Where the statement is true, circle **T**; where it is false, circle **F**.

1.   T   F   The red scare of 1919–1920 brought the United States to the brink of war with the revolutionary Communist government in Russia.

2.   T   F   The Sacco-Vanzetti case aroused worldwide protest because of alleged prejudice by the judge and jury against the atheistic immigrant defendants.

3.   T   F   The revived Ku Klux Klan remained a powerful force in American politics until the onset of the Great Depression.

4.   T   F   The Immigration Act of 1924, for the first time, severely limited the numbers of immigrants and discriminated against those from eastern and southern Europe.

5.   T   F   Some intellectuals, like Horace Kallen and Randolph Bourne, believed that immigrants should be able to retain elements of their own cultures and thus contribute to a more diverse and cosmopolitan America.

6.   T   F   One major consequence of prohibition was the rise of organized crime that controlled liquor distribution as well as drugs, gambling, and prostitution.

7.   T   F   The Scopes trial verdict acquitted biology teacher John Thomas Scopes and overturned the Tennessee law prohibiting the teaching of evolution in the schools.

8.   T   F   Two major innovations of the new consumer economy were mass advertising and the ability to purchase goods on credit without paying the full price immediately.

9.   T   F   The automobile had major social and cultural effects in weakening family life and offering new freedom to women and youth.

10. T F   D.W. Griffiths' film, *The Birth of a Nation*, was the first major Hollywood production to present African Americans in a positive light.

11. T F   The 1920s saw attempts to restore stricter standards of sexual behavior, especially for women.

12. T F   The Harlem Renaissance and the rise of jazz both reflected a new racial pride among African Americans.

13. T F   The most prominent writers of the 1920s upheld the moral virtues of small-town American life against the critical attitudes and moral questioning of the big cities.

14. T F   Many American writers and artists of the 1920s sought escape from what they saw as the narrow culture of the United States by moving abroad to Mexico.

15. T F   The real estate and stock market booms of the 1920s were fueled by large amounts of risky speculation and excessive credit.

B. Multiple Choice

Select the best answer and circle the corresponding letter.

1. The red scare of the early 1920s was initially set off by
    a. the Sacco-Vanzetti case.
    b. the rise of the radical Industrial Workers of the World.
    c. the Bolshevik revolution in Russia.
    d. an influx of radical immigrants.
    e. the revelation of American Communist infiltration of the federal government.

2. Besides attacking minorities like Catholics, blacks, and Jews, the Ku Klux Klan of the 1920s opposed contemporary cultural changes, such as
    a. evolution and birth control.
    b. prohibition and higher education.
    c. automobiles and airplanes.
    d. patriotism and immigration restriction.
    e. novels and modern architecture.

3. The quota system established for immigration in the 1920s was based partly on the idea that
    a. many of the political refugees from war-torn Europe were likely radicals or communists.
    b. immigrants from northern and western Europe were superior to those from southern and eastern Europe.
    c. the era of European immigration would be replaced by immigration from Latin America.
    d. immigration should be based on family connections, education, and job skills, not ethnic group.
    e. the United States was becoming increasingly overpopulated.

4. Progressive intellectuals, like Horace Kallen and Randolph Bourne, differed from most Americans of the 1920s in believing that
    a. the continuing divisions of language and religion among the working class enabled employers to exploit workers and crush unions.
    b. southern and eastern European cultures were as sophisticated as those from northern and western Europe.
    c. racial and economic justice was more important that cultural issues.
    d. immigrants should be able to preserve elements of their culture and not be forced to conform to a single American model.
    e. the U.S. government should recognize more than one official language.

5.   One major impact of prohibition was

    a.   a rise in criminal organizations that supplied illegal liquor.

    b.   an improvement in family relations and the general moral tone of society.

    c.   a turn from alcohol to other forms of substance abuse.

    d.   the rise of voluntary self-help organizations like Alcoholics Anonymous.

    e.   a heightened respect for law enforcement at the local, state, and federal levels.

6.   The essential issue in the Scopes trial was whether

    a.   scientists ought to be allowed to investigate the biological origins of humanity.

    b.   the teachings of Darwin could be reconciled with those of religion.

    c.   Darwinian evolutionary science could be taught in the public schools.

    d.   Fundamentalist Protestants could use public school facilities for their meetings.

    e.   the teaching of Darwinism would inevitably lead to sex education in the schools.

7.   The term *Fordism* was widely used to describe businessman Henry Ford's innovation of

    a.   Ford's anti-Semitism and hostility to education.

    b.   applying the internal combustion engine to a vehicle that the ordinary person could own.

    c.   a system of time and motion studies designed to improve efficiency in manufacturing.

    d.   assembly-line mass production of identical, relatively cheap manufactured goods.

    e.   permitting customers to purchase automobiles on credit with little money down.

8.   One of the primary social effects of the new automobile age was a

    a.   growing migration from cities to smaller towns and rural areas.

    b.   strengthening of intergenerational ties among parents, children, and grandchildren.

    c.   tightening of restrictions on women.

    d.   closing of the gap between the working class and the wealthy.

    e.   weakening of traditional family ties between parents and youth.

9.   Radio and the movies both had the cultural effect of

    a.   increasing Americans' interest in history and literature.

    b. enabling the sophisticated culture of the wealthy elite to spread to the masses.

    c.   encouraging producers of culture to adapt their products to a wide a variety of individual tastes.

    d.   encouraging local creativity and ending cultural dependence on a few big cities.

    e.   increasing standardized mass culture and weakening traditional forms of family and neighborhood culture.

10.   Among the major changes vigorously pursued by many American women in the 1920s were

    a.   expanded voting rights and political equality.

    b.   economic equality and equal pay for equal work.

    c.   social reform and family welfare.

    d.   leadership in national business and politics.

    e.   opportunities for adventure and sexual liberation.

11.   The primary achievement of Marcus Garvey's Universal Negro Improvement Association was its

    a.   promotion of black jazz and blues.

    b.   positive impact on black racial pride.

    c.   economic program of economic development in Harlem.

    d.   successful transportation of numerous America blacks to Africa.

    e.   formation of an organization designed to promote racial integration and equality.

12. H.L. Mencken's magazine, *American Mercury*, appealed to many young literary rebels by
    a. encouraging American writers to migrate abroad to Paris.
    b. promoting a program of progressive economic and social reform.
    c. its regular publication of sexually explicit writing and images.
    d. attacking the American middle class, patriotism, and Puritan do-gooders.
    e. its popular appeal to a great variety of Americans.
13. Many of the prominent new writers of the 1920s were
    a. fascinated by their historical roots in old New England.
    b. disgusted with European domination of American culture.
    c. interested especially in nature and social reform.
    d. rooted in the traditions and values of the South.
    e. highly critical of traditional American Puritanism and small-town life.
14. The center of the African-American literary and cultural revival of the 1920s was
    a. Atlanta.
    b. New Orleans.
    c. Chicago.
    d. Harlem, in New York City.
    e. Paris.
15. During the 1920s, Treasury Secretary Andrew Mellon and the Republican Congress pursued the economic policy of
    a. encouraging stock and real estate speculation.
    b. permitting the federal debt to grow substantially in order to stimulate the economy.
    c. cutting taxes for the wealthy and shifting the tax burden to the middle class.
    d. promoting higher wages so that the lower income groups could purchase goods and keep the economy growing.
    e. favoring old industries, like textiles and steel, over new industries, like consumer appliance manufacturing.

C. Identification

Supply the correct identification for each numbered description.

1. _____ The public panic of 1919–1920, spawned by fear of Bolshevik revolution, that resulted in the arrest and deportation of many political radicals

2. _____ Hooded defenders of Anglo-Saxon and Protestant values against immigrants, Catholics, and Jews

3. _____ Restrictive legislation of 1924 that reduced the number of newcomers to the United States and discriminated against immigrants from southern and eastern Europe

4. _____ Theory advocated by Bourne, Kallen, and others that immigrants should be able to retain elements of their traditions within a diverse America, rather than being forced to melt all differences

5. _____ National policy created by the passage of the Eighteenth Amendment, which led to widespread lawbreaking and the rise of organized crime

6. _____ Legal battle over teaching evolution that pitted modern science against Fundamentalist religion

7. _____ Henry Ford's cheap, rugged, mass-produced automobile

8. _____   D. W. Griffiths' epic film of 1915 about the Reconstruction era that prompted protests and boycotts by African Americans

9. _____   One of the few new consumer products of the 1920s that encouraged people to stay at home rather than pulling them away from home and family

10. _____   Movement led by feminist Margaret Sanger that contributed to changing sexual behaviors, especially for women

11. _____   Syncopated style of music created by blacks that first attained widespread national popularity in the 1920s

12. _____   Marcus Garvey's self-help organization that proposed to the resettlement of blacks in Africa

13. _____   H. L. Mencken's monthly magazine that led the literary attack on traditional moral values, the middle class, and Puritanism

14. _____   F. Scott Fitzgerald's influential first novel of 1920 that celebrated youth and helped set the tone for the emerging jazz age of the decade

15. _____   The explosion of creative expression in a district of New York City that encouraged African American artists, writers, and musicians to celebrate their racial pride

D. Matching People, Places, and Events

Match the person, place, or event in the left column with the proper description in the right column by inserting the correct letter on the blank line.

1. ___ A. Mitchell Palmer

2. ___ Nicola Sacco and Bartolomeo Vanzetti

3. ___ Al Capone

4. ___ John Dewey

5. ___ William Jennings Bryan

6. ___ Henry Ford

7. ___ Bruce Barton

8. ___ Langston Hughes

9. ___ Charles A. Lindbergh

10. ___ Marcus Garvey

11. ___ Randolph Bourne

12. ___ H. L. Mencken

13. ___ F. Scott Fitzgerald

14. ___ Ernest Hemingway

15. ___ Gertrude Stein

a. The Poet Laureate of Harlem and author of *The Weary Blues*

b. Innovative writer whose novels reflected the disillusionment of many Americans with propaganda and patriotic idealism

c. Italian American anarchists whose trial and execution aroused widespread protest

d. Mechanical genius and organizer of the mass-produced automobile industry

e. U.S. attorney general who rounded up thousands of alleged Bolsheviks in the red scare of 1919–1920

f. Baltimore writer who criticized the supposedly narrow and hypocritical values of American society

g. Top gangster of the 1920s, eventually convicted of income-tax evasion

h. Former presidential candidate who led the fight against evolution at the 1925 Scopes trial

i. Experimental writer whose Paris salon became a gathering place for American writers and artists in the 1920s

j. A leader of the new advertising industry, author of a pro-business interpretation of Jesus in *The Man Nobody Knows*

k. Cosmopolitan intellectual who advocated cultural pluralism and said America should be "not a nationality but a trans-nationality"

l. Leading American philosopher and proponent of progressive education

m. Wholesome, shy aviation pioneer who became a cultural hero of the 1920s for his pathbreaking flight

n. Minnesota-born writer whose novels were especially popular with young people in the 1920s

o. Jamaican-born leader who enhanced African American pride despite his failed migration plans

E. Putting Things in Order

Put the following events in correct order by numbering them from 1 to 5.

1. _____   The trial of a Tennessee high-school biology teacher symbolizes a national conflict over values of religion and science.

2. _____   Fear of the Bolshevik revolution sparks a crusade against radicals and Communists in America.

3. _____   A modest young man becomes a national hero by accomplishing a bold feat of aviation.

4. _____   Two Italian immigrants are convicted of murder and robbery, provoking charges of prejudice against the judge and jury.

5. _____   A new immigration law tightens up earlier emergency restrictions and imposes discriminatory quotas against the New Immigrants.

F. Matching Cause and Effect

Match the historical cause in the left column with the proper effect in the right column by writing the correct letter on the blank line.

Cause	**Effect**
1. ____ American fear of Bolshevism	a. Caused the rise of the Ku Klux Klan and the imposition of immigration restrictions
2. ____ Nativist American fear of immigrants and Catholics	

3. ____   Prohibition

4. ____   The automobile industry

5. ____   The radio

6. ____   Rising prosperity, new technologies, and the ideas of Sigmund Freud

7. ____   Resentment against conventional small-town morality

8. ____   The economic boom of the 1920s

9. ____   The ability to buy stocks with only a small down payment

10. ____   Andrew Mellon's tax policies

b.   Caused many influential writers of the 1920s to criticize traditional values and search for new moral standards

c.   Caused the red scare and the deportation of foreign radicals

d.   Enabled many ordinary citizens to join in a speculative Wall Street boom

e.   Stimulated highway construction, petroleum production, and other related industries

f.   Helped stimulate mass attention to sports and entertainment while spreading the reach of advertising

g.   Reduced the tax burden on the wealthy and contributed to the stock-market boom

h.   Greatly raised the incomes and living standards of many Americans

i.   Created a new atmosphere of sexual frankness and liberation, especially among the young

j.   Helped spawn bootlegging and large-scale organized crime

G. Developing Historical Skills

Understanding Cultural Developments in Historical Context

The first part of this chapter describes the major social and economic changes of the 1920s. The second part describes the cultural developments that also occurred in the 1920s. Since the artists, writers, and others who produced the culture and ideas of the period were living amidst these very same social changes, your knowledge of the historical context can help you understand why they created the kind of works they did.

Answer the following questions:

1.   In what ways were the movies, for all their glamour, similar to the automobile industry as developed by Henry Ford?

2.   How did new technological and economic innovations like the automobile (pp. 781–785) and social changes like urbanization help bring about the cultural liberation of women?

3. In what ways did the novels of F. Scott Fitzgerald (pp.792–793) or musical developments like jazz (pp. 790–791) especially appeal to people living amid the social and economic changes of the 1920s? Did these cultural developments simply mirror existing politics and society, or were they in some ways a challenge to them?

4. Why were writers like H. L. Mencken, Sinclair Lewis, Sherwood Anderson, and others (pp.792–793) so harshly critical of American middle-class and small-town life in their work? Why did such writers strike a popular chord in the 1920s?

PART III: APPLYING WHAT YOU HAVE LEARNED

1. How and why did America turn toward domestic isolation and social conservatism in the 1920s?

2. How was the character of American culture affected by the social and political changes of the 1920s? (Include both white ethnic groups and blacks in your discussion.)

3. Why was immigration, which had been part of American experience for many generations, seen as such a great threat to American identity and culture in the prosperous 1920s? How did the severe and discriminatory immigration restriction laws passed in the 1920s affect the country?

4. Why did critics, like Horace Kallen and Randolph Bourne, dislike the pressure on immigrants to Americanize and join the melting pot? What kind of future America did their ideals of cultural pluralism promote. Why was this view not widely accepted in the 1920s?

5. How did the Eighteenth Amendment outlawing alcohol both reflect and deepen the cultural divisions in the United States, including urban-rural conflicts?

6. How did some of the major public events of the 1920s reflect national disagreements over fundamental social, cultural, and religious values?

7. How did the automobile and other new products create a mass-consumption economy in the 1920s?

8. How did the new films, literature, and music of the 1920s affect American values in areas of religion, sexuality, and family life?

9. How and why did African Americans in the Harlem Renaissance and elsewhere begin celebrating racial pride and the New Negro in the 1920s? Was Marcus Garvey's movement to encourage black migration to Africa an expression of that same spirit or a reflection of the still-harsh oppression that most blacks experienced?

10. In what ways were the twenties a vigorous social and cultural reaction against the progressive movement in the decades leading up to World War I (see Chapters 29, 30, and 31)? Was this hostility to progressivism primarily a result of disillusionment with the outcome of the war or a reflection of the limits of progressive reform itself?

CHAPTER 32

The Politics of Boom and Bust, 1920–1932

PART I: REVIEWING THE CHAPTER

A. Checklist of Learning Objectives

After mastering this chapter, you should be able to:

1. Analyze the domestic political conservatism and economic prosperity of the 1920s.

2. Explain the Republican administrations' policies of isolationism, disarmament, and high-tariff protectionism.

3. Compare the easygoing corruption of the Harding administration with the straight-laced uprightness of his successor Coolidge.

4. Describe the international economic tangle of loans, war debts, and reparations, and indicate how the United States tried to address it.

5. Discuss how Hoover went from being a symbol of twenties business success to a symbol of depression failure.

6. Describe the stock market crash of 1929, and explain the deeper causes of the Great Depression.

7. Indicate how Hoover's response to the depression reflected a combination of old-time rugged individualism and the new view that the federal government had some responsibility for the economy.

B. Glossary

To build your social science vocabulary, familiarize yourself with the following terms.

1. **nationalization** Ownership of the major means of production by the national or federal government. ". . . wartime government operation of the lines might lead to nationalization."

2. **dreadnought** A heavily armored battleship with large batteries of twelve-inch guns. ". . . Secretary Hughes startled the delegates . . . with a comprehensive, concrete plan for . . . scrapping some of the huge dreadnoughts. . . ."

3. **accomplice** An associate or partner of a criminal who shares some degree of guilt. ". . . he and his accomplices looted the government to the tune of about $200 million. . . ."

4. **reparations** Compensation by a defeated nation for damage done to civilians and their property during a war. "Overshadowing all other foreign-policy problems . . . was . . . a complicated tangle of private loans, Allied war debt, and German reparations payments."

5. **pump priming** In economics, the spending or lending of a small amount of funds in order to stimulate a larger flow of economic activity. "'Pump-priming' loans by the RFC were no doubt of widespread benefit. . . ."

PART II: CHECKING YOUR PROGRESS

A. True-False

Where the statement is true, circle **T**; where it is false, circle **F**.

1. T   F   The most corrupt members of Harding's cabinet were the secretaries of state and the treasury.

2. T   F   The Republican administrations of the 1920s believed in strict enforcement of antitrust laws to maintain strong business competition.

3. T   F   The Republican administrations of the 1920s pursued an isolationist policy toward national security by engaging in a large military buildup.

4. T   F   The high tariff policies of the 1920s enhanced American prosperity but crippled international trade and Europe's economic recovery from World War I.

5. T   F   Calvin Coolidge's image of honesty and thrift helped restore public confidence in the government after the Harding administration scandals.

6. T   F   One sector of the American economy that did not share the prosperity of the 1920s was agriculture.

7. T   F   The major sources of support for liberal third-party presidential candidate Robert La Follette in the election of 1924 were among the urban working class and in the South

8. T   F   The main exception to America's isolationist foreign policy in the 1920s was continuing U.S. armed intervention in the Caribbean and Central America.

9. T   F   Britain, France, and America's other Allies vigorously protested U.S. demands for repayment of loans made during World War I.

10. T   F   In the election of 1928, Democratic nominee Al Smith's urban, Catholic, and wet background cost him support from many traditionally Democratic southern voters.

11. T   F   The Hawley-Smoot Tariff strengthened the trend toward expanded international trade and economic cooperation.

12. T   F   The American economic collapse during the Great Depression was the most severe suffered by any major industrial nation in the 1930s.

13. T   F   The Great Depression was caused partly by overexpansion of credit and excessive consumer debt.

14. T   F   Throughout his term, Hoover consistently adhered to his firm belief that the federal government should play no role in providing economic relief and assisting the recovery from the Depression.

15. T   F   Hoover's harsh use of the U.S. Army to disperse the veterans' Bonus Army from Washington brought him widespread condemnation.

B. Multiple Choice

Select the best answer and circle the corresponding letter.

1. As president, Warren G. Harding proved to be
    a. thoughtful and ambitious but impractical.
    b. an able administrator and diplomat but a poor politician.
    c. politically competent and concerned for the welfare of ordinary people.
    d. weak-willed and tolerant of corruption among his friends and his cabinet.
    e. better at managing domestic policy than foreign policy.

2. The relationship between government and big business advocated by the Republican presidents of the 1920s was that
    a. regulation of business should be weakened and the government should actively promote business profits.
    b. federal regulation should take precedence over state and local government.
    c. antitrust laws should be vigorously enforced to prevent monopolies.
    d. the government should retain a role in operating key businesses like the railroads and utilities.
    e. the government should keep hands off business and actively promote laissez-faire.

3. Two groups that suffered severe political setbacks in the immediate post–World War I environment were
    a. Protestants and Jews.
    b. organized labor and blacks.
    c. small businesses and farmers.
    d. women and city dwellers.
    e. southerners and Midwesterners.

4. Which two terms best describe the Harding and Coolidge administrations' approach to foreign policy?
    a. Internationalism and moralism
    b. Interventionism and militarism
    c. Isolationism and disarmament
    d. Balance of power and alliance-seeking
    e. Imperialism and racism

5. The proposed ratio of 5:5:3 in the Washington Disarmament Conference of 1921–1922 referred to the
    a. ratio of American, British, and Japanese troops to be maintained in China.
    b. respective number of votes Britain, France, and the United States would have in the League of Nations.
    c. allowable ratio of battleships and carriers among the United States, Britain, and Japan.
    d. number of nations from Europe, the Americas, and Asia, respectively, that would have to ratify the disarmament treaties before they went into effect.
    e. number of negotiators that the United States, Britain, and Japan sent to the conference.

6. The very high tariff rates of the 1920s had the primary economic effect of
    a. stimulating the formation of common markets among the major industrial nations.
    b. causing severe deflation in the United States and Europe.
    c. turning American trade away from Europe and toward Asia.
    d. stimulating American technological developments and raising wages.
    e. causing the Europeans to erect their own tariff barriers and thus severely reduce international trade

7. The central scandal of Teapot Dome involved members of Harding's cabinet who

    a. sold spoiled foodstuffs to the army and navy.
    b. took bribes for leasing federal oil lands.
    c. violated prohibition by tolerating gangster liquor deals.
    d. stuffed ballot boxes and played dirty tricks on campaign opponents.
    e. took expensive trips at taxpayer expense.

8. The farm bloc's favorite solution to the severe drop in prices that caused farmers' economic suffering in the 1920s was

    a. direct federal assistance to encourage farmers not to grow grain or cotton.
    b. for the federal government to buy up agricultural surpluses at higher prices and sell them abroad.
    c. for the United States to impose high tariffs on agricultural imports from foreign countries.
    d. for farmers to form producers' unions to obtain higher prices from consumers.
    e. for farmers to switch from corn, cotton, and wheat to more profitable crops.

9. Besides deep divisions within the Democratic party, the elections of 1924 revealed

    a. Coolidge's inability to attain Harding's level of personal popularity.
    b. the close political division between Republicans and Democrats.
    c. the turn of the solid South from the Democrats to the Republicans.
    d. the rise of liberalism within the Democratic party.
    e. that the progressive movement was much weaker than it had been before World War I.

10. The international economic crisis caused by unpaid war reparations and loans was partially resolved by

    a. private American bank loans to Germany that enabled Germany to pay war reparations.
    b. forgiving the Allied loans and German reparations.
    c. the creation of a new international economic system by the League of Nations.
    d. the rise of Mussolini and Hitler.
    e. forcing Germany to pay off the Allied loans to the United States.

11. Al Smith's Roman Catholicism and opposition to prohibition hurt him especially

    a. among northeasterners
    b. among ethnic voters.
    c. among African Americans.
    d. among women voters.
    e. in the South.

12. In the political campaign of 1928, Herbert Hoover revealed himself to be

    a. a charismatic and eloquent campaigner.
    b. a combination of nineteenth-century small-town virtues with big business efficiency.
    c. willing to engage in anti-Catholic rhetoric to defeat Al Smith.
    d. hostile to new forms of technology and progress.
    e. interested primarily in foreign policy.

13. One important cause of the great stock market crash of 1929 was

    a. overexpansion of production and credit beyond people's ability to pay for goods.
    b. a tight money policy that made it difficult to obtain loans.
    c. the lack of tariff protection for American markets from foreign competitors.
    d. excessive government regulation of business.
    e. the agricultural depression that had weakened the American farm economy.

14. The sky-high Hawley-Smoot Tariff of 1930 had the economic effect of
    a. providing valuable protection for hard-pressed American manufacturers.
    b. lowering the value of American currency in international money markets.
    c. crippling international trade and deepening the depression.
    d. forcing foreign governments to negotiate fairer trade agreements.
    e. raising so much revenue that the federal government was running surpluses..

15. The federal agency that Hoover established in order to provide pump-priming loans to business was the
    a. Tennessee Valley Authority.
    b. Bonus Expeditionary Force.
    c. Grain Stabilization Corporation.
    d. American Legion.
    e. Reconstruction Finance Corporation.

C. Identification

Supply the correct identification for each numbered description.

1. _____ Poker-playing cronies from Harding's native state who contributed to the morally loose and corrupt atmosphere in his administration

2. _____ Supreme Court ruling that removed women's workplace protection, invalidated a minimum wage for women, and undermined the earlier Court decision in *Muller* v. *Oregon*

3. _____ World War I veterans' group that vigorously promoted militant patriotism, political conservatism, and economic benefits for former servicemen

4. _____ Agreement emerging from the Washington Disarmament Conference that reduced naval strength and established a 5:5:3 ratio of warships among the major naval powers

5. _____ Toothless international agreement of 1928 that pledged nations to outlaw war

6. _____ Naval oil reserve in Wyoming that gave its name to one of the major Harding administration scandals

7. _____ Farm proposal of the 1920s, passed by Congress but vetoed by the president, that provided for the federal government to buy farm surpluses and sell them abroad

8. _____ American-sponsored arrangement for rescheduling German reparations payments that opened the way to private American bank loans to Germany.

9. _____ Southern Democrats who turned against their party's wet, Catholic nominee and voted for the Republicans in 1928

10. _____ Sky-high tariff bill of 1930 that deepened the depression and caused international financial chaos

11. _____ The climactic day of the October 1929 Wall Street stock-market crash

12. _____ Depression shantytowns, named after the president whom many blamed for their financial distress

13. _____ Hoover-sponsored federal agency that provided loans to hard-pressed banks and businesses after 1932

14. _____   Encampment of unemployed veterans who were driven out of Washington by General Douglas MacArthur's forces in 1932

15. _____   The Chinese province invaded and overrun by the Japanese army in 1932

D. Matching People, Places, and Events

Match the person, place, or event in the left column with the proper description in the right column by inserting the correct letter on the blank line.

1. ___ Warren G. Harding

2. ___ Charles Evans Hughes

3. ___ Andrew Mellon

4. ___ Henry Sinclair

5. ___ John Davis

6. ___ Albert B. Fall

7. ___ Harry Daugherty

8. ___ Calvin Coolidge

9. ___ Robert La Follette

10. ___ Herbert Hoover

11. ___ Al Smith

12. ___ Black Tuesday

13. ___ Charles Dawes

14. ___ Douglas MacArthur

15. ___ Henry Stimson

a. The worst single event of the great stock market crash of 1929

b. Negotiator of a plan to reschedule German reparations payments and Calvin Coolidge's vice president after 1925

c. The "Happy Warrior" who attracted votes in the cities but lost them in the South

d. Harding's interior secretary, convicted of taking bribes for leases on federal oil reserves

e. Weak, compromise Democratic candidate in 1924

f. U.S. attorney general and a member of Harding's corrupt Ohio Gang who was forced to resign in administration scandals

g. Strong-minded leader of Harding's cabinet and initiator of major naval agreements

h. Wealthy industrialist and conservative secretary of the treasury in the 1920s

i. Weak-willed president whose easygoing ways opened the door to widespread corruption in his administration

j. Hoover's secretary of state, who sought sanctions against Japan for its aggression in Manchuria

k. Secretary of commerce, through much of the 1920s, whose reputation for economic genius became a casualty of the Great Depression

l. Leader of a liberal third-party insurgency who attracted little support outside the farm belt

m. Wealthy oilman who bribed cabinet officials in the Teapot Dome scandal

n. Commander of the troops who forcefully ousted the army of unemployed veterans from Washington in 1932

o. Tight-lipped Vermonter who promoted frugality and pro-business policies during his presidency

E. Putting Things in Order

Put the following events in correct order by numbering them from 1 to 5.

1. _____ Amid economic collapse, Congress raises tariff barriers to new heights and thereby deepens the depression.

2. _____ An American-sponsored plan to ease German reparations payments provides a temporarily successful approach to the international war-debt tangle.

3. _____ An American-sponsored international conference surprisingly reduces naval armaments and stabilizes Far Eastern power relations.

4. _____ The prosperous economic bubble of the 1920s suddenly bursts, setting off a sustained period of hardship.

5. _____ A large number of corrupt dealings and scandals become public knowledge just as the president who presided over them is replaced by his impeccably honest successor.

F. Matching Cause and Effect

Match the historical cause in the left column with the proper effect in the right column by writing the correct letter on the blank line.

Cause	Effect
1. ___ Republican pro-business policies	a. Led to a Republican landslide in the election of 1928
2. ___ American concern about the arms race and the danger of war	b. Weakened labor unions and prevented the enforcement of progressive antitrust legislation
3. ___ The high-tariff Fordney-McCumber Law of 1922	c. Plunged the United States into the worst economic depression in its history
4. ___ The loose moral atmosphere of Harding's Washington	d. Drove crop prices down and created a rural economic depression
5. ___ The improved farm efficiency and production of the 1920s	e. Led to the successful Washington Disarmament Conference and the Five Power Naval Agreement of 1922
6. ___ America's demand for complete repayment of the Allies' war debt	
7. ___ Hoover's media campaign and Smith's political liabilities	

8. ___   The stock-market crash

9. ___   Domestic overexpansion of production and dried-up international trade

10. ___   Hoover's limited efforts at federally sponsored relief and recovery

f.   Encouraged numerous federal officials to engage in corrupt dealings

g.   Helped cause the stock-market crash and deepen the Great Depression

h.   Failed to end the depression but did prevent more serious economic suffering

i.   Sustained American prosperity, but pushed Europe into economic protectionism and turmoil

j.   Aroused British and French anger and toughened their demands for German war reparations

G. Developing Historical Skills

Reading Diagrams

Sometimes a schematic drawing or diagram can help explain a complicated historical process in a simpler way than words. The international financial tangle of the 1920s is an exceptionally complicated affair, but examining the diagram on p. 808 makes it much easier to understand.

Answer the following questions.

1.   What two roles did Americans play in the process?

2.   What economic relationship did Great Britain and France have with Germany?

3.   To whom did Britain owe war debts? To whom did France owe war debts?

4.   Why was credit from American bankers so essential to all the European powers? Can you explain what happened when that credit was suddenly cut off after the stock-market crash of 1929?

PART III: APPLYING WHAT YOU HAVE LEARNED

1.   What basic economic and political policies were pursued by the three conservative Republican administrations of the 1920s?

2.   What were the causes and effects of America's international economic and political isolationism in the 1920s?

3.   What weakness existed beneath the surface of the general 1920s prosperity? How did these weaknesses help cause the Great Depression?

4.   Why were liberal or progressive politics so weak in the 1920s? Discuss the strengths and weaknesses of La Follette and Smith as challengers to the Republicans in 1924 and 1928.

5.   The three Republican presidents of the 1920s are usually lumped together as essentially identical in outlook. Is that an accurate way to view them? What differences, if any, in style and policy, existed among Harding, Coolidge, and Hoover?

6.   What were the economic and social effects of the Great Depression on the American people? Why did so many of the unemployed blame themselves rather than economic forces for their inability to find work?

7.   How did President Hoover attempt to balance his belief in rugged individualism with the economic necessities of the time? Why do historians today, more than people of the time, tend to see Hoover as a more tragic figure, rather than a heartless or cruel president?

8.   Which economic policies of the 1920s and 1930s helped cause and deepen the Depression. Since the depression soon became worldwide, did the Depression's fundamental causes lie inside or outside the United States?

9.   How could the economic and political conservatism of the 1920s coincide with the great cultural and intellectual innovations of the same decade (see Chapter 31)? Was it fitting or ironic that someone as straight-laced and traditional as Calvin Coolidge should preside over an age of jazz, gangsterism, and Hollywood?

10. Why did American intervention in Latin America in the 1920s run contrary to the general turn toward isolationism and indifference to the outside world?

CHAPTER 33

The Great Depression and the New Deal, 1933–1939

PART I: REVIEWING THE CHAPTER

A. Checklist of Learning Objectives

After mastering this chapter, you should be able to:

1. Describe the rise of Franklin Roosevelt to the presidency in 1932 and the important role that Eleanor Roosevelt played in the Roosevelt administration.

2. Describe each of the early New Deal three R goals—relief, recovery, and reform—and indicate what major efforts were made to achieve each goal.

3. Describe the New Deal's effect on labor and labor organizations.

4. Discuss the early New Deal's efforts to organize business and agriculture in the NRA and the AAA, and indicate what directions Roosevelt took after those two agencies were declared unconstitutional.

5. Explain why Roosevelt became so frustrated with the conservative Supreme Court, and how his Court-packing plan backfired and weakened the political momentum of the New Deal.

6. Explain how Roosevelt mobilized a New Deal political coalition that included the South, Catholics, Jews, African Americans, and women.

7. Describe and analyze the arguments presented by both critics and defenders of the New Deal.

B. Glossary

To build your social science vocabulary, familiarize yourself with the following terms.

1. **dispossessed** The economically deprived. ". . . she . . . emerged as a champion of the dispossessed. . . ."

2. **rubberstamp** To approve a plan or law quickly or routinely, without examination. ". . . it was ready to rubberstamp bills drafted by White House advisors. . . ."

3. **blank check** Referring to permission to use an unlimited amount of money or authority. ". . . Congress gave the president extraordinary blank-check powers. . . ."

4. **foreign exchange** The transfer of credits or accounts between the citizens or financial institutions of different nations. "The new law clothed the president with power to regulate banking transactions and foreign exchange. . . ."

5. **hoarding** Secretly storing up quantities of goods or money. "Roosevelt moved swiftly . . . to protect the melting gold reserve and to prevent panicky hoarding."

6. **boondoggling** Engaging in trivial or useless work; any enterprise characterized by such work. "Tens of thousands of jobless were employed at . . . make-work tasks, which were dubbed 'boondoggling.' "

7. **Fascist (Fascism)** A political system or philosophy that advocates a mass-based party dictatorship, extreme nationalism, racism, and the glorification of war. "Fear of Long's becoming a fascist dictator ended. . . ."

8. **parity** Equivalence in monetary value under different conditions; specifically, in the United States, the price for farm products that would give them the same purchasing power as in the period 1909–1914. ". . . this agency was to establish 'parity prices' for basic commodities."

9. **holding company** A company that controls the stocks and securities of another company. "New Dealers . . . directed their fire at public utility holding companies. . . ."

10. **collective bargaining** Bargaining between an employer and his or her organized work force over hours, wages, and other conditions of employment. "The NRA blue eagles, with their call for collective bargaining, had been a godsend. . . ."

11. **jurisdictional** Concerning the proper sphere in which authority may be exercised. ". . . bitter and annoying jurisdictional feuding involving strikes continued. . . ."

12. **checks and balances** In American politics, the interlocking system of divided and counter-weighted authority among the executive, legislative, and judicial branches of government. ". . . Roosevelt was savagely condemned for attempting to break down the delicate checks and balances. . . ."

13. **pinko** Disparaging term for someone who is not completely a "red," or Communist, but is alleged to be sympathetic to communism. "Critics deplored the employment of 'crackpot' college professors, leftist 'pinkos.'. . ."

14. **deficit spending** The spending of public funds beyond the amount of income. "Despite some $20 billion poured out in six years of deficit spending. . . ."

15. **left** (or **left-wing**) In politics, groups or parties that traditionally advocate progress, social change, greater economic and social equality, and the welfare of the common worker. (The **right** or **right-wing** is traditionally groups or parties that advocate adherence to tradition, established authorities, and an acceptance of some degree of economic and social hierarchy.) "He may even have headed off a more radical swing to the left. . . ."

PART II: CHECKING YOUR PROGRESS

A. True-False

Where the statement is true, circle **T**; where it is false, circle **F**.

1. T F Roosevelt's call for a New Deal in the 1932 campaign included attacks on the Hoover deficits and a promise to balance the federal budget.

2. T F Eleanor Roosevelt had little experience with social reform and women's concerns before her husband was elected president.

3. T F Congress rushed to pass many of the early New Deal programs that granted large emergency powers to the president.

4. T F In designing the New Deal, Roosevelt and his advisers avoided drawing on European models that might smack of socialism to Americans.

5.   T F   The Civilian Conservation Corps (CCC) and the Public Works Administration (PWA) were both designed to reform American business practices.

6.   T F   Two early New Deal programs, the National Recovery Administration (NRA) and the Agricultural Adjustment Administration (AAA), were both declared unconstitutional by the Supreme Court.

7.   T F   Even amidst the worst of the Great Depression, most Americans did not worry that the United States would follow Italy or Germany in giving a dictator power to solve the crisis.

8.   T F   The New Deal opened new opportunities for women through appointment to government offices and the new social sciences.

9.   T F   The Tennessee Valley Authority (TVA) was designed primarily to aid in conserving water and soil resources in eroded hill areas.

10. T F   The Committee for Industrial Organization (CIO) used sympathetic New Deal laws to unionize many unskilled workers previously ignored by the American Federation of Labor (AF of L).

11. T F   Roosevelt's political coalition rested heavily on lower-income groups, including African Americans, Jews, Catholics, and southerners.

12. T F   After Roosevelt's Court-packing plan failed, the conservative Supreme Court continued to strike down New Deal legislation just as it had before.

13. T F   The U.S. Social Security System created by the New Deal provided more comprehensive social welfare insurance than anything available in Europe at the time.

14. T F   The New Deal more than doubled the U.S. national debt through deficit spending.

15. T F   By 1939, the New Deal had largely solved the major depression problem of unemployment.

B. Multiple Choice

Select the best answer and circle the corresponding letter.

1.   Franklin Roosevelt's presidential campaign in 1932
   a.   called for large-scale federal spending to reduce unemployment and restore prosperity.
   b.   focused primarily on issues of international trade.
   c.   promised to aid the "forgotten man" by balancing the federal budget and ending deficits.
   d.   emphasized that there were no simple solutions to recovering from the Depression.
   e.   declared that curing the Depression would require the president to exercise unprecedented power over the economy.

2.   Even before FDR won the White House, Eleanor Roosevelt had become an influential figure in her own right by advocating the causes of
   a.   blacks and people with disabilities.
   b.   consumer protection and environmentalism.
   c.   farmers and ranchers.
   d.   immigrant ethnic groups and Roman Catholics.
   e.   women and the poorer classes.

3. The Roosevelt landslide of 1932 included the shift into the Democratic camp of traditionally Republican

    a.   New Englanders.
    b.   African Americans.
    c.   labor unions.
    d.   southerners.
    e.   Hispanics.

4. Roosevelt's first bold action during the Hundred Days was

    a.   taking the nation off the gold standard.
    b.   taking federal control of the railroads.
    c.   legalizing unions and strikes.
    d.   doubling relief for the unemployed.
    e.   closing all the banks and declaring a national bank holiday.

5. The primary purpose of the Civilian Conservation Corps (CCC) was to

    a.   restore unproductive farmland to productive use.
    b.   protect wildlife and the environment.
    c.   provide better-trained workers for industry.
    d.   provide jobs and experience for unemployed young people.
    e.   construct public buildings, shelters, and trails in the National Forests.

6. Strong political challenges to Roosevelt came from extremist critics like

    a.   Herbert Hoover and Al Smith.
    b.   Frances Perkins and Harry Hopkins.
    c.   Henry Ford and Mary McLeod Bethune.
    d.   John Steinbeck and John L. Lewis.
    e.   Father Charles Coughlin and Huey Long.

7. Roosevelt's National Recovery Administration (NRA) ended when

    a.   Dr. Francis Townsend attacked it as unfair to the elderly.
    b.   Congress refused to provide further funding for it.
    c.   it came to be considered too expensive for the results achieved.
    d.   the Supreme Court declared it unconstitutional.
    e.   it was caught engaging in wasteful and corrupt spending.

8. Roosevelt's Agricultural Adjustment Administration met especially sharp criticism because it

    a.   failed to raise farm prices.
    b.   actually contributed to soil erosion on the Great Plains.
    c.   raised prices by paying farmers to slaughter animals and not grow crops.
    d.   relied too much on private bank loans to aid farmers.
    e.   favored southern cotton and sugar growers at the expense of Midwestern grain farmers.

9. In addition to the natural forces of drought and wind, the Dust Bowl of the 1930s was also caused by

    a.   Roosevelt's AAA farm policies.
    b.   excessive use of dry farming and mechanization techniques on marginal land.
    c.   southwestern farmers' tendency to plant crops only every other year.
    d.   the drying up of underground aquifers used to irrigate the Great Plains.
    e.   the repeated failure of large-scale dam projects to bring water to the region.

10. The so-called Indian New Deal included an emphasis on
    a. local tribal self-government and recovery of Indian identity and culture.
    b. the distribution of tribal lands to individual Indian landowners.
    c. the migration of Indians from rural reservations to the cities.
    d. programs to encourage businesses like gambling casinos to locate on Indian lands.
    e. creating a common Indian identity beyond identifying with a particular tribe.

11. The daring New Deal program that attempted simultaneously to provide flood control, electric power, and economic development occurred in the valley of the
    a. Columbia River.
    b. Colorado River.
    c. Hudson River.
    d. Tennessee River.
    e. Missouri River.

12. The Social Security Act of 1935 provided for
    a. electricity and conservation for rural areas.
    b. pensions for the elderly, the blind, and unemployment insurance for workers.
    c. assistance for low-income public housing and social services.
    d. insurance for catastrophic medical expenses.
    e. social welfare protections for the poor whether they were able to work or not.

13. The new labor organization that flourished under Depression conditions with the New Deal's legal backing was the
    a. Knights of Labor.
    b. American Federation of Labor.
    c. National Labor Relations Board.
    d. Committee for Industrial Organization.
    e. United Mine Workers.

14. Among the key groups that made up the powerful Roosevelt coalition in the election of 1936 and for many decades afterward were
    a. African Americans, southerners, and Catholics.
    b. Republicans, New Englanders, and Old Immigrants.
    c. Midwesterners, small-town residents, and Presbyterians.
    d. businessmen, prohibitionists, and Coughlinites.
    e. westerners, farmers, and miners.

15. Roosevelt's attempt to pack the Supreme Court with his supporters proved extremely costly because
    a. the Court members he appointed still failed to support the New Deal.
    b. Congress began proceedings to impeach him.
    c. it revealed that he could not stand up to sharp political opposition.
    d. many of his New Deal supporters turned to back Huey Long.
    e. its failure took away much of the political momentum of the New Deal.

C. Identification

Supply the correct identification for each numbered description.

1. _____   Phrase used to describe all of Franklin Roosevelt's policies and programs to combat the Great Depression

2. _____   FDR's reform-minded intellectual advisers, who conceived much of the New Deal legislation

3. _____ Popular term for the special session of Congress in early 1933 that rapidly passed vast quantities of Roosevelt-initiated legislation and handed the president sweeping power

4. _____ The early New Deal agency that worked to solve the problems of unemployment and conservation by employing youth in reforestation and other beneficial tasks

5. _____ Large federal employment program, established in 1935 under Harry Hopkins, that provided jobs in areas from road building to art

6. _____ Widely displayed symbol of the National Recovery Administration (NRA), which attempted to reorganize and reform U.S. industry

7. _____ New Deal farm agency that attempted to raise prices by paying farmers to reduce their production of crops and animals

8. _____ The drought-stricken plains areas from which hundreds of thousands of Okies and Arkies were driven during the Great Depression

9. _____ New Deal agency that aroused strong conservative criticism by producing low-cost electrical power while providing full employment, soil conservation, and low cost housing to an entire region

10. _____ New Deal program that financed old-age pensions, unemployment insurance, and other forms of income assistance

11. _____ The new union group that organized large numbers of unskilled workers with the help of the Wagner Act and the National Labor Relations Board

12. _____ New Deal agency established to provide a public watchdog against deception and fraud in stock trading

13. _____ Organization of wealthy Republicans and conservative Democrats whose attacks on the New Deal caused Roosevelt to denounce them as economic royalists in the campaign of 1936

14. _____ Roosevelt's highly criticized scheme for gaining Supreme Court approval of New Deal legislation

15. _____ Economic theory of British economist who held that governments should run deliberate deficits to aid the economy in times of depression

D. Matching People, Places, and Events

Match the person, place, or event in the left column with the proper description in the right column by inserting the correct letter on the blank line.

1. ___ Franklin D. Roosevelt

2. ___ Eleanor Roosevelt

3. ___ Francis E. Townsend

4. ___ Harry Hopkins

5. ___ Father Coughlin

6. ___ Huey "Kingfish" Long

7. ___ George W. Norris

a. Republican who carried only two states in a futile campaign against "The Champ" in 1936

b. The "microphone messiah" of Michigan whose mass radio appeals turned anti–New Deal and anti-Semitic

c. Writer whose best-selling novel portrayed the suffering of dust bowl Okies in the Thirties

d. As Director of Minority Affairs for the National Youth Administration, the highest black official in the Roosevelt administration

8. ___ Harold Ickes

9. ___ John Steinbeck

10. ___ John L. Lewis

11. ___ Frances Perkins

12. ___ Alfred M. Landon

13. ___ Ruth Benedict

14. ___ John Maynard Keynes

15. ___ Mary McLeod Bethune

e. Presidential wife who became an effective lobbyist for the poor during the New Deal

f. Louisiana senator and popular mass agitator who promised to make "every man a king" at the expense of the wealthy

g. Former New York governor who roused the nation to action against the depression with his appeal to the "forgotten man"

h. Roosevelt's secretary of labor, America's first female cabinet member

i. Prominent 1930s social scientist who argued that each culture produced its own type of personality

j. Former New York social worker who became an influential FDR adviser and head of several New Deal agencies

k. Former bull moose progressive who spent billions of dollars on public building projects while carefully guarding against waste

l. Leader of senior citizen movement who called for the federal government to pay $200 a month to everyone over sixty

m. British economist whose theories helped justify New Deal deficit spending

n. Vigorously progressive senator from Nebraska whose passionate advocacy helped bring about the New Deal's Tennessee Valley Authority

o. Domineering boss of the mine workers' union who launched the CIO

E. Putting Things in Order

Put the following events in correct order by numbering them from 1 to 5.

1. _____ FDR devalues the dollar to about sixty cents in gold in an attempt to raise domestic prices.

2. _____ Congress passes numerous far-reaching laws under the pressure of a national crisis and strong presidential leadership.

3. _____ Republican attempts to attack the New Deal fall flat, and FDR wins reelection in a landslide.

4. _____ FDR's frustration at the conservative Supreme Court's overturning of New Deal legislation leads him to make a drastic proposal.

5. _____ Passage of new federal pro-labor legislation opens the way for a new union group and successful mass labor organizing.

F. Matching Cause and Effect

Match the historical cause in the left column with the proper effect in the right column by writing the correct letter on the blank line.

Cause

1. ____ The lame-duck period from November 1932 to March 1933

2. ____ Roosevelt's leadership during the Hundred Days

3. ____ The Civilian Conservation Corps, the Works Progress Administration, and the Civil Works Administration

4. ____ New Deal farm programs like the AAA

5. ____ The Tennessee Valley Authority

6. ____ The Wagner (National Labor Relations) Act

7. ____ FDR's political appeals to workers, African Americans, southerners, and "New Immigrants"

8. ____ The Supreme Court's conservative rulings against New Deal legislation

9. ____ Roosevelt's attempt to pack the Supreme Court

10. ____ The rapid cutback in federal pump-priming spending in 1937

Effect

a. Succeeded in raising farm prices but met strong opposition from many conservatives

b. Encouraged the CIO to organize large numbers of unskilled workers

c. May have pushed the Court toward more liberal rulings but badly hurt FDR politically

d. Caused a sharp Roosevelt Depression that brought unemployment back up to catastrophic levels

e. Caused a political paralysis that nearly halted the U.S. economy

f. Provided federal economic planning, conservation, cheap electricity, and jobs to a poverty-stricken region

g. Provided federal jobs for unemployed workers in conservation, construction, the arts, and other areas

h. Caused Roosevelt to propose a plan to pack the Supreme Court

i. Pushed a remarkable number of laws through Congress and restored the nation's confidence

j. Forged a powerful political coalition that made the Democrats the majority party

G. Developing Historical Skills

Reading Charts

Charts can classify complex information for ready reference. In this chapter, they are an effective way to present the many New Deal laws, agencies, and programs. The chart dealing with the Hundred Days is on p. 827, and that dealing with the later New Deal on p. 831.

Answer the following questions.

1. Which Hundred Days agency whose primary purpose was recovery also contributed to relief and reform?

2. List three Hundred Days actions that were aimed primarily at recovery.

3. List three later New Deal measures aimed primarily at reform.

4. Which later New Deal law aimed primarily at relief also contributed to recovery and reform?

5. Which was the last of the later New Deal laws aimed primarily at providing relief?

6. Compare the two charts. What can you conclude about the Hundred Days compared to the later New Deal, in relation to their relative emphasis on the three goals of relief, recovery, and reform? In which of the areas do you see the most continuity of purpose?

H. Map Mastery

Map Discrimination

Using the maps and charts in Chapter 34, answer the following questions.

1. *TVA Area*: In which four states was most of the Tennessee Valley Authority located?

2. *TVA Area*: How many major TVA dams were located in (a) Tennessee and (b) Alabama?

3. *Labor Union Membership in Selected Countries, 1913–2001*: Which two major industrialized nations had the lowest percentage of unionized workers before the onset of the Great Depression in 1930? Which two had the highest percentage of unionized workers?

4. *Labor Union Membership in Selected Countries, 1913–2001*: Which two nations had the lowest percentage of unionized workers in 1950, after the Great Depression and World War II. Which two nations had the highest percentage of such workers in 1950?

Map Challenge

Using *Labor Union Membership in Selected Countries, 1913–2001*: Write a brief essay comparing the growth of organized labor during the Depression and the following decade—1930–1950—with the growth of unionization in other industrialized nations. How has the percentage of unionized American workers altered in comparison to other nations since 1950? What might explain such differences?

PART III: APPLYING WHAT YOU HAVE LEARNED

1.   What qualities did FDR bring to the presidency, and how did he display them during the New Deal years? What particular role did Eleanor Roosevelt play in FDR's political success?

2.   How did the early New Deal legislation attempt to achieve the three goals of relief, recovery, and reform?

3.   Which of the New Deal's many programs to reform the economy and alleviate the depression was the most successful, and why? (You may identify and discuss more than one.) Which was least successful, and why?

4.   Were direct federal efforts to provide work for the unemployed—such as the Civilian Conservation Corps, the Works Progress Administration, and the Public Works Administration—justified either in terms of their immediate benefits to workers or as means of stimulating the economy. Why or why not?

5.   Why did the New Deal arouse such opposition from conservatives, including those on the Supreme Court?

6.   Discuss the political components of the Roosevelt coalition, formed in the 1930s. What did the New Deal offer to the diverse elements of this coalition?

7.   Was the New Deal essentially a conservative attempt to save American capitalism from collapse, a radical change in traditional American antigovernment beliefs, or a moderate liberal response to a unique crisis?

8.   How was the New Deal a culmination of the era of progressive reform, and how did it differ from the pre–World War I progressive era (see Chapters 28 and 29)?

9.   One of the strongest arguments that proponents of the New Deal make was that it saved Depression-plagued America from the radical right-wing or left-wing dictatorships that seized power in much of Europe. Was the United States ever in danger of turning to fascism or communism if there had been no New Deal or if Roosevelt and his policies had failed. In what ways did the demagogues of the 1930s, like Coughlin, Long, and Townsend, resemble European radical leaders, and in what ways were they different?

10.   Critics of the New Deal have often pointed out that it did not really solve the great Depression problem of unemployment; only World War II did that. Did the New Deal's other positive effects—such as in Social Security, labor rights, and regulation of the stock market—counter-balance its inability to overcome the central problem of unemployment?

CHAPTER 34

Franklin D. Roosevelt and the Shadow of War, 1933–1941

PART I: REVIEWING THE CHAPTER

A. Checklist of Learning Objectives

After mastering this chapter, you should be able to:

1. Describe Franklin Roosevelt's early isolationist policies, and explain their political and economic effects.

2. Explain how American isolationism dominated U.S. policy in the mid-1930s.

3. Explain how America gradually began to respond to the threat from totalitarian aggression, while still trying to stay neutral.

4. Describe Roosevelt's increasingly bold moves toward aiding Britain in the fight against Hitler and the sharp disagreements these efforts caused at home.

5. Indicate how the United States responded to Nazi anti-Semitism in the 1930s, and why it was slow to open its arms to refugees from Hitler's Germany.

6. Discuss the events and diplomatic issues in the growing Japanese-American confrontation that led up to Pearl Harbor.

B. Glossary

To build your social science vocabulary, familiarize yourself with the following terms.

1. **exchange rate** The monetary ratio according to which one currency is convertible into another, for instance, American dollars vis-à-vis German deutschmarks, which determines their value relative to one another. "Exchange-rate stabilization was essential to revival of world trade. . . ."

2. **militarist** Someone who glorifies military values or institutions and extends them into the political and social spheres. "Yet in Tokyo, Japanese militarists were calculating that they had little to fear. . . ."

3. **totalitarianism** A political system of absolute control, in which all social, moral, and religious values and institutions are put in direct service of the state. "Post-1918 chaos in Europe, followed by the Great Depression, fostered the ominous spread of totalitarianism."

4. **quarantine** In politics, isolating a nation by refusing to have economic or diplomatic dealings with it. ". . . they feared that a moral quarantine would lead to a shooting quarantine."

5. **division** The major unit of military organization, usually consisting of about 3,000 to 10,000 soldiers, into which most modern armies are organized. " . . . he sent his mechanized divisions crashing into Poland at dawn on September 1, 1939."

6. **unilateral** In politics, concerning a policy or action undertaken by only one nation. "This ancient dictum [was] hitherto unilateral. . . ."

7.   **multilateral** In international diplomacy, referring to a policy or action undertaken by more than one nation. "Now multilateral, [the Monroe Doctrine bludgeon] was to be wielded by twenty-one pairs of American hands. . . ."

8.   **steppes** The largely treeless great plains of southeastern Europe and western Asia. "The two fiends could now slit each other's throats on the icy steppes of Russia."

9.   **convoy (v.)** To escort militarily, for purposes of protection. The escorting ships or troops are called a **convoy (n.)**. "Roosevelt made the fateful decision to convoy in July 1941."

10. **warlord** An armed leader or ruler who maintains power by continually waging war, often against other similar rulers or local military leaders, without constitutional authority or legal legitimacy. ". . . Roosevelt had resolutely held off an embargo, lest he goad the Tokyo warlords. . . ."

11. *hara-kiri* Traditional Japanese ritual suicide. "Japan's *hara-kiri* gamble in Hawaii paid off only in the short run."

PART II: CHECKING YOUR PROGRESS

A. True-False

Where the statement is true, circle **T**; where it is false, circle **F**.

1.   T   F   Roosevelt's policy toward the 1933 London Economic Conference showed his concern for establishing a stable international economic order.

2.   T   F   Roosevelt adhered to his Good Neighbor principle of nonintervention in Latin America, even when Mexico seized American oil companies in 1938.

3.   T   F   American isolationism was caused partly by deep disillusionment with U.S. participation in World War I.

4.   T   F   The Neutrality Acts of the mid-1930s prevented Americans from lending money or selling weapons to warring nations and from sailing on belligerent ships.

5.   T   F   Despite the neutrality laws, the United States government provided assistance and sent unofficial military units to defend the democratic Spanish Loyalist government in its Civil War with rebel fascist General Francisco Franco.

6.   T   F   America's isolationist mood began to swing toward interventionism in response to Roosevelt's Quarantine speech and Japan's attack on the U.S. gunboat *Panay* in 1937.

7.   T   F   The United States attempted to dissuade the Western European democracies from pursuing their policy of appeasing Hitler's aggressive demands at the Munich Conference and after.

8.   T   F   The cash-and-carry Neutrality Act of 1939 allowed America to aid the Allies without making loans or transporting weapons on U.S. ships.

9.   T   F   The fall of France to Hitler in 1940 strengthened U.S. determination to stay neutral.

10. T   F   Isolationists argued that economic and military aid to Britain would inevitably lead to U.S. involvement in the European war.

11. T   F   Republican presidential nominee Wendell Willkie joined the isolationist attack on Roosevelt's pro-Britain policy in the 1940 campaign.

12. T   F   The 1941 Lend-Lease Act marked the effective abandonment of U.S. neutrality and the beginning of naval clashes with Germany.

13. T F   The Atlantic Charter was an agreement on future war aims signed by Great Britain, the United States, and the Soviet Union.

14. T F   U.S. warships were already being attacked and sunk in clashes with the German navy before Pearl Harbor.

15. T F   The focal point of conflict between the United States and Japan in the pre–Pearl Harbor negotiations was Japan's demand that the Philippines be freed from U.S. colonial rule.

B. Multiple Choice

Select the best answer and circle the corresponding letter.

1. Roosevelt torpedoed the international London Economic Conference of 1933 because he
    a. wanted to concentrate primarily on the recovery of the American domestic economy.
    b. saw the hand of Hitler and Mussolini behind the conference's proposals.
    c. was firmly committed to the gold standard.
    d. wanted economic cooperation only between the United States and Britain, not the rest of Europe.
    e. resented the role of European bankers in bringing on the Great Depression and feared their return to influence.

2. Seeking to withdraw from overseas commitments and colonial expense, the United States, in 1934, promised future independence to
    a. Puerto Rico.
    b. the Virgin Islands.
    c. American Samoa.
    d. Cuba.
    e. the Philippines.

3. Roosevelt's Good Neighbor policy toward Latin America included
    a. a substantial program of American economic aid for Latin American countries.
    b. a renunciation of American intervention in Mexico or elsewhere in the region.
    c. an American military presence to block growing German influence in Argentina and Brazil.
    d. an American pledge to transfer the Panama Canal to Panama by the year 2000.
    e. opening American markets to Latin exports of cotton, coffee, and rubber.

4. The immediate response of most Americans to the rise of the fascist dictators Mussolini and Hitler was
    a. a call for a new military alliance to contain aggression.
    b. a focus on political cooperation with Britain and the Soviet Union.
    c. support for the Spanish government against fascist rebels.
    d. a deeper commitment to remain isolated from European problems.
    e. a willingness to aid Italian and German refugees from the totalitarian regimes.

5. The Neutrality Acts of 1935, 1936, and 1937 essentially required that
    a. United States remain neutral in any war between Britain and Germany.
    b. no Americans sail on belligerent ships, sell munitions, or make loans to nations at war.
    c. no belligerent power could conduct propaganda campaigns, sell goods, or make loans within the United States.
    d. the United States as a neutral power intervene to end the wars in China and Ethiopia and the Spanish Civil War.
    e. German Americans, Italian Americans, and Japanese Americans all had to declare their loyalty to the United States and not send aid or give support to the aggressors.

6. The effect of the strict American arms embargo during the civil war between the Loyalist Spanish government and Franco's fascist rebels was to

    a. encourage a negotiated political settlement between the warring parties.
    b. strengthen the Spanish government's ability to resist Franco.
    c. push Britain and the Soviet Union to intervene in the Spanish Civil War.
    d. cripple the democratic Loyalist government while the Italians and Germans armed Franco.
    e. encourage American arms merchants to sell their heaviest weapons to the Soviet Union.

7. The policy of appeasing the Fascist dictators reached its low point in 1938, when Britain and France sold out Czechoslovakia to Hitler in the conference at

    a. Geneva.
    b. Versailles.
    c. Munich.
    d. Prague.
    e. Paris.

8. The cash-and-carry Neutrality Act of 1939 was cleverly designed to

    a. guarantee that American policy would not benefit either side in World War II.
    b. enable American merchants to provide loans and ships to the Allies without violating neutrality laws.
    c. prepare America for involvement in the war.
    d. aid Britain and France by letting them buy supplies and munitions in the United States without involving American loans or ships.
    e. permit American banks to loan cash to Britain and France but not provide credit.

9. The destroyers-for-bases deal of 1940 provided that

    a. the United States would give Britain fifty American destroyers in exchange for eight British bases in North America.
    b. the United States would give Britain new bases in North America in exchange for fifty British destroyers.
    c. if America entered the war, it would receive eight bases in Britain in exchange for American destroyers.
    d. the British would transfer captured French destroyers to the United States in exchange for the use of American bases in East Asia.
    e. American destroyers would have complete access to eight British naval bases around the world.

10. The twin events that precipitated a clear change in American foreign policy from neutrality to active, though nonbelligerent, support of the Allied cause were the

    a. Munich Conference and the invasion of Poland.
    b. Nazis' *Kristallnacht* and Mussolini's backdoor invasion of France.
    c. fall of Poland and the invasion of Norway.
    d. invasion of the Soviet Union and the German submarine attacks on American shipping.
    e. fall of France and the Battle of Britain.

11. In the campaign of 1940, the Republican nominee Willkie essentially agreed with Roosevelt on the issue of

    a. the New Deal.
    b. the third term.
    c. Roosevelt's use of power in office.
    d. foreign policy.
    e. upholding the Neutrality Acts of 1935, 1936, and 1937.

12. The Lend-Lease Act clearly marked
    a. the end of isolationist opposition to Roosevelt's foreign policy.
    b. an end to the pretense of American neutrality between Britain and Germany.
    c. a secret Roosevelt plan to involve the United States in war with Japan.
    d. the beginning of opposition in Congress to Roosevelt's foreign policy.
    e. the American public's realization that a war with Germany was now inevitable.
13. The provisions of the Atlantic Charter, signed by Roosevelt and Churchill in 1941, included
    a. self-determination for oppressed peoples and a new international peacekeeping organization.
    b. a permanent alliance between Britain, the United States, and the Soviet Union.
    c. a pledge to rid the world of dictators and to establish democratic governments in Germany and Italy.
    d. an agreement to oppose Soviet communism, but only after Hitler was defeated.
    e. a joint commitment to end the British Empire and U.S. domination of Latin America through the Monroe Doctrine.
14. By the fall of 1940, over a year before Pearl Harbor, American warships were being regularly attacked by German destroyers near the coast of
    a. Spain.
    b. Ireland.
    c. the southeastern United States.
    d. Canada.
    e. Iceland.
15. The key issue that caused the negotiations between the United States and Japan to fail just before Pearl Harbor was
    a. the refusal of the Japanese to withdraw their navy from Hawaiian waters.
    b. America's insistence on its right to expand naval power in Asia.
    c. the Japanese refusal to withdraw from China.
    d. the Japanese refusal to guarantee the security of the Philippines.
    e. Japan's unwillingness to loosen its harsh rule in Korea.

C. Identification

Supply the correct identification for each numbered description.

1. _____ International economic conference on stabilizing currency that was sabotaged by FDR

2. _____ Nation to which the U.S. promised independence in the Tydings-McDuffie Act of 1934

3. _____ FDR's repudiation of Theodore Roosevelt's Corollary to the Monroe Doctrine, stating his intention to work cooperatively with Latin American nations

4. _____ A series of laws enacted by Congress in the mid-1930s that attempted to prevent any American involvement in future overseas wars

5. _____ Conflict between the rebel fascist forces of General Francisco Franco and the Loyalist government that severely tested U.S. neutrality legislation

6. _____ Roosevelt's 1937 speech that proposed strong U.S. measures against overseas aggressors

7. _____ European diplomatic conference in 1938, where Britain and France yielded to Hitler's demands for Czechoslovakia

8. _____   Term for the British-French policy of attempting to prevent war by granting German demands

9. _____   Leading U.S. group advocating American support for Britain in the fight against Hitler

10. _____   Leading isolationist group advocating that America focus on continental defense and non-involvement with the European war

11. _____   Controversial 1941 law that made America the arsenal of democracy by providing supposedly temporary military material assistance to Britain

12. _____   A devastating night of Nazi attacks on Jewish businesses and synagogues that signaled a deepening of anti-Semitism and caused revulsion in the United States

13. _____   U.S.–British agreement of August 1941 to promote democracy and establish a new international organization for peace

14. _____   U.S. destroyer sunk by German submarines off the coast of Iceland in October 1941, with the loss of over a hundred men

15. _____   Major American Pacific naval base devastated in a surprise attack in December 1941

D. Matching People, Places, and Events

Match the person, place, or event in the left column with the proper description in the right column by inserting the correct letter on the blank line.

1. ____ Cordell Hull

2. ____ Adolf Hitler

3. ____ Benito Mussolini

4. ____ Gerald Nye

5. ____ Francisco Franco

6. ____ Abraham Lincoln brigade

7. ____ Czechoslovakia

8. ____ Poland

9. ____ France

10. ____ Charles A. Lindbergh

11. ____ Wendell Willkie

12. ____ Winston Churchill

13. ____ Joseph Stalin

14. ____ Iceland

15. ____ Hawaii

a. Courageous prime minister who led Britain's lonely resistance to Hitler

b. Leader of the America First organization and chief spokesman for U.S. isolationism

c. Young American volunteers who went to fight for Loyalist Spain against Franco's Spanish fascist rebels.

d. Dynamic dark horse Republican presidential nominee who attacked FDR only on domestic policy

e. Fanatical fascist leader of Germany whose aggressions forced the United States to abandon its neutrality

f. Instigator of 1934 Senate hearings that castigated World War I munitions manufacturers as "merchants of death"

g. Nation whose sudden fall to Hitler in 1940 pushed the United States closer to direct aid to Britain

h. Site of a naval base where Japan launched a devastating surprise attack on the United States

i.   North Atlantic nation near whose
      waters U.S. destroyers came under
      Nazi submarine attack

j.   Small East European democracy
      betrayed into Hitler's hands at Munich

k.   The lesser partner of the Rome-Berlin
      Axis who invaded Ethiopia and joined
      the war against France and Britain

l.   FDR's secretary of state, who
      promoted reciprocal trade agreements,
      especially with Latin America

m.   Russian dictator who first helped Hitler
      destroy Poland before becoming a
      victim of Nazi aggression in 1941

n.   East European nation whose September
      1939 invasion by Hitler set off World
      War II in Europe

o.   Fascist rebel against the Spanish
      Loyalist government

E. Putting Things in Order

Put the following events in correct order by numbering them from 1 to 5.

1. _____   FDR puts domestic recovery ahead of international economics, torpedoing a
                   major monetary conference.

2. _____   Western democracies try to appease Hitler by sacrificing Czechoslovakia, but
                   his appetite for conquest remains undiminished.

3. _____   Already engaged against Hitler in the Atlantic, the United States is plunged
                   into World War II by a surprise attack in the Pacific.

4. _____   The fall of France pushes FDR into providing increasingly open aid to Britain.

5. _____   Japan invades China and attacks an American vessel, but the United States
                   sticks to its neutrality principles.

F. Matching Cause and Effect

Match the historical cause in the left column with the proper effect in the right column by writing the
correct letter on the blank line.

Cause	Effect
1. ___ FDR's refusal to support international economic cooperation in the 1930s	a. prevented Roosevelt and the United States from admitting many Jewish refugees from Nazism into the United States
2. ___ Roosevelt's Good Neighbor policy	
3. ___ Bad memories of World War I and revelations about arms merchants	

4. ___ The U.S. Neutrality Acts of the 1930s

5. ___ Japanese aggression against China in 1937

6. ___ Hitler's invasion of Poland

7. ___ The fall of France in 1940

8. ___ Willkie's support for FDR's pro-British foreign policy

9. ___ The U.S. embargo on oil and other supplies to Japan

10. ___ Restrictive immigration laws and the hostility of the State Department and southern Democrats

b. Prompted FDR to make his Quarantine Speech, proposing strong action against aggressors

c. Brought new respect for the United States and for democracy in Latin America

d. Shocked the United States into enacting conscription and making the destroyers-for-bases deal

e. Forced Japan to either accept U.S. demands regarding China or go to war

f. Caused the United States to institute a cash-and-carry policy for providing aid to Britain

g. Deepened the worldwide depression and aided the rise of fascist dictators

h. Actually aided fascist dictators in carrying out their aggressions in Ethiopia, Spain, and China.

i. Promoted U.S. isolationism and the passage of several Neutrality Acts in the mid-1930s

j. Kept the 1940 presidential campaign from becoming a bitter national debate

G. Developing Historical Skills

Reading Text for Sequence and Context

In learning to read for and remember the historical sequence of events, it is often helpful to look for the context in which they occurred.

In the first list below are several major events discussed in the chapter. The second list contains the immediate contexts in which those events occurred. First, link the event to the appropriate context by putting a number from the bottom list to the right of the proper event. Then put the event-with-context in the proper sequence by writing numbers 1 to 7 in the spaces to the left.

Order	Event	Context
_____	Destroyer-for-bases deal	_____
_____	Atlantic Charter	_____
_____	Good Neighbor policy	_____
_____	U.S. Neutrality Acts of 1935–1936	_____
_____	Pearl Harbor	_____
_____	Lend-lease	_____
_____	Munich Conference	_____

Context

1.   Failure of U.S.–Japanese negotiations

2.   Decline of U.S. investment in Latin America

3.   Nye Hearings and Italy's invasion of Ethiopia

4.   Britain's near-defeat from German bombing

5.   The fall of France

6.   Hitler's threats to go to war

7.   Hitler's invasion of Russia

H. Map Mastery

Map Discrimination

Using the maps and charts in Chapter 34, answer the following questions.

1.   *Presidential Election of 1940*: In the 1940 election, how many electoral votes did Willkie win west of the Mississippi River?

2.   *Presidential Election of 1940*: How many electoral votes did Willkie win east of the Mississippi River?

3.   *Main Flow of Lend-Lease Aid*: Which continent received the most U.S. lend-lease aid?

4.   *Main Flow of Lend-Lease Aid*: Which nation received lend-lease aid by way of both the Atlantic and Pacific oceans?

PART III: APPLYING WHAT YOU HAVE LEARNED

1.   How and why did the United States attempt to isolate itself from foreign troubles in the early and mid-1930s?

2.   Discuss the effects of the U.S. neutrality laws of the 1930s on both American foreign policy and the international situation in Europe and East Asia.

3.   How did the fascist dictators' continually expanding aggression gradually erode the U.S. commitment to neutrality and isolationism?

4.   How did Roosevelt manage to move the United States toward providing effective aid to Britain while slowly undercutting isolationist opposition?

5.   Why was American so slow and reluctant to aid Jewish and other refugees from Nazi Germany? Would there have been effective ways to have helped European Jews before the onset of World War II?

6.   The Spanish Civil War is often called "the dress rehearsal for World War II." To what degree is this description accurate? Could the United States and the other democratic powers have successfully prevented the fall of democratic Spain to Franco? Or might it have drawn them even earlier into a Europe-wide war?

7.   Was American entry into World War II, with both Germany and Japan, inevitable? Is it possible the U.S. might have been able to fight either Germany or Japan, while avoiding armed conflict with the other?

8.   How did the process of American entry into World War II compare with the way the country got into World War I (see Chapter 30). How were the Neutrality Acts aimed at the conditions of 1914–1917, and why did they prove ineffective under the conditions of the 1930s?

9.   Argue for or against: America's foreign policy from 1933 to 1939 was fundamentally shaped by domestic issues and concerns, particularly the Great Depression.

10.   Isolationists and hostile critics in 1940–1941, and even after World War II, charged Franklin Roosevelt with deliberately and sometimes deceitfully manipulating events and public opinion so as to lead the United States into war. What factual basis, if any, is there for such a charge? Which of Roosevelt's words and actions tend to refute it?

CHAPTER 35

America in World War II, 1941–1945

PART I: REVIEWING THE CHAPTER

A. Checklist of Learning Objectives

After mastering this chapter, you should be able to:

1. Indicate how America reacted to Pearl Harbor and prepared to wage war against both Germany and Japan.

2. Describe the mobilization of the American economy for war and the mobilization of manpower and womanpower for both the military and wartime production.

3. Describe the war's effects on American society, including regional migration, race relations, and women's roles.

4. Explain the early Japanese successes in East Asia and the Pacific, and the American strategy for countering them.

5. Describe the early Allied invasion of North Africa and Italy, the strategic tensions with the Soviet Union over the Second Front, and the invasion of Normandy in 1944.

6. Discuss FDR's successful 1944 campaign against Thomas Dewey for a fourth term and his controversial choice of a new vice president.

7. Explain the final military efforts that brought Allied victory in Europe and Asia and the significance of the atomic bomb.

B. Glossary

To build your social science vocabulary, familiarize yourself with the following terms.

1. **concentration camp** A place of confinement for prisoners or others a government considers dangerous or undesirable. "The Washington top command . . . forcibly herded them together in concentration camps. . . ."

2. *bracero* A Mexican farm laborer temporarily brought into the United States. "The *bracero* program outlived the war by some twenty years. . . ."

3. **U-boat** A German submarine (from the German *Unterseeboot*). "Not until the spring of 1943 did the Allies . . . have the upper hand against the U-boat."

4. **depose(d); deposition** Forcibly remove from office or position. "Mussolini was deposed, and Italy surrendered unconditionally soon thereafter."

5. **beachhead** The first position on a beach secured by an invading force and used to land further troops and supplies. "The Allied beachhead, at first clung to with fingertips, was gradually enlarged, consolidated, and reinforced."

6. **underground** A secret or illegal movement organized in a country to resist or overthrow the government. "With the assistance of the French 'underground,' Paris was liberated. . . ."

7. **acclamation** A general and unanimous action of approval or nomination by a large public body, without a vote. "He was nominated at Chicago on the first ballot by acclamation."

8. **bastion** A fortified stronghold, often including earthworks or stoneworks, that guards against enemy attack. ". . . the 101st Airborne Division had stood firm at the vital bastion of Bastogne."

9. **genocide** The systematic extermination or killing of an entire people. "The Washington government had long been informed about Hitler's campaign of genocide against the Jews. . . ."

10. **bazooka** A metal-tubed weapon from which armor-piercing rockets are electronically fired. "The enemy was almost literally smothered by bayonets, bullets, bazookas, and bombs."

PART II: CHECKING YOUR PROGRESS

A. True-False

Where the statement is true, circle **T**; where it is false, circle **F**.

1. T F America's major strategic decision in World War II was to attack Japan first, while holding off Hitler's Germany until later.

2. T F A substantial minority of Americans, particularly those of German, Japanese, and Italian descent, opposed American entry into World War II.

3. T F Government-run rationing and wage-price controls contributed to America's ability to meet the economic challenges of the war.

4. T F New sources of labor such as women and Mexican *braceros* helped overcome the human-resources shortage during World War II.

5. T F World War II stimulated massive black migration to the North and West and encouraged black demands for greater equality.

6. T F A majority of women who worked in wartime factories stayed in the labor force after the war ended.

7. T F American citizens at home had to endure serious economic deprivations during World War II.

8. T F The Japanese navy established its domination of the Pacific sea-lanes in the 1942 battles of Coral Sea and Midway.

9. T F The American strategy in the Pacific was to encircle Japan by flank movements from Burma and Alaska.

10. T F While their Soviet ally was still reeling from Hitler's invasion in the first years of the war, Britain and the United States bore the heaviest burden of Allied ground fighting and casualties.

11. T F By pushing for complete conquest and total destruction of the German government, the Allied policy of unconditional surrender guaranteed that Germany's economy and society would have to be rebuilt from the ground up after the war.

12. T F At the Teheran Conference in 1943, Stalin, Churchill, and Roosevelt planned the D-Day invasion and developed the final strategy for winning the war.

13. T F Liberal Democrats rallied to dump Vice President Henry Wallace from FDR's ticket in 1944 and replace him with Senator Harry S Truman.

14. T   F   Franklin Roosevelt's death caused a period of hesitation in the Allied war effort and raised German hopes of a negotiated settlement of the war.

15. T   F   The United States modified its demand for unconditional surrender by allowing Japan to keep its emperor, Hirohito.

B. Multiple Choice

Select the best answer and circle the corresponding letter.

1. The fundamental American strategic decision of World War II was to

   a. attack Germany and Japan simultaneously with equal force.
   b. concentrate naval forces in the Pacific and ground forces in Europe.
   c. attack Germany first, while using just enough strength to hold off Japan.
   d. attack Germany and Japan from the back door routes of North Africa and China.
   e. secure control of North Africa, the Middle East, and India so Germany and Japan could not unite their forces.

2. The major exception to the relatively good American civil liberties record during World War II was the harsh treatment of

   a. American fascist groups.
   b. native Hawaiians.
   c. Mexican Americans.
   d. German Americans.
   e. Japanese Americans.

3. Wartime inflation and shortages of crucial goods were kept partly in check by

   a. government price controls and rationing.
   b. government takeover of critical factories and railroads.
   c. special bonuses to farmers and workers to increase production.
   d. importation of additional fuel and food from Latin America.
   e. decreasing the money supply and releasing federal emergency stockpiles to the public.

4. The Bracero Program, created by the federal government during World War II, was aimed to

   a. encourage Mexican American women to join the work force by providing government child care.
   b. enable Mexican immigrants to take over the homes and farms of interned Japanese Americans.
   c. relieve the agricultural labor shortage by bringing in temporary workers from Mexico.
   d. counteract the growing tension between Latinos and Anglos in California and the Southwest.
   e. draft Latinos and American Indians into the military.

5. Compared to British and Soviet women during and after World War II, American women

   a. were less likely to work for wages in the wartime economy.
   b. worked more often in heavy-industry war plants.
   c. were a higher percentage of the nation's armed forces.
   d. were more ready to put their children into federally run child care.
   e. more often stayed in paid employment following the war's end.

6. The Fair Employment Practices Commission was designed to

   a. prevent discrimination against blacks in wartime industries.
   b. guarantee all regions of the country an opportunity to compete for defense contracts.
   c. prevent discrimination in employment against women.
   d. guarantee that those who had been unemployed longest would be the first hired.
   e. guarantee the right of workers to organize and strike if necessary.

7. The wartime migration of rural southern African Americans to northern and western urban factories was dramatically accelerated after the war by the invention of

   a. the cotton gin.
   b. the gasoline-powered mechanical combine.
   c. synthetic fibers, such as nylon, that largely replaced cotton cloth.
   d. television.
   e. the mechanical cotton picker.

8. Besides African Americans, another traditionally rural group, which used service in the armed forces as a springboard to postwar urban life was

   a. Scandinavian Americans.
   b. New England farmers.
   c. Indians.
   d. Japanese Americans.
   e. Mexican migrant laborers.

9. The 1942 battles of Bataan and Corregidor in the Philippines marked the beginning of

   a. Japanese conquest of key Pacific islands.
   b. the American comeback from the terrible defeat at Pearl Harbor.
   c. air warfare conducted from the decks of aircraft carriers.
   d. brutal tropical warfare in which atrocities were committed on both sides.
   e. the rebellion of Filipinos and others against cruel Japanese rule.

10. The essential American strategy in the Pacific called for

    a. securing bases in China from which to bomb the Japanese home islands.
    b. carrying the war into Southeast Asia from Australia and New Guinea.
    c. advancing on as broad a front as possible all across the Pacific.
    d. island hopping by capturing only the most strategic Japanese bases and bypassing the rest.
    e. seizing rapid control of islands near Japan so that the Japanese home islands could be bombed.

11. The U.S.–British demand for unconditional surrender of Germany and Japan was

    a. a sign of the Western Allies' confidence in its ultimate victory.
    b. designed to weaken Japan's and Germany's will to resist.
    c. a sign of the Western Allies' eagerness to reassure the Soviets in the absence of a Second Front.
    d. developed in close cooperation with the Soviet Union.
    e. aimed at encouraging German and Japanese dissidents to overthrow their governments.

12. The American conquest of Guam and other islands in the Marianas in 1944 was especially important because it

    a. halted the Japanese advance in the Pacific.
    b. was the first time that the United States had reconquered its own territories from Japanese rule.
    c. paved the way for the American reconquest of the Philippines.
    d. indicated that the Japanese would surrender without an invasion of the home island.
    e. made possible round-the-clock bombing of Japan from land bases.

13. The most difficult and brutal European fighting for American forces through most of 1943 occurred in

    a. France.
    b. Italy.
    c. North Africa.
    d. Belgium.
    e. the Philippines.

14. Hitler's last-ditch effort to stop the British and American advance in the west occurred at the Battle of

    a. Normandy.
    b. Château-Thierry.
    c. Rome.
    d. the Bulge.
    e. El Alamein.

15. The second American atomic bomb was dropped on the Japanese city of

    a. Nagasaki.
    b. Hiroshima.
    c. Kyoto.
    d. Okinawa.
    e. Tokyo.

C. Identification

Supply the correct identification for each numbered description.

1. _____ A U.S. minority that was forced into concentration camps during World War II

2. _____ A federal agency that coordinated U.S. industry and successfully mobilized the economy to produce vast quantities of military supplies

3. _____ Women's units of the army and navy during World War II
   _____

4. _____ Government arrangement whereby substantial numbers of Mexican workers were temporarily brought into the United States to provide agricultural labor

5. _____ Symbolic personification of female laborers who took factory jobs in order to sustain U.S. production during World War II

6. _____ The federal agency established to guarantee opportunities for African American employment in World War II industries

7. _____ U.S.–owned Pacific archipelago seized by Japan in the early months of World War II

8. _____ Crucial naval battle of June 1942, in which U.S. Admiral Chester Nimitz blocked the Japanese attempt to conquer a strategic island near Hawaii

9. _____ Controversial U.S.–British demand on Germany and Japan that substituted for a second front

10. _____ Site of 1943 Roosevelt-Churchill conference in North Africa, at which the Big Two planned the invasion of Italy and further steps in the Pacific war

11. _____ Iranian capital where Roosevelt, Churchill, and Stalin met to plan D-Day in coordination with Russian strategy against Hitler in the East

12. _____ The beginning of the Allied invasion of France in June 1944

13. _____ The December 1944 German offensive that marked Hitler's last chance to stop the Allied advance

14. _____ The last two heavily defended Japanese islands conquered by the United States near the end of World War II in 1945
   _____

15. _____ The top-secret project to develop the atomic bomb

D. Matching People, Places, and Events

Match the person, place, or event in the left column with the proper description in the right column by inserting the correct letter on the blank line.

1. ____ Henry J. Kaiser

2. ____ John L. Lewis

3. ____ A. Philip Randolph

4. ____ Erwin Rommel

5. ____ Jiang Jieshi (Chiang Kai-shek)

6. ____ Douglas MacArthur

7. ____ Chester W. Nimitz

8. ____ Dwight D. Eisenhower

9. ____ Winston Churchill

10. ____ Joseph Stalin

11. ____ Thomas E. Dewey

12. ____ Henry A. Wallace

13. ____ Harry S Truman

14. ____ Albert Einstein

15. ____ Hirohito

a. Commander of the Allied military assault against Hitler in North Africa and France

b. Japanese emperor who was allowed to stay on his throne, despite unconditional surrender policy

c. FDR's liberal vice president during most of World War II, dumped from the ticket in 1944

d. The Allied leader who constantly pressured the United States and Britain to open a second front against Hitler

e. Top German general in North Africa whose advance was finally halted at El Alamein by British General Montgomery

f. Leading American industrialist and shipbuilder during World War II

g. Commander of the U.S. Army in the Pacific during World War II, who fulfilled his promise to return to the Philippines

h. Inconspicuous former senator from Missouri who was suddenly catapulted to national and world leadership on April 12, 1945

i. Tough head of the United Mine Workers, whose work stoppages precipitated antistrike laws

j. Commander of the U.S. naval forces in the Pacific and brilliant strategist of the island-hopping campaign

k. Allied leader who met with FDR to plan strategy at Casablanca and Teheran

l. German-born physicist who helped persuade Roosevelt to develop the atomic bomb

m. Republican presidential nominee in 1944 who failed in his effort to deny FDR a fourth term

n. Head of the Brotherhood of Sleeping Car Porters whose threatened march on Washington opened job opportunities for blacks during World War II

o. U.S. ally who resisted Japanese advances in China during World War II

E. Putting Things in Order

Put the following events in correct order by numbering them from 1 to 4.

1. _____ The United States and Britain invade Italy and topple Mussolini from power.

2. _____ Japan surrenders after two atomic bombs are dropped.

3. _____ The United States enters World War II and begins to "fight Hitler first."

4. _____ The United States stops the Japanese advance in the Pacific and attacks Germany in North Africa.

F. Matching Cause and Effect

Match the historical cause in the left column with the proper effect in the right column by writing the correct letter on the blank line.

Cause	**Effect**
1. ___ The surprise Japanese attack at Pearl Harbor	a. Kept the Western Allies from establishing a second front in France until June 1944
2. ___ Fear that Japanese Americans would aid Japan in invading the United States	b. Slowed the powerful Japanese advance in the Pacific in 1942
3. ___ Efficient organization by the War Production Board	c. Enabled the United States to furnish itself and its allies with abundant military supplies
4. ___ The mechanical cotton picker and wartime labor demand	d. Enabled the United States to set up key bomber bases while bypassing heavily fortified Japanese-held islands
5. ___ Women's role in wartime production	e. Drew millions of African Americans from the rural South to the urban North
6. ___ American resistance in the Philippines and the Battle of the Coral Sea	f. Resulted in Senator Harry S Truman's becoming FDR's fourth-term running mate in 1944
7. ___ The American strategy of leapfrogging toward Japan	g. Created a temporary, but not a permanent, transformation in gender roles for most women
8. ___ The British fear of sustaining heavy casualties in ground fighting	h. Caused innocent American citizens to be rounded up and put in concentration camps
9. ___ Conservative Democrats' hostility to liberal vice president Henry Wallace	
10. ___ Japan's refusal to surrender after the Potsdam Conference in July 1945	

       i.   Created a strong sense of American national unity during World War II

       j.   Led the United States to drop the atomic bomb on Hiroshima in August 1945

G. Developing Historical Skills

Reading Maps for Routes and Strategy

In order to understand the events and strategies of war, careful reading of military maps is essential. Attention to the routes and dates of the Allied armies, presented in the map of *World War II in Europe and North Africa, 1939–1945* on p. 893, will help you grasp the essentials of Allied strategy and the importance of the postponement of the second front in the west, as described in the text. Answer the following questions.

1.   Where were (a) the Russians and (b) the Western Allies Britain and America each fighting in January and February of 1943?

2.   Approximately where were the central Russian armies when the British and Americans invaded Sicily?

3.   Approximately where were the central Russian armies when the British and Americans invaded Normandy in June 1944?

4.   It took approximately ten months for the British and Americans to get from the Normandy beaches to the Elbe River in central Germany. How long did it take the Russians to get from Warsaw to Berlin?

5.   Besides north-central Germany, where else did the British, American, and Russian invasion routes converge? From what two countries were the British and Americans coming? From what country was the southern Russian army coming?

H. Map Mastery

Map Discrimination

Using the maps and charts in Chapter 35, answer the following questions.

1.   *Internal Migration in the United States During World War II*: During World War II, what was the approximate net migration of civilian population from the East to the West? (Net migration is the number of westward migrants minus the number of those who moved east.)

2.   *Internal Migration in the United States During World War II*: Of the nine fastest-growing cities during the 1940s, how many were located in the West and South? (Consider Washington, D.C., as a southern city.)

3.   *Internal Migration in the United States During World War II*: Which were the two fastest-growing cities in the North?

4.   *United States Thrusts in the Pacific, 1942–1945*: Which two of the following territories were not wholly or partially controlled by Japan at the height of Japanese conquest: India, the Philippines, Australia, Netherlands Indies, Thailand, and New Guinea?

5.   *World War II in Europe and North Africa, 1939–1945*: From which North African territory did the Allies launch their invasion of Italy?

6.   *World War II in Europe and North Africa, 1939–1945*: As the Russian armies crossed into Germany from the east, which three Axis-occupied East European countries did they move through?

7.   *World War II in Europe and North Africa, 1939–1945*: As the Western Allied armies crossed into Germany from the west, which three Axis-occupied West European countries did they liberate and move through? (Do not count Luxembourg.)

8. *World War II in Europe and North Africa, 1939–1945*: Along which river in Germany did the Western Allied armies meet the Russians?

Map Challenge

Using the maps of both the Pacific (p. 888) and European (p. 893) theaters in World War II, write an essay explaining the principal movements of Allied armies and navies in relation to the principal Allied strategies of the war determined in the ABC–1 agreement and the various wartime exchanges and meetings among American, British, and Soviet leaders.

PART III: APPLYING WHAT YOU HAVE LEARNED

1. What effects did World War II have on the American economy? What role did American industry and agriculture play in the war?

2. What role did American women play during World War II? Why did the war prove to be ultimately less of a turning point in the advancement of women's full equality than some expected or hoped?

3. Most Americans, and the United States government, now regard the internment of Japanese Americans during World War II as an injustice and unnecessary. Why was there so little opposition to it at the time?

4. Ever since World War II, historians and other scholars have commonly spoken of "postwar American society." How was American society different after the war from before? Were these changes all direct or indirect results of the war, or would many have occurred without it?

5. How did the United States and its allies develop and carry out their strategy for defeating Italy, Germany, and Japan?

6. The text says that the American and British demand for unconditional surrender was actually a sign of weakness. Why? What were the effects of this policy, both during and after the war? Would there have been any benefits to permitting the Germany government to survive in some form, without Hitler? Was the agreement to permit Hirohito to remain as emperor of Japan as wise decision?

7. What were the costs of World War II, and what were its effects on America's role in the world?

8. Compare America's role in World War I—domestically, militarily, and diplomatically—with its role in World War II (see Chapter 30). What accounts for the differences in America's participation in the two wars?

9. Examine the controversy over the atomic bomb in the context of the whole conduct of World War II on both sides. Is it correct to say that the bomb did not mark a change in the character of warfare against civilians, but only its scope? Despite the larger casualties in other bombings, why did the bombings of Hiroshima and Nagasaki stir a greater concern?

10. World War II has sometimes been called "the good war." Is this an accurate label? Why or why not?

CHAPTER 36

The Cold War Begins, 1945–1952

PART I: REVIEWING THE CHAPTER

A. Checklist of Learning Objectives

After mastering this chapter, you should be able to:

1. Explain the causes and consequences of the post–World War II economic boom.

2. Describe the large postwar migrations to the Sunbelt and the suburbs.

3. Explain changes in American society and culture brought about by the baby boom.

4. Explain the origin and causes of the emerging conflict between the United States and the Soviet Union after Germany's defeat and Truman's accession to the presidency.

5. Describe the early U.S.-Soviet Cold War conflicts over Germany and Eastern Europe, and explain why the United Nations proved largely ineffectual in addressing them.

6. Discuss the American theory and practice of containment, as reflected in the Truman Doctrine, the Marshall Plan, and NATO.

7. Describe the concern about Soviet spying and communist subversion within the United States and the increasing climate of fear it engendered.

8. Describe the expansion of the Cold War to East Asia, including the Chinese communist revolution and the Korean War.

B. Glossary

To build your social science vocabulary, familiarize yourself with the following terms.

1. **gross national product** The total value of a nation's annual output of goods and services. "Real gross national product (GNP) slumped sickeningly in 1946 and 1947. . . ."

2. **agribusiness** Farming and related activities considered as commercial enterprises, especially large corporate agricultural ventures. ". . . consolidation produced giant agribusinesses able to employ costly machinery."

3. **population curve** The varying size and age structure of a given nation or other group, measured over time. "This boom-or-bust cycle of births begot a bulging wave along the American population curve."

4. **precinct** The smallest subdivision of a city, as it is organized for purposes of police administration, politics, voting, and so on. "He then tried his hand at precinct-level Missouri politics. . . ."

5. **protégé** Someone under the patronage, protection, or tutelage of another person or group. "Though a protégé of a notorious political machine in Kansas City, he had managed to keep his own hands clean."

6. **superpower** One of the two overwhelmingly dominant international powers after World War II—the United States and the Soviet Union. "More specific understandings among the wartime allies—especially the two emerging superpowers—awaited the arrival of peace."

7. **exchange rates** The ratios at which the currencies of two or more countries are traded, which express their values relative to one another. ". . . the International Monetary Fund (IMF) [was established] to encourage world trade by regulating currency exchange rates."

8. **underdeveloped** Economically and industrially deficient. "They also founded the International Bank for Reconstruction and Development . . . to promote economic growth in war-ravaged and underdeveloped areas."

9. **military occupation** The holding and control of a territory and its citizenry by the conquering forces of another nation. ". . . Germany had been divided at war's end into four military occupation zones. . . ."

10. **containment** In international affairs, the blocking of another nation's expansion through the application of military and political pressure short of war. "Truman's piecemeal responses . . . took on intellectual coherence in 1947, with the formulation of the 'containment doctrine.' "

11. **communist-fronter** One who belongs to an ostensibly independent political, economic, or social organization that is secretly controlled by the Communist party. ". . . he was nominated . . . by . . . a bizarre collection of disgruntled former New Dealers . . . and communist-fronters."

12. **Politburo** The small ruling executive body that controlled the Central Committee of the Soviet Communist party, and hence dictated the political policies of the Soviet, Chinese, and other Communist parties (from "Political Bureau"). "This so-called Pied Piper of the Politburo took an apparently pro-Soviet line. . . ."

13. **perimeter** The outer boundary of a defined territory. ". . . Korea was outside the essential United States defense perimeter in the Pacific."

PART II: CHECKING YOUR PROGRESS

A. True-False

Where the statement is true, circle **T**; where it is false, circle **F**.

1. T F The American consumer economy began to grow dramatically as soon as World War II ended, during the years 1945 to 1950.

2. T F The postwar economic boom was especially fueled by military spending and cheap energy.

3. T F The enormous American population migrations of the immediate postwar era strengthened the traditional family and inter-generational forms of child-rearing.

4. T F The economic and population growth of the Sunbelt occurred because the South relied less than the North did on federal government spending for its economic well-being.

5. T F In the decades after World War II most big American cities became heavily populated by minorities, while the new suburbs were almost entirely white.

6. T F Government housing policies played a role in creating a high degree of residential segregation in the cities and new suburbs.

7. T F The inexperienced new president Harry S Truman relied heavily on his advisors and often dodged responsibility for difficult decisions.

8.   T   F   The new United Nations proved more effective than the old League of Nations because its effective power was concentrated in the Security Council, made up of the great powers.

9.   T   F   The Soviet Union wanted to build a strong, neutral German state after World War II, while the Western Allies feared a Nazi revival and sought a weak or divided Germany.

10.   T   F   The Truman Doctrine was initiated in response to threatened Soviet gains in Iran and Afghanistan.

11.   T   F   The Marshall Plan was developed primarily as a response to the possible Soviet military invasion of Western Europe.

12.   T   F   The fundamental purpose of NATO was to end the historical feuds among the European nations of Britain, France, Italy, and Germany.

13.   T   F   The postwar hunt for communist subversion was supposedly aimed at rooting out American communists from positions in government and teaching.

14.   T   F   Truman defeated Dewey in 1948 partly because of the deep splits within the Republican party that year.

15.   T   F   Truman fired General MacArthur because MacArthur wanted to expand the Korean War and publicly criticized the president for refusing to use nuclear weapons against China.

B. Multiple Choice

Select the best answer and circle the corresponding letter.

1. Besides giving educational benefits to returning veterans, the Servicemen's Readjustment Act of 1944 (the GI Bill of Rights) was partly intended to
   a. prevent returning soldiers from flooding the job market.
   b. provide American colleges with a new source of income.
   c. keep the GIs' military skills in high readiness for the Cold War.
   d. help to slow down the inflationary economy that developed at the end of World War II.
   e. make sure that veterans' benefits were spent on education rather than on scarce housing.

2. Perhaps the greatest beneficiaries of the post–World War II economic boom were
   a. the industrial inner cities.
   b. farm laborers.
   c. labor unions.
   d. women.
   e. Mexican Americans.

3. Among the primary causes of the long postwar economic expansion were
   a. foreign investment and international trade.
   b. military spending and cheap energy.
   c. labor's wage restraint and the growing number of small businesses.
   d. government economic planning and investment.
   e. low bank interest rates and foreign investment.

4.   The two regions that gained most in population and new industry in the postwar economic expansion were the

    a.   Pacific Northwest and New England.
    b.   Northeast and South.
    c.   Midwest and West.
    d.   Southeast and Appalachia.
    e. South and West.

5.   The federal government played a large role in the growth of the Sunbelt through

    a.   federal subsidies to southern and western agriculture.
    b.   its policies supporting civil rights and equal opportunity for minorities.
    c.   its lower-costs housing loans to veterans who would settle in that region.
    d.   its financial support of the aerospace and defense industries.
    e.   its promotion of high energy costs that drove people away from the cold-weather North.

6.   Among the federal policies that contributed to the huge postwar migration from the inner cities to the suburbs were

    a.   civil rights laws guaranteeing integrated housing in the suburbs.
    b.   public housing and Social Security.
    c.   military and public-works spending.
    d.   direct subsidies to homebuilders for planned suburban communities.
    e.   housing-mortgage tax deductions and federally built highways.

7.   The postwar baby-boom population expansion contributed to the

    a.   sharp rise in elementary school enrollments in the 1970s.
    b.   strains on the Social Security system in the 1950s.
    c.   popular youth culture of the 1960s.
    d.   expanding job opportunities of the 1980s.
    e.   more rapid growth of multi-unit rental housing compared with home ownership.

8.   Among President Harry Truman's most valuable qualities as a leader was his

    a.   considerable experience in international affairs.
    b.   personal courage, authenticity, and sense of responsibility for big decisions.
    c.   intolerance of pettiness or corruption among his subordinates.
    d.   patience and willingness to compromise with honest critics.
    e.   willingness to hand over responsibility for big decisions to his cabinet members.

9.   Which of the following was *not* among the causes of the Cold War between the United States and the Soviet Union?

    a.   The Americans and Soviets had both been relatively isolated from world affairs before World War II.
    b.   The U.S. call for an open world clashed with the Soviets' insistence on controlling a sphere of interest in Eastern Europe.
    c.   The Soviets supported an end to European colonialism in the Third World, while the Americans helped their Allies put down colonial rebellions.
    d.   The Americans and Soviets both had a missionary ideology that tried to spread their ideas to other nations.
    e.   The Soviets were resentful of America's slowness in opening a second front and abrupt cancellation of lend-lease.

10. Which of the following was *not* among the successful achievements of the new United Nations?

    a. Preserving peace in Iran, Kashmir, and other world places of crisis
    b. Guiding former European colonies to independence
    c. Creating the new Jewish state of Israel
    d. Controlling atomic energy and containing the spread of nuclear weapons
    e. Promoting international health, science, and education

11. A crucial early development of the Cold War occurred when

    a. Germany was divided into an East Germany under Soviet control and a pro-American West Germany.
    b. American and Soviet forces nearly engaged in armed clashes in Austria.
    c. the Soviets crushed anticommunist rebellions in Poland and Hungary.
    d. the pro-Soviet French and Italian Communist parties attempted revolutions against their own governments.
    e. the Soviet Union announced that it would seek to develop atomic bombs and nuclear missiles.

12. The NATO alliance represented an historic departure from traditional American foreign policy because it

    a. departed from the principles of the Monroe Doctrine.
    b. committed the United States to guaranteeing the permanent subordination of Germany.
    c. gave command of American soldiers to officers from other countries.
    d. meant establishing military bases outside the territory of the continental United States.
    e. committed the United States to a permanent military alliance with other nations.

13. The Truman Doctrine originally developed because of the dangerous communist threat to

    a. Turkey and Greece.
    b. France and West Germany.
    c. Iran and Afghanistan.
    d. Poland and Hungary.
    e. Korea and Japan.

14. Senator Joseph McCarthy's anticommunist crusade was first directed primarily against

    a. Soviet spies inside the United States.
    b. potential internal Communist party takeovers of France and Italy.
    c. the Chinese communists.
    d. the alleged employment of American communists by the United States government.
    e. local school boards that employed atheist and homosexual teachers.

15. President Harry Truman fired General Douglas MacArthur from his command of American forces in East Asia because

    a. MacArthur had bungled the invasion of Inchon.
    b. MacArthur refused to accept the idea of American forces being under United Nations control.
    c. MacArthur wanted to widen the Korean War by bombing Communist China and publicly criticized the president.
    d. MacArthur was effectively seizing power as the military dictator of South Korea.
    e. Truman learned that MacArthur was planning to run against him for the presidency in 1952.

C. Identification

Supply the correct identification for each numbered description.

1. _____   Popular name for the Servicemen's Readjustment Act that provided education and economic assistance to former soldiers

2. _____   Shorthand name for the southern and western regions of the United States that experienced the highest rates of growth after World War II

3. _____   New York suburb where postwar builders pioneered the techniques of mass home construction

4. _____   Term for the dramatic rise in U.S. births that began immediately after World War II

5. _____   Big Three wartime conference that later became the focus of charges that Roosevelt had sold out Eastern Europe to the Soviet communists

6. _____   The extended post–World War II confrontation between the United States and the Soviet Union that stopped just short of a shooting war

7. _____   Meeting of Western Allies during World War II that established the economic structures to promote recovery and enhance FDR's vision of an open world

8. _____   New international organization that experienced some early successes in diplomatic and cultural areas but failed in areas like atomic arms control

9. _____   Allied-organized judicial tribunal that convicted and executed top Nazi leaders for war crimes

10. _____   American-sponsored effort that provided substantial funds for the economic relief and recovery of Western Europe

11. _____   The new anti-Soviet organization of Western nations that ended the long-time American tradition of not joining permanent military alliances

12. _____   Jiang Jieshi's (Chiang Kai-shek's) pro-American forces, which lost the Chinese civil war to Mao Zedong's (Mao Tse-tung's) communists in 1949

13. _____   Key U.S. government memorandum that militarized American foreign policy and indicated national faith in the economy's capacity to sustain large military expenditures

14. _____   U.S. House of Representatives committee that took the lead in investigating alleged procommunist agents such as Alger Hiss

15. _____   The dividing line between North and South Korea, across which the fighting between communists and United Nations forces ebbed and flowed during the Korean War

D. Matching People, Places, and Events

Match the person, place, or event in the left column with the proper description in the right column by inserting the correct letter on the blank line.

1. ___   Benjamin Spock

2. ___   Hermann Goering

3. ___   Joseph Stalin

4. ___   Julius and Ethel Rosenberg

5. ___   Jiang Jieshi (Chiang Kai-shek)

6. ___   George F. Kennan

a.   Top Nazi official who committed suicide after being convicted in war-crimes trials

b.   Physician who provided advice on child rearing to baby-boomers' parents after World War II

c.   Young California congressman whose investigation of Alger Hiss spurred fears of communist influence in

7. ____ Mao Zedong (Mao Tse-tung)

8. ____ George C. Marshall

9. ____ J. Robert Oppenheimer

10. ____ Reinhold Niebuhr

11. ____ Richard Nixon

12. ____ Joseph McCarthy

13. ____ Henry A. Wallace

14. ____ Strom Thurmond

15. ____ Douglas MacArthur

America

d. Chinese Nationalist leader whose corrupt and ineffective government fell to communist rebels in 1949

e. Originator of a massive program for the economic relief and recovery of devastated Europe

f. American military commander in Korea fired by President Harry Truman

g. Former vice president of the United States whose 1948 campaign as a pro-Soviet liberal split the Democratic Party

h. Leading American theologian who advocated Christian realism and the use of force if necessary to maintain justice against Nazi or Stalinist evil

i. Wisconsin senator whose charges of communist infiltration of the U.S. government deepened the anti-red atmosphere of the early 1950s

j. Former scientific director of the Manhattan Project who joined Albert Einstein in opposing development of the hydrogen bomb

k. The tough leader whose violation of agreements in Eastern Europe and Germany helped launch the Cold War

l. Leader of the Chinese Communists whose revolutionary army seized power in China in 1949

m. Americans convicted and executed for spying and passing atomic secrets to the Soviet Union

n. Southern segregationist who led Dixiecrat presidential campaign against Truman in 1948

o. Brilliant U.S. specialist on the Soviet Union and originator of the theory that U.S. policy should be to contain the Soviet Union

E. Putting Things in Order

Put the following events in correct order by numbering them from 1 to 5.

1. _____ The threatened communist takeover of Greece prompts a presidential request for aid and a worldwide effort to stop communism.

2. _____ The collapse of Jiang Jieshi's (Chiang Kai-shek's) corrupt government means victory for Mao Zedong's (Mao Tse-tung's) communists and a setback for U.S. policy in Asia.

3. _____ A new president takes charge of American foreign policy amid growing tension between America and its ally, the Soviet Union.

4. _____ A "give-'em-hell" campaign by an underdog candidate overcomes a three-way split in his own party and defeats his overconfident opponent.

5. _____ Communists go on the offensive in a divided Asian nation, drawing the United States into a brutal and indecisive war.

F. Matching Cause and Effect

Match the historical cause in the left column with the proper effect in the right column by writing the correct letter on the blank line.

Cause	**Effect**
1. ___ Cheap energy, military spending, and rising productivity	a. Caused an era of unprecedented growth in American prosperity from 1950 to 1970
2. ___ The mechanization and consolidation of agriculture	b. Drew millions of white and black Americans to the Sunbelt after World War II
3. ___ Job opportunities, warm climates, and improved race relations	c. Led to the proclamation of the Truman Doctrine and hundreds of millions of dollars in aid for anticommunist governments
4. ___ White flight to the suburbs	
5. ___ The post–World War II baby boom	
6. ___ The American airlift to West Berlin	d. Led to the organization of the permanent NATO alliance
7. ___ The British withdrawal from communist-threatened Greece	e. Caused the rise of big commercial agribusiness and spelled the near-disappearance of the traditional family farm
8. ___ The threat of Soviet invasion or U.S. isolationist withdrawal from Europe	
9. ___ General MacArthur's reform-oriented rule of occupied Japan	f. Aroused Republican charges that Democrats Truman and Acheson had lost China
10. ___ Mao Zedong's (Mao Tse-tung's) defeat of Jiang Jieshi (Chiang Kai-shek)	g. Broke a Soviet ground blockade and established American determination to resist further Soviet advance

    h.   Left America's cities heavily populated by racial minorities

    i.   Led to the firm establishment of Japanese democracy and the beginnings of a great Japanese economic advance

    j.   Caused much school building in the 1950s, a youth culture in the 1960s, and a growing concern about aging in the 1980s

G. Developing Historical Skills

Reading a Bar Graph

Read the bar graph of *National Defense Budget* on p. 914 and answer the following questions.

1.   In what census year, after World War II, did the defense budget first decline as a percentage of the federal budget and a percentage of GNP?

2.   In what census year, after 1960, was the defense budget the same fraction of GNP as it was in 1950?

3.   Which decade, after World War II, saw the largest increase in actual dollar outlays for defense?

4.   By approximately what percentage of the federal budget did the defense budget increase from 1950 to 1960? By roughly what percentage did it decrease from 1970 to 1980? By what percentage did it increase from 1980 to 1990? By about what percentage did it decrease from 1990 to 1999?

H. Map Mastery

Map Discrimination

Using the maps and charts in Chapter 36, answer the following questions.

1.   *Postwar Partition of Germany*: Which of the Big Four had the smallest occupation zone in postwar Germany?

2. *Postwar Partition of Germany*: Which of the three Western occupation zones was closest to Berlin?

3. *Postwar Partition of Germany*: Which two other nations did the American occupation zone border on?

4. *The Shifting Front in Korea*: When General MacArthur attacked at Inchon, did he land above or below the thirty-eighth parallel?

5. *The Shifting Front in Korea*: Besides China, what other nation bordering North Korea presented a potential threat to American forces?

6. *The Shifting Front in Korea*: After the armistice—signed on July 27, 1953—which of the two Koreas had made very slight territorial gains in the Korean War?

Map Challenge

Using the map of *Distribution of Population Increase, 1950–2005* on p. 916, write an essay explaining the differences in the regional impact of post–World War II migration and population growth from 1950 to 2005. What states and regions exhibited exceptions to the general patterns of growth?

PART III: APPLYING WHAT YOU HAVE LEARNED

1. Why did the American economy soar from 1950 to 1970? How did this new, widely distributed affluence alter the American way of life?

2. Describe how the population movements from the Northeast to the Sunbelt, and from inner cities to the suburbs, altered major features of American society as well as its center of gravity. Which of these two migrations do you regard as the more significant, and why?

3. What were the immediate conflicts and deeper causes that led the United States and the Soviet Union to go from being allies to bitter Cold War rivals?

4. Explain the steps that led to the long-term involvement of the United States in major overseas military commitments and expenditures, including NATO and the Korean War. How did expanding military power and the Cold War affect American society and its ideas?

5. Discuss President Harry Truman's role as a leader in both international and domestic affairs from 1945 to 1952. Does Truman deserve to be considered a great president? Why or why not?

6. Why did World War II—unlike World War I—lead to a permanent end to American isolationism (see Chapter 30)?

7. Was the spread of nuclear weapons from the United States to the Soviet Union, and then to other nations, simply inevitable once the technology was known? How, if at all, could nuclear proliferation have been prevented?

8. Why did America's growing international struggle against the Soviet Union so quickly lead to a fear of communist subversion within the United States. Would it have been possible to have rationally tried to stop Soviet spying without creating an indiscriminate witch hunt? To what extent was the anticommunist crusade really concerned about American national security, and to what extent was it simply persecuting people perceived as different?

9. Compared to the total victory and unconditional surrender of World War II, the Korean War led to a frustrating stalemate and armed hostile peace. What made Korea a different sort of war? Why was MacArthur's claim that "there is no substitute for victory" problematic in the case of Korea?

10. Was the early Cold War primarily an ideological crusade of democracy against international communism and its totalitarian ideas, or was it essentially an American defense of its national security and economic interests against the direct threat of the Soviet Union? Support your answer by considering some of the key events of the early Cold War, including the Korean War.

CHAPTER 37

The Eisenhower Era, 1952–1960

PART I: REVIEWING THE CHAPTER

A. Checklist of Learning Objectives

After mastering this chapter, you should be able to:

1. Describe the changes in the American consumer economy in the 1950s and their relationship to the rise of popular mass culture.

2. Describe the Republicans' return to power under Eisenhower and the rise and decline of McCarthyism.

3. Trace the emergence of the civil rights movement in the 1950s and its initial impact on American race relations and the nation's image abroad.

4. Describe the practice of Eisenhower Republicanism in the 1950s, including domestic consequences of the Cold War.

5. Outline the Eisenhower-Dulles approach to the Cold War and the nuclear arms race with the Soviet Union.

6. Indicate how Eisenhower's foreign policy was implemented in Vietnam, the Middle East, and Cuba.

7. Describe the issues and outcome of the tight Kennedy-Nixon presidential campaign of 1960.

8. Summarize the major changes in American culture in the 1950s, including the rise of Jewish, southern, and African American writers and playwrights.

B. Glossary

To build your social science vocabulary, familiarize yourself with the following terms.

1. **Pentecostal** A family of Protestant Christian churches that emphasize a "second baptism" of the holy spirit, speaking in tongues, faith healing, and intense emotionalism in worship. "'Televangelists' like the Baptist Billy Graham, the Pentecostal Holiness preacher Oral Roberts."

2. **McCarthyism** The practice of making sweeping, unfounded charges against innocent people with consequent loss of reputation, job, and so on. "But 'McCarthyism' has passed into the English language as a label for the dangerous forces of unfairness. . . ."

3. **universalism** The belief in the fundamental moral and social unity of humankind, and its transcendence of particular national or local cultural differences " . . . published a bestseller in 1943, *One World*, which advocated a new postwar era of racially-blind universalism."

4. **taboo** A social prohibition or rule that results from strict tradition or convention. ". . . Warren shocked the president and other traditionalists with his active judicial intervention in previously taboo social issues."

5. **sheikdom** Small, traditional tribal territory ruled by a **sheik**, an hereditary Arab chieftain. "The poor, sandy sheikdoms increasingly resolved to reap for themselves the lion's share of the enormous oil wealth. . . ."

6. **jury tampering** The felony of bribing, threatening, or otherwise interfering with the autonomous deliberations and decisions of a jury. "Convicted of jury tampering, Hoffa served part of his sentence before disappearing without a trace. . . ."

7. **secondary boycott** A boycott of goods, aimed not at the employer or company directly involved in a dispute but at those who do business with that company. "The new law also prohibited 'secondary boycotts' and certain kinds of picketing."

8. **thermonuclear** Concerning the heat released in nuclear fission; specifically, the use of that heat in hydrogen bombs. "Thermonuclear suicide seemed nearer in July 1958. . . ."

9. **confiscation** The seizure of property by a public authority, often as a penalty. "Castro retaliated with further wholesale confiscations of Yankee property. . . ."

10. **iconoclastic** Literally, a breaking of sacred images; hence, by extension, any action that assaults ideas or principles held in reverence or high regard. "Gore Vidal penned . . . several impish and always iconoclastic works. . . ."

PART II: CHECKING YOUR PROGRESS

A. True-False

Where the statement is true, circle **T**; where it is false, circle **F**.

1. T F The growth of aerospace industries in the 1950s meant the continued expansion of blue collar jobs and a rise in union membership.

2. T F The rise of television and other forms of mass entertainment in the 1950s undermined the cultural influence of religion and religious leaders.

3. T F Senator Joseph McCarthy's great power and capacity to destroy careers finally collapsed when he attacked the U.S. Army.

4. T F The effective use of television by the Eisenhower-Nixon campaign in 1952 demonstrated the power of the new medium to bypass older political structures.

5. T F The Supreme Court ruled in *Brown* v. *Board of Education* that black schools had to receive additional funding in order to guarantee that racially separate education would be truly equal.

6. T F Martin Luther King, Jr., argued that the civil rights movement needed to cast aside the influence of the traditionally conservative African American churches.

7. T F President Eisenhower and Secretary of State John Foster Dulles's Cold War strategy was to expand conventional weapons and troop deployments in Western Europe in order to contain the Soviet Union.

8. T F In the Suez crisis of 1956, the United States backed the French and British invasion of Egypt in order to guarantee the flow of oil from the Middle East.

9. T F The Soviet launch of the Sputnik satellite in 1957 fueled criticism of the American educational system and led to federal funding for advancing the sciences and foreign languages.

10. T F The Paris summit conference of 1960 between President Eisenhower and Soviet premier Khrushchev signaled the first major thaw in the Cold War.

11. T F The strict American embargo on all trade with Cuba was precipitated by Castro's confiscation of American property for his land reform program.

12. T F Senator Kennedy was able to successfully neutralize the issue of his Roman Catholicism during the 1960 campaign.

13. T F In his foreign policies, Dwight Eisenhower attempted to avoid threats to peace without the extensive use of American military power.

14. T F World War II sparked a great literary outpouring of sober, realistic novels about the realities of warfare.

15. T F Post–World War II American literature was enriched by African American novelists like Ralph Ellison and Jewish novelists like Saul Bellow.

B. Multiple Choice

Select the best answer and circle the corresponding letter.

1. A key economic transformation of the 1950s was the
   a. displacement of large corporations by smaller entrepreneurial businesses.
   b. decline in the percentage of women in the paid labor force.
   c. turn from World War II military and defense industries to civilian production.
   d. replacement of mass consumer production by targeted marketing aimed at particular segments of the population.
   e. growth of white collar office jobs that increasingly replaced blue collar factory labor.

2. During the 1950s, a majority of American women were
   a. working in blue-collar factory or service jobs.
   b. married, raising children, and not employed outside the home.
   c. pursuing training and education to prepare them for the new high technology positions.
   d. agitating for federal child care and other assistance to enable them to assume a larger place in the work force.
   e. single, divorced, or widowed.

3. The primary force shaping the new consumerism and mass popular culture of the 1950s was
   a. the computer.
   b. erotic magazines like *Playboy*.
   c. television.
   d. evangelical Protestantism.
   e. sports.

4. In the 1952 Republican presidential campaign, the war hero Dwight Eisenhower stayed above the battle and left the task of attacking Democratic candidate Governor Adlai E. Stevenson as soft on Communism to
   a. Senator Joseph McCarthy.
   b. vice presidential candidate Senator Richard Nixon.
   c. General Douglas MacArthur.
   d. future Secretary of State John Foster Dulles.
   e. Governor Earl Warren of California.

5. As president, Eisenhower enjoyed great popularity by presenting a leadership style of

    a. reassurance, sincerity, and optimism.
    b. aggressiveness, boldness, and energy.
    c. political shrewdness, economic knowledge, and hands-on management.
    d. vision, imagination, and moral leadership.
    e. charisma, vigor, and charm.

6. The Korean War ended with

    a. an agreement to unify and neutralize Korea.
    b. a peace treaty that provided for withdrawal of American and Chinese forces from Korea.
    c. an American and South Korean military victory.
    d. a stalemated armistice and the continued hostile division of North and South Korea.
    e. the withdrawal of all American and Chinese troops from the Korean peninsula.

7. President Eisenhower's fundamental attitude and policy toward Senator Joseph McCarthy was

    a. to tolerate McCarthy's attacks on Democrats, but prevent him from having influence within the Eisenhower administration.
    b. public distance from McCarthyism, but private admiration for McCarthy himself.
    c. to attack McCarthy as a threat to civil liberties and American traditions of fairness.
    d. private loathing, but public unwillingness to challenge McCarthy's power.
    e. to develop a U.S. Army plan to destroy McCarthy's power through televised hearings.

8. The precipitating event that led to the rise of Dr. Martin Luther King, Jr. as the most prominent civil rights leader was the

    a. lynching of Emmett Till.
    b. Little Rock school crisis.
    c. Montgomery bus boycott.
    d. passage of the 1957 Civil Rights Act.
    e. lunch counter sit-in movement.

9. European criticism of widespread American racism and segregation was especially strengthened in the 1950s by

    a. black soldiers' attacks on the U.S. government when stationed in Europe.
    b. Soviet and American Communists' attacks on U.S. racial attitudes.
    c. the Supreme Court's decisions upholding segregated schools.
    d. U.S. government mistreatment of black artists like Paul Robeson and Josephine Baker.
    e. the prohibition on black participation in major league sports.

10. Martin Luther King, Jr.'s own civil rights organization, the SCLC, rested on the institutional foundation of

    a. black businesses.
    b. labor unions.
    c. black colleges.
    d. northern philanthropic foundations.
    e. black churches.

11. President Dwight Eisenhower's basic approach to domestic economic policy was to

    a. seek to overturn the Democratic New Deal.
    b. propose major new federal social programs.
    c. turn most New Deal programs over to the states.
    d. trim back some New Deal programs but keep most in place.
    e. make business and labor equal partners with government in maintaining a strong economy.

12. During the Suez crisis of 1956, President Eisenhower used America's great oil power to

    a. break the power of the new OPEC organization of petroleum-producing states.
    b. force the Arab nationalist Nasser to back down from his seizure of the Suez Canal.
    c. force Britain, France, and Israel to withdraw their troops from Egypt.
    d. guarantee that the United States would not become dependent on Middle Eastern oil.
    e. prop up pro-American Arab monarchies in Saudi Arabia and Iraq.

13. The United States first became involved in Vietnam by

    a. providing economic aid to the democratic Vietnamese government of Ngo Dinh Diem.
    b. providing economic aid to the French colonialists fighting Ho Chi Minh.
    c. providing aid to Ho Chi Minh in his fight against the French colonialists.
    d. sending American bombers to defend the French at Dien Bien Phu.
    e. supporting Chinese Nationalists in their attempt to regain power in China.

14. Senator John F. Kennedy's principal issue against Vice President Richard Nixon in the campaign of 1960 was that

    a. as a Catholic, he would better be able to deal with Catholic Latin America.
    b. the United States should seek a nuclear disarmament agreement with the Soviets.
    c. the United States had fallen behind the Soviet Union in prestige and power.
    d. the Eisenhower administration had failed to work hard enough for desegregation.
    e. Nixon was a cynical political opportunist who might abuse power if he became president.

15. One major breakthrough in American literature in the early post–World War II years was

    a. the realistic depiction of war and industrial poverty.
    b. angry social criticism of the American dream.
    c. satirical and comic novels by Jewish writers.
    d. an optimistic vision of nature and love in the work of American poets and playwrights.
    e. a literary renaissance among Latino writers and playwrights.

C. Identification

Supply the correct identification for each numbered description.

1. _____ Term for making ruthless and unfair charges against opponents, such as those leveled by a red-hunting Wisconsin senator in the 1950s

2. _____ Supreme Court ruling that overturned the old *Plessy* v. *Ferguson* principle that black public facilities could be "separate but equal"

3. _____ The doctrine upon which Eisenhower and Dulles based American nuclear policy in the 1950s

4. _____ Nonviolent direct action, led by Martin Luther King, Jr., that launched the civil rights movement into major prominence

5. _____ The British-and-French-owned waterway whose nationalization by Egyptian President Nasser triggered a major Middle East crisis

6. _____ A soviet scientific achievement that set off a wave of American concern about Soviet superiority in science and education

7. _____ Swedish scholar Gunnar Myrdal's powerful book highlighting the conflict between America's high democratic ideals and its treatment of its black citizens

8. _____ High-flying American spy plane, whose downing in 1960 destroyed a summit and heightened Cold War tensions

9. _____ The Eisenhower administration's massive roundup and deportation of nearly a million illegal Mexican immigrants in 1954

10. _____ Betty Friedan's 1963 book that launched a revolution against the suburban cult of domesticity that reigned in the 1950s

D. Matching People, Places, and Events

Match the person, place, or event in the left column with the proper description in the right column by inserting the correct letter on the blank line.

1. ___ Dwight D. Eisenhower

2. ___ Joseph R. McCarthy

3. ___ Earl Warren

4. ___ Martin Luther King, Jr.

5. ___ Ho Chi Minh

6. ___ Ngo Dinh Diem

7. ___ Betty Friedan

8. ___ Adlai E. Stevenson

9. ___ Billy Graham

10. ___ James R. Hoffa

11. ___ John Foster Dulles

12. ___ Nikita Khrushchev

13. ___ Fidel Castro

14. ___ Richard Nixon

15. ___ John F. Kennedy

a. Eloquent Democratic presidential candidate who was twice swamped by a popular Republican war hero

b. Anticommunist leader who set up a pro-American government to block Ho Chi Minh's expected takeover of all Vietnam

c. Latin American revolutionary who became economically and militarily dependent on the Soviet Union

d. Eisenhower's tough-talking secretary of state who wanted to roll back communism

e. Red-hunter turned world-traveling diplomat who narrowly missed becoming president in 1960

f. Black minister whose 1955 Montgomery bus boycott made him the leader of the civil rights movement

g. The soldier who kept the nation at peace for most of his two terms and ended up warning America about the military-industrial complex

h. Popular religious evangelical who effectively used the new medium of television

i. Youthful politician who combined television appeal with traditional big-city Democratic politics to squeak out a victory in 1960

j. Blustery Soviet leader who frequently challenged Eisenhower with both threats and diplomacy

k. Reckless and power-hungry demagogue who intimidated even President Eisenhower before his bubble burst

l.   A Vietnamese nationalist and communist whose defeat of the French led to calls for American military intervention in Vietnam

m.   Writer whose 1963 book signaled the beginnings of more extensive feminist protest

n.   Tough Teamster-union boss whose corrupt actions helped lead to passage of the Landrum-Griffin Act

o.   Controversial jurist who led the Supreme Court into previously off-limits social and racial issues

E. Putting Things in Order

Put the following events in correct order by numbering them from 1 to 5.

1. _____   Major crises in Eastern Europe and the Middle East create severe challenges or Eisenhower's foreign policy.

2. _____   An American plane is downed over the Soviet Union, disrupting a summit and rechilling the Cold War.

3. _____   Eisenhower refuses to use American troops to prevent a communist victory over a colonial power in Asia.

4. _____   Eisenhower orders federal troops to enforce a Supreme Court ruling over strong resistance from state officials.

5. _____   Eisenhower's meeting with Soviet leader Khrushchev marks the first real sign of a thaw in the Cold War.

F. Matching Cause and Effect

Match the historical cause in the left column with the proper effect in the right column by writing the correct letter on the blank line.

Cause	**Effect**
1. ___ Joseph McCarthy's attacks on the U.S. Army	a. Set off massive resistance to integration in most parts of the Deep South
2. ___ *Brown* v. *Board of Education*	
3. ___ Governor Orval Faubus's use of the National Guard to prevent integration	b. Led to continuing nuclear tests and the extension of the arms race
4. ___ The 1956 Hungarian revolt	c. Caused the United States to begin backing an anticommunist regime in South Vietnam
5. ___ The Communist Vietnamese victory over the French in 1954	
6. ___ Nasser's nationalization of the Suez Canal	d. Created widespread resentment of the United States in parts of the Western Hemisphere

7. ___ The fears of both the United States and the Soviet Union that the other nation was gaining a lead in rocketry and weapons

8. ___ The mistreatment of American black artists like Paul Robeson and Josephine Baker and their own protests

9. ___ American intervention in Latin America and support for anti-communist dictators in that region

10. ___ Kennedy's television glamour and traditional political skills

e. Forced Secretary of State Dulles to abandon his plans to roll back communism

f. Exposed the senator's irresponsibility and brought about his downfall

g. Forced President Eisenhower to send federal troops to Little Rock

h. Led to increasingly harsh international criticism of America's racial policies.

i. Enabled the Democrats to win a narrow electoral victory in 1960

j. Led to the 1956 British-French-Israeli invasion of Egypt

G. Developing Historical Skills

Comparing and Interpreting Election Maps

Carefully read and compare the maps for the elections of 1952 (p. 949) and 1960 (p. 965). Answer the following questions.

1. Which was the only non-southern (border) state to vote for both the Democrats Stevenson in 1952 and Kennedy in 1960?

2. Which three southern states (states of the old Confederacy) voted for Republicans, Eisenhower in 1952 and Nixon in 1960?

3. Which was the only southern (former Confederate) state to switch from Republican (Eisenhower) in 1952 to Democratic (Kennedy) in 1960? Which was the only border state to switch from Republican in 1952 to Democratic in 1956?

4. How many more electoral votes did Kennedy get in the West (counting Hawaii, but not counting Texas) in 1960 than Stevenson got in the same region in 1952?

5. How many electoral votes did Kennedy win in 1960 from southern states that Stevenson also carried in 1952? (Note the divided electoral vote in one state.)

PART III: APPLYING WHAT YOU HAVE LEARNED

1. In what ways was the Eisenhower era a time of caution and conservatism, and in what ways was it a time of dynamic economic, social, and cultural change?

2. American blacks had suffered and often protested segregation and discrimination since the end of Reconstruction, but without result. Why did the civil rights movement finally began to gain public attention and influence in the 1950s?

3. Besides *Brown* v. *Board of Education* and the Montgomery bus boycott, which were the most important breakthroughs in civil rights and race relations of the late 1940s and 1950s?

4. How did Eisenhower balance assertiveness and restraint in his foreign policies in Vietnam, Europe, and the Middle East?

5. How did such an irresponsible figure as Senator Joseph McCarthy gain enormous power for a brief period of time in the early 1950s, and then rapidly fall into powerlessness and disgrace? Was McCarthy a unique phenomenon of that time playing on Americans' Cold Wars fears, or could such a witch-hunting atmosphere return with another such leader?

6. What were the dynamics of the Cold War with the Soviet Union in the 1950s, and how did Eisenhower and Khrushchev combine confrontation and conversation in their relationship?

7. How did America's far-flung international responsibilities shape the U.S. economy and society in the Eisenhower era? Was the American way of life fundamentally altered by the nation's new superpower status, or did it remain largely sheltered from world affairs?

8. How did television and other innovations of the consumer age affect American politics, society, and culture in the 1950s?

9. Despite widespread power and affluence, the 1950s were often described as an "age of anxiety." What were the major sources of anxiety and conflict that stirred beneath the surface of the time? Could they have been addressed more effectively by Eisenhower and other national leaders? Why or why not?

10. Argue for or against: American politics, society, and culture in the 1950s were all stagnant and narrow, and did not address the real social problems facing the country.

CHAPTER 38

The Stormy Sixties, 1960–1968

PART I: REVIEWING THE CHAPTER

A. Checklist of Learning Objectives

After mastering this chapter, you should be able to:

1. Describe the high expectations stirred by Kennedy's New Frontier and his limited success in achieving his domestic objectives.

2. Analyze the theory of Kennedy's doctrine of flexible response to communist challenges around the world and its dangerous application in Vietnam.

3. Describe Johnson's succession to the presidency in 1963, his electoral landslide over Goldwater in 1964, and his Great Society successes of 1965.

4. Discuss the course of the black movement of the 1960s, from civil rights to Black Power.

5. Outline the steps by which Johnson led the United States deeper into the Vietnam quagmire.

6. Explain how the Vietnam War brought turmoil to American society and eventually drove Johnson and the divided Democrats from power in 1968.

7. Describe the youthful cultural rebellions of the 1960s in the United States and around the world, and indicate which of their features quickly faded and which endured.

B. Glossary

To build your social science vocabulary, familiarize yourself with the following terms.

1. **free world** During the Cold War, the noncommunist democracies of the Western world, as opposed to the communist states. "But to the free world the 'Wall of Shame' looked like a gigantic enclosure around a concentration camp."

2. **nuclear proliferation** The spreading of nuclear weapons to nations that have not previously had them. "Despite the perils of nuclear proliferation or Soviet domination, de Gaulle demanded an independent Europe. . . ."

3. **exile** A person who has been banished or driven from her or his country by the authorities. "He had inherited . . . a CIA-backed scheme to topple Fidel Castro from power by invading Cuba with anticommunist exiles."

4. **peaceful coexistence** The principle or policy that communists and noncommunists—specifically, the United States and the Soviet Union—ought to live together without trying to dominate or destroy each other. "Kennedy thus tried to lay the foundations for a realistic policy of peaceful coexistence with the Soviet Union."

5. **détente** In international affairs, a period of relaxed agreement in areas of mutual interest. "Here were the modest origins of the policy that later came to be known as 'détente.' "

6. **sit-in** A demonstration in which people occupy a facility for a sustained period to achieve political or economic goals. "Following the wave of sit-ins that surged across the South. . . ."

7. **establishment** The ruling inner circle of a nation and its principal institutions. "Goldwater's forces had . . . rid[den] roughshod over the moderate Republican 'eastern establishment.'"

8. **literacy test** A literacy examination that a person must pass before being allowed to vote. "Ballot-denying devices like the poll tax, literacy tests, and barefaced discrimination still barred black people from the political process."

9. **ghetto** The district of a city where members of a religious or racial minority are forced to live, either by legal restriction or by informal social pressure. (Originally, ghettoes were enclosed Jewish districts in Europe.) ". . . a bloody riot exploded in Watts, a black ghetto in Los Angeles."

10. **black separatism** The doctrine that blacks in the United States ought to separate themselves from whites, either in separate institutions or in a separate political territory. ". . . Malcolm X trumpeted black separatism. . . ."

11. **hawk** During the Vietnam War, someone who favored vigorous prosecution or escalation of the conflict. "If the United States were to cut and run from Vietnam, claimed prowar 'hawks,' other nations would doubt America's word. . . ."

12. **dove** During the Vietnam War, someone who opposed the war and favored de-escalation or withdrawal by the United States. "New flocks of antiwar 'doves' were hatching daily."

13. **militant** In politics, someone who pursues political goals in a belligerent way, often using paramilitary means. "Other militants . . . shouted obscenities. . . ."

14. **dissident** Someone who dissents, especially from an established or normative institution or position. ". . . Spiro T. Agnew [was] noted for his tough stands against dissidents and black militants."

15. **coattails** In politics, the ability of a popular candidate at the top of a ticket to transfer some of his or her support to lesser candidates on the same ticket. "Nixon was . . . the first president-elect since 1848 not to bring in on his coattails at least one house of Congress. . . ."

PART II: CHECKING YOUR PROGRESS

A. True-False

Where the statement is true, circle **T**; where it is false, circle **F**.

1. T F Kennedy's pledge to land a man on the moon by the end of the 1960s was primarily an attempt to restore America's damaged prestige in the missile-and-space race with the Soviet Union.

2. T F The Kennedy doctrine of flexible response was applied primarily to the effort to contain potential Soviet expansion into central and western Europe.

3. T F The successful U.S.-supported coup against the corrupt Diem regime in South Vietnam enabled a more democratic South Vietnamese government to take a stronger role in defeating the Communist Viet Cong.

4. T F Kennedy financed and trained the Cuban rebels involved in the Bay of Pigs invasion, but refused to intervene directly with American troops or planes when their invasion failed.

5. T F   The Soviets' humiliation in the Cuban missile crisis resulted in Khrushchev's ouster and a new round of military competition between the United States and the Soviet Union.

6. T F   Even after Martin Luther King's civil rights demonstrators were viciously attacked in Birmingham in 1963, President Kennedy stayed aloof and urged restraint and caution by African American leaders.

7. T F   Johnson passed his major Great Society legislation like Medicare and Medicaid only by compromising with Republicans and conservative southern Democrats in Congress.

8. T F   The Gulf of Tonkin Resolution authorized the president to respond to naval attacks but kept the power to make war in Vietnam firmly in the hands of Congress.

9. T F   Johnson's Great Society immigration reforms ended the discriminatory quotes in place since the 1920s and opened America's doors to millions of immigrants from Asia and Latin America.

10. T F   The culmination of the nonviolent civil rights movement was the passage of the Civil Rights Act of 1964 and the Voting Rights Act of 1965.

11. T F   The urban riots of the late 1960s demonstrated that the South had vehemently resisted the civil rights movement's efforts to integrate southern schools and neighborhoods.

12. T F   The insurgent antiwar campaigns of Senators Eugene McCarthy and Robert Kennedy forced Johnson to withdraw as a presidential candidate and de-escalate the Vietnam War.

13. T F   The bitter Democratic divisions over Vietnam enabled Richard Nixon to win the presidency with a minority of popular votes and no clear policy mandate.

14. T F   The youth rebellion of the 1960s and the political crisis of 1968 were caused by the unique events and conditions in the United States at that time.

15. T F   One major American institution largely unaffected by the cultural upheaval of the 1960s was the conservative Roman Catholic Church.

B. Multiple Choice

Select the best answer and circle the corresponding letter.

1. President Kennedy's New Frontier proposals for increased federal educational aid and medical assistance to the elderly
    a. succeeded because of his skill in legislative bargaining.
    b. were traded away in exchange for passage of the bill establishing the Peace Corps.
    c. were stalled by strong opposition in Congress from Republicans and southern Democrats.
    d. were strongly opposed by business interests.
    e. were essentially abandoned because of Kennedy's concentration on foreign policy.
2. The industry that engaged in a bitter conflict with President Kennedy over price increases was the
    a. airline industry.
    b. health care industry.
    c. steel industry.
    d. oil industry.
    e. banking industry.

3. The fundamental strategic and military policy pursued by the Kennedy administration was to
   a. develop a flexible response to fighting brushfire wars in the Third World.
   b. threaten massive nuclear retaliation against any communist advances.
   c. build up heavy conventional armed forces in Western Europe against the threat of a Soviet invasion.
   d. provide military assistance to client states in the Third World so that they could fight proxy wars without the need of American forces.
   e. arm and train rebels to overthrow the Soviet puppet regimes in Eastern Europe.

4. The Kennedy administration suffered a major foreign policy disaster when
   a. Middle East governments sharply raised the price of imported oil.
   b. American-backed Cuban rebels were defeated by Castro's Cuban army at the Bay of Pigs.
   c. Khrushchev forced the United States to remove its missiles from Turkey during the Cuban missile crisis.
   d. American Green Beret guerrilla forces began suffering heavy casualties in the jungles of Vietnam.
   e. Britain and France both withdrew from NATO and developed their own nuclear forces.

5. The Cuban missile crisis ended when
   a. the American-backed Cuban invaders were defeated at the Bay of Pigs.
   b. the United States agreed to allow Soviet missiles in Cuba as long as they were not armed with nuclear weapons.
   c. Nikita Khrushchev was overthrown, and the new Soviet leader Brezhnev called for an end to the nuclear arms race.
   d. the United States and the Soviet Union agreed that Cuba should become neutral in the Cold War.
   e. the Soviets agreed to pull all missiles out of Cuba and the United States agreed not to invade Cuba.

6. The Kennedy administration was pushed into taking a stronger stand on civil rights by
   a. the civil rights movement, led by the Freedom Riders and Martin Luther King, Jr.
   b. realizing the political advantages of enabling blacks to vote.
   c. pressure from foreign governments and the United Nations.
   d. the threat of violent race riots in northern cities.
   e. civic and business leaders who saw racial conflict as disruptive to the economy.

7. One major reason why Lyndon Johnson won an overwhelming landslide victory in the 1964 election was that
   a. he repudiated many of the policies of the unpopular Kennedy administration.
   b. he promised to take a tough stand in opposing communist aggression in Vietnam.
   c. he successfully portrayed Republican candidate Senator Barry Goldwater as a trigger-happy extremist.
   d. Johnson had achieved considerable personal popularity with the electorate.
   e. his economic plans promised to deliver the nation from hard economic times.

8. President Johnson was more successful than President Kennedy in pushing economic and civil rights reforms through Congress because
   a. he was better at explaining the purposes of the laws in his speeches.
   b. the Democrats gained overwhelming control of Congress in the landslide of 1964.
   c. Republicans were more willing to cooperate with Johnson than with Kennedy.
   d. Johnson was better able to swing southern Democrats behind his proposals.
   e. he was not distracted by foreign policy crises in Vietnam and Latin America.

9. The Civil Rights Act of 1965 guaranteed

    a. desegregation in interstate transportation.
    b. job opportunities for African Americans.
    c. desegregation of high schools and colleges.
    d. voting rights for African Americans.
    e. equal opportunity in housing and an end to discriminatory real estate practices.

10. Which of the following was *not* among Lyndon Johnson's Great Society achievements?

    a. Federal aid to education
    b. Civil rights and voting rights for blacks
    c. Federally funded medical care for the elderly and the poor
    d. Clean water and clean air legislation
    e. Immigration liberalization and reform

11. Which of the following was *not* among the political problems that the Johnson administration faced in waging the Vietnam War?

    a. Growing doubts among some within the administration itself about the wisdom of the war
    b. Strong opposition from world opinion and many of America's allies
    c. Political opposition and draft resistance inside the United States
    d. The weakness and corruption of frequently changing South Vietnamese governments
    e. The threat that some South Vietnamese government would simply ask the Americans to leave

12. Opposition to the Vietnam War in Congress was centered in the

    a. House Foreign Affairs Committee.
    b. Senate Armed Services Committee.
    c. Republican leadership of the House and Senate.
    d. Senate Foreign Relations Committee.
    e. New York congressional delegation led by Senator Robert Kennedy.

13. The two antiwar candidates whose strong political showing forced Johnson to withdraw from the 1968 presidential race were

    a. Nelson Rockefeller and Ronald Reagan.
    b. Eugene McCarthy and Robert Kennedy.
    c. J. William Fulbright and George McGovern.
    d. George Wallace and Curtis LeMay.
    e. Richard Nixon and Spiro Agnew.

14. Which of the following was *not* among the political upheavals and crises that occurred around the world in 1968?

    a. The anticommunist uprising against Fidel Castro's rule in Cuba.
    b. The Prague spring revolt in Czechoslovakia and its crushing by Soviet tanks
    c. French student and worker revolts that nearly overthrew the French government
    d. The student rebellions at Columbia University and many other American campuses
    e. The antiwar political campaigns of Senators Eugene McCarthy and Robert Kennedy

15. One dominant theme of the 1960s youth culture that had deep roots in American history was

    a. conflict between the generations.
    b. distrust and hostility toward authority.
    c. the widespread use of mind-altering drugs.
    d. a positive view of sexual experimentation.
    e. interracial collaboration and marriage.

C. Identification

Supply the correct identification for each numbered description.

1. _____ Kennedy administration program that sent youthful American volunteers to work in underdeveloped countries

2. _____ High barrier between East and West, erected during the 1961 Berlin crisis

3. _____ Shorthand term for Kennedy administration's policies aimed at "getting America moving again"

4. _____ An attempt to provide American aid for democratic reform in Latin America that met with much disappointment and frustration

5. _____ Site where anti-Castro guerrilla forces failed in their U.S.-sponsored invasion

6. _____ Tense confrontation between Kennedy and Khrushchev that nearly led to nuclear war in October 1962

7. _____ Civil rights demonstrators who sought to desegregate public facilities like bus stations by traveling through the South

8. _____ LBJ's broad program of welfare legislation and social reform that swept through Congress in 1965

9. _____ The 1964 congressional action that became a blank check for the Vietnam War

10. _____ Law, spurred by Martin Luther King, Jr.'s march from Selma to Montgomery, that guaranteed rights originally given blacks under the Fifteenth Amendment

11. _____ Racial slogan that signaled a growing challenge to King's nonviolent civil rights movement by militant younger blacks

12. _____ The Vietnamese New Year celebration, during which the communists launched a heavy offensive against the United States in 1968

13. _____ Brief, dramatic war between Israel and neighboring Arab states that led to Israeli conquest and control of the Palestinian West Bank and Gaza

14. _____ Student organization that moved from nonviolent protest to underground terrorism within a few years

15. _____ Site of an off-duty police raid in 1969 that spurred gay and lesbian activism

D. Matching People, Places, and Events

Match the person, place, or event in the left column with the proper description in the right column by inserting the correct letter on the blank line.

1. ___ John F. Kennedy

2. ___ Robert S. McNamara

3. ___ Nikita Khrushchev

4. ___ Martin Luther King, Jr.

5. ___ Lyndon B. Johnson

6. ___ Barry M. Goldwater

7. ___ James Meredith

a. First black student admitted to the University of Mississippi, shot during a civil rights march in 1966

b. Cabinet officer who promoted flexible response, but came to doubt the wisdom of the Vietnam War he had presided over

8. ____   Malcolm X

9. ____   J. William Fulbright

10. ____   Eugene J. McCarthy

11. ____   Robert F. Kennedy

12. ____   Richard M. Nixon

13. ____   George C. Wallace

14. ____   Hubert Humphrey

15. ____   Allen Ginsberg

c.   New York senator whose antiwar campaign for the presidency was ended by an assassin's bullet in June 1968

d.   Former vice president who staged a remarkable political comeback to win presidential election in 1968

e.   Charismatic Black Muslim leader who promoted separatism in the early 1960s

f.   Minnesota senator whose antiwar Children's Crusade helped force Johnson to alter his Vietnam policies

g.   Chair of the Senate Foreign Relations Committee and leader of congressional opposition to the Vietnam War

h.   Nonviolent black leader whose advocacy of peaceful change came under attack from militants after 1965

i.   Vice president whose loyalty to LBJ's Vietnam policies sent him down to defeat in the 1968 presidential election

j.   Charismatic president whose brief administration experienced domestic stalemate and foreign confrontations with communism

k.   Third-party candidate whose conservative, hawkish 1968 campaign won 9 million votes and carried five states

l.   Aggressive Soviet leader whose failed gamble of putting missiles in Cuba cost him his job

m.   Beat poet of the 1950s whose hostility to materialism and establishment values helped lay groundwork for 1960s counterculture

n.   Conservative Republican whose crushing defeat opened the way for the liberal Great Society programs

o.   Brilliant legislative operator whose domestic achievements in social welfare and civil rights fell under the shadow of his Vietnam disaster

E. Putting Things in Order

Put the following events in correct order by numbering them from 1 to 5.

1. _____ A southern Texas populist replaces a Harvard-educated Irish American in the White House.

2. _____ An American-sponsored anticommunist invasion of Cuba fails.

3. _____ Kennedy successfully risks nuclear confrontation to thwart Khrushchev's placement of Russian missiles in Cuba.

4. _____ A candidate running on a peace platform obtains a congressional blank check for subsequent expanded military actions against the Communist Vietnamese.

5. _____ Communist military assaults, political divisions between hawks and doves, and assassinations of national leaders form the backdrop for a turbulent election year.

F. Matching Cause and Effect

Match the historical cause in the left column with the proper effect in the right column by writing the correct letter on the blank line.

Cause		Effect	
1. ___	Kennedy's unhappiness with the corrupt Diem regime	a.	Pushed Johnson into withdrawing as a presidential candidate in 1968
2. ___	Khrushchev's placement of missiles in Cuba	b.	Brought ever-rising American casualties and a strengthened will to resist on the part of the communist Vietnamese
3. ___	Johnson's landslide victory over Goldwater in 1964	c.	Led to a U.S.-encouraged coup and greater political instability in South Vietnam
4. ___	The Gulf of Tonkin Resolution	d.	Helped push through historic civil rights legislation in 1964 and 1965
5. ___	Martin Luther King, Jr.'s civil rights marches	e.	Brought along huge Democratic congressional majorities that passed a fistful of Great Society laws
6. ___	Angry discontent in northern black ghettos		
7. ___	American escalation of the Vietnam War	f.	Helped Nixon win a minority victory over his divided opposition
8. ___	The communist Vietnamese Tet Offensive in 1968	g.	Became the questionable legal basis for all of Johnson's further escalation of the Vietnam War
9. ___	Senator Eugene McCarthy's strong antiwar campaign	h.	Led to a humiliating defeat when Kennedy forced the Soviet Union to back down
10. ___	The deep Democratic Party divisions over Vietnam	i.	Sparked urban riots and the growth of the militant Black Power movement

j.   Led to an American military request for 200,000 more troops as well as growing public discontent with the Vietnam War

G. Developing Historical Skills

Interpreting Line Graphs

Read the line graph of *Poverty in the United States* on p. 987 carefully and answer the following questions.

1.   In what year did the number of people below the poverty line return to approximately the same level it had been at in 1964?

2.   In what two years did the percentage of the American population below the poverty line reach its lowest point since 1960?

3.   Between what years did the absolute numbers of people below the poverty line rise slightly at the same time those in poverty declined slightly as a percentage of the total population? What would explain this difference?

4.   The number of people in poverty in 1966 was about the same as the number in poverty in which subsequent year?

H. Map Mastery

Map Discrimination

Using the maps and charts in Chapter 38, answer the following questions.

1.   *Vietnam and Southeast Asia*: Besides North Vietnam, which two other Southeast Asian countries bordered on South Vietnam?

2.   *Presidential Election of 1964*: How many electoral votes did Barry Goldwater win outside the Deep South in 1964?

3. *Presidential Election of 1968*: What four northeastern states did Nixon carry in 1968?

4. *Presidential Election of 1968*: Which five states outside the Northeast did Humphrey carry in 1968? (One of them is not in the continental United States.)

Map Challenge

After pushing through Congress the Civil Rights Act of 1964 and the Voting Rights Act of 1965, President Lyndon Johnson is said to have remarked that as a result "the Democratic party will lose the South for at least an entire generation." Using the electoral maps of the five elections of 1952, 1960, 1964, and 1968 (pp. 949, 965, 986, and 996 in Chapters 37 and 38), write a brief essay describing the changing fortunes of the Republican and Democratic parties in different regions of the country from 1952 to 1968. To what extent did the emerging pattern of dramatically shifting party loyalties in 1964 and 1968 suggest that Johnson may have been right. Are there any other factors that may help explain these changes?

PART III: APPLYING WHAT YOU HAVE LEARNED

1. What successes and failures did Kennedy's New Frontier experience at home and abroad?

2. President Kennedy's pledge to "land a man on the moon in this decade," which was successfully fulfilled by the Apollo moon landing in 1969, was a dramatic assertion of America's global power and technological leadership of the world. How important was the space program to the New Frontier, and to America's image of itself? Did the Apollo project and the moon landing still retain its luster after Vietnam and the social upheavals of the 1960s?

3. Compare and contrast Kennedy and Johnson as presidential leaders in the 1960s. Why did Kennedy come to be remembered so fondly by many Americans, and Johnson not, even though Kennedy's accomplishments in office were very slim compared to Johnson's enormous Great Society achievements?

4. What led the United States to become so deeply involved in the Vietnam War? (See Chapters 36 and 37 for background on the Cold War, anticolonialism, and earlier events in Vietnam.)

5. How did the civil rights movement move from its difficult beginnings in the 1950s and early 1960s to great successes in 1964–1965. Why did it encounter increasing criticism and opposition from both black militants and the forces of white backlash (represented by George C. Wallace) so soon after its greatest triumphs?

6. Compare and contrast Martin Luther King, Jr., and Malcolm X as black leaders. Was the emphasis on black pride and self-determination that Malcolm represented really opposed to King's ideals, or did it just address a different set of problems more deeply rooted in northern ghettos than in southern segregation? Why did so many blacks—and whites—begin to criticize King's emphasis on absolute nonviolence in the freedom struggle?

7. Why did the Vietnam War, and the domestic opposition to it, come to dominate American politics in the 1960s?

8. In later decades, many historians came to interpret the upheavals of 1968, in the United States and elsewhere around the world, as the end of the postwar era. Is this an accurate interpretation? Why did authority of all kinds—and not just political authority—come under assault in this period?

9. When the Democratic party tore itself apart over the Vietnam War and other issues in the late 1960s, the winner proved to be the forces of an emerging conservatism led by Richard Nixon and George Wallace. How and why did conservatism emerge so rapidly from the seemingly devastating Goldwater defeat in the election of 1964?

10. What, if anything, was valuable about the radical social movements of the 1960s, such as those led by Students for a Democratic Society? What was most destructive and negative? Did such movements have any long-term impact?

11. How was the cultural upheaval of the 1960s related to the political and social changes of the decade? Is the youth rebellion best seen as a response to immediate events, or as a consequence of such longer-term forces as the population bulge and economic prosperity? What were the long-term results of the counterculture in all its varieties?

CHAPTER 39

The Stalemated Seventies, 1968–1980

PART I: REVIEWING THE CHAPTER

A. Checklist of Learning Objectives

After mastering this chapter, you should be able to:

1. Describe Nixon's foreign policy in relation to Vietnam, the Soviet Union, and Communist China.

2. Analyze Nixon's domestic policies, his opposition to the "Warren Court," his southern strategy, and his landslide victory against George McGovern in 1972.

3. Examine the political and economic tensions created by the secret bombing of Cambodia, the American withdrawal from Vietnam, and the first Arab oil embargo.

4. Discuss the Watergate scandals, Nixon's resignation, and Ford's unelected presidency.

5. Explain the closely intertwined economic, energy, and Middle East crises of the 1970s and why both Republican and Democratic administrations were unable to address them successfully.

6. Describe the racial tensions of the 1970s, especially over school busing and affirmative action.

7. Discuss the rise of second-wave feminism in the United States and elsewhere, and the conservative resistance to it that blocked the Equal Rights Amendment.

8. Indicate how Jimmy Carter's outsider presidency fell into political disarray, culminating in the Iranian hostage crisis humiliation.

B. Glossary

To build your social science vocabulary, familiarize yourself with the following terms.

1. **moratorium** A period in which economic or social activity is suspended, often to achieve certain defined goals. "Antiwar protestors staged a massive national Vietnam moratorium in October 1969. . . ."

2. **Marxism** The doctrines of Karl Marx, advocated or followed by worldwide communist parties and by some democratic socialists. "The two great communist powers . . . were clashing bitterly over their rival interpretations of Marxism."

3. **anti-ballistic missile** A defensive missile designed to intercept and destroy an offensive missile in flight. "The first major achievement was an anti-ballistic missile (ABM) treaty. . . ."

4. **devaluation** In economics, steps taken to reduce the purchasing power of a given unit of currency in relation to foreign currencies. " . . . he next stunned the world by taking the United States off the gold standard and devaluing the dollar."

5. **foray** a single, defined movement or attack by a military unit. "The most disturbing feature of these sky forays. . . ."

6. **Kremlin** The extensive palace complex in Moscow that houses the Soviet (Russian) government; hence, a shorthand term for the Soviet or Russian government. "Believing that the Kremlin was poised to fly combat troops to the Suez area. . . ."

7. **attorney general** The presidentially appointed head of the Department of Justice and chief legal officer of the federal government. ". . . firing his own special prosecutor . . . as well as his attorney general and deputy attorney general. . . ."

8. **executive privilege** In American government, the claim that certain information known to the president or the executive branch of government should be unavailable to Congress or the courts because of the principle of separation of powers. " . . . the Supreme Court unanimously ruled that "executive privilege" gave him no right to withhold evidence. . . ."

9. **recession** A moderate and short-term economic downturn, less severe than a depression. (Economists define a recession as two consecutive quarters: that is, six months, of declining gross domestic product.) "Lines of automobiles at service stations lengthened as tempers shortened and a business recession deepened."

10. **born-again** The evangelical Christian belief in a spiritual renewal or rebirth, involving a personal experience of conversion and a commitment to moral transformation. ". . . this born-again Baptist touched many people with his down-home sincerity."

11. **balance of payments** The net ratio, expressed as a positive or negative sum, of a nation's exports in relation to its imports. (It may be calculated in relation to one particular foreign nation, or to all foreign states collectively.) "The soaring bill for imported oil plunged America's balance of payments deeply into the red. . . ."

12. **commando** Member of a small, elite military force trained to carry out difficult missions, often inside territory controlled by the enemy. "A highly trained commando team penetrated deep into Iran's sandy interior."

PART II: CHECKING YOUR PROGRESS

A. True-False

Where the statement is true, circle **T**; where it is false, circle **F**.

1. T F Nixon's Vietnamization policy was aimed at bringing an immediate negotiated end to the Vietnam War.

2. T F The roaring inflation of the 1970s was fundamentally caused by President Johnson's decision to fight the Vietnam War and fund the Great Society programs without raising taxes to pay for them.

3. T F Nixon's 1970 invasion of Cambodia provoked vehement domestic protests and intensified political clashes between hawks and doves.

4. T F Nixon's and Kissinger's diplomacy attempted to play the Soviet Union and China off against each other in order to enhance America's position in Vietnam and elsewhere.

5. T F The Warren Supreme Court's decisions on sexual freedom, rights of accused criminals, and school prayer stirred fierce attacks by President Nixon and political conservatives.

6. T F Nixon consistently opposed a greater federal government role in environmental protection and worker safety issues.

7. T F The burning issue in the 1972 Nixon-McGovern campaign was inflation and the management of the economy.

8.   T   F   Congress initially supported President Nixon's bombing campaign against Cambodia as the only way to save South Vietnam from defeat.

9.   T   F   The 1973 Paris agreement on Vietnam provided for a cease-fire and American withdrawal but did not really end the civil war among the Vietnamese.

10.   T   F   The 1973 Arab-Israeli War and OPEC-led rise in the price of oil greatly accelerated the inflation that began in the wake of the Vietnam War.

11.   T   F   Republican leaders in Congress strenuously opposed Nixon's resignation and urged him to fight to stay in office even after the Watergate tapes were released.

12.   T   F   President Gerald Ford immediately set out to reverse the Nixon-Kissinger policy of détente toward the Soviet Union.

13.   T   F   The feminist movement's successes in advancing women's economic and educational opportunities culminated in the passage of the Equal Rights Amendment (ERA).

14.   T   F   President Carter's declaration that America's problems were due to a "moral and spiritual crisis" aroused strong public support for his proposals to decrease dependency on Middle Eastern oil.

15.   T   F   The Iranian revolution against the pro-American shah brought the United States into a bitter confrontation with the new, militant Muslim leaders of that country.

B. Multiple Choice

Select the best answer and circle the corresponding letter.

1.   Which of the following was *not* a cause of the growing economic slowdown and crises of the 1970s?
   a.   Lyndon Johnson's refusal to raise taxes to pay for the Vietnam War and the Great Society
   b.   The declining productivity of the average American worker
   c.   The growth in tariffs and trade barriers between the United States and Europe
   d.   Sharply rising oil prices and the end of America's energy independence
   e.   The competitive advantage of modern German and Japanese manufacturers compared to older American technologies

2.   The essential principle of President Nixon's Vietnamization policy was that
   a.   the United States would accept a unified but neutral Vietnam.
   b.   the United States would escalate the war in Vietnam but withdraw from Cambodia and Laos.
   c.   the United States would gradually withdraw ground troops, while supporting the South Vietnamese war effort.
   d.   the United States would seek a negotiated settlement of the war.
   e.   China would restrain North Vietnamese aggression, while the United States withdrew from South Vietnam.

3.   The antiwar movement exploded dramatically in 1970 when
   a.   the massacre of civilians at My Lai by some U.S. soldiers was revealed.
   b.   Nixon ordered further bombing of North Vietnam.
   c.   the communist Vietnamese staged their Tet Offensive against American forces.
   d.   Nixon ordered an invasion of Cambodia.
   e.   several U.S. army units refused to continue fighting.

4. President Nixon and Secretary of State Kissinger successfully pressured the Soviet Union into making diplomatic deals with the United States by

    a. playing the China card by opening U.S. diplomacy and trade with the Soviets' rival communist power.
    b. using American economic aid as an incentive for the Soviets.
    c. threatening to attack Soviet allies such as Cuba and Vietnam.
    d. drastically increasing spending on nuclear weapons and missiles.
    e. building an anti-ballistic missile system that effectively neutralized the Soviet nuclear threat.

5. The Supreme Court came under sharp political attack in the 1970s, especially because of its rulings on

    a. antitrust laws and labor rights.
    b. voting rights and election laws.
    c. foreign trade and business regulation.
    d. environmental laws and immigrants' rights.
    e. criminal defendants' rights and prayer in public schools.

6. The most controversial element of Nixon's Philadelphia Plan was

    a. its guarantees of women's equal right to employment in the construction trades.
    b. the extension of affirmative action to promote the employment of minorities and women as social groups rather than individuals.
    c. its insistence that employers and labor provide financial compensation to individuals who had suffered discrimination.
    d. its attempt to get around Supreme Court decisions prohibiting racial and sexual discrimination by business and labor.
    e. its requirement that private businesses had to hire based on affirmative action, while government was exempt.

7. The two areas where President Nixon created powerful new federal agencies that directly impinged on business operations were

    a. workforce education and training and private pension policies.
    b. automobile safety and urban planning.
    c. civil rights and women's rights.
    d. environmental protection and occupational health and safety.
    e. workplace child care and executive compensation.

8. The War Powers Act was passed by Congress specifically in response to

    a. the Watergate scandal.
    b. President Nixon's secret bombing of Cambodia.
    c. the continuing war in Vietnam.
    d. Nixon's willingness to send U.S. troops to support Israel in the Six-Day War.
    e. the use of American troops for peacekeeping in the Middle East.

9. The most serious of the many corrupt Nixon administration practices, exposed by the Senate Watergate Committee, was

    a. the acceptance of illegal payments by foreign governments.
    b. bribes to congressmen and senators.
    c. the illegal use of the Federal Bureau of Investigation and the Central Intelligence Agency to cover up White House crimes and harass Nixon's enemies.
    d. the illegal use of the Environmental Protection Agency and the Occupational Safety and Health Administration to force businesses to contribute to Nixon's election campaign.
    e. the payment of kickbacks from businesses awarded federal contracts.

10. The Arab oil embargo of 1973–1974 and its aftermath dramatically affected the American economy by

   a. forcing America to turn to alternative energy sources.
   b. leading the United States to expand oil drilling in Alaska and in offshore oil fields.
   c. increasing American investment in the Middle East.
   d. ending the era of cheap energy and igniting a raging inflation.
   e. enabling Arab governments to gain substantial control of major American businesses.

11. President Gerald Ford's most controversial decision in the White House was

   a. appointing New York Governor Nelson Rockefeller as his new vice president.
   b. imposing federal wage and price controls to dampen double-digit inflation.
   c. signing the third basket of human rights guarantees in the Helsinki accords.
   d. refusing to send American ground troops back into South Vietnam.
   e. granting a complete pardon to Richard Nixon for all crimes he may have committed.

12. Despite numerous successes for women in the 1970s, the feminist movement suffered a severe setback when

   a. the Supreme Court began to oppose the extension of women's rights.
   b. the Equal Rights Amendment failed to achieve ratification by the states.
   c. Congress refused to extend women's right to an equal education to the area of athletics.
   d. moderate and radical feminists began to attack each other over whether gender differences should be totally eradicated.
   e. the declining economy created a growing gap between men's and women's earning power.

13. The conservative antifeminist movement attacked the Equal Rights Amendment by arguing that it would

   a. lead to the establishment of nongendered dress codes.
   b. force an end to women-only colleges.
   c. require equal pay for equal work by men and women.
   d. make abortion rights the law of the land.
   e. end traditional workplace protections for women and undermine the family.

14. President Jimmy Carter's political support plummeted when he

   a. supported Iranian militants in their overthrow of the Shah of Iran.
   b. called for the use of alternative energy to end America's dependence on Middle Eastern oil.
   c. told Americans in a speech that their excessive concern for material goods had led to a moral and spiritual crisis.
   d. negotiated a peace treaty between Israel and Egypt.
   e. established full diplomatic relations with Communist China.

15. President Carter's greatest foreign policy failure was his

   a. negotiation of the Panama Canal treaties.
   b. inadequate response to the Soviet invasion of Afghanistan.
   c. inability to get other Arab states besides Egypt to make peace with Israel.
   d. reinstitution of registration of all young men for the military draft.
   e. inability to end the Iranian revolutionaries' seizure of American hostages.

C. Identification

Supply the correct identification for each numbered description.

1. _____ Nixon's policy of withdrawing American troops from Vietnam, while providing aid for the South Vietnamese to fight the war

2. _____ The Ohio university where four students were killed during protests against the 1970 invasion of Cambodia

3. _____ Top-secret documents, published by the *New York Times* in 1971, that showed the blunders and deceptions that led the United States into the Vietnam War

4. _____ Site of massacre by American soldiers of Vietnamese civilians.

5. _____ Nixon's regionally-focused plan to win reelection by curbing the Supreme Court's judicial activism and soft-pedaling civil rights

6. _____ Term for the new group-oriented affirmative action policy promoted by the Nixon administration

7. _____ A Washington office complex whose name was applied to the widespread corruption and crimes of the Nixon administration

8. _____ The law, passed in reaction to the secret Cambodia bombing, that restricted presidential use of troops overseas without congressional authorization

9. _____ Powerful new federal agency established to enforce the Clean Air Act, the Clean Water Act, and other similar laws.

10. _____ Nixon-Ford-Kissinger policy of seeking relaxed tensions with the Soviet Union through trade and arms limitation

11. _____ International agreement of 1975, signed by President Ford, that settled postwar European boundaries and attempted to guarantee human rights in Eastern Europe

12. _____ Proposed constitutional amendment promoting women's rights that fell short of ratification

13. _____ Supreme Court decision that declared women's right to choose abortion.

14. _____ President Jimmy Carter's 1979 speech that blamed Americans' excessive materialism for causing a national "moral and spiritual crisis"

15. _____ The action by Iranian revolutionary militants that aroused worldwide outrage and further crippled Jimmy Carter's presidency

D. Matching People, Places, and Events

Match the person, place, or event in the left column with the proper description in the right column by inserting the correct letter on the blank line.

1. ____ Richard Nixon

2. ____ Spiro Agnew

3. ____ Rachel Carson

4. ____ Daniel Ellsberg

5. ____ Henry Kissinger

6. ____ Earl Warren

7. ____ George McGovern

8. ____ Phyllis Schlafly

9. ____ Gerald Ford

10. ____ John Dean

a. Nixon appointee as Chief Justice of the Supreme Court who failed to overturn earlier liberal Court decisions as Nixon hoped

b. The first appointed vice president of the United States who became the first unelected president

c. Supreme Court justice whose judicial activism came under increasing attack by conservatives

d. Nixon's tough-talking conservative vice president, who was forced to resign in 1973 for taking bribes and kickbacks

11. ___ James Earl Carter

12. ___ Warren Burger

13. ___ Allen Bakke

14. ___ Shah of Iran

15. ___ Anwar Sadat

e. Talented diplomatic negotiator and leading architect of détente with the Soviet Union during the Nixon and Ford administrations

f. Egyptian leader who signed the Camp David accords with Israel

g. California medical school applicant whose case led a divided Supreme Court to uphold limited forms of affirmative action for minorities

h. Environmental writer whose book, *Silent Spring*, helped encourage laws like the Clean Water Act and the Endangered Species Act

i. South Dakota senator whose antiwar campaign was swamped by Nixon

j. Former Georgia governor whose presidency was plagued by economic difficulties and a crisis in Iran

k. Former Pentagon official who leaked the Pentagon Papers

l. Winner of an overwhelming electoral victory who was forced from office by the threat of impeachment

m. White House lawyer whose dramatic charges against Nixon were validated by the Watergate tapes

n. Conservative activist who led a successful movement to stop ratification of the Equal Rights Amendment

o. Repressive pro-Western ruler whose 1979 overthrow precipitated a crisis for the United States

E. Putting Things in Order

Put the following events in correct order by numbering them from 1 to 6.

1. _____ The overthrow of a dictatorial shah leads to an economic and political crisis for President Carter and the United States.

2. _____ An impeachment-threatened president resigns, and his appointed vice president takes over the White House.

3. _____ A U.S. president travels to Beijing (Peking) and Moscow, opening a new era of improved diplomatic relations with the communist powers.

4. _____ The American invasion of a communist stronghold near Vietnam creates domestic turmoil in the United States.

5. _____ The signing of an agreement with North Vietnam leads to the final withdrawal of American troops from Vietnam.

6. _____ A plainspoken former governor becomes president by campaigning against
F. Matching Cause and Effect

F. Matching Cause and Effect

Match the historical cause in the left column with the proper effect in the right column by writing the correct letter on the blank line.

Cause

1. ___ Nixon's Vietnamization policy

2. ___ The U.S. invasion and bombing of Cambodia

3. ___ Nixon's trips to Beijing (Peking) and Moscow

4. ___ The Warren Court's judicial activism

5. ___ Pressure on Moscow and renewed bombing of North Vietnam

6. ___ The growing successes of the women's movement in areas of employment and education

7. ___ Nixon's tape-recorded words ordering the Watergate cover-up

8. ___ The communist Vietnamese offensive in 1975

9. ___ The Soviet invasion of Afghanistan

10. ___ The 1979 revolution in Iran

Effect

a. Spawned a powerful backlash that halted federal day care efforts and the Equal Rights Amendment

b. Caused Senate defeat of the SALT II treaty and the end of détente with Moscow

c. Brought about gradual U.S. troop withdrawal but extended the Vietnam War for four more years

d. Prompted conservative protests and Nixon's appointment of less activist justices

e. Led to the taking of American hostages and new economic and energy troubles for the United States

f. Brought about a cease-fire and the withdrawal of American troops from Vietnam in 1973

g. Caused protests on U.S. campuses and congressional attempts to restrain presidential war powers

h. Brought an era of relaxed international tensions and new trade agreements

i. Caused the collapse of South Vietnam and the flight of many refugees to the United States

j. Proved the president's guilt and forced him to resign or be impeached

G. Developing Historical Skills

Understanding Political Cartoons

The more controversial a major political figure, the more likely he or she is to be the subject of political cartoons. Richard Nixon was such a controversial figure, and the cartoons in this chapter show several views of him. Answer the following questions.

1. What is the view of Nixon's diplomacy in the cartoon *Balancing Act* on p. 1007? What is the significance of his unusual balance bar?

2. In the cartoon of *Nixon, the "Law-and-Order-Man"* on p. 1014, what aspect of Nixon's earlier career is satirized? What details suggest the cartoonist's view of Nixon's Watergate strategy?

3. In the cartoon *Who Lost Vietnam* on p. 1016, Nixon is satirized, but less harshly than in the other cartoons. What changes the perspective on him here?

PART III: APPLYING WHAT YOU HAVE LEARNED

1. Was the Nixon-Kissinger foreign policy of détente with the Soviet Union and engagement with Communist China fundamentally a great success? What were its major accomplishments, and what were its limitations?

2. In what ways did Nixon's domestic policies appeal to Americans' racial and economic fears, and in what ways did he positively address problems like inflation, discrimination, environmental degradation, and worker safety?

3. What were Nixon's fundamental goals in waging the Vietnam War from 1969 to 1973? Did he achieve them? Why did the secret bombing and invasion of Cambodia cause such a furious reaction by Congress and the public?

4. How did Nixon fall from the political heights of 1972 to his forced resignation in 1974? What were the political consequences of Watergate?

5. How did both Republican and Democratic administrations of the 1970s attempt to cope with the interrelated problems of energy, economics, and the Middle East? Why were they so largely unsuccessful in addressing these concerns?

6. How and why did the United States become increasingly involved in the political and economic affairs of the Middle East during the 1970s?

7. Why did the American public eventually become so disillusioned with the policy of détente toward the Soviet Union? Was the policy itself fundamentally flawed from the beginning, or was it Soviet misbehavior and aggression that destroyed an originally wise policy?

8. The American public had high hopes for Jimmy Carter as an honest and well-intentioned president who could clean up Washington after the corruption of Watergate. Why did Carter's presidency come to be seen as such a failure? Was Carter largely a victim of events he could not control, or did his own outlook and policies contribute to his failures in the White House?

9. In what ways were the foreign policy and economic issues of the 1970s similar to those of the whole post–World War II era, and in what ways were they different (see Chapters 36, 37, and 38)?

10. It is sometimes said that the recent American disillusionment and even cynicism about politics dates to the paired tribulations of Vietnam and Watergate. Why were these two events so deeply unsettling to traditional American views of democracy and government? Is the linking of the two events accurate, or were there fundamental differences between them?

CHAPTER 40

The Resurgence of Conservatism, 1981–1992

PART I: REVIEWING THE CHAPTER

A. Checklist of Learning Objectives

After mastering this chapter, you should be able to:

1. Describe the rise of Reagan and the New Right in the 1980s, including their effective use of social issues like abortion, affirmative action, and homosexuality.

2. Explain the Reagan revolution in economic policy, and indicate its immediate and long-term consequences.

3. Describe the revival of the Cold War in Reagan's first term and the consequences of Reagan's tough stands toward the Soviet Union.

4. Discuss the growing American entanglement in Central American and Middle Eastern troubles in the 1980s, including the Iran-Contra Affair.

5. Describe the change in Soviet policies initiated by Mikhail Gorbachev and Reagan's second-term turn to negotiation with the Soviets.

6. Analyze the growing power of the religious right in American politics and the battles over abortion and other issues before the Supreme Court.

7. Describe the end of the Cold War and its complex consequences for America's foreign relations and domestic economy.

8. Explain America's growing involvement in the Middle East, including the First Persian Gulf War and its aftermath.

B. Glossary

To build your social science vocabulary, familiarize yourself with the following terms.

1. **neoconservatives (neoconservatism)** Political activists and thinkers, mostly former liberals, who turned to a defense of traditional social and moral values and a strongly anticommunist foreign policy in the 1970s and 1980s. "Though Reagan was no intellectual, he drew on the ideas of a small but influential group of thinkers known as 'neoconservatives.'"

2. **supply side** In economics, the theory that investment incentives such as lowered federal spending and tax cuts will stimulate economic growth and increased employment. "But at first 'supply-side' economics seemed to be a beautiful theory mugged by a gang of brutal facts. . . ."

3. **red ink** Referring to a deficit in a financial account, with expenditures or debts larger than income or assets. "Ironically, this conservative president thereby plunged the government into a red-ink bath of deficit spending. . . ."

4. **oligarchs** A small, elite class of authoritarian rulers. ". . . the aging oligarchs in the Kremlin. . . ."

5. **welfare state** The political system, typical of modern industrial societies, in which government assumes responsibility for the economic well-being of its citizens by providing social benefits. "They achieved, in short, Reagan's highest political objective: the containment of the welfare state."

6. **leveraged buy-out** The purchase of one company by another using money borrowed on the expectation of selling a portion of assets after the acquisition. "A wave of mergers, acquisitions, and leveraged buy-outs washed over Wall Street. . . ."

7. **logistical (adj.) (logistics (n.)**Relating to the organization and movement of substantial quantities of people and material in connection with some defined objective. "In a logistical operation of astonishing complexity, the United States spearheaded a massive international military deployment on the sandy Arabian peninsula."

PART II: CHECKING YOUR PROGRESS

A. True-False

Where the statement is true, circle **T**; where it is false, circle **F**.

1. T   F   Ronald Reagan successfully attacked big government as the enemy rather than the friend of the common man.

2. T   F   Reagan's landslide victory over Carter in 1980 did not have the coattails to bring his fellow Republicans into office.

3. T   F   Once in office, Reagan backed away from most of his ideologically conservative election promises and concentrated on practical management of the economy and relations with the Russians.

4. T   F   The fact that Reagan's supply-side economic proposals bogged down in Congress demonstrated the continuing stalemate between Congress and the executive branch.

5. T   F   Reagan's vigorous free-market economic and hard-line stance against the Soviet Union was opposed by all of America's traditional European allies.

6. T   F   Part of Reagan's strategy in confronting the Soviet Union was to raise U.S. military expenditures to enormous heights that he believed the Soviets could not match.

7. T   F   Reagan pursued a tough policy of military intervention and aid in opposition to leftist governments in Central America and the Caribbean.

8. T   F   Soviet leader Mikhail Gorbachev's policies of *glasnost* and *perestroika* helped reduce Soviet-American conflict in Reagan's second term.

9. T   F   The Iran-Contra Affair involved the secret exchange of weapons to Iran in exchange for the release of American hostages and the illegal transfer of the profits to Nicaraguan rebels.

10. T   F   The failure of Reaganomics to deliver a balanced federal budget actually served Reagan's political goal of curbing the liberal welfare state.

11. T   F   The powerful new religious right borrowed many of its tactics and organizing methods from the new left of the 1960s.

12. T   F   The Supreme Court cases of *Webster* v. *Reproductive Health Services* and *Casey* v. *Planned Parenthood* carved out compromises that softened the conflict between pro-life and pro-choice forces.

13. T   F   The collapse of the Soviet Communist government led to the overthrow of the puppet communist regimes throughout Eastern Europe.

14. T   F   The overthrow of communism in Eastern Europe and the Soviet Union led to vicious fighting among previously repressed ethnic groups.

15. T   F   The First Persian Gulf War achieved its primary goal of liberating Kuwait but left Saddam Hussein in power in Iraq.

B. Multiple Choice

Select the best answer and circle the corresponding letter.

1. In the 1980 national elections
    a. Ronald Reagan declared that as a conservative he would not seek drastic changes in American foreign or domestic policy.
    b. Ronald Reagan won the presidency, but both houses of Congress retained Democratic party majorities.
    c. third-party candidate John Anderson nearly forced the election into the House of Representatives.
    d. Ronald Reagan won the presidency by the closest margin since the Kennedy-Nixon election of 1960.
    e. Senator Edward Kennedy's primary challenge to incumbent President Carter revealed the divisions and weakness of the Democratic party.

2. Ronald Reagan was similar to Franklin D. Roosevelt in that both presidents
    a. disliked big business.
    b. championed the common person against vast impersonal menaces.
    c. came from privileged backgrounds and family wealth.
    d. favored social engineering by the government.
    e. emphasized hands-on management skills rather than ideology.

3. Ronald Reagan differed from Franklin D. Roosevelt because Reagan
    a. said big business was the enemy of the common person, while Roosevelt declared that the problem was big government.
    b. appealed to the working class, while Roosevelt appealed primarily to the rich.
    c. advocated a populist political philosophy and Roosevelt did not.
    d. branded big government as the enemy of the common person, while Roosevelt said that big business was the major foe.
    e. was effective in using the media to appeal directly to the American people, while Roosevelt was less successful as a media communicator.

4. Conservative Democrats who helped Ronald Reagan pass his budget and tax-cutting legislation were called
    a. boll weevils.
    b. Sagebrush rebels.
    c. scalawags.
    d. neoconservatives.
    e. Contras.

5. The one area of the federal government activity that Ronald Reagan spent lavishly on was
    a. farm programs.
    b. social security.
    c. defense.
    d. education.
    e. environmental protection.

6. Reagan's fundamental principle in negotiating with the Soviet Union was to
    a. trade America's minor interests for major concessions from the Soviets.
    b. negotiate only from a position of overwhelming military superiority.
    c. negotiate only in cooperation with the Western European allies.
    d. insist on greater human rights and economic freedoms as conditions of the negotiations.
    e. demand that the Soviets tear down the Berlin Wall in exchange for nuclear arms agreements.
7. President Reagan formed a strong personal and political partnership with British Prime Minister Margaret Thatcher based upon
    a. Reagan's admiration and support for the idea of female leadership in high office.
    b. their belief in cultivating support for Western policies from Third World countries.
    c. their common devotion to protecting the social safety net for those left behind by technological change.
    d. their shared support for a stronger role for religion in public and political life.
    e. their mutual support for vigorous free-market economics and tough confrontation with the Soviet Union.
8. Reagan's key agreements with Soviet leader Mikhail Gorbachev provided for
    a. the eventual end of communism inside the Soviet Union.
    b. a major reduction in both Soviet and American nuclear weapons and intercontinental missiles.
    c. the opening of Soviet markets to American businesses.
    d. an end to Soviet and American sponsorship of governments and rebels in the Third World.
    e. the banning of all intermediate-range nuclear missiles from Europe.
9. In the bitter 1980s war between Islamic revolutionary Iran and Iraqi dictator Saddam Hussein, the United States
    a. maintained strict neutrality and an arms embargo on both sides.
    b. secretly supported the Iranians in hopes that they could overthrow Saddam Hussein.
    c. ended up supplying weapons to both sides.
    d. tried to negotiate a peaceful settlement of the war.
    e. threatened the use of military force to prevent a victory by Saddam Hussein.
10. The religious right movement of the 1980s adopted many ideas and tactics from the 1960s new left such as
    a. advertising in newspapers and television.
    b. practicing identity politics, consciousness raising, and civil disobedience.
    c. taking over traditional political party machines from within.
    d. wearing Native American clothing and hairstyles.
    e. relying on charismatic personal leaders rather than ideology.
11. Among the issues that many religious right activists were most concerned about were
    a. abortion and gay rights.
    b. taxation and economic development.
    c. U.S. foreign policy in the Middle East.
    d. Medicare and Social Security.
    e. energy and environmental protection.
12. The 1989 Supreme Court decision that upheld some state restrictions on a woman's right to have an abortion was
    a. *Roe* v. *Wade.*
    b. *Webster* v. *Reproductive Health Services.*
    c. *Brown* v. *Board of Education.*
    d. the *Miranda* decision.
    e. *Martin* v. *Wilks.*

13. In which of the following communist nations did mass protests, demanding liberty and democracy, in the years 1989–1991 completely fail?

    a. The Soviet Union
    b. East Germany
    c. China
    d. Poland
    e. Cuba

14. The great success achieved by American and Allied forces in the 1991 Persian Gulf War was the

    a. overthrow of Saddam Hussein.
    b. liberation of Kuwait from Iraqi rule.
    c. freeing of the Kurds from Iraqi oppression.
    d. achievement of an enduring peace in the Middle East.
    e. formation of a strong American-Arab alliance against Islamic extremism.

15. The bitter hearings over the confirmation of Clarence Thomas to the U.S. Supreme Court revealed

    a. the continuing strong appeal of the antipornography issue.
    b. the continued American public fear of interracial sexual relations.
    c. President George H.W. Bush's attempt to steer the Supreme Court in a moderate direction.
    d. the American public's disgust at hearing public testimony about sexual harassment.
    e. a growing gender gap, with more women turning away from Republican social policies.

C. Identification

Supply the correct identification for each numbered description.

1. _____   Influential group of intellectuals, led by Irving Kristol and Norman Podhoretz, who provided key ideas for the Reagan Revolution

2. _____   California ballot initiative of 1978 that set the stage for the tax revolt that Reagan rode to victory in 1980

3. _____   The economic theory of Reaganomics that emphasized cutting taxes and government spending in order to stimulate investment, productivity, and economic growth by private enterprise

4. _____   Term for young urban professionals of the 1980s who flaunted their wealth through conspicuous consumer spending

5. _____   Conservative southern Democrats who supported Reagan's economic policies in Congress

6. _____   Polish labor union crushed by the communist-imposed martial-law regime in 1983

7. _____   The twin policies of openness and restructuring by which Soviet leader Mikhail _____   Gorbachev attempted to reform the Communist system

8. _____   The leftist revolutionary rulers of Nicaragua, strongly opposed by the Reagan administration

9. _____   Right-wing rebels against radical Nicaraguan government, secretly funded by profits of U.S. arms sales to Iran

10. _____   The scandal, carried out by Reagan administration officials, in which weapons were sold to Iran in exchange for the release of American hostages, the profits used to fund Nicaraguan rebels

11. _____   Reagan's proposed space-based nuclear defense system, nicknamed "Star Wars"

12. _____   Leading organization of the new religious right, led by Reverend Jerry Falwell

13. _____   Physical symbol of the Cold War and divided Europe that came down in 1989

14. _____   The central location in Beijing, China, where demonstrators demanding greater freedom and democracy were brutally crushed by government tanks in spring 1989

15. _____   Code name for the military operation of the hundred-hour war that drove Saddam Hussein out of Kuwait

D. Matching People, Places, and Events

Match the person, place, or event in the left column with the proper description in the right column by inserting the correct letter on the blank line.

1. ___ Jimmy Carter

2. ___ Edward Kennedy

3. ___ Ronald Reagan

4. ___ Margaret Thatcher

5. ___ Sandra Day O'Connor

6. ___ Mikhail Gorbachev

7. ___ George H. W. Bush

8. ___ Norman Podhoretz

9. ___ Saddam Hussein

10. ___ Anita Hill

11. ___ Walter Mondale

12. ___ Geraldine Ferraro

13. ___ Jerry Falwell

14. ___ Norman Schwartzkopf

15. ___ Clarence Thomas

a. Prominent evangelical minister, leader of the Moral Majority

b. University of Oklahoma law professor who charged Clarence Thomas with sexual harassment during bitter 1991 Supreme Court hearings

c. Soviet leader whose summit meetings with Reagan achieved an arms-control breakthrough in 1987

d. Jimmy Carter's vice president who lost badly to Ronald Reagan in the 1984 election

e. Iraqi dictator defeated by the United States and its allies in the Persian Gulf War

f. Brilliant legal scholar appointed by Reagan as the first woman justice on the Supreme Court

g. Well-meaning president who was swamped by the 1980 Reagan landslide but later won the Nobel Peace Prize

h. Leading neoconservative intellectual who attacked excesses of 1960s liberalism and provided ideological support for Ronald Reagan

i. First woman to be nominated to a major party ticket as Democratic vice-presidential candidate in 1984

j. Successful commander of American forces in the First Persian Gulf War

k. Liberal Democratic senator whose opposition to Carter helped divide the Democrats in 1980

l. Long-time Republican political figure who defeated Dukakis for the presidency in 1988

m. Controversial Supreme Court justice who narrowly won confirmation despite charges of sexual harassment

n. British Prime Minister of the 1980s whose support of free-market economics and tough anticommunism made her Ronald Reagan's closest partner

o. Political darling of Republican conservatives who won landslide election victories in 1980 and 1984

E. Putting Things in Order

Put the following events in correct order by numbering them from 1 to 6.

1. _____   Reagan easily wins reelection by overwhelming divided Democrats.

2. _____   The United States and its allies defeat Iraq in the Persian Gulf War.

3. _____   President Jimmy Carter loses in a landslide to former actor and California governor Ronald Reagan.

4. _____   Reagan's supply-side economic programs pass through Congress, cutting taxes and federal spending.

5. _____   George Herbert Walker Bush defeats Michael Dukakis in a "referendum on Reaganism."

6. _____   The Soviet Union dissolves into Russia and other new nations, many plagued by fierce ethnic conflicts

F. Matching Cause and Effect

Match the historical cause in the left column with the proper effect in the right column by writing the correct letter on the blank line.

Cause	Effect
1. ___ The intellectual movement called neoconservatism	a. Led to a break-off of arms-control talks, U.S. economic sanctions against Poland, and growing anxiety in Western Europe
2. ___ Reagan's crusade against big government and social spending	b. Brought about an overwhelming Republican victory in the 1984 presidential election
3. ___ By 1983, Reagan's supply-side economic policies	

4. ___ The revival of the Cold War in the early eighties

5. ___ Continued political turmoil and war in Lebanon

6. ___ Reagan's hostility to leftist governments in Central America and the Caribbean

7. ___ Reagan's personal popularity and Democratic divisions

8. ___ Reagan's "Star Wars" plan for defensive missile systems in space

9. ___ The huge federal budget deficits of the 1980s

10. ___ Reagan's and Bush's appointments of conservative justices to the Supreme Court

11. ___ The Reagan administration's frustration with hostages and bans on aid to Nicaraguan rebels

12. ___ Dissident movements like that of Solidarity in Poland

13. ___ The widespread student protests in China's Tiananmen Square in 1989

14. ___ Saddam Hussein's invasion of Kuwait

15. ___ Anita Hill's charges of sexual harassment against Supreme Court nominee Clarence Thomas

c. Resulted in the failure of the American marines' peacekeeping mission in 1983

d. Helped curb affirmative action and limit the right to abortion

e. Led to sharp cuts in both taxes and federal social programs in 1981

f. Strained relations with America's European allies

g. Curbed inflation and spurred economic growth but also caused sky-high deficits and interest rates

h. Prompted Congress to pass the Gramm-Rudman-Hollings Act calling for automatic spending cuts and a balanced budget by 1991

i. Helped fuel Ronald Reagan's successful presidential campaign in 1980

j. Caused the U.S. invasion of Grenada and the CIA-engineered mining of Nicaraguan harbors

k. Led to the overthrow of communist puppet governments in Eastern Europe

l. Brought the killing of many people by tanks and machine guns and a re-assertion of harsh Communist Party rule

m. Brought a large American army to the Arabian peninsula and naval forces to the Persian Gulf

n. Caused a bitter Senate hearing and a growing gender gap between Republicans and Democrats

o. Led to the Iran-contra affair

G. Developing Historical Skills

Using Chronologies

Properly read, chronologies provide handy tools for understanding not only the sequence of events but also their historical relations.

Examine the Chronology for this chapter (p. 1053), and answer the following questions.

1.   In which year did a number of events indicate deep Soviet-American tension and a revived Cold War?

2.   How many years did it take after the first Reagan-Gorbachev summit to reach agreement on the INF treaty?

3.   List three events prior to the Persian Gulf War in 1991 that reflect growing American involvement in the Middle East.

4.   List three events between the imposition of sanctions against Poland (1981) and the dissolution of the Soviet Union (1991) that show the progress in easing Cold War tensions.

PART III: APPLYING WHAT YOU HAVE LEARNED

1.   What caused the rise of Reagan and the new right in the 1980s, and how did their conservative movement fundamentally reshape American politics?

2.   What were the goals of Reagan's supply-side economic policies, and what were those policies' short-term and long-term effects?

3.   What led to the revival of the Cold War in the early 1980s, and how did Ronald Reagan turn the conflict with the Soviet Union to American advantage?

4.   Why did the Reagan administration pursue its policy of opposing leftists in Central America and the Caribbean so fervently, to the point of funding the Nicaraguan Contras with arms sale profits from Iran? Was this primarily motivated by ideological anticommunism, or by fear of the Soviet Union gaining a strategic foothold in the Americas?

5.   How and why did religious and moral issues rather suddenly jump to the forefront of American politics and law in the 1980s?

6.   Many historians have compared the Reagan revolution with Franklin Roosevelt's New Deal because of the way it seemed to transform radically American economics and politics. Is this a valid comparison? Is it correct to see the Reagan legacy as a complete reversal of the New Deal, or of the Great Society of Lyndon Johnson?

7. Trace the evolution of the Supreme Court from the dominant days of the Warren Court in the 1960s (see Chapter 39) to the more conservative Court of the late 1980s. Why did Supreme Court decisions and judicial appointments become such focal points of political controversy in this period? In what ways did the Supreme Court "follow the election returns." In what ways did it resist narrowly political pressures?

8. To what extent were American policies responsible for the overthrow of communism in Eastern Europe and the Soviet Union in 1989–1991.

9. Was the first Persian Gulf War fundamentally based on America's Wilsonian foreign policy of promoting democracy, liberty, and self-determination for small nations (in this case, Kuwait), or was it primarily a defense of national self-interest, such as in protecting oil supplies and strengthening America's allies in the Middle East? Use evidence from the chapter to support your answer.

10. What were the opportunities and problems created by America's new status as the sole superpower after the end of the Cold War and the dissolution of the Soviet Union?

CHAPTER 41

America Confronts the Post-Cold War Era, 1992–2009

PART I: REVIEWING THE CHAPTER

A. Checklist of Learning Objectives

After mastering this chapter, you should be able to:

1. Describe the major domestic developments of the Clinton administration, including Clinton's attempts to govern as a New Democrat and the fierce partisan warfare against him conducted by Gingrich Republicans.

2. Discuss the causes and consequences of the violence that plagued American society in the 1990s.

3. Discuss America's challenges in developing a foreign policy in the post–Cold War environment, including the U.S. intervention in the Balkans and the continuing failure to achieve peace in the Middle East.

4. Describe the disputed 2000 election between Albert Gore, Jr. and George W. Bush, and indicate how and why American politics remained sharply polarized the first decade of the twenty-first century.

5. Discuss the impact of the September 11 terrorist attacks on American society and global involvements, including the wars in Afghanistan and Iraq.

6. Describe President George Bush's domestic and foreign policies, and explain why they met increasing opposition after Bush's victory in the 2004 election.

7. Indicate how both Democrats and Republicans attempted to respond to the concerns about the economy and the Iraq War, and identify each nominated presidential candidate strongly advocating change from the Bush administration.

B. Glossary

To build your social science vocabulary, familiarize yourself with the following terms.

1. **sect** A separatist religious group that claims for itself exclusive knowledge of truth and a superior method of salvation over all other religious organizations. "That showdown ended in the destruction of the sect's compound and the deaths of many Branch Davidians. . . ."

2. **paramilitary** Unauthorized or voluntary groups that employ military organization, methods, and equipment outside the official military system of command and organization. "These episodes brought to light a lurid and secretive underground of paramilitary private 'militias.' . . ."

3. **protectionism (protectionists)** The policy of promoting high tariff taxes on imported goods or services in order that domestic producers can sell at lower prices than foreign manufacturers or service providers. " . . . he reversed his own stand in the 1992 election campaign and bucked the opposition of protectionists in his own party. . . . "

4. **vouchers** Officially granted certificates for benefits of a particular kind, redeemable by a designated agency or service provider. "Bush championed private-sector initiatives, such as school vouchers. . . ."

5. **junta** From Latin America politics: a small armed group, usually military officers, who seize power and rule as a collective dictatorship. " . . . surely it was better to have the buck stop with the judges, not with a junta."

6. **autocratic (autocracy)** Relating to authoritarian or repressive government or institutional practices. "There was little evidence that Saddam's downfall might topple other autocratic regimes in the region."

PART II: CHECKING YOUR PROGRESS

A. True-False

Where the statement is true, circle **T**; where it is false, circle **F**.

1. T F Bill Clinton's presentation of himself as a New Democrat was designed to emphasize his commitment to reversing past Democratic party positions on civil rights.

2. T F After victory in the 1994 congressional elections, the militant conservatism of Speaker Newt Gingrich stumbled when it shut down the federal government for a time.

3. T F Clinton's liberal reforms put conservative Republicans on the defensive and led to substantial Democratic gains in the 1994 mid-term Congressional elections.

4. T F The Oklahoma City bombing of 1995, the Columbine High School shootings of 1999, and the Virginia Tech killings of 2007 led Congress to pass strong restrictions on handguns and other weapons.

5. T F The struggling economy of the 1990s led President Clinton to support increased protectionism and restrictions on the export of American jobs overseas.

6. T F The Clinton administration's major foreign policy success came in negotiating a peace settlement between Israelis and Palestinians in the Middle East.

7. T F The two charges on which President Clinton was impeached and then acquitted were perjury before a grand jury and obstruction of justice.

8. T F In the 2000 election, George W. Bush defeated Albert Gore in the Electoral College but not in the popular vote.

9. T F Once in office, President George W. Bush pursued strongly conservative policies on abortion, the environment, and taxes.

10. T F Osama bin Laden, the mastermind of the September 11 terrorist attacks, was an Afghan Taliban leader who had originally fought the Soviet invasion of his country.

11. T F The United Nations, in 1993, declined to authorize the use of force against Iraq to compel compliance with its resolutions.

12. T F The USA-Patriot Act, passed in response to September 11, authorized the detention and deportation of immigrants suspected of terrorism.

13. T F President George Bush's second-term proposal to privatize Social Security received strong support from liberals and senior citizens' groups.

14.   T   F   A major source of President George Bush's declining popular approval rating came from the federal government's inadequate response to the devastation of Hurricane Katrina.

15.   T   F   The primary cause of the Democrats' strong showing in the 2006 mid-term election was discontent with Bush's education and trade policies.

B. Multiple Choice

Select the best answer and circle the corresponding letter.

1.   Bill Clinton defeated incumbent President George Bush in 1992 by focusing especially on the issue of

    a.   women's rights and gay rights.
    b.   the environment.
    c.   the economy.
    d.   health care.
    e.   education

2.   In 1992, businessman H. Ross Perot made the strongest showing of any third-party presidential candidate since Theodore Roosevelt by winning approximately _____ percent of the popular vote.

    a.   5
    b.   10
    c.   20
    d.   40
    e.   50

3.   Two areas where President Clinton's initial attempts at liberal reform failed badly were

    a.   free trade and welfare reform.
    b.   the environment and consumer protection.
    c.   health care and gay service in the military.
    d.   affirmative action and education funding.
    e.   gun control and deficit reduction.

4.   Two areas where the Clinton administration achieved success in domestic affairs were

    a.   health care and gay rights.
    b.   political campaign reform and term limits.
    c.   gun control and deficit reduction.
    d.   immigration reform and improved race relations.
    e.   environmental protection and stock market regulation.

5.   The assault on the Branch Davidian compound in Waco, Texas, and the bombing of the Oklahoma City federal building were both extreme, violent expressions of a wider 1990s atmosphere of

    a.   religious belief in the imminent end of the world.
    b.   disillusionment with government and hostility to politicians.
    c.   hostility to free market capitalism.
    d.   anger toward ethnic minorities and immigrants.
    e.   tolerance for foreign terrorist assaults on the United States.

6. The new Republican congressional majority, led by House Speaker Newt Gingrich, caused a severe backlash in favor of President Clinton in 1995 when it
   a. restricted unfunded mandates imposed on state and local governments.
   b. supported the Welfare Reform Act, cutting welfare benefits and requiring recipients to seek employment.
   c. tried to restrict illegal immigration.
   d. attempted to prohibit sex education in the public schools.
   e. shut down the federal government for a time and proposed sending children on welfare to orphanages.

7. Despite the great prosperity of the 1990s economy, President Clinton experienced controversy and strong opposition to his policy of
   a. expanding global free trade and supporting the World Trade Organization.
   b. reducing the power and benefits of American unions.
   c. imposing regulations on the highly speculative dot.com Internet businesses and their stock offerings.
   d. demanding that China allow full human rights in exchange for greater American trade.
   e. increasing the minimum wage for lower income workers.

8. The Democratic minority's fundamental defense of the impeachment charges against President Clinton was that
   a. Clinton had not committed the acts with which he was charged.
   b. Clinton's actions were personal failings that did not rise to the constitutional level of high crimes and misdemeanors.
   c. Newt Gingrich and other leading Republicans had also engaged in sexual misconduct.
   d. the nation could not afford to remove an incumbent president during a time of international crisis.
   e. the special prosecutor Kenneth Starr did not understand the changes in contemporary Americans' attitudes toward sexuality.

9. Victory in the 2000 presidential election was eventually awarded to George W. Bush when
   a. the Florida legislature awarded that state's electoral votes to Bush.
   b. the Supreme Court ruled in Bush's favor that Florida's hand counting of ballots was illegal.
   c. Al Gore conceded that it was impossible for him to win.
   d. a joint session of Congress declared Bush the winner.
   e. a thorough recount showed that Bush had won the state.

10. One of George W. Bush's first vigorously conservative and nationalistic actions in office was to repudiate American participation in the
    a. International Atomic Energy Agency.
    b. United Nations World Health Organization.
    c. International Criminal Court and the Geneva Conventions on the treatment of prisoners.
    d. Kyoto Global Warming Treaty.
    e. international Law of the Sea Treaty.

11. The fundamentalist Islamic party that ruled Afghanistan and shielded Osama bin Laden prior to the September 11 attacks was
    a. the Party of God.
    b. Al Qaeda.
    c. Hamas.
    d. the Baath Party.
    e. the Taliban.

12. Which of the following was *not* among the reasons offered by President George W. Bush for America's 2003 invasion of Iraq?
    a. Possible Iraqi involvement in the September 11 attacks
    b. The need for the U.S. to control Iraqi oil supplies
    c. Saddam Hussein's possession of weapons of mass destruction
    d. The idea that the creation of a peaceful, democratic Iraq would inspire hope and reform throughout the Middle East
    e. Saddam Hussein's cruel oppression of his own people
13. Which of the following was *not* among the controversial Bush administration actions that led to increased polarization between supporters and opponents of the administration?
    a. Attorney General Ashcroft's zealous enforcement of the USA-Patriot Act
    b. Bush's strong anti-abortion policies
    c. The reduction of benefits for Gulf War veterans
    d. Approaches to gay and lesbian rights
    e. Bush's response to the devastation caused by Hurricane Katrina.

C. Identification

Supply the correct identification for each numbered description.

1. _____ Centrist Democratic organization that promoted Bill Clinton's candidacy as a New Democrat

2. _____ Shorthand phrase for compromise policy that emerged after Clinton's failed attempt to end ban on gays and lesbians in the military

3. _____ Fundamentalist group whose compound in Waco, Texas, was assaulted by federal agents in 1993

4. _____ Colorado high school where a deadly shooting in 1999 stirred a national movement against guns and gun violence

5. _____ Conservative campaign platform that led to a sweeping Republican victory in the 1994 mid-term elections

6. _____ Controversial free trade agreement between the United States, Mexico, and Canada that virtually eliminated trade barriers between the three nations.

7. _____ International trade organization that prompted strong protests from antiglobal trade forces in the late 1990s.

8. _____ Caribbean nation where Clinton sent twenty thousand American troops to restore ousted President Jean-Bertrand Aristide to power

9. _____ The sexual scandal involving a young White House intern that led to impeachment but not conviction of President Clinton

10. _____ Third party, led by environmentalist Ralph Nader, that took votes from Democratic presidential nominee Albert Gore in 2000 election

11. _____ Constitutional institution for choosing presidents that came under severe criticism after the 2000 popular vote winner failed to win the office

12. _____ The other site of direct attack by terrorists on September 11, 2001, besides the twin towers of the World Trade Center

13. _____ The international terrorist network headed by Osama bin Laden

14. _____   Controversial law restricting civil liberties, passed in the immediate aftermath of the September 11 attacks

15. _____   Iraqi prison where alleged American abuse of Iraqi prisoners inflamed anti-American sentiment in Iraq and beyond

D. Matching People, Places, and Events

Match the person, place, or event in the left column with the proper description in the right column by inserting the correct letter on the blank line.

1. _____ William J. Clinton

2. _____ H. Ross Perot

3. _____ Hillary Rodham Clinton

4. _____ Robert Dole

5. _____ Newt Gingrich

6. _____ John McCain

7. _____ Slobodan Milosevic

8. _____ Monica Lewinsky

9. _____ William Rehnquist

10. _____ Al Gore

11. _____ George W. Bush

12. _____ Richard Cheney

13. _____ Osama bin Laden

14. _____ Saddam Hussein

15. _____ Barack Obama

a. Young White House intern whose sexual affair with President Clinton led to his impeachment

b. President Clinton's loyal vice president who won the most popular votes but lost the election of 2000

c. George W. Bush's vice president who vigorously promoted conservative domestic policies and the invasion of Iraq

d. Texas billionaire who won nearly 20 percent of the popular vote as third-party candidate in 1992

e. Illinois senator who became the first African American to be elected president, in 2008

f. Serbian president who conducted vicious ethnic cleansing campaigns and was eventually forced from office

g. Son of a former president whose narrow election as president in 2000 did not prevent him from pursuing a strong conservative agenda in office

h. The first baby boomer president who was the first Democrat elected to two full terms since Franklin Roosevelt

i. Long-time Iraqi dictator who was overthrown by invading American armies in 2003

j. First presidential spouse to be given major policy responsibilities and to win election to the United States Senate

k. Fiery Republican Speaker of the House who led his party to great victory in 1994 but resigned after Republican losses in 1998

l. Wealthy Saudi Arabian exile who formed a global terrorist network that assaulted the United States

m. Veteran reform-minded senator who won the Republican Party presidential nomination in 2008

n. 1996 Republican presidential nominee who was soundly defeated by Bill Clinton

o. Chief Justice of the United States who presided at the impeachment trial of President Clinton

E. Putting Things in Order

Put the following events in correct order by numbering them from 1 to 5

1. _____ George W. Bush loses the popular vote but wins the presidency with a majority of the Electoral College.

2. _____ Republicans win a majority in the House of Representatives after Newt Gingrich promotes the strongly conservative Contract with America.

3. _____ Arkansas Governor Bill Clinton defeats incumbent President George H. W. Bush.

4. _____ With authorization from the U.S. Congress, but not the United Nations, President George Bush launches a preemptive American invasion of Iraq.

5. _____ Terrorists conduct the first major attack on American soil in two hundred years.

PART III: APPLYING WHAT YOU HAVE LEARNED

1. Was Bill Clinton's election in 1992 a positive mandate for change, or was it primarily a repudiation of the first Bush administration's record on the economy?

2. How did the antigovernment mood of the 1990s affect both Bill Clinton and his Republican opponents? In what ways did Clinton attempt to uphold traditional Democratic themes, and in what ways did he serve to consolidate the conservative Bush-Reagan era?

3. What new foreign policy challenges did the United States face after the end of the Cold War?

4. What were the greatest foreign policy successes and failures of the Clinton administration in the 1990s?

5. Why was there so much antigovernment rhetoric, political action, and even violence in the 1990s? To what extent did the Clinton administration attempt to counter this mood, and to what extent did it bend to it?

6.   Argue for or against: the presidential election of 2000, despite its controversies, demonstrated the strength and resiliency of America's democracy.

7.   What was the impact of the September 11, 2001, terrorist attacks on America's national priorities and foreign policies? Is it true that everything changed after September 11, or were there significant areas in which America's global aims remained essentially the same?

8.   What caused the increased polarization in American politics in the early 2000s? Is it appropriate to align this polarization with the two political parties and their respective strengths in red states and blue states? Are there significant issues that have not been affected by this political polarization?

9.   What were the Bush administration's primary justifications for the Iraq War? Why did Americans find the military and political environment in Iraq so much more difficult than expected?

10.   How did President Bush spend the political capital that he said he had accumulated through his victory in the 2004 election.

CHAPTER 42

The American People Face a New Century

PART I: REVIEWING THE CHAPTER

A. Checklist of Learning Objectives

After mastering this chapter, you should be able to:

1. Describe the changing shape of the American economy and work force and the new social and ethical challenges facing the United States in a global economy dominated by high technology and scientific innovation.

2. Explain the impact of the feminist revolution on women's roles and on American society as a whole.

3. Analyze the changing structure and character of American families, and explain the social consequences of the aging of America.

4. Describe the impact of the great wave of immigration from Asia and Latin America since the 1970s and the challenge it posed to the traditional ideals of the melting pot.

5. Describe the difficulties and challenges facing American cities, including the increasing split between central cities and outer suburbs.

6. Describe the changing condition of African Americans in American politics and society, including the impact of economic differences within the African American community.

7. Describe the impact of the information technology revolution on American economics, communications, and culture.

8. Discuss the major developments in American thought, culture, and the arts since the 1970s.

B. Glossary

To build your social science vocabulary, familiarize yourself with the following terms.

1. **biosphere** The earth's entire network of living plants and organisms, conceived as an interconnected whole. ". . . the fragile ecological balance of the wondrous biosphere in which human-kind was delicately suspended."

2. **nuclear family** A parent or parents and their immediate offspring. "The nuclear family, once prized as the foundation of society. . . ."

3. **undocumented** Lacking official certification of status as a legal immigrant or resident alien. ". . . attempted to choke off illegal entry by penalizing employers of undocumented aliens. . . ."

4. **amnesty** An official governmental act in which some general category of offenders is declared immune from punishment. ". . . by granting amnesty to many of those already here."

5. **civil trial** A trial before a judge or jury instigated by a private lawsuit in which one party seeks relief, compensation, or damages from another. A **criminal trial** is instigated by an indictment for criminal law violations brought by a state prosecutor on behalf of the government ("the people"); it may result in fines, imprisonment, or execution. "In a later civil trial, another jury found Simpson liable for the 'wrongful deaths' of his former wife and another victim."

6. **blogosphere** Term for the collective dynamic, environment and interaction of all those who produce information and opinion by writing Internet "weblogs," or **blogs.** "As the 'blogosphere' grew, it posed a major challenge to the traditional media. . . ."

PART II: CHECKING YOUR PROGRESS

A. True-False

Where the statement is true, circle **T**; where it is false, circle **F**.

1. T F   The communications and genetics revolutions in postwar America created new social and moral dilemmas as well as widespread economic growth.

2. T F   After World War II, America's leading research universities concentrated on basic research and scholarship, while scientists in private industry focused on applied research and product development.

3. T F   The gap between America's wealthiest citizens and its poorest continued to grow in the 1990s and early 2000s.

4. T F   By the year 2006, almost all women without children at home were employed, but a majority of mothers with small children remained outside the workplace.

5. T F   One of the greatest issues affecting the character of American families in the 1990s and after was the growing poverty of the nation's elderly.

6. T F   One factor that made Hispanic immigration to the United States unique was the close proximity of Mexican Americans to their former homeland across the border.

7. T F   Immigrants contributed more in federal income and excise taxes than they consumed in benefits.

8. T F   By the mid-1990s, a majority of Americans lived in suburbs rather than central cities or rural areas.

9. T F   Reactions to the O.J. Simpson case and the controversial 2000 election in Florida demonstrated that both whites and blacks were increasingly able to make political judgments without considering race.

10. T F   African Americans attained considerable success in being elected to both local and national political leadership positions in the late twentieth and early twenty-first centuries.

11. T F   President George Bush's plan to provide a path to citizenship for illegal aliens received strong support from Democrats and Republicans alike.

12. T F   The rise of television and rock music caused a sharp decline in the number of Americans who patronized the high culture of museums and symphony orchestras.

13. T F   The tradition of fictional and nonfiction writing about the American West declined sharply in the late twentieth century.

14. T   F   The center of the American and international art world after World War II was San Francisco.

15. T   F   The greatest challenge to American values posed by the terrorist attacks of September 11, 2001, was how to maintain national security without eroding traditional freedoms and isolating the United States in the world.

B. Multiple Choice

Select the best answer and circle the corresponding letter.

1. The flagship business of the heavy industrial economy of the early twentieth century was the
    a. International Business Machines Company.
    b. Microsoft Corporation.
    c. U.S. Steel Corporation.
    d. General Mills Corporation.
    e. Union Pacific Railroad.

2. The primary engine driving the U.S. economy of the early twenty-first century is
    a. alternative energy development.
    b. corporate mergers and acquisitions.
    c. scientific research.
    d. international investment in American companies.
    e. labor union activism.

3. An example of ethical controversy surrounding fundamental scientific research in the first decade of the twenty-first century concerned
    a. stem cell research using human embryos.
    b. biological research on increasing plant yields.
    c. artificial computer aids to human intelligence.
    d. artificial insemination and organ transplants.
    e. pharmaceutical drugs designed to treat depression.

4. One of the greatest concerns regarding the continuing success of American science and engineering was that
    a. America's research universities were being crippled by antiscientific ideologies.
    b. American industry no longer sought to take advantage of scientific breakthroughs.
    c. women and minorities were still largely unable to pursue scientific careers.
    d. the United States was no longer producing enough scientists or even attracting top scientists from abroad.
    e. there were few remaining frontiers where fundamental scientific advance could occur.

5. The most striking development in the American economic structure in the 1990s and 2000s was the
    a. growing inequality between rich and poor.
    b. slow general decline in the American standard of living.
    c. growing reliance on investments and real estate rather than jobs for income.
    d. increasing concentration of wealth in certain regions and affluent suburbs.
    e. concentration of high tech investment in the older cities of the Northeast and Midwest.

6. Which of the following was *not* among the causes of the income gap in the United States?
    a. Intensifying global economic competition
    b. The shrinkage in manufacturing jobs for unskilled and semiskilled labor
    c. The decline of labor unions
    d. The entry of large numbers of women into the work force
    e. The increasing tendency of educated workers to marry one another

7. The most dramatic change in the patterns of women's employment from the 1950s to the 2000s was
    a.   the end of heavy occupational segregation in certain female-dominated job categories.
    b.   that the majority of mothers with young children went to work outside the home.
    c.   that women made greater employment gains when they were educated in all-female schools and colleges.
    d.   that married women worked at a higher rate than single women.
    e.   that women made greater economic gains when they operated small businesses from their homes than when they were employed in the workforce.

8. Perhaps the most significant sign of the pressures on the traditional American family in the late twentieth century was that
    a.   television no longer accurately portrayed family situations.
    b.   a majority of children no longer lived with their birth parents.
    c.   immigrant families were less stable than those of traditional old stock Americans.
    d.   the elderly were no longer likely to live with their adult children.
    e.   families were increasingly slow to form at all.

9. The increasingly longer lives of America's senior citizens were often eased by the
    a.   ability of the potent elderly lobby to obtain government benefits for seniors.
    b.   willingness of younger generations to provide income support for aged parents.
    c.   large-scale migration of senior citizens to the West Coast.
    d.   more positive portrayals of the elderly in movies and television.
    e.   growing equality of income among seniors caused by private pension programs.

10. The most serious problem caused by federal programs like Social Security and Medicare in the twenty-first century was likely to be that
    a.   benefits could not keep up with rising inflation.
    b.   the Social Security and Medicare trust funds would exercise too great a control over the economy.
    c.   benefits for large numbers of retiring baby boomers would create generational conflict with younger workers.
    d.   the health care system could no longer meet the rising demand for services to the elderly.
    e.   American businesses would no longer contribute to retirement or health care accounts.

11. The new immigrants of the late twentieth and early twenty-first centuries came to the United States primarily because they
    a.   wanted jobs and economic opportunities unavailable in their homelands.
    b.   were fleeing religious and political repression.
    c.   admired American cultural and intellectual achievements.
    d.   wanted to strengthen the minority voting bloc in the United States.
    e.   regarded national borders as increasingly irrelevant in the global economy.

12. The largest group of the new immigrants came from
    a.   East Asia.
    b.   Mexico and other Latin American countries.
    c.   Africa and the Middle East.
    d.   South Asia.
    e.   the Caribbean.

13. Which of the following was *not* a significant result of the Internet revolution in early twenty-first century?

    a. An economic boom in high-tech dot.com companies
    b. A democratization of information and communication
    c. The weakening of traditional, mainstream print media
    d. The rapid dispersal of both information and misinformation through the "blogosphere"
    e. A decline of visual media in favor of electronic reading and writing

14. The primary goals of modern multiculturalists was to

    a. end traditional American national literature and culture.
    b. make Spanish an official American language equal to English.
    c. preserve and promote distinct ethnic and racial cultures in the United States rather than emphasize a common American identity and culture.
    d. emphasize the human rights and human values common to all people regardless of nationality.
    e. promote minority education and media as a means of bringing about radical social change.

15. The most striking development in American literature in the past two decades has been the

    a. importance of the literature of fantasy, absurdism and black comedy.
    b. rise of writers from once-marginal regions and ethnic groups.
    c. focus on themes of nostalgia and lost innocence.
    d. rise of social realism and attention to working-class stories.
    e. avoidance of attention to sensitive sexual and racial issues.

C. Identification

Supply the correct identification for each numbered description.

1. _____ The computer corporation that symbolized the U.S. economy in the 1990s much as U.S. Steel did in 1900

2. _____ Health care program for the elderly, enacted in 1965, that created large economic demands on the American economy by the 1990s

3. _____ Law of 1986 that granted amnesty to past illegal immigrants and penalized employers of future illegal workers

4. _____ The largest of the new immigrant groups

5. _____ Organization, headed by César Chavez, that worked to improve conditions for migrant workers

6. _____ City where major racial disturbance erupted in 1992

7. _____ American region that saw a particularly rich literary revival beginning in the 1980s

8. _____ Tax-funded federal agency, created in 1965, that provided support for American art and artists

9. _____ Avant-garde painting movement pioneered by Jackson Pollock and others in the 1940s and 1950s

10. _____ Oil tanker whose 1989 spill off the coast of Alaska sparked deep concern over oil drilling and transportation on the world's oceans

D. Matching People, Places, and Events

Match the person, place, or event in the left column with the proper description in the right column by inserting the correct letter on the blank line.

1. ___ O. J. Simpson
2. ___ L. Douglas Wilder
3. ___ Barack Obama
4. ___ Larry McMurtry
5. ___ Norman MacLean
6. ___ August Wilson
7. ___ Toni Morrison
8. ___ N. Scott Momaday
9. ___ David Mamet
10. ___ Eve Ensler
11. ___ Jackson Pollock
12. ___ Frank Gehry

a. Leading Indian writer, author of *House Made of Dawn*

b. Pioneer artistic creator of abstract expressionism in the 1940s and 1950s

c. The first African American state governor

d. Leading twenty-first century American architect whose works, like the Disney Concert Hall, used fanciful metallic forms

e. Feminist playwright whose *Vagina Monologues* blended comedy and sharp social commentary

f. Playwright who deployed gritty American slang in socially critical dramas like *Glengarry Glen Ross*

g. Former football star whose murder trial became a focus of racial tension

h. Author of *Beloved* and winner of the Nobel Prize for Literature

i. Western writer who portrayed small towns in *Last Picture Show* and the cattle-drive era in *Lonesome Dove*

j. First African American elected president of the United States

k. African American playwright who portrayed the psychological costs of the northern migration

l. Former English professor who wrote memorable tales of his Montana boyhood

E. Putting Things in Order

Put the following events in correct order by numbering them from 1 to 5.

1. _____ F. Douglas Wilder is elected the first African American governor.

2. _____ Congress passes the Immigration Reform and Control Act to try to thwart illegal immigration.

3. _____   Jackson Pollock and others pioneer abstract expressionism and the leading form of modern American painting.

4. _____   Los Angeles experiences a major riot as the result of a racial incident involving police brutality.

5. _____   California voters approve Proposition 209 in an attempt to overturn affirmative-action policies.

F. Matching Cause and Effect

Match the historical cause in the left column with the proper effect in the right column by writing the correct letter on the blank line.

Cause	**Effect**
1. ___ Decline of manufacturing jobs and higher pay for educated workers	a. Made the American southwest increasingly a bicultural zone
2. ___ The computer revolution and the new trend toward genetic engineering	b. Changed both child-rearing patterns and men's social roles
3. ___ Expanding economic opportunities for women	c. Led to sharp attacks on Eurocentrism in American education
4. ___ Rise of the median age of the population since the 1970s	d. Contributed to sharply increased income inequality in the United States
5. ___ Growing numbers and political power for Hispanic Americans	e. Made the elderly a powerful political force
6. ___ The growth of the African American middle class and their migration to the suburbs	f. Further isolated the poverty-stricken lower class in the inner cities
	g. Made New York City the art capital of the world
7. ___ Poverty and economic upheavals in Latin America and Asia	h. Created the highest rates of immigration to the United States since the early 1900s
8. ___ The resentment against many affirmative action measures	
9. ___ The reaction against integration and the rise of multiculturalism	i. Led California voters to pass measures restricting the use of racial categories
10. ___ The success of modernist American art movements since the 1940s	j. Expanded the economy but threatened many traditional jobs while creating new ethical dilemmas for society

PART III: APPLYING WHAT YOU HAVE LEARNED

1. What were the consequences of the dramatically changed American economy as the United States advanced into the early twenty-first century?

2. What caused the rapidly increasing gap between rich and poor in America? Was this disparity a direct result of economic and social policies, or was it a largely unavoidable consequence of the changes in business, education, and social structure in the period 1980–2007?

3. How did women's new economic opportunities affect American society? What barriers to women's complete economic equality proved most difficult to overcome?

4. How did the new immigration and the rise of ethnic minorities transform American society by the beginning of the twenty-first century? Were the effects of the new immigration similar to that of earlier waves of immigration or fundamentally different?

5. How were the changes in American society reflected in literature and the arts in the late twentieth and early twenty-first centuries?

6. What is the central social and moral challenge America faces in the first half of the twenty-first century? How is the way the nation approaches that challenge shaped by American history, and how does understanding that history contribute to addressing that challenge in productive ways?

7. How did the Internet revolution transform the American economy, communications, and education? What were the most positive results of the explosion of Internet communication? What were some of its problems and dangers?

8. How does the relative uniqueness of America's history and culture affect its relationship to such increasingly international issues as economic development, the environment, immigration, and terrorism?